The New Publicity Kit

The New Publicity Kit

JEANETTE SMITH

John Wiley & Sons, Inc.

New York • *Chichester* • *Brisbane* • *Toronto* • *Singapore*

Credits:

Figures 8.1, 8.8, 8.13, 8.14, 8.15, 8.17, and 8.18 reprinted with permission of Michael Fineman, Fineman Associates, San Francisco, CA.

Figure 8.2 reprinted with permission of Gabriella S. Klein, Communications Concepts Unlimited, Racine, WI.

Figures 8.4 and 8.16 reprinted with permission of Elizabeth Hays, Davis-Hays & Company, Inc., Maywood, NJ.

Figures 8.5 and 8.6 reprinted with permission of Anne Klein & Associates, Inc., Mt. Laurel, NJ.

Figure 8.19 reprinted with permission of Deen & Black Public Relations, Sacramento, CA.

Pages 63, 82, 143 (Figure 8.20), 212: Reprinted with permission of *The Dallas Morning News*.

Page 13: Bill Hosokawa, "Readers Representative," reprinted with permission of the *Rocky Mountain News*.

Page 36: Bob Greene, the *Chicago Tribune*, reprinted by permission of Tribune Media Services.

Pages 84–85: Reprinted by permission of *Editor & Publisher* magazine.

Pages 70–71, 101–102, 267, 282, 291: Copyright © 1990 by The New York Times Company, reprinted by permission.

This text is printed on acid-free paper.

This publication is designed to provide accurate and authoritative information in regard to the subject matter covered. It is sold with the understanding that the publisher is not engaged in rendering legal, accounting, or other professional services. If legal advice or other expert assistance is required, the services of a competent professional person should be sought.

Library of Congress Cataloging-in-Publication Data:

Smith, Jeanette.
    The new publicity kit / Jeanette Smith.
        p.   cm.
    ISBN 0-471-08003-9 (cloth).—ISBN 0-471-08014-4 (pbk.)
    1. Industrial publicity—United States.   2. Small business—United
    States—Management.   3. Publicity.   4. Nonprofit organizations—
    United States—Management.   I. Title.
    HD59.S519   1995
    659—dc20   94-41429

Printed in the United States of America

10 9 8 7 6 5 4 3 2 1

Preface

This book is meant to convey information as in a good conversation. When a business friend offers to coach you in a particular operation or procedure, that person doesn't read you a textbook—you and your friend *talk*. In this case it's a one-person conversation whereby the business friend hopes to have anticipated your questions about what you need and want to know.

So let's sit down and talk.

There are a couple of things you should know straightaway. First, for those who already have a copy of *The Publicity Kit, The **New** Publicity Kit* is much, much more than an expanded revision. For instance, beyond explaining and urging you to adapt to the new technology that's exploding throughout all communications media and can literally mean the difference between success and failure of a publicity program, it provides a big cat to accompany you all the way to locking in that success.

A *cat*? Well, we call it a *copycat*, and it may be one of the two most helpful features in the book. The cat has taken up residence in a chapter called A Copycatter's Primer: Your "Lessen Plan" For Making Publicity Release Writing Easier. Here, the heads of prominent publicity agencies in various areas of the country, offer advice and examples that are comparable to their sitting down with you, as how-to instructors, to talk you through the process.

Another genuinely valuable feature is also a "lessen plan," in how to assemble, construct, and deliver video news releases (VNRs) that are the only acceptable format these days for achieving television publicity. And with the arrival and explosion of "menu" programmed cable television, which focuses on "narrowcasting," television publicity is becoming almost as easy to achieve for the smallest businesses as print publicity has been in the past.

This book is meant to be marked up with both pen and highlighter, and tagged with sticky notes to indicate places you want to return to. Einstein knew the importance of not cluttering the mind. It's said that when he was asked for his telephone number he had to go to the phone book to look it up because, he said, he never cluttered his mind with information he could find somewhere else.

Don't clutter your mind. Use this book as cartoonists Wise and Aldrich recommend in "Real Life Adventures"—as an "Owners Manual: [a place] to look to find out what you did that you shouldn't have done, and what you should have done that you didn't."

Contents

1

Media Are Reinventing Themselves

Now it's time to reinvent publicity

In the Key of Gee!

Things were moving fast enough when Benjamin Disraeli was Britain's prime minister for him to declare "Change is constant!" Today, however, the world is changing at a speed that can be intimidating. Nothing is changing faster than the ways in which media are reinventing themselves. So let's take a long look at *the edge of the future*, because these high-tech changes mean that publicity and advertising must reinvent themselves too.

But don't be intimidated. The fountain pen paved the way for the ballpoint pen. The vacuum tube heralded the transistor. And wire photo transmission—invented about 60 years ago—paved the way for the fax machine, which turned newspapers into instant visual recorders of events. When you take that long look forward, you'll find that much of the new technology is merely electronic forms of things that have been in use all along. The obstacle has always been that people have difficulty foreseeing what will follow.

Today we have a vice president of the United States—the first in history—who holds live, interactive news conferences on an international computer network. Some are calling him the "cyber veep" (from the new-tech word *cybernetics*). And when business and media people, many of whom have thought for years that government is populated by lumbering, dumb dinosaurs, see the VP demonstrating such technical prowess, they begin to think, "Wow, I guess we'd better get with it!"

John Cole, in a letter to the editor published in *The Dallas Morning News*, summed it up nicely. "Change is inevitable, and you can either be swept aside by it, go along with it, or become a master of it." He went on to admonish those who try to stick with only what they know. "I can just hear [a person] 100 years ago, talking about how the telephone is so complex because you have to remember all those numbers, and how the telegraph was so much better because you could just take your message down to the telegraph office and have it sent!"

(Perhaps Disraeli was called "Dizzy"—honest!—because he thought changes were coming so dizzyingly fast in his day.)

The Infobahn—A Cutting-Edge Technology

You can't turn on a news program, pick up a newspaper, or scan the comics without seeing or hearing something about the "information superhighway." The term has been beaten to death. (Perhaps we could nickname it the "infobahn" just for a little break now and then.)

In Mell Lazarus's "Miss Peach" comic strip, one of the kids tells another, "I don't believe it's important to learn all the junk they're trying to teach us. . . ." The other kid says, "Too bad. Someday you'll wind up trying to hitch-hike along the information superhighway."

And a secretary sits one-fingering her typewriter while the caption below the Wise and Aldrich "Real Life Adventures" cartoon states, "Information superhighway-wise, most of us are still on little dirt roads."

So what is this superhighway? There doesn't seem to be any single definition. There certainly are no maps, and no one seems to know where the road goes, but everyone can hardly wait to get there. And everyone wants to talk about it. Early in 1994 there was a convention at the University of California at Los Angeles called—what else?—*The Superhighway Summit*. It brought together all the telecommunication giants, including Vice President Al Gore, to talk about a revolution.

Cyberspace

Cyberspace is another overworked term. It's merely the global web of computer networks. One of the reasons for the growth of these networks is that computers that cost $5,000 five years ago cost only $900 today.

If you believe the talk that comes out of all the computer tech conventions, you believe that computers, telephones, and TVs will meet in our living rooms any day now. Well, not exactly, as the Hertz commercial says. It likely will be the turn of the century before "asynchronous transfer mode" (ATM) is able to unify the different characteristics of voice, data, and video communications and bring this technology to everyone's home and office.

It may take that long just to learn the language! You have to understand such words as *hermeneutic compulsion*, *morphology*, and *simulcrums*.

High tech has come along more slowly for newspapers, which until now have been the principal publicity and advertising medium for small businesses. But changes that came much faster in television are now romping along at a mind-boggling speed for newspapers too.

Take heart, though. Many of the changes are just electronic versions of things you've used all along. These are merely faster, smarter, more versatile ways of working. Instead of hand-gathered, typed collections of media lists and demographic, geographic, and psychographic information about your customers or clients, today there are on-line data bases that tell you whether this medium or that one, this cable channel or that one, is best for your purposes.

New Tech Benefits

The new technologies have unlimited numbers and kinds of benefits. For example, video news releases (VNRs) are relatively new on the publicity front. They present a completely new way to get television stations to use publicity stories, but preparing them requires more than merely sitting down at a keyboard and typing out a release. Wholly new information is now available to organizations that distribute their news via VNRs. There are explicit "bar-coded" monitoring checks that lock in the time, the date, the station and city, and the number of seconds used. You are able to tell exactly where, when, by whom, and how much of your VNR was used. This feature, called "encoding," is explained in detail in Chapter 16.

Publicity Defined

Before we look at what these new technologies mean to the production of publicity—and advertising—and learn ways to put them to your best use, let's look at what publicity is.

It has been said that publicity is nothing more than doing the right thing and telling about it.

The city of Miami was virtually unknown before the late publicity master, Steve Hanagan, brought it to world prominence with a publicity program that focused on using the dateline "Miami" in publicity stories describing the good, fun things happening there and the benefits from visiting, working, and living in the Florida beach town.

Simply, *publicity* is the principal tool used in wooing and winning *public* opinion to achieve good *public* relations. Notice the prominence of the word *public*? A good public image, established through positive publicity, shows up on the profit side of the ledger.

Publicity tells the story a business, a nonprofit group, or a person wants the *public* to know. It is the face your organization presents, through media, to the *public*.

Public Image

Remember these names: Tonya Harding, Whitewater, David Koresch, BCCI banking, double agent Aldrich Ames, Exxon? If this were a word-association test, what would come to mind? You might immediately recognize that each name has attracted enormous publicity—the kind a small business or a nonprofit group hopes never to acquire. It is far easier and much more pleasant to produce beneficial, productive publicity than it is to turn a poor image into a better one. The latter task, however, is also a function of publicity.

"Remember this," cautioned the late public relations counsel and publicity director Herb Baus "What is *believed* about an organization can be more important than what is true about an organization."

A Publicity Crisis

"Spin doctors," part of the current jargon, refers to some of today's public relations specialists. They are available for hire to put a particular, desired spin on a situation that is or could be seen in a different light.

The New York Daily News, when faced with a crippling, perhaps deadly, labor dispute in 1988, decided not to chance shooting itself in the foot. It called in a spin expert.

This professional specialized in publicity and public relations for nuclear power clients and had fronted for GPU Nuclear Corporation, which was responsible for the worst nuclear power accident in U.S. history at Three Mile Island. She became the most visible face of *The Daily News* management and prevented the second-largest, at the time, metropolitan daily newspaper in the United States from literally destroying itself. She followed the "minimax" principle, minimizing the negative while maximizing the positive, to keep the paper's best possible face before the public.

The strategy worked, although other factors—such as the economy and severely lowered advertising and circulation, which later forced a number of newspapers to close down—eventually caused *The Daily News* to declare bankruptcy. In January 1993, however, it was purchased by Mortimer Zuckerman, who owns *U.S. News & World Report* and *Atlantic Monthly*, and today it is showing a substantial operating profit.

The Media as Publicity Channels

Media are the communications channels used to present your organization's story to the public: print, electronic, and word-of-mouth. The most popular media are newspapers, radio, television, and direct mail. Print media also include magazines, flyers, brochures, and newsletters.

Don't discount the effect of print media vehicles, because, as the publisher of *Family Weekly* magazine stated, "Television may have become our eyes and ears and our public meeting space, but print continues to be our memory."

Memory can't be trusted, and your customers, clients, and constituents can't get from television or radio spots (as they can from print sources) hard-copy clippings of your telephone number and address to tuck into a pocket or an address book. Nor can television and radio give them coupons to mail-order something you are offering. Furthermore, printed stories are collectible proof that can later become the base for a documented background or history of the organization. (See Appendix D for information about subscribing to a clipping service.)

It's Not Rumor—Even Newspapers Are Going Ninja!

Currently, there are interactive media, audiotex, videotex, and cyberspace. And right now, today, there are PNs—personal newspapers.

Michael Conniff, an *Editor & Publisher* magazine columnist, said it best (about newspapers): "The Dinosaur is starting to Dance!" Five years ago, he says, the high priests of telecommunications were ready to pronounce last rites over ink and paper. Newspapers were a dinosaur waiting for the asteroid to hit terra firma and to put the whole creaking breed out of its misery for good.

"Flip the dial to five years later," says Conniff, "and we find God-fearing people who are wondering who slipped the steroids to the dinosaur. Telecommunications is the continuing story of newspapers on steroids in the 1990s.

"We are not talking futurespeak here. We are talking about thousands of newspapers, and we are not just talking about the voice information services known as audiotex.

"No, we are talking about an explosion of media exploration unprecedented in the history of any medium, and that includes the megabyte types in the Silicon Valley."

Conniff, who also is an editor for The Kelsey Group, a market research and consulting firm, says that newspapers are the pioneers in audiotex, videotex, fax, on-line, and even multimedia services. "There is not a single industry in America so committed to reinventing itself as newspapers are today," he says.

For Road Scholars

Picture a newsPAPER with no paper, that you can take with you in the car.

Knight-Ridder, the second largest newspaper group, after Gannett, is one of the most aggressive developers of what is called "Newspapers on Demand," which includes becoming interactive and "decoupling" from paper.

Knight-Ridder has developed a hand-held computer screen, which consumers can get if they subscribe to the news "paper." This device is in the form of a flat tablet about the size and thickness of a Time magazine. Instead of pulling out the morning paper, the reader grabs the tablet, switches it on, and a newspaper front page appears. Using a pen, the reader can call up stories, flip pages, shop the ads, skim the business and sports pages, and browse the comics. Readers also can "clip" items electronically to save as they save coupons or stories from a regular paper, or to send electronically to another person. Incredibly, with the miracle of modern electronics and video, graphics can be animated in 3-D with sound, so the reader can turn a photo into a television news replay.

Because the tablet can also be voice activated, the reader can take it in the car on the way to work, issue a command, "Give me the business news," and hear the top stories played back in sound. It all adds up to an interactive newspaper that has been decoupled from paper.

The man in charge of all this for Knight-Ridder, Roger Fidler, calls it "mediamorphosis" and says the tablet will be available in 1995. It will cost the newspapers' subscribers extra—probably about $1,000. If the price is too high for some, they can lease a tablet, in the same way they subscribe to cable services.

Yes, they're still called newspapers. But what will these media forms be called when they've "decoupled" from paper? Maybe the name will stay. After all, we still say we "dial" phone numbers—not that we "punch" numbers!

Fidler says that newspapers of the future will retain some form of ink on paper. "My assumption is that print and electronic newspapers will coexist for several decades; there will not be a sudden and complete mediamorphosis."

The Future Is Here—In San Jose

In May 1994, The San Jose (California) Mercury News began what it calls electronic extensions of its newsPAPER—on-line copies of news, updates, news conference transcripts, movie and theater schedules, and much more—at a significant expense to Knight-Ridder, its parent company.

A story in The New York Times reported that Mercury News subscribers pay basic fees of $2.95 for telephone and fax service and $9.95 a month for the computer service that is part of the America Online System. On-line subscribers can read news as it is printed in the newspaper, but few editors believe readers use the service for that purpose, *The Times* reports. The reason for their belief is that the system is cumbersome, as compared with a printed newspaper, and does not include photographs or graphics alongside the text.

But on-line subscribers can also use code numbers printed in the newspaper every day to call up material that doesn't get into print. And for an extra charge, subscribers can get articles from the paper's past coverage.

A service to be added possibly in 1995, allows readers without computers to punch in the same codes to obtain information by fax. It also lets readers simply listen to news features over the phone.

The Times reports that *The Mercury News* has hired special editors, called "senders," to scour the wire services for reports to augment the content of the printed newspaper. (Doesn't that tell you something? If a newspaper the size of the *Mercury News*—circulation is more than 300,000—must hire senders just to fill its need for added information, then, if your publicity information is sufficiently interesting and properly prepared, it will be used in even the larger newspapers that previously didn't have space for small business news.)

Knight-Ridder is betting a large fortune that this is the way to go and that readers *will* appreciate and buy.

Another Dinosaur is Dying

The best thinking, currently, is that the new electronic "newspaper" won't involve big, concentrated news staffs in centralized office buildings. The huge printing presses used today will become dinosaurs too old to do much dancing.

Another dinosaur—virtually extinct—is kids on bikes tossing papers on front lawns. The reason: The time between printing the last page and the paper's arrival on a subscriber's doorstep or at the newsstand is as long or longer than it was 50 years ago. According to Fidler, at time of arrival most of the news in morning editions is between 10 and 30 hours old.

Such developments put greater pressures on publicity people. They must produce news and copy formats that are capable of efficiently adapting to both print and electronic media. That, however, is what the new edition of this book is all about: showing you how to do it and making the transition easy.

The Yes and "Know" of Publicity for Businesses and Nonprofits

Publicity is a critical part of an effective, productive, and successful nonprofit operation. If your constituency is ignorant of your existence, it will be impossible for you to provide service to them. And no matter how well organized and well managed your company is, it will fail to accomplish its mission. Furthermore, positive publicity helps establish credibility, an essential ingredient for nonprofit organizations in attracting grants, donors, and volunteers.

The success of for-profit businesses also depends on potential customers' and clients' awareness of the organization's existence and their receptiveness to it. Businesses, however, have greater access to advertising to help attract public awareness, because they usually have greater incomes and larger operating budgets. Advertising, publicity, and public relations should be regular operating expenses for for-profit organizations.

Good publicity helps to establish credibility: this is true for both businesses and nonprofit groups. And credibility establishes trustworthiness and reliability, along with the feeling that the organization is worthy of confidence—all qualities that are absolutely essential in today's value-skeptical society. An honorable, re-spected reputation is money in the bank.

It's important, then, to have a full understanding of what publicity is, how it differs from public relations and advertising, and what is required to act as the publicity practitioner for your organization. In-depth explanations of strategies for dealing with high-tech advances will be given throughout this book.

Publicity's Function, Task, and Job

The *function* of publicity is to win as much goodwill for an organization or an individual as possible. The *task* of publicity is to promote the good and true and to have the public reject what is untrue. The *job* of publicity is to tell the story through a variety of media. Just as different tools are used to construct a building, publicity requires a variety of media to further the particular interest or image of an organization or to solve a publicity problem.

Publicity Is News

Publicity is *news* of interest to many people. It can create an image for a person-ality, an organization, a government, or a city (as in the case of Miami). There is even a hotdog stand in Los Angeles that has its own paid publicity agent, and because so many celebrities patronize the place, the publicity circulated is news of interest to many people.

Publicity in Every Organization

Because publicity basically is news, your work boils down to examining the count-less human-interest stories and information found in every group of people and in every organization. The stories are just waiting to be dug out, properly dressed up, and made available to news media.

As you gain practice, you will find yourself looking at every event, person, and experience with the question: Would this be interesting to enough readers or viewers to make it a good publicity story? You also will be looking for the unusual and the unexpected for possible feature stories.

Feature stories? News stories? There are differences, but both can produce publicity for your group. (The differences between the two and how to write these kinds of stories are covered in Chapters 6 and 7.)

The Differences Between Publicity and Public Relations

Publicity is part of an overall public relations (PR) plan—often the most visual part. So take a short detour here and look at what public relations is, particularly as compared with publicity. The facetious explanation given in *Orben's Current Comedy* is: "Public Relations is the fine art of making sure that something is no sooner done than said."

Some of the confusion in establishing that the two are not synonymous comes from such errors as found in books that explain PR as "telling your story." That's what publicity does; public relations is much more. Even professionals have a difficult time explaining or defining public relations. In a regional meeting of the Public Relations Society of America at Southern Methodist University's School of Continuing Education, the first handout of the session provided 34 definitions of public relations! Confusion comes from the fact that "PR deals with an intangible, hard-to-define commodity—information," according to Dr. Roy Busby, professor of journalism at the University of North Texas.

Jeffrey Goodell, a New York-based business writer, acknowledges the problem of defining public relations in an article in *The New York Times Magazine*. The story is about Hill & Knowlton, one of the biggest public relations companies in the world. Goodell wrote:

> *Given the fact that even people who have been in the business for years can't agree on what to call their profession, it's no surprise that outsiders often misunderstand how public relations works. . . . The distinction between journalism and public relations is sometimes blurred.*
>
> *Many public relations professionals are, in fact, former journalists who have been lured to the other side of the fence (usually by a hefty increase in salary).*

When you speak of publicity, a person readily understands that you are telling your story through some form of media. But when you use the term *public relations*, to many this also means *publicity*.

Public Relations Defined

Public relations can be a speakers' bureau or public polls or a survey to create credibility and goodwill. It can be an open house; telephone-answering techniques; personal contact by representatives; training institutes for staff; policy interpretations; newsletters; employee, client/customer, grantsmaker, or pressure-group relations; audiovisual presentations; direct mailings; fund raisers—and more.

The Hard Sell and the Soft Sell

Public relations has two sides, as Jeffrey Goodell points out in a *New York Times Magazine* article: "The hard sell and the soft sell. . . . The softer, less glamorous side of public relations is full of mundane tasks like writing newsletters and annual reports. . . . The hard sell is typified by what is known as 'crisis management' and is one of the most lucrative aspects of the business.

"The hard sell brings in the big bucks because it not only covers no-holds-barred corporate warfare, with millions of dollars on the line, but it also includes accidents and scandals." The hard sell also pays the highest salaries because the job is spelled "S-T-R-E-S-S"—in capital letters. A joke in the industry says that one crisis management specialist was fired because his ulcer healed, and his boss thought he'd lost interest in his job."

In an article entitled "PR Superstars: 100 of the Brightest," in *Public Relations*

Quarterly, the principal criterion was not earnings (although most of these super-stars are believed to earn more than $100,000 a year), but successful results. The article says, "They succeed at doing what many other PR people don't even think to try."

Public Relations and Publicity

Of course, public relations includes publicity, which often is a major portion of PR and usually the most visible part. Properly utilized, public relations can reinforce advertising, expand message reach, establish or add credibility, generate excitement and support, tell the whole story, reach distinct and special audiences, and create public acceptance.

"The public relations professional must be listener, interpreter, and communicator. He or she must know WHAT to say. WHO to say it to, HOW best to say it, and WHY it ought to be said. He must possess the instincts of the businessman, the skills of the journalist, and the foresight of the psychologist." That excellent description, given by Herbert H. Rozoff in the *Public Relations Journal*, says a good deal about the importance of public relations.

Publicity and PR as Distinct from Advertising

Public relations reinforces advertising. And though advertising can be public relations, public relations is *not* advertising. Nor is publicity advertising.

Publicity may be confused with or thought of as advertising by the uninitiated. Most certainly it is not—although you might stretch your definition to say it is advertising you cannot buy. However, please *never* think of publicity as free advertising. There is no money value to publicity space. In fact, in credible media, money cannot buy it under any circumstances.

Another point to keep in mind is that people tend to give greater value to something that is purchased. The value of good publicity, however, which is free, is immeasurable. Not only do readers tend to put more trust in printed news than in advertising, but publicity can also be one of your most cost-effective marketing tools.

Don't Try to Disguise Advertising as "News"

Advertising is sponsor-purchased space or time in which you present your message to attract public attention or patronage to a product, an organization, or an idea.

Publicity is a message—about a product or a service, an organization or a person, or an idea—that is prepared strictly within the parameters of newspaper or broadcast news and distributed to the news departments (instead of to the advertising departments) of daily or weekly newspapers or broadcast media, *without payment* to the media.

An editor receives hundreds of publicity stories each day, most of them labeled "News." A good portion of these march briskly across the desk and into a wastebasket, because the editor considers them attempts to get free ads that should have been bought and paid for. Advertising, after all, pays most of the editor's salary and the medium's bills.

Newspapers Are no Different from Other Media

People sometimes mistakenly regard a newspaper as purely a public service, operating solely to provide information to readers. Information is *one* of its services, but a newspaper is strictly a free-enterprise business that must make a profit to survive. It won't be around long if it doesn't. (For a better understanding of newspapers, see Chapter 19.)

Newspaper revenues come, basically, from two sources:

1. Circulation (sale of copies)
2. Advertising (sale of space)

In almost all cases, ads provide more than half of the total revenue, usually about two-thirds.

Although broadcast media do not use as large an amount of publicity as do newspapers, don't ask or expect radio or television to use, as news, information that belongs in a paid commercial. Radio and television media do, however, provide time for public service announcements (PSAs). (Preparing and distributing PSAs are dealt with in Chapter 18.)

Publicists as Newspaper "Staffers"

How much of the published news and feature material in newspapers comes from publicity sources? A study conducted among newspaper editors by Ury-Sigmond Public Relations a few years ago indicated that 21 percent of the nonadvertising contents of newspapers comes from publicity sources. However, the study also produced the statistic that 81 percent of the news and feature material received from these sources is *rejected*. Only 6 percent is used as written.

A sizable number of newspeople—print and electronic—look upon publicity people as extensions of their staffs, covering news areas that the medium could not otherwise afford to cover. When you hand a legitimate news story to an editor, he or she appreciates it. The editor knows that the lifeblood of a newspaper is news in which the public is interested. But he or she also knows that there is no way the staff, no matter how large, can cover everything that happens.

So, in effect, you become a member of an editor's reporting staff, *if* the editor can rely on you as a dependable and discriminating news source. The other side of the coin is that the editor can fire you as a reporter by tossing your material into the wastebasket if he or she has reason to doubt your integrity or accuracy.

The Yes and "Know" of Being a Publicity Representative

This book is the road map to your destination. However, *you* must be the vehicle to get your organization there. If you are the owner or chief executive of the organization, you have incentive to do the best possible job so that the results will show up on the profit side of the ledger. As an entrepreneur, you may have no desire whatever to use the knowledge and expertise you are acquiring to produce publicity for any reason other than to benefit your own organization.

There are other users of this book, however, who have been appointed by their employers, or selected as volunteers in a nonprofit organization, to do the job.

Someone once said that there is no limit to what the boss can do if he or she puts someone else's mind to it!

Your Personal Benefits

No matter how you acquired the job—by election, by appointment as chairman of the publicity committee, or by the boss pointing a finger and saying, "You do it"—you are lucky. Ultimately, the better you know the field of publicity, the better you serve your own ends. For staffers, there can be personal good fortune in this appointment.

As a publicity chairperson or staffer you will learn things and make contacts that can last and profit you for a lifetime. You may need to call on these skills and contacts at times to create publicity or when something happens to cause "bad press" for your organization. As a staffer, you may even decide you like the job well enough to add it to your career skills. It certainly never hurts a resume to include publicity writing and production. And it certainly never hurts an executive who wishes to move up or on, to let it to be known that he or she has "profit-able" publicity experience. Employers often see these attributes as valuable, which can be the deciding factor over competitors who have otherwise equal abilities. Non-profit organizations actively seek these skills among their volunteers. In other words, don't discount this opportunity. It can turn into a rewarding, even gainful, activity.

Some who progress through this book, from enthusiastic beginner to competent paraprofessional, may wish to seek full-time employment in the field. For such people, publicity might be likened to a penthouse with a great view of the entire field of communications: solid background in publicity equips a person to work in any communications medium.

If you have no desire to enter the field, publicity work produces another asset that can be highly worthwhile in a climb up the career ladder. Concise, clear communication, an absolute necessity in publicity writing, is the mark of an effective communicator, which, in business, is a prime requisite for success. David Ogilvy (of Ogilvy & Mather, one of the nation's best-known advertising firms), in his book *The Unpublished David Ogilvy*, tells how important this ability is.

- *The better you write, the higher you go in Ogilvy & Mather. People who THINK well, WRITE well.*
- *Wooly minded people write wooly memos, wooly letters, and wooly speeches.*
- *Good writing is NOT a natural gift. You have to LEARN to write well.*

If you decide you want to explore publicity as a career, there is one more rewarding benefit: it is one of the higher-paying branches of print journalism.

No matter whether you look to publicity as a vocation or as part of your job, the goal is similar to a medical doctor's, except that your *first* dedication is to *increase* health. Your job description would call for you to do the following:

- Solve problems
- Observe symptoms
- Diagnose causes
- Prescribe solutions

In case of the illness of your organization, you must also alleviate pain to the best of your ability.

Your Qualifications as a Publicist

You can't be a cowboy if you can't ride a horse! And you can't be a publicist—volunteer, appointed, or paid—unless you have the qualifications. What are they? Basically, there are only four:

1. A nose for news
2. An ability to present the news
3. Energy to do the work
4. Integrity

Nose for News. Nosing out the news for a publicity release merely takes a little thought. But fleshing out bare-bones facts to present a meaty, interesting news release requires hunting for unusual angles, adding an original twist, and sometimes digging deep to locate information beyond obvious facts.

You will be surprised to see how soon you begin to develop a news sense and to know instinctively when a happening is news and when it isn't. One of the best ways to develop this sense is to study your newspapers. Notice the kinds of stories used and which ones go on special pages (page one; community-news page; business, family, club, and sports pages; etc.).

The ease with which a nose for news can be acquired is treated in greater detail in Chapter 8, "A Copycatter's Primer."

Ability to Present News.   An ability to present the news requires knowledge of the mechanical production of copy to certain specifications. Anyone able to correctly use and type the English language can follow these specifications, which are spelled out in Chapter 6.

Energy to Do the Work.   Energy to do the work encompasses the sheer stamina needed for digging out and collecting the news—then typing, typing, and more typing. (A publicist must have a typewriter, a word processor, a computer and printer, or someone to do the typing. This is essential.)

Integrity.   Integrity is the most important quality you must have. If an editor does not have faith that the information you give him or her is true and correct in details and that it will not backfire on him or her when printed, the editor cannot be expected to use the material. Your job is to win public confidence in your organization through publicity. If the information in a release is found to be incorrect, untrue, or inaccurate, you will destroy credibility and confidence in your organization. At the same time, you will destroy your own credibility with the publication that you are hoping will use the information.

Tale of a Publicity Default

Of all sad words of tongue or pen, what of the job well done that might have been? The following story illustrates the point well. In a "Readers' Representative" column in the Denver *Rocky Mountain News*, Bill Hosokawa detailed what can happen to an important news story when an organization's responsible parties don't provide sufficient information to the newspaper.

The event was the Hispanic Annual Salute (HAS) Award Dinner, with 16 organizations acting as cosponsors and more than a thousand people attending. Total coverage was six paragraphs on page 28 the day *after* the function.

Hosakawa stated that there was "no denying the event was worthy of this newspaper's attention and was undercovered." After questioning the newspaper's city editor, he explained why it happened. The editor had the following to say:

In researching how this story came to be, I find that we received only a routine news release telling us the salute was going to be held. Neither the assistant city editor who assigned the story, nor the reporter who covered it, remember anything about the news release that indicated the event was anything out of the ordinary. It would have been immensely helpful to have had complete information in advance. We had no communication from [HAS] individuals or others that would have told us this was an important event. In fact, our ongoing effort to be sensitive to events and issues that directly affect minority readers was responsible for our covering the salute at all.

The chairman of HAS contended that a press kit about the event, with photographs of the honorees, was sent to the *News* some weeks before the banquet. Hosokawa believes, however, that "the matter unfortunately fell between the cracks or, more accurately, was buried under the mountain of material that arrives daily."

That this example (of what can happen on both sides of the publicity fence) was made public is unique. Seldom does a company or a nonprofit organization know why its releases aren't used, and it tends to place the blame on the newspaper. In this case, the matter was given public attention through the "Reader's Representative" column. A disgruntled reader had written to the column to question the newspaper's coverage of such an important event within the Hispanic community.

What this incident says to anyone and everyone who prepares publicity for his or her organization is that there can be no relaxation in following the guidelines on publicizing a staged event. (See Chapter 13.) And it shouts the advice most loudly to nonprofit organizations who depend so heavily on unpaid volunteers to perform their important jobs.

Something else this story says is that the publicity was highly important to the entire Hispanic community, and especially vital to HAS and to the volunteers who did all the work in preparing and carrying out the event. What is so disheartening for them is that the newspaper would have done considerably more in recognition of its Hispanic readership if only it had known about the event in advance, and if only the publicity job had been properly handled.

So, try not to shoot yourself in the foot. Stay on top of things all the way through to the end of a story. Newspapers *want* your news!

The story also illustrates that, as your group's publicity representative, you must do the job to the best of your training and ability, or you let your group and a lot of other people down. The purpose of this book is to show you how to do the best job possible.

Disadvantages of Publicity Work

Although you may be able to start with very few qualifications, publicity work isn't an easy job. You seldom will be completely satisfied with the job you do, no matter how well you perform. You'll know that you could have done more, if you had had more of the following:

* Help
* Time
* Money

You'll rarely or probably never, have the satisfaction of receiving a byline or even of getting the credit for a story that may appear word-for-word as you wrote it. The story may even appear under someone else's byline!

There are benefits, though. If you take your job seriously and approach it as a learning experience, there is much that will serve you well, if ever you wish to enter the for-pay business of professional publicity.

Copycatting 101

There's a skill you'll want to develop to cut publicity release writing to its simplest—call it "copycatting." Or you can think of it as using OPB—using Other People's Brains.

Gathering material to put together your own customized Copycat Kit, which you'll easily master in Chapter 8, is an ongoing project that should be started *immediately*. Copycatting is explained at this point so that you will know right from the start the way it works and the kinds of information you should start gathering *now*.

A copycat file can be your idea bank. It's where you can stockpile and store an unlimited supply of information to stimulate thinking about potential publicity news releases and feature stories. It can be a cupboard of ideas to start productive brainstorming sessions. But its most important function is that it can be your easy-as-fill-in-the-blanks hard copy examples of how to write your publicity releases.

It works this way: Each time you have a release to write, check your copycat file and find a newspaper or magazine story similar to the one you want to write. Just change it to fit your own circumstances. In other words, you don't have to reinvent the wheel each time, and you don't have to be a trained writer.

For now, just collect materials. You can hold them in an expanding file pocket, an oversized envelope, or a cardboard or plastic box. In Chapter 8 we'll show you how to turn them into a "cache register" for your publicity program.

Your Cache Register Stash

Start immediately to gather examples of various types of information from newspapers, business journals, and magazines. Watch for stories about:

* New board members
* New executives, managers, and department heads
* New products or new services announcements
* Awards to companies, nonprofit groups, employees or volunteers

- Product or services improvements
- Research results
- Sponsorships or tie-ins between companies, charities, and education, or with other nonprofits
- Mergers or acquisitions
- Expansions
- Grants awards
- Image builders
- Relocations
- Special events

As you work through the information presented in Chapters 2 to 7, you undoubtedly will think of other kinds of information that are or will be applicable to your organization's present and future publicity plans.

Even if you intend to send releases only to small dailies or weeklies, don't confine your collection to models from those papers. Often the writing and information content in large metropolitan newspapers are better, so they can serve your copycatting efforts better. In addition, larger dailies may print a broader scope of stories that ultimately can provide more ideas for your publicity idea cache. When you travel out of town, pick up newspapers from other cities and include examples from them.

As you gather your samples, you'll doubtless notice that each newspaper—large or small—has its own style. Stories in The New York *Times* are decidedly different from those in the *Ventura* (California) *County Star-Free Press*. Those in the *Chicago Tribune* are different from stories and features in the *Mason City* (Iowa) *Globe-Gazette* or the *DeKalb* (Missouri) *County Record-Herald*.

You also may notice that stories in business sections are different from those on the sports pages or in the sections where charity events and nonprofits' activities appear. Some papers—*The New York Times*, for example—use longer, more detailed news stories. Most, however, use brief, concise reports.

Collect *everything* you think might be useable. It's always easier to toss than to gather.

2

Analysis of a News Story

How different types of news require
specific styles of writing

Straight News as Facts

One of America's preeminent editors, Lester Markel, said it best:

What you see is news,
what you know is background,
what you feel is opinion.

What he didn't say is that straight news is *Facts*. But not just bare-bone facts, as Mark Twain showed us.

The story is that early in Mark Twain's training as a news reporter, he was warned to keep strictly to fact and to never report anything that he couldn't verify personally. Shortly after receiving this warning, he was assigned to cover an important social event, and this was his account:

A woman giving the name of Mrs. James Jones, who is reported to be one of the society leaders of the city, is said to have given what is purported to be a party yesterday to a number of alleged ladies. The hostess claims to be the wife of a reputed attorney.

You get his point: News is the reporting of facts, and the main purpose of news is to present information. *But,* the first canon of newswriting is to make things easy for the reader—easy to understand and to digest. The trick is to flesh out bare-bones facts with descriptive detail that makes the reader see and feel the story—and *want* to read it.

There are, basically, three kinds of articles in newspapers: news stories, feature stories, and editorials. An editor will appreciate submission of the first two as publicity releases, but not the third. Read the paper's editorials, but don't submit them.

(Most publicity for small businesses and nonprofits is submitted to newspapers, because newspapers are more apt to use it. However, the principles that determine what is news and what are the elements of a news story are the same for all media.

Specific information about publicity for radio, television, and cable is covered in Chapters 15 and 16.)

Editorials as the Newspaper's Domain

Editorials are the exclusive domain of a newspaper's management, in which its own opinions and advice are presented. With tongue firmly in cheek, Ralph Schoenstein in *Saturday Review* demonstrated the primary purposes of editorials: to stimulate thinking, stir discussion, and arouse action. "Journalists have been writing editorials," Schoenstein observed, "since the *Eden Examiner* said:"

> *Things have come to a pretty pass when it's unsafe to walk on the Garden's fashionable East side.*
>
> *It is hoped that the Power-That-Be will do more than merely deport Mr. Cain and others of his ilk. May we therefore suggest that remedial legislation also be forthcoming from Him to curb this shocking outbreak of terror that poses an ever-present threat to the security of the entire fallen world.*

Newspapers rarely use editorials that are not staff-written or solicited as guest editorials. (Of course, there is no rule against getting to know the editorial page editor and suggesting that he or she write the editorial you have in mind.)

Publicity Releases as News

Most publicity releases fall into the news-story category. Every news item that enters a newspaper office passes into the hands of the newspaper's editors—people with great responsibilities. The editors scan the reams of copy received daily to find the best and most interesting news stories for their readers. It is their job to sift, sort, trim, and, from all the news and features flowing in from all parts of the world, fashion a complete newspaper.

So before you go to the trouble of writing a news release, think about what it will contain and whether it really is news, so that it can at least compete for placement in a newspaper's limited news hole (news space).

The Two Types of News Stories

Publicity, then, is news, of which there are two types: spot news and created news.

Spot News

Spot News is spontaneous, usually beyond your control, and certainly not of your making. An example is the injury or death of a visitor at a company-sponsored event. The publicity derived would not be beneficial, so your principal functions as your organization's press agent would be to try to mitigate the harmful impact resulting from such an uncontrollable event and to assist the media in every possible way to do their jobs in covering it. An excellent guideline for your role here is to be helpful, obliging, and honest. Don't be a "suppress" agent!

Created News

Created news comes from a created event or happening that produces controlled publicity: meetings, elections, appointments of individuals to higher organization positions, performances, or almost any kind of happening. Assignment of con-tracts, new services, new products, new programs, new projects, awards, and rec-ognition of or by affiliates—all are material for news stories.

Truly created news may come from a strictly staged event: a benefit, an open house, a reception, a training program, a community-interaction accomplishment and so on. The main disadvantage to such a staged media event is that it is time-consuming and costly for you and your organization. A lot of work and money are needed to produce an event so compelling that news teams will flock to your door. (See Chapter 13 for more about staged events.)

The Basic Elements of News: Names, Times, and Events

An editor looks at each release with one thing in mind: Is it legitimate news of interest to a large number of readers? Ask yourself: To how many people is this story of interest? Then you can better understand the editor's problem in measur-ing the newsworthiness of each piece of copy submitted to him or her.

If you are looking for publicity for a commercial product or service, you must also ask yourself whether the release really is a news item—or is it advertising? You can be sure that if the editor smells an attempt to pass off, as news, advertising that should be paid for, he or she will toss your release quicker than you can say, "Pub-licity is *not* free advertising."

Evaluation Test for a News Release

Here, are some general "test" questions to help you evaluate any information you plan to send as a news release:

- Is the item of interest to at least 10 percent of the publication's readers or to the readers of the particular section to which you will direct it (e.g., business, family, magazine, sports, etc.)?
- Is it timely? Past events are history, not news. *The Wall Street Journal* states it well in one of its self-promotion ads: "Dedicated to the proposition that news does not improve with age."
- Does it include names of people? Better still, does it include names of well-known people? Experience has taught editors that people are their own favorite subjects, and that names, names, and more names help build cir-culation. Readers like to see what prominent people are doing, and they also like seeing their own names in print—in positive ways—and will buy extra copies of editions in which they are mentioned. The greater the sales of papers, the higher the advertising rates and the greater the profits, some of which may become salary increases for editors.
- Does it have a local angle? (The importance of this point is discussed in a section of this chapter, "Changes in News Writing.")
- Does it have a human-interest angle? *Human interest* is a hard-to-define element that has to do with events in human life. Human interest appeals

to the emotions, the part of the consciousness that involves feeling or sensibility. Love, fear, sadness, and laughter are emotions that can provide human-interest for stories.

- Is it an ad? In the beginning, until you are totally familiar with how publicity differs from advertising, don an imaginary editor's hat and try putting yourself in his or her place. Examine the subject matter with a critical eye to decide whether it should go to the editor or to the advertising department. (For more information about advertising, see Chapters 17 and 18.)

Newspaper Space Limitations

Even if your news release passes all of the above "test" questions, it still may not be printed. It may have to be forfeited because it arrives on a particularly heavy news day when there is little room for much else.

Although the space limitations for newspapers aren't nearly as constricting as the time limits for television and radio, there's another factor that relates to whether your news release is used: the reams and reams of releases that come in each day— far more than can possibly be used in the allotted space, no matter the amount of news space available. By way of proving this point, a reporter took all the press releases the newspaper received in one 24-hour period and pasted them together. They added up to the distance around 16 city blocks, and that didn't include wire-service copy and reporters' stories—only press releases!

To filter out the chaff along with the overload, editors screen stories through the exercise of experienced judgment. You may sometimes disagree with their judgment; you may feel space is wasted on items that do not interest you. But remember, the editors are attempting to meet the needs of *all* their readers—people of varying ages, occupations, incomes, and educations, and, hence, of varying interests.

Basics of a News Story

A news story should be all of the following:

- *Factual.* You naturally want every story you give to an editor to be as accurate and impartial as a story prepared by one of his or her own reporters. (Publicists aren't expected to include downside information in a release. They *are* expected to respond with honesty when a reporter or editor seeks such information to expand coverage of the release.)
- *Timely.* One of the oldest newsroom sayings is so old it's reached cliché standing: Yesterday's news is history.
- *Interesting.* Try to appeal to the largest possible number of readers.
- *Objective.* Straight news must never include the writer's opinion. (Some feature stories, usually written in the first person, do include the writer's observations and opinions.)
- *Written in an* inverted pyramid *format* (as described in more detail in Chapter 6). Facts should be arranged in the order of importance; the most important facts are always stated first. Figure 2.1 illustrates the use of the inverted pyramid format in a short news story and a long news story.

FIGURE 2.1   News Story Structure

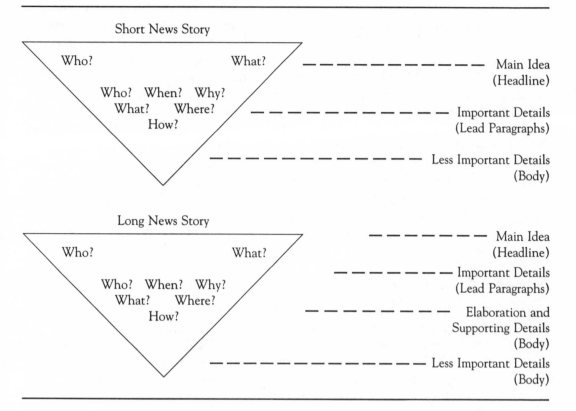

Components of a News Story

In general, the structure of a news story (as illustrated in Figure 2.1) is the opposite of that for other literary forms. In a straight-news story, "it's what's up top that counts."

Former CBS newsman Walter Cronkite has often been quoted as saying that television news is a headline service. Instead of minimizing the depth and significance of television news reports, the statement actually recognizes the importance of headlines. In effect, a headline is a news bulletin. Each *headline* should be a summary of an article's contents, but it also can be a newspaper's "commercial" to attract readers to the story.

Headlines are written so that busy people may glance through a book-sized newspaper and obtain the meat of the day's news within a few minutes. Headlines together with *leads* give readers the main points of stories.

(In Chapter 6 you'll learn the importance and effectiveness of using headlines on your news release copy to attract the eye, the attention, and the interest of the editor into whose hands your release falls, and to increase its chances of being read and used.)

In a straight-news story there is no buildup to a climax as in feature-news writing (covered in Chapter 7). The writer boils the story down to its principal facts and lays them all out, right in the lead sentence or paragraphs.

Journalism instructors tell their students that a lead (pronounced "leed") is the heart of a news story. This is fact because it's what gives busy readers a summary of what follows and, after the headline, is what attracts readers to a story. It is meant to answer at once what busy readers who have only a few minutes, want to know immediately: What happened? Who did it? When, where, why and how?

To include these 5 Ws and the H, the lead may extend over a couple of paragraphs, but it's where a copyreader or editor can cut the story if news space becomes tight, and it will still tell readers essentially what happened.

The *body* of a news article explains in more detail the facts covered in the lead, and each paragraph diminishes in importance to the end. Paragraphs are short, usually no more than 50 or 60 words, because big blocks of type in narrow-width columns have a gray, uninteresting look and are difficult to read.

There is no excuse for dullness in writing the story. A mere catalog of facts is not a news story. As pioneer newspaper publisher E.W. Scripps told young reporters years ago, "There is really no such thing as an uninteresting story. There are only reporters who do not know how to present it in an interesting manner."

Newspaper Writing Style

Before you sit down to write your first news release, study newspaper writing style. Learn a newspaper's usual style of abbreviation, capitalization, and spelling.

If you will submit only to local papers, the job is relatively easy. Study those local newspapers. If, however, you will be sending releases throughout a broader area, there also is an easy way to learn the style of most newspapers.

There are three "bibles" of style that are found in virtually every newsroom in this country:

- United Press International Stylebook: The Authoritative Handbook for Writers, Editors & News Directors.

  By United Press International Staff. This is a reference used by UPI editors and writers, newspaper editors and reporters, and publicity writers. It is a goldmine of information about such things as writing style, usage, spelling, punctuation, capitalization, and more.
- *The Associated Press Stylebook and Libel Manual.* This is much more than a stylebook. It also provides a section about libel for people who write for newspapers, or who offer newsletters or any other information in print that is distributed to the public.
- *The Elements of Style,* by William Strunk, Jr., and E. B. White, is published by the Macmillan Publishing Company. This tiny booklet (approximately 4- by- 7 inches, 84 pages) is more than a newspaper stylebook. It is also concerned with what is correct or acceptable in the use of English. It concentrates on fundamentals: the rules of usage and principles of composition most commonly violated. This resource should be in the hands of every person who must communicate in writing for *any* purpose.

Writing Principles

Many schoolbook writing rules are broken by practical reporters and editors who know that their product—the newspaper—must sell. To do that, the writing style must be alive and kicking. Good newswriting is vivid, clear, concise, and simple.

Accuracy, simplicity, and objectivity are essential in newswriting. It is equally important for the reporter and the publicity writer to keep personal opinions out of news stories; the expression of opinion is the privilege of the editorial pages and feature stories. Straight-news must be kept as factual as the human condition permits.

Errors in names haunt editors. A minor matter? Not to an editor whose readers say, "If they can't get the *name* right, can I believe anything they print?" Take that question to heart. Write it on your mirror where you'll see it every morning, and apply it to your releases—both news and features. Remember, an editor will be asking, "If that organization can't get small facts right, can I count on any of the information they send me to be correct?"

Definition of News

There are no formula specifications; there is no categorical definition of what news is. As with the word *love*, there is no completely satisfactory definition for the word *news*.

It is almost easier to define what is *not* news. It is not gossip. It is not opinion.

A former editor of the Palo Alto *Times*, Manchester Bodi, offered this definition: "News is what everybody wants to know. It's what a lot of people should know, but they'd rather not. It's what some people don't want other people to know. It's what makes you wise, ignorant, happy, discontented, frustrated, satisfied. In other words, news is just about everything. Or nothing!"

Perhaps a better understanding of what news is, comes from looking at the factors that guide reporters and editors in writing and editing it, as set forth by a journalism instructor, Dr. DeWayne B. Johnson, in a publication he wrote for *The Outlook* (Santa Monica, California) that was used by area teachers in *The Outlook's* "Newspapers in Education" program.

Significance or consequence. *The meaning of the news, the impact of the news, has a bearing on whether or not it is news. A peace feeler. A rumored entente. Editors look for meaning and so should readers. What is the long-range significance?*

Magnitude. *How big is it? In selecting news, editors are forced to gauge the "size" of the item, whether it be of a border clash, an auto crash, or an earthquake. An earthquake killing five in Timbuktu seems small in Southern California, but would seem big if it happened here on Wilshire Boulevard.*

Proximity. *The nearer the event, the more likely it is to be accepted here as news. Five dead in an auto crash in Timbuktu means nothing to readers on the Pacific Coast Highway. One fatality on a downtown Santa Monica street is worthy of notice.*

Progress. *An item indicating some small gain by the human race qualifies an item as news. A new serum, a more effective way of teaching, a landing on another planet, education, science. Progress enters the concept of what makes news.*

Timeliness. *News is an extremely perishable item—it is news because it is happening now. The "news peg" is the thing that makes it news today.*

Unusualness. *News features, human-interest stories fall in this category and win a place in the "news hole" of the newspaper.*

There are other ways of dissecting the news, but those in the preceding paragraphs are meant to provide you with a jumping-off place to help you understand, rather than to give you definite answers.

Changes in News Writing

The high-tech structural changes that are smacking newspapers right and left are fairly obvious. Less apparent are changes in writing styles.

Accentuate the Local

Robert C. Jeffrey, dean of the College of Communication at the University of Texas at Austin, summed it up this way: "News is being redefined." Because 70 percent of a newspaper's revenue is generated locally, local issues are continuing to increase in importance.

While newspapers may no longer be the chief dispensers of news, Jeffrey said, they cannot be equaled in explanatory and analytical coverage, *especially at the local level.*

Abe Peck, a professor at one of the country's outstanding journalism schools, said that reporting Desert Storm in 1991 was a last-stand blitzkrieg against the "newspaper way" of reporting and writing. The Medill School of Journalism professor went on to explain, "Real-time TV footage (however shallow), niche publishing (however narrow), merely mortal profits and old formats bouncing off complicated issues have left newspaper audiences restless; the product too often is boring or trivial."

Senior writer Charles Madigan, of the *Chicago Tribune*, explains: "We're trying to get a narrative, non-traditional treatment of news stories. We can't do what television does today."

Readers Were Balking—And Walking

There is a new mindset among readers. Ray Champney, owner of RJC, International, an Irving, Texas-based company, untangles the problem. "News releases in the past used to be announcements that something had happened. Now the news has to go deeper. Now people want to know, why does it happen? what does it do? what does it mean? why is this good for me, a reader? It used to be enough to simply announce that things were taking place, that new programs were being put into place. Now television does that for us."

Champney, who provides publicity as well as advertising services for clients, says news is different today partially because the way in which business is being conducted is different. He cites an example:

Discount Shuttle is one of our clients. Discount Shuttle is a direct competitor with

Super Shuttle. Both of them service the airports, the hotels, provide tours, and have vans that run around the Dallas/Fort Worth area.

In the past, it would have been news that Discount Shuttle was going to be a direct competitor of Super Shuttle, serving the same customers' needs. Such a news release might still get a blurb here and there.

But to get real news space, questions have to be answered and sufficient information must be included: What is the real reason for Discount Shuttle? The news release has to spell out that Discount Shuttle—and the very name implies it—exists in order to give a competitive choice to the consumer along with good performance and an excellent service level at an affordable price. In addition to merely providing airport services, our client also provides specialized services because consumers are demanding it. For instance, they've put together service programs with restaurants where they take groups of up to 10 people to a restaurant, deliver them, and pick them up. The news story is that they are providing individualized services. They're catering to the local community whereas before these types of services catered only to business travelers. They still cater to business travelers, but they've added layers of service on top of that. That's the news of today. That is the kind of information people respond to when they read the news.

More important from your point of view, the information Champney describes is the kind of information editors respond to these days. That's the kind of release that gets used.

Champney also believes that advertisers are responsible for the discoveries that created the changes in news reporting. Advertisers were forced to find exactly what the public wants, he says. And now newspapers, which rely so heavily on advertising, have been forced to bow to public preferences in order to hang on to readers, who are the reason advertisers advertise in their medium.

Times They Are A-Changin'

So what does this mean with respect to writing your publicity releases? Abe Peck sets it forth for editors. He could have said it for your benefit, too. Take notice!

- Put away the castor oil. During the "Front Page" [movie] era, many stories were high on color, low on fact. Accuracy improved, but the prototypical news article became uninterpretative, bloodless. The citizenry was expected to read out of public duty. Analysis and fine writing [has to be used] to lure them back.
- Inject more point(s) of view. Point of view is the essence of a good feature.
- Exit the land of the pyramids. The inverted pyramid story, with its who/why/where up top, displays the essential facts for readers . . . but overuse turns too many papers into one-note Johnnies.
- Enhance, don't obscure. Highlight writing that's both provocative and evocative. "I constantly have to remind myself to hear the word *story* in newspaper story."

There's much more to come on the subject of changes at newspapers—in content, structure, and writing. Change is a theme that runs throughout this book.

Basic Steps to a Successful Publicity Program

What you need to know and do to get your publicity program off the ground

PLAN AHEAd

Of course, you can follow Arthur's advice in Mell Lazarus's "Miss Peach" comic strip—"Never make plans. That way, you won't start worrying ahead of time."

Or you can use the hit-and-miss or hit-and-score approach. There's nothing really wrong with this if you achieve your objectives.

Or—and this is by far the most reliable approach—you can attain the publicity you hope for with a *planned*, outlined program that will bring better results *and make your job easier.*

Publicity "Planagement" Program

Success for an organization could be spelled "p-l-a-n-n-i-n-g," and planning results in profits. "Business without profit is not business, any more than a pickle is candy," was a saying of American industrialist Charles F. Abbott. This chapter will help you set up a "planagement" program to assure success and profits from your publicity efforts.

A large portion of the business community is made up of entrepreneurs, contract workers, and contingency workers who have been forced out of big businesses, points out Ray Champney, owner of RJC, International, a marketing agency. "A substantial number of people who are now small business people formerly were big company people. The executives who were managers, upper- and mid-level managers, now are entrepreneurs. "These people," says Champney, "have worked and succeeded in the past according to the big company structure." Many of today's businesspeople, who came from big businesses, aren't trained in the do-it-yourself method of business planning—or publicity program planning.

Figuring the Value of Publicity

It's not possible to put a $ figure on publicity, but a properly *planned* publicity program can greatly increase the profit to which Charles Abbott referred.

John Baroody, marketing director for *Automobile* magazine, circulation 550,000, says, "No one has ever totally quantified what it's [publicity's] worth in dollars or sales. But if you could ever get your hands around it, it would be an overwhelming number, I'm sure."

"Some national clipping services count the number of mentions a company or its products are getting as a result of PR efforts," an *Advertising Age* article states. "Still marketers wonder about how much a newspaper paragraph is worth. And how much should it cost?"

The comparison in *Ad Age* continues. "When the price for a single color page ad in a publication such as *Car & Driver* or *Motor Trend* runs in the $50,000 range, PR must seem like the next best thing to free. The cost of spending the day with a half-dozen journalists could be as low as picking up the tab for lunch."

Keep in mind, however, that there is a downside. If a reporter is left with a negative impression, the cost can be immense. "PR is very inexpensive compared to advertising," says Earl Hesterberg, vice president and general manager of Nissan Division. "You can't spend as much on PR in a whole year as you spend on one batch of television commercials." Furthermore, Hesterberg points out, "Magazine articles rank above advertising in the customers' lists of reasons for influences that lead to buying [a product]."

The big payoff for a PR/publicity campaign for Chrysler, which is applicable to just about any small business's campaign, is that, typically, readers of the "buff" magazines—beyond reporters—are discerning enthusiasts whose opinions are valued and sought by family and friends. So, as a result of the publicity, there's a trickle-down effect created by their recommendations.

Step 1. Questions for your Public Relations Plan

Every for-profit or nonprofit organization has public relations—either good or bad. The late highly esteemed public relations counsel and journalist Herb Baus advised, "Everything that the organization can do to improve its public relations will improve its ability to get results and realize the objectives for which it exists."

In developing a plan and policy for achieving *good* public relations—and, ultimately, good publicity—it is essential to ask and to answer three simple questions:

- What impression and effect do we want to make on the public?
- What do we want the public to do?
  Respect the organization's credibility and integrity?
  Respond more positively to sales messages?
  Link the organization's name with its product or service?
  Give money?
  Volunteer time and skills?
- What specific actions must be taken by the public if we are to achieve our objectives?

These questions must be given adequate thought and research in order to set your goals and objectives in Step 4.

Step 2. Know Your Organization

If you are the entrepreneur or the head of an organization, you undoubtedly know the group intimately. If, however, you have been appointed to do the publicity job, then you should research the organization, its employees, and the people who serve and are served by it. Keep the information handy for reuse time and time again.

One of the best ways to acquire the information you desire and to uncover problems is to develop a questionnaire for "intake interviews." (Regular interviewing techniques and recommendations for gathering information and writing publicity releases are included in Chapter 6.) Talk to customers, clients, volunteers, strangers—anyone who will give you a different point of view concerning your business or nonprofit. Essential information includes answers to the following questions:

- Why was the company/organization founded? When? By whom?
- What has it accomplished?
- What is being done now?
- What are future plans?
- Who are the board members, management, and department heads (also staff, if the organization is a volunteer group)? List names, correctly spelled, addresses, geographic areas, and a bit of identifying information about each person, such as title, awards, former positions, community projects, or any other large or small claims to recognition. In the case of board members, name each person's company, corporation, government agency, or whatever place he or she earns a living. If the person is retired, give the name of the organization from which he or she is retired.
- Do you know and have handy (in written form) the company's slogan and upcoming projects or, if it is a nonprofit organization, its goals and objectives?

You will use portions of this information in every release you write. Having it easily accessible will save hours later when an editor or a reporter calls for additional information or verification.

Step 3. Lay Out A Plan

Get a plan. This often is the first advice given to someone starting a business, and it is no less important to the person starting a publicity program.

If you are an entrepreneur, perhaps you were given the "get a plan" start-up advice when you first began your company. Like thousands of others, you sat down at your computer and batted out something impressive. Then you filed it away, and you've been too busy to look at it since you got the company off the ground and flying. However, your publicity program plan will become a well-used road map that you refer to regularly to keep you on-route and to get you where you want to go.

All successful organizations have both short-term and long-term plans. A realistic first-time publicity program might be based on a one-year plan. After you get your feet wet and have a better understanding of how to prepare and attain publicity, you can assure a successful ongoing publicity program by developing short-range, midrange, and long-range plans.

If you have been appointed to the job, you definitely will want to discuss with the organization's management exactly what your publicity program should accomplish.

If you are the boss, you still may wish to present your program to your management committee for suggestions and endorsement. After all, this is the foundation of your entire publicity strategy, and your overall approach should be set to accomplish the goals of the entire organization. Others' brains can add perspective. Moreover, it is well known that involving subordinates by enlisting their advice and help assures greater interest and enthusiasm.

Publicity Budget. Our twenty-eighth president, Woodrow Wilson, is often quoted as proclaiming: "The way to stop financial 'joyriding' is to arrest the chauffeur, not the automobile." Don't get arrested for not having a publicity budget or for not working within it! A budget is a very important part of a realistic publicity plan. Cost push and demand pull often create the bottom line in designing a practical publicity plan.

This is the time, then, to think about the help you will need. If yours is a for-profit organization, the cost of assigning the help you require, a factor in the budget, is a management decision.

If you are head of the organization, you must realistically evaluate how much of your time you can devote to carry out your plan and how much you must assign to others. Be prudent about the amount of additional time beyond your own that will be needed.

If you represent a nonprofit organization and the help you require will come from volunteers, delegating tasks is not a budget matter.

Program Committee. Even if you feel you can handle the job alone for a nonprofit organization, it is wise to have an assisting committee from which succeeding publicity representatives may be chosen. No matter what others may tell you—for instance, that the best committee consists of three people, two of whom are absent—don't believe it. Serving on a committee permits others to gain a working knowledge of the procedures that will make for better representation in future years. As the late Dave Gottlieb, a president of the American Newspaper Publishers Association's Research Institute, quipped, "There ain't no one of us that's as smart as the all of us."

Brainstorming Sessions. Before we exercise, we take time to stretch our muscles. Before we rush into a publicity plan/program, it helps to stretch a little. Brainstorming is a stretch before the planning exercise.

Brainstorming with others who are knowledgeable about your plans and goals is almost always productive, and who could be better to conduct brainstorming sessions with than your publicity committee? The team approach has many benefits. (Appendix C provides guidance in conducting brainstorming sessions.)

Other cost factors must be estimated and included in your budget: possible video news release (VNR) and radio news release (RNR) production expenses, distribution costs, costs of photos, and so on. These cost estimates will be governed by your release schedule, which is detailed in Step 7: "Schedule Releases."

Hand-Me-Downs.   There is one other item that is valuable for businesses, but is an *essential* part of every publicity plan for a nonprofit: hand-me-downs. If you have ever served as a committee chair, you will understand the need to include pass-along items and information. When each new publicity representative starts a term of service with no information or resources from his or her predecessor, the work must be performed as if the organization had never before existed. Such situations say to the media that the organization isn't very efficient—which immediately brings forth the question, "If they're not efficient within their group, are they efficient in gathering the information for their releases and can I rely on it?"

Make plans to systematize your work in a notebook for your successor. Add to your media list (which you will learn to compile in Chapter 4) the "Who-to's," along with a few notes about each of the media people with whom you deal and their preferences (i.e., "He wants only local names, local angles," or "She won't use . . . ," and so on.)

As you send out each news release, file a copy in the notebook. Not only your successor, but *you* will find it extremely helpful if you attach copies of the clippings of the final, published story to the original releases. Your release, together with the published story, not only shows the fruits of your efforts, but more important, reveals how an editor changed your copy. This will help you adapt future releases to achieve greater acceptance and to know what types of releases were the most effective. This material becomes a ready-reference file and an efficient textbook and report to turn over to the next person who fills the position.

Crisis Communications.   Texans like to say that there were so many heroes at the Alamo because there was no back door. Be sure your plan has a back door—include provisions for crisis communications.

No one expects misfortune, adversity, or calamity, and an organization never knows whether or when a crisis may occur. The American Airlines flight attendant strike was a reminder for larger companies everywhere to design or update their crisis communications plans.

Strikes and other kinds of crises also happen to small businesses and nonprofit groups. Even the YMCA and the Boy Scouts and Girl Scouts have had their "bad press" problems. Every plan should follow the Scouts' well-known motto—"Be Prepared."

A booklet by a PR authority is well worth its $5.00 cost in developing your organization's crisis communications plans. The booklet gives a 10-step process that includes a checklist of 50 specific options to activate the plan. Some of the steps cover the following topics:

- Maintaining a continually updated Fact Sheet
- Preparing a first response statement of concern
- Maintaining a continually updated media list that fits your organization's size and kind

- Planning for and deciding who should be named to a crisis team immediately following a crisis.

Other integral groundwork—such as setting aside a "headquarters" office and follow up procedures—should be outlined so that when the need arises, the how-to is laid out in the publicity plan.

To order the booklet, *Don't Panic! An Instant Guide To Crisis Communications,* by Alan Caruba, write to:

Caruba Organization
Box 40
Maplewood, NJ 07040

Step 4. Set Your Publicity Goals

A *goal* is a statement of broad direction or interest that is general, timeless, and always determined by needs. (Tips for writing effective goals and objectives are included in Appendix B.) The general purpose of almost every publicity campaign and public relations program is to improve communication.

Set down your publicity goals with the full knowledge, understanding, approval, and pledged support of management or leadership. Make sure that the purposes and desired achievements of your publicity program are clear.

Among an organization's publicity goals may be the following:

- To win recognition and public awareness of a specific service, product, project, event, program, or function
- To gain prestige and dignity for the group; to establish, build, or improve image, reputation, and credibility
- To bring public recognition to a product or a service
- To attract attention to a program or a policy
- To find a solution(s) to the problem(s) uncovered through "intake interviews"
- To attract and enlist volunteers
- To bring a specific event or happening to the attention of the public and to encourage attendance
- To give recognition to board members, executives, and employees for special activities outside the workplace or for awards won

Choose a realistic number of goals—two, three, or possibly four overall goals—that can be accomplished within the time span of your plan, with the amount of help and funds available.

Step 5. Write Objectives

With your goals set, write objectives for each that define specific, measurable, and attainable end results. Objectives are different from goals, in that the emphasis for goals is always on accomplishment whereas objectives focus on specifics. Write out your objectives to show the specifics of exactly what will be done, when it will be done, by whom, and what end result will be accomplished. (Tips for writing effective goals and objectives are in Appendix B.)

Be realistic! Set publicity objectives according to the available time and capabilities, of you and your staff or committee, and also according to your budget. Answer the following questions before you begin writing your objectives:

- How much publicity does you group need? (The important word is *need*, not *desire*. Again, be realistic.)
- How much time can you invest in doing the work?
- How much money is in your budget for costs of production and mailing, photos, and staff? (This may be the most important question to answer.)
- Is this a continuing, ongoing effort, or a one-shot event?
- Does the organization's need call for weekly, monthly, or only occasional releases?

Step 6. Analyze Your Target Audience

At this time, when media are reinventing themselves—and therefore the information they present is more "niche" targeted—it is necessary to know precisely which audience(s) each medium is attempting to attract and—equally important—the audience(s) you wish to target. Advertisers have found this determination to be essential before buying space or time when "menu" publishing and broadcast "narrow-casting" are the new order among the media. Although you won't be paying for space or time as advertisers must do, it is equally important that you, as your organization's publicity practitioner, know WHO your audiences should be, and WHERE to locate them. (Detailed information about HOW to gather audience analysis data is presented in Chapter 4.)

Step 7. Schedule Releases—Including Photos

Reaching the public through publicity is often like trying to catch the attention of a hibernating dinosaur. Not only may the dinosaur seem to be sleeping so soundly that it cannot hear, but its skin can be so thick that it might need a number of nudges before it even notices the existence of a specific organization.

How quickly the "dinosaur" wakes up is directly related to the numbers and kinds of news releases an organization sends out. A single news item or feature story may reach a considerable number of people, but one print or broadcast story, no matter how widely circulated, will not create a significant or lasting awareness. In other words, you must take the initiative, and initiative in publicity usually means news releases—a continuing, ongoing, regular schedule of news releases.

Pro Bono Work. It would be nice if advertising and public relations agencies offered their services pro bono to nonprofits. Some do, of course. But the need is far greater than the opportunities.

An excellent way to attract publicity for a for-profit is to help a nonprofit. Not only does the commercial group reap the sincere gratitude of the nonprofit, which is usually splendid at saying "thanks," but the news media like stories of this kind and are happy to give credit where it's due.

One idea that would be particularly appropriate for a bank is to arrange to place foodbank barrels in the bank's lobby, then negotiate a deal with the local newspaper for free ad space, and write news releases—on the bank's letterhead, of course—soliciting public support.

Another idea might be to hold a half-day media relations workshop for all nonprofits in town. Invite key print and broadcast editors for a panel discussion, and PR agency representatives to present the basics of conducting successful publicity programs. Provide press releases, press kits, and fact sheets for media reporters who attend, and send these materials to those who don't cover the event. Not only will the event give your commercial organization its share of publicity through promoting the event, it will also allow you to meet and gain the respect of a variety of media people.

There is an unlimited number of *pro bono* projects that can be appropriate and fruitful. Why not call a brainstorming session with your staff and see what creative ideas you come up with?

News Release Timetable.   Set a timetable for the year's publicity, including photos for the print media and VNRs and RNRs for electronic news media if they are included in your schedule. Make your schedules for releases and photos at the same time so that you can consult print editors about assigning space for your important news stories. Some papers assign stories and photos of major events as much as six months to a year in advance; broadcast media work within much closer time frames. Plan to line up major layouts as early as possible. Keep in mind, when planning your publicity schedule, that the speed with which the public takes notice of your organization's work—no matter how important the work—is in direct proportion to the amount of the information you generate.

When your schedule is outlined, evaluate it to decide what items are of primary importance in overall organization plans, and arrange them according to priority. With the schedule set down, you now are able to discuss intelligently with editors your space requests, problems, and extended plans.

Step 8. Meet the Press

The next step is to introduce yourself. In publicity, it's not only what you know, but sometimes equally important, who knows you!

A delightful "Ziggy" cartoon by Tom Wilson recognizes this "law." The cartoon says, "Business success is easy. . . . All you need is good old American know-who!"

Chapter 4 tells you how to make a media list—a "know-who" inventory of newspeople to whom you will introduce yourself. Chapter 5 presents in detail ways and means to meet and work in harmony with the media.

A Letter or a Visit?   The manner in which you introduce yourself depends largely on the size of the newspapers and broadcast stations in your area. If you are working with smaller (weekly, suburban, or rural) media, you may wish to introduce yourself in person. If your targets are large metropolitan dailies and television stations, it is a better idea to address letters to each one. (Most metropolitan print and broadcast facilities have such strict security systems in place that you undoubtedly will not be admitted without an appointment, and an appointment is difficult to get unless the person you wish to meet knows you.)

Draft a letter of introduction that you can send to everyone you plan to meet personally. However, for each person, make an individually typed, individually addressed letter. (That is, send an individually addressed, individually typed or computer printout—not handwritten—letter to *each* person. Not a carbon, not a photocopy. Each letter must be an original, to any editor, reporter, or columnist on your media list whom you expect to contact for any reason during the forthcoming year.)

If you are a top executive, your letter can briefly state that you intend to send publicity releases, and that at some point—when your schedule and the individual's schedule permit—you look forward to meeting her or him. You can also state that in the meantime, you will appreciate any information that can help you conform your releases to his or her requirements. Mention that you are enclosing a self-addressed, stamped envelope (SASE) for his or her convenience. Follow the same procedure if radio, television, and cable publicity or public service announcements (PSAs) are included in your plans. (Details on producing publicity and PSAs for broadcast are presented in Chapters 15 and 16.)

If you are a staffer or a volunteer, your letter should state that you are the new publicity representative for your organization and that you wish to learn anything and everything that can help you make your releases conform to the editor's requirements. Mention that you are looking forward to meeting her or him when you submit your first copy. Also mention that you are aware of deadline times and will arrange to arrive at a time when he or she is off deadline.

Contact Information.   Include with—or in—your letter of introduction, the address(es) and telephone and fax number(s) where you may be reached. If you have a direct-dial number, specify it. The letter itself should carry this information, but the enclosure of a business card or a typed telephone index card for the person's file is a thoughtful gesture.

It never hurts to give an additional name and phone number, in the letter and on the index card, of someone who is informed about your organization and who is familiar with its publicity program. For a news release, this can mean the difference between being used or being tossed if you are not immediately available when there is a need for verification or for additional information by a newswriter trying to meet a deadline.

Pertinent Data and Fact Sheets.   Attach to your letter of introduction a list of names: board members, major executives (with titles), and any other persons of importance in the organization. If you represent a nonprofit organization, this is an excellent opportunity to send an up-to-date directory of members. At the very least, send the names of new officers and committee chairpersons and their *correct* addresses and phone numbers.

Also enclose a brochure or a typed fact sheet about the organization. (How to prepare a fact sheet is examined in Chapter 11, "Hard-Copy Press Kit Preparation.") Many editors keep files of such information.

In addition to these items, include an *undetailed* schedule of publicity plans for the coming year, listed with the corresponding events that will be the basis for the news stories.

Follow-Up Contact.   After you have made your initial contacts, wait about a week or ten days, then give each person a call and request an opportunity to meet him or her. Instead of sending a directory or a list of board members and major executives with your letter of introduction, you might carry it with you to use as a conversation opener.

In regard to phone calls, however, remember that you won't make any Brownie points if you call when an editor is trying to get the paper out. So keep in mind this general rule of thumb for contacting newspapers: Evening papers are on dead-line in the morning—editors are actually not off the hook and a little relaxed until about 2:00 P.M.; morning newspapers have a reverse schedule, working afternoons and early evenings for a usual midnight deadline. Catch evening newspaper people in mid-or late- afternoon. Contact morning paper people before they start the deadline crunch. (The best time to contact television news people is discussed in Chapter 16.)

Press or Media?   How do you speak to—and of—these people when you write or meet them? In the *Chicago Tribune*, nationally syndicated columnist Bob Greene gave some indication about the way newspaper people feel about getting lumped together with electronic newspeople: "There was a time before the word *media* became a part of the national vocabulary, when you were a newspaperman or a television reporter or a radio guy, and you were considered part of 'the press'." Greene went on to say that he thinks he knows exactly when this changed:

> In 1968, at the national political conventions, when reporters were given cardboard identification tags to wear around their necks, the tags had "Press" imprinted on them. At the 1972 national political conventions, however, the press tags were passed out—only they said "Media." The reason I recall this is that I remember being confused. I didn't understand what the word meant, and I didn't even know how to pronounce it. Other reporters were puzzled, too, but the forces behind the conventions explained that there were so many television correspondents and broad-cast technicians on hand that the convention officials had decided to switch from "Press" to "Media."

Bob Greene's grumbling gives you a hint that it may be more expedient to identify newspaper people as "the press" and to identify radio and television people as "the media."

(*Press release* is a term widely used by publicists, particularly those who come from newspapers. However, it implies the exclusion of electronic newspeople. Although you will seldom send publicity releases to television stations, because their time limitations rarely permit use of news items from small businesses or nonprofits, you undoubtedly will include cable and radio stations in your release list. Therefore, you may wish to use the more generic term, *news release*.)

Analysis of an Example Shows Publicity is Better, Cheaper Than Advertising

Chrysler Corporation definitely is *not* a small business. Call it a megacorp. Yet sometimes the best copycatting comes from adapting what the Big Guys do. After all, they've spent jillions to rent the best brains available. It's sort of like using stories from the largest metropolitan dailies as models for the news stories and features a small businessperson writes for the hometown paper.

So let's use the example of Chrysler's publicity and PR efforts to introduce their 1993 line. The story is told in *Advertising Age*.

Working months ahead of the car's public introduction, Chrysler's PR teams exposed journalists to the project. Reporters and photographers were introduced to engineers for open discussions. *Ad Age* reported that by the time they went on sale in the fall, photos of the cars were on covers and pages of automotive magazines—in automotive jargon, called "buff books"—accompanied by almost universally upbeat feature stories. The media and car buffs were well acquainted with the new line long before it was available for sale.

This is using public relations and publicity to win the attention of special auto publications' writers who, in turn, have the attention of millions of car buff readers across the country. Copycatting the procedures and methods used by Chrysler can be done across the board in any similar situation and in any field.

You Have a Plan . . . Now Set it in Putty!

If you're expecting that the plan you've drafted will have a short shelf life, that's good. You don't want to set it in cement; you want to be able to remold it easily. Annual reviews of any plan—on a *monthly* basis—is the best assurance of an effective program.

Look it over. Gloat a little. You may not think that your plan is a barn-burner, but it's not bad . . . if you don't mind that it's probably not perfect.

There's a story from *The Joyful Newsletter*, reported in *Reader's Digest*, that shows how good planning could have produced some much-coveted publicity:

> Moses had a press agent named Sam. When he and his people got to the Red Sea, Moses called for Sam and asked, "Where are the boats?"
>
> "Oh, I'm sorry, Moses," Sam said. "I was so busy with the press releases, I forgot to order the boats."
>
> "You idiot!" Moses exclaimed. "What do you want me to do—raise my staff and ask God to part the Red Sea?"
>
> "Hey, boss," Sam said, "if you can do that, I could get you two pages in the Old Testament."

4

Your Media List

How to ensure that your news will
get to the right people

The Cable Explosion Adds a New Measure to Media Lists

This may be your first personal brush with the fact that media changes have gone ballistic! Here, where you start to put together a list of media that will serve your publicity purposes best, is where it may hit hard that your list need no longer be made up of only newspapers. (Previously, television news coverage was limited to the doings of mighty corporations or to business scandals, because airtime is so limited.) Now there are 500 channel choices among cable stations, which makes it conceivable that even small businesses can find electronic video news outlets that will use their releases.

The job of constructing a media release list has grown, but the potential for securing publicity has grown too. Getting your message out is essential—if people don't know about your organization, how can they buy your product or subscribe to your service?—so lining up the best places to direct that message is an absolutely indispensable part of the job.

Consistent Flow of News Releases

Someone once said that a newspaper is the keyhole to the world. To misquote the quote: Your *media list* is the world's keyhole to your organization.

A consistent flow of publicity releases establishes the fact that your organization is alive and active, and the law of percentages as to how many releases actually are used clicks into place. Salespeople know about percentage laws: one is that, on average, a certain number of calls produces a certain number of sales. Of course, other factors, such as the quality of the product, influence percentages. Similar percentage laws will work for you if the quality of your releases meets media requirements for content and format—*and if you direct those releases to the right media.*

To accomplish your mission—to assure that an appropriate percentage of your releases is used—you must get your message out on a regular, ongoing basis. A single printed news or feature story, no matter how lengthy or how interesting, reaches a certain number of people but misses many others. One news story will not create a lasting awareness.

"Business is much too serious a thing to be left to chief executive officers," says Douglas K. Ramsey in *The Corporate Warriors*. Knowing the seriousness of this task, you may decide to assign the business of preparing your organization's media list to a member of your staff. Remember, before you make the appointment, that the assignment is an essential part in developing a successful publicity program. It carries considerable responsibility.

A Key to Good Media Coverage

You cannot conduct a publicity program without a media list. It can be as small as a personal-contact roll call of a few people at a local newspaper and, perhaps, at a radio and cable station or two, and at a business journal; or it can be as extensive as a national or international mailing list or satellite media tour list. (Seldom do small or even mid-sized businesses have reason to distribute news nationally or internationally. Occasionally, however, a news or feature story merits arranging a "satellite tour." Chapter 16 includes information about how and when to arrange one.)

The size of the media list is determined by your publicity program plans—and, of course, by your publicity budget. The sophistication of its preparation can be decided by answers to a couple of questions: Is this a continuing, ongoing effort or a one-shot happening? Does your publicity plan call for weekly, monthly, or only occasional news releases?

Whether your media list is kept in a loose-leaf notebook, filed on index cards large enough to accommodate the information you catalog, or maintained in a computerized data bank, it is your organization's *customized* directory of press and broadcast contacts. Not only is a well-maintained media list an essential component of a publicity program, it saves time, energy, and resources. As a publicity-release list, it should include every news outlet that will effectively reach the people you want your organization's message to address.

A New Factor Has Entered the Picture

The fact that there are so *many* cable stations has forced them to program themselves as magazines, and radio stations have learned is the most effective way. Each caters to distinct groups of viewers, exactly the opposite from the across-the-board mass audiences that commercial television attracts. This is called "narrowcasting" or "menu" television.

Today, with the numbers of media outlets so expanded, including them all is far too costly. It will pay you to think like an advertiser in compiling your media list. The most successful small business advertisers no longer place advertising in mass market media; they aim their advertising messages to exactly those people who want or need their product or service. They do their homework in advance and have an accurate sense of what their customers' interests, wants, and needs are, then they locate the highly vertical media that cater to these customers' special interests, wants, and needs. Advertisers also know the age segments into which their customers fit, because radio, cable, and many magazines count their audiences by explicit age segments. It doesn't make much sense for an advertiser to pay for time on an all-rock music station when he wants to sell health care insurance or recreational vehicles to retirees. The same is true for publicity. If you sell RVs, why waste precious time—and mailing costs—to write and send publicity to publications and broadcasters that your target group never reads or listens to? If you're not familiar with your market, take a little time and get acquainted before you make up a media list. There is a section at the end of this chapter that tells how to gather data and target audience analysis information—*the way advertisers do it.*

Separate Lists for Releases and Advertising

If your media list or a portion of it will be used for placement of advertising, keep the advertising portion separate.

There are good reasons for keeping separate lists. Never, *never* send your publicity release through the advertising department of any publication, no matter how many ad dollars you spend with the publication. Often businesspeople who spend substantial amounts of advertising money feel that the expenditure should buy them some privilege in the editorial sections. The integrity of news judgment is a matter of great pride among editors and reporters. There is deep resentment at the thought that anyone might attempt to influence the publication's decision as to what constitutes proper editorial material. You can be sure, however, that if you spend big bucks for ad space in a specific newspaper, the paper's editors will have noticed the frequency or the size of your ads.

(We're not referring here to media that use "advertorials," which are paid ads presented in an editorial format. By law, this kind of advertising in broadcast media must be labeled as advertisements, and credible newspapers and magazines go out of their way to label such messages as advertisements, so that listeners or readers don't confuse them with actual editorial content.)

Publicity Media List

Media selection, as discussed in this chapter, is focused exclusively on uses for publicity purposes. Depending on the extent and diversity of the types of news and feature releases you expect to circulate, your media list can be arranged to meet selective, specific, individualized needs and thereby save distribution time, energy, and costs.

The following sections not only assist you in decisions about who and what to include in your media list, but also give you the mechanics for preparing and efficiently maintaining it.

Ready-Made Lists

Robert Frost laid it right out. He said, "The world is full of willing people; some willing to work . . . the rest willing to let them." But why do all that work yourself when someone else already may have done it for you? Try using OPB—Other People's Brains—which is just another way of saying, why reinvent the wheel? If someone has already prepared a media list and it will fit your needs, why not use it? Or why not edit a ready-made list to fit your specific requirements?

Some cities have media guides, often published by the local public relations association or the chamber of commerce. You can learn whether there is such a guide by calling these offices or a local public relations firm. If no guide exists, you may be able to get names from organizations you work with or from the PR department of a board member's company. If all else fails, you can develop your own list from scratch.

Resources for a Media-List

Most telephone book Yellow Pages give names, addresses, and phone numbers of area newspapers, some of which you may not be familiar with. Although you probably know the names of major area television stations, there may also be radio and cable stations you've never heard of.

If you plan to release items to media beyond the range of your telephone book, other sources of information are available, each offering different kinds of information about various media. The best-known directories are:

- *Editor & Publisher International Year Book*
- *Bacon's Publicity Checker*
- *Standard Rate & Data Service, Inc.*
- *Gale Directory of Publications and Broadcast Media*
- *The Standard Periodical Directory*
- *Ulrich's International Periodicals Directory*

Your local library may have copies of one or more of these directories, but they often don't have current editions, which means the data are outdated. However, a local public relations or advertising firm may give you access to its copies. A better idea might be to call the local division of a public relations association and ask which PR agency might be willing to let you use a directory. (Appendix D gives information on how these directories differ and how one or another can meet your information needs; it also lists broadcasting directories and provides ordering information.)

If you have access to a computer, there is a double-barreled resource: *Bates Directory of U.S. Daily Newspapers* and *Bates Directory of U.S. Weekly Newspapers.* These are doubly valuable because they also print out mailing labels addressed to thousands of newspapers, television, and radio stations—for less than $50 each list. Moreover, it does not require high-level computer knowledge to use them.

For more information, call or write:

> International Features
> 8 South J Street
> P.O. Box 1349
> Lake Worth, FL 33460
> 407/582-8320

Obviously, you will want to send your news releases to newspapers with readerships fitting your consumer profile that are as large as possible and that are *appropriate* for your information. The same is equally true for broadcast media. However, don't hesitate to include them all if you are the least bit uncertain about their readership or listener bases. It is better to send information where it is not needed than not to send it where it may be used.

Large metropolitan areas may have more than one major daily newspaper. Because large papers serve the news interests of such broad geographical areas and cover international, national, and local events of areawide significance and impact, you may find it difficult to place news items that involve small companies or volunteer organizations. In these areas, it is important to include other newspapers on your media list, such as suburban and weekly newspapers. Rarely if ever will broadcast media use news items from small businesses. Smaller, independent stations, however, are more likely than large stations to use a nonprofit organization's public service announcements.

Develop a Magazine List Through Another Resource

For many years most magazines, such as *Liberty, Life, Look,* and *Saturday Evening Post,* were intended for general interest, mass audiences. Then "niche" publishing answered the call by advertisers for publications that directly targeted their individual audiences. Today, with 22,000 magazines in circulation in the United States, you undoubtedly can find one or more magazines that are focused specifically and directly on the interests of your market, no matter how narrow those interests are.

The question of how it is economically feasible to publish for such small groups of readers was addressed recently at a convention in Los Angeles. The answer came from Terry Spohn, senior acquisitions editor for Kalmbach, publisher of a collection of magazines that cater to special interests ranging from dollhouses and model railroads to geological sciences and astronomy.

Each of the company's magazines has its own staff, though some resources, such as the art department, are shared. But the principle reason they can publish profitably in such small numbers is because, Spohn says, "there are some pretty accurate demographic studies on who buys what. It's relatively easy to isolate special-interest groups and say, 'This one is large enough to support a magazine.' "

The same kinds of demographic studies are available to you, so that you can know *who* your consumers are. Then you target them through just such media as those published by Kalmbach Publishing.

Magazines have special editorial requirements, so a different version of your release may be necessary. *Writer's Market* and other similar directories also available at most libraries give information about specific editorial requirements and the nature of the audience each magazine plays to. There are some broad-interest magazines, but most, like radio and cable, have narrow subject matter boundaries. And, if magazines fit your publicity plan, don't forget to include city and regional magazines to reach people in a specific geographic area.

Cable Numbers Are Exploding

We may not know for years to come where cable stations' narrow focuses will take them. Some years ago, the same thing happened with magazines. Television, to a certain degree, has followed the same path as magazines. There are general interest, mass audience, commercial TV stations, and there are highly vertical specialty stations that cater exclusively to religious, ethnic, or other specialty programming.

And then there are cable networks and stations. Cable, like radio, has all-news stations—even all-news networks! But it remains to be proven whether the numbers of all-news stations will escalate or decline, whether the public's sometimes fickle nature will want more and more news stations available on a 24-hour basis, or will turn their interests more toward entertainment. At this point, in addition to ABC, CBS, NBC, and Fox for mass audience, commercial network news, there are CNN, CNBC, MTVG, VH-1, Headline News, and more on cable.

The cable industry is virtually blasting off. For example, Westcott Communications, headquartered in Dallas, grew from one network in 1986 to nineteen networks in 1993. That's *networks*, not stations!

Undoubtedly, there are one or more networks beyond the news networks that may be interested in your news. Here are a couple of examples:

- LTCN—the Long Term Care Network—undoubtedly is interested in pharmaceutical information for older people, or anything that will enrich long-term care or improve geropsychiatric treatment
- The Fire & Emergency Television Network (FETN), which directs its programming to such things as "E-med" training, survival skills, firefighter safety, hazard communication, and more. This network, like many others, presents its own news broadcasts following most of its programs. If you have a product or service or event in which firefighters and EMT personnel would be interested, this cable network should be on your media list.

With a little digging, you may find cable networks that attract exactly the people you want to reach. And those networks probably are exceedingly hungry for your news. But you must do the investigating—and it must be ongoing, because new networks, like those of Westcott Communications, are coming on-line continually.

Keep tuned! These are just some of the reasons your entire publicity plan—including your media list—must remain flexible.

Suburban and Weekly Newspapers

If you plan to send publicity releases within a large metropolitan area, it's important to include neighborhood and suburban newspapers that are published daily or weekly, as mentioned previously. In the Los Angeles area alone, there are more than 300 of these small papers. Such papers, often family owned, are major sources of information to people outside metropolitan areas. Often, the owner is also the editor, and sometimes a reporter and the advertising manager as well. Editors of smaller papers are constantly searching for news items about people or happenings in their circulation areas, and they appreciate getting these items as events occur.

Other Outlets for Nonprofits

Beyond straight-news stories, there are other areas for publicity that clubs and charitable organizations should explore. In Southern California, for example, many metropolitan and community newspapers, weekly and monthly magazines and tabloids, and college and university newspapers offer organizations an opportunity to publicize events through community bulletin board columns, calendar listings, business calendars, and society and family activity columns. A review of the media in your geographical area, to find ways you can use your information, is well worth the extra effort.

Business Newspapers.   The business-newspaper trade association, American Business Press, Inc., estimates that at least 8 out of 10 businesspeople in responsible positions regularly read one or more specialized business publications. According to the U.S. Small Business Administration, these readers—whether they are owners or employees—are looking for new ideas, new equipment, new materials, new finished products, anything that will help them to do their jobs better and increase profits for their companies.

An ad for *The Network of City Business Journals* lays it on the line: "We have a different approach to digging up business stories than the daily newspaper." It represents more than 60 business journals nationwide and is worth exploring to locate business publications to add to your media list.

Business newspapers may be receptive to your news releases. They have relatively small circulations, typically below 50,000, and some may distribute only a few thousand copies. But they provide intensive coverage of the industry, trade, or profession for which they are published. It is likely that you will find one or several business newspapers in your field of interest. But be sure to check out the papers you include so that you can modify your releases to meet their criteria, and note alongside the listings the specifics required.

School Newspapers and Newsletters.   Don't forget to add to your media list the newsletters of other for-profit or nonprofit organizations, as well as individuals who are in a position to spread the word.

Depending, of course, on the nature of your campaign and on the types and ages of the people you wish to reach, also consider including area high school, college, and university newspapers.

Other Media.   If you are setting up or sponsoring a new or special program in a school, or if your staff or employees are working with students in constructive ways, you may wish to check school district information offices to locate parent-teacher organizations, called PTAs or PTOs, for bulletins or other such publications where you can get publicity. Churches distribute newsletters, bulletins, and/or small newspapers. If you anticipate releases that would be appropriate and appealing to members of such institutions, include them in your media list.

There are other special "communities" that use print as a means of communicating with their members or participants. It may take some digging to locate their names and addresses, but it also may be well worth the effort.

Specific Contact Names and Titles

To acquire specific contact names for area newspapers, pick up several copies of recent issues. An examination of the papers, their content, and their mastheads usually provides the listing information you need. A telephone call will get you specific names, titles, and direct-dial telephone numbers, which can be important when a hurried news call to a specific person is warranted. Create a file of these publications for future reference—not only for names of editors and columnists, but also for types of information they carry and the styles of writing they use.

The Newspaper Directory "Bible."   If you plan to work with other than local people and publications, go to the library and ask the reference librarian to direct you to a current copy of *Editor & Publisher International Year Book*. This book is the most complete and authentic directory of the newspaper business. It includes information about newspaper executives and department editors (business, financial, sports, food, etc.) and a recently added section, "Who's Where." It also includes listings for the following:

- News, picture (photo), and press services,
- Feature, news, and picture syndicate services,
- Newspaper-distributed magazine sections,
- Weekly and suburban newspapers; and much more.

Each year the July issue of *Editor & Publisher* magazine is devoted to syndicates and includes a valuable directory of newspaper columnists.

When preparing your list of weekly newspapers, you may need to find out if some or all are published by a single company. (This information, too, is listed in *Editor & Publisher International Year Book*.) If so, all releases may be edited by one editor, and therefore only one copy of a release may be required. However, each release should specifically set forth, in the top portion of its first page, the names of the newspapers to which the release is directed. (Be sure to make note of all the newspapers as part of your listing, and include a reminder to specify which newspapers you wish to include for each release.)

On the other hand, each weekly may have its own editor and require a separate release to each paper. (Write a reminder to this effect alongside the listing.)

All this is information you must dig out for yourself. It's not easily located in any one directory.

General Titles.   If you are unable to find a specific name of an editor or reporter to whom to send your releases, the following generic list will suffice, but don't count on generic-name mailings achieving anywhere near the "use percentage" of releases that are directed to correctly named recipients.

- City Desk, for daily newspapers (city editors assign stories).
- Local News Desk, for wire services and periodicals.
- Business Editor, Financial Editor, Women's Editor, Sports Editor, or any other section editors who are appropriate recipients of your publicity news.
- Photo Desk, for newspapers, wire services, and periodicals.
- Editor, for weekly newspapers.
- News Assignment Desk, for radio, television, and cable.
  (The titles of specific people to contact at television stations are included in Chapter 16.)

Verification and Spelling of Names

Some of the tips you will receive throughout this book on how to get along with the media stress getting the names of media contact people right—and then spelling them correctly. This is just common sense. Every news contact wants to be addressed by his or her own name and title—not by a predecessor's—and no one likes to see his name misspelled. *Editor & Publisher International Year Book* lists names and titles of people who work for each publication. This information is correct at the time of the directory's publication deadline. However, there can be many changes in personnel after even only a few weeks. Check by phone, if you can, to verify the name and title and the correct spelling of both for each person on your media list.

Double-Planting

Another tip—no, make it a rule—is never to send the same release to more than one person at each newspaper. It is relatively easy to make enemies when two editors use the same story in different sections of one day's newspaper, only to find that you sent the same release to both of them. This is called *double-planting*. If your list includes more than one person at each publication (city editor, business page editor, and others), be sure to remember to choose *one* individual to whom you direct each release. Again, a reminder note alongside a listing can be helpful.

Media List Mechanics

For reasons that will become apparent, it is best to separate your media list into separate categories for print and broadcast. (One reason is that the format for each medium is totally different.) In this way, you can more easily eliminate broadcast media when they are inappropriate or send only to business editors, weeklies, high school and college newspapers, or any other individual category according to the nature of the information in each release. However, when the information is appropriate for all groups, the separate categories can be merged easily. (If you have access to a computer, these separations and mergings are made even easier.)

Start your media list (in separate sections) by filling in the blanks in Figures 4.1 through 4.3. After you have acquired the basics, you can refine each section of your list to precisely fit your organization's needs. Until you finalize each section, you may wish to keep individual outlets on file cards that can be shuffled or replaced as needed. Actually, if you keep a manual mailing list—as opposed to one compiled and printed by computer—it will undoubtedly be easier to keep all entries on file cards for editing purposes. Personnel changes, even mergers and address changes, call for continuing updates.

Other types of information should be gathered for each broadcast station. For radio and cable, identify and make note of each station's audience: its average age and format (e.g., all ages, contemporary, rock, news, sports, talk, etc.). For radio, cable, and television, make note of the type and length of material they prefer:

FIGURE 4.1   Media-List Information Sheet (Newspapers)

Name of newspaper: _____

Address: _____

Telephone: _____

Name of editor/reporter/columnist interested in our operations:

_____

Other(s) to contact under other circumstances:

_____

_____

_____

_____

Publication day (if a weekly or suburban): _____

Deadlines: _____

_____

_____

_____

_____

_____

_____

_____

_____

_____

_____

_____

_____

_____

FIGURE 4.2   Media-List Information Sheet (High School and College Newspapers)

Name of newspaper: _____

Contact: _____

_____

Address: _____

_____

Telephone: _____

_____

_____

_____

_____

_____

_____

_____

_____

_____

_____

_____

_____

_____

_____

_____

_____

_____

_____

_____

_____

FIGURE 4.3   Media-List Information Sheet (Broadcast Media)
(See Chapter 16 for list of broadcast news editors.)

Name of television or radio station: _____

Call letters and dial location: _____

Address: _____

Telephone: _____

Average age/format (radio and cable only): _____

Public Service Director: _____

Preferred length/preferred material: _____

Pubic affairs program: Make arrangements to be on show through (name):

_____

_____

_____

_____

_____

_____

_____

_____

_____

_____

_____

_____

_____

_____

_____

_____

_____

_____

Examples (for radio, cable, or television)

Uses accompanying descriptive photos or videos

Uses/prefers VNRs

15 seconds for community calendar

30 seconds for public service spots (PSAs)

Copy with basic information for community calendar

Scripts for PSA spots

Two-week lead time for community calendar

Six-to-eight-week lead time for PSA spots

Prefers pretaped PSAs; does (does not) tape

Bulletin board program twice every hour during which PSAs are played; maximum time 10 seconds

(More information about broadcast publicity is presented in Chapters 15 and 16.)

Once you've developed your media list, it should be updated regularly, with additions and deletions made as changes happen.

Include Fax Numbers

Sometimes information can and should be faxed. There may be times when a reporter or an editor needs additional information quickly. Faxing it is not only fast, but more reliable than a telephone message. Timing is another element that dictates whether to fax a release. All releases that are not for the current edition should be mailed or delivered. But fax a release if the information in it should be presented immediately or if there is some kind of change in a previously distributed release, such as cancellation or postponement of an event.

While you're checking directories for listings, notice whether a fax number is listed, and, if so, add it to your listings. For example, recently the *New York Daily News* listed a fax number; *The New York Times*, *Wall Street Journal*, *New York Post*, and *The Dallas Morning News* did not. This seems to make a quiet statement about the publication's receptiveness to faxed messages.

Mailing Label Efficiency Tips

Use the following tips to produce mailing labels:

- When your list is as complete as possible and if you type it manually, prepare it on carbon labels or copier labels.
- Create a copier master sheet of media names and addresses that can be reproduced on pregummed pages of labels. (These can be readily applied to envelopes.)
- Make several sets of mailing labels. An emergency release can create a real crisis if you find that a set of labels must be produced before the release can be distributed.

- If you have access to computer-processed labels, put your media list on a disk so that it can be edited, corrected, or printed at a moment's notice.
- Be *sure* that every person's name and title and every publication's name and address are *correct*—no typos, no misspellings.
- VNRs and RNRs should be hand addressed, as recommended in Chapter 16.

How to Gather Information About Your Audience

You have to know a lot about the people in your market, including what they read and listen to, in order to get your publicity message to them.

Small business advertisers have learned to sketch as accurate a profile of their present and potential customers as possible before they attempt to buy space for ads. And when they know their customers' interests, wants, and needs, then they can ferret out the specific media that reach those consumers. Age, by groups, is a significant part of the final profile.

In other words, if you don't know who you want to talk to—through advertising or publicity—how are you going to locate the niche-type media that will reach them?

There are data gathering services, but they probably cost more than your budget allows. Actually, there are better ways. *Listen* to people with whom you do business now; listen at every opportunity you have, in your shop or your office, and listen to what your staff tells you about the people you do business with.

Personal interviews are time-consuming—no doubt about it—and they do not produce large numbers of responses. But they do give you straight answers as to what they are thinking, believing, doing—and buying. The easiest people to get to are your present customers, but total strangers are most likely to give you totally candid answers.

The more information you can gather from available resources, the less you must gather in other ways. Your own records probably show names, addresses, records of purchases, complaints or returns, frequency of purchases, and the length of time the individual has been or was a customer.

If you have an 800 or 900 telephone number, your telephone bill gives you a tailored list of consumers' telephone numbers. Using a cross-reference directory, you can locate the name and address of each person who was interested enough to make a call. It's difficult to imagine a better list at any price—and this one's free!

A Generic Fill-In-The-Blanks Profile

Only you know exactly the information you need, but you'll get a major portion of it by completing the following form (from *The Advertising Kit: A Complete Guide for Small Businesses* by Jeanette Smith. Lexington Books/Macmillan.). You can add or delete specific categories and customize it to apply to your organization and your patrons.

AGE: _____ teen, _____ 20–25, _____ 26–35, _____ 36–49, _____ 50–65, _____ 66–older

SEX: _____ GEOGRAPHIC LOCATION: _____

INCOME LEVEL: _____ EDUCATION LEVEL: _____

MARITAL STATUS: _____ SIZE OF FAMILY: _____

OCCUPATION: _____ white collar; _____ homemaker; _____ blue collar

ETHNIC BACKGROUND: _____ black; _____ Hispanic; _____ white; _____ Japanese; _____ Chinese; _____ Korean; _____ other (If ethnic background is important, don't list merely Asian. Break out divisions, because each group is distinct.)

PURCHASE CRITERIA: _____ price oriented; _____ style oriented

RESIDENCE: _____ owns; _____ rents; _____ house; _____ apartment

_____ Owns vehicle: _____ Type of vehicle

_____ Uses public transportation

AVERAGE DISTANCE TRAVELED TO REACH BUSINESS LOCATION: _____ ½ mile or less; _____ 2 miles or less; _____ 2–10 miles; _____ 10 miles or more

_____ Has; _____ Has not PREVIOUSLY PURCHASED (our) PRODUCT/SERVICE

PURCHASE(s) made by: _____ cash; _____ check; _____ store credit card; _____ other credit card; _____ billing

FREQUENCY OF PURCHASE: _____ daily; _____ weekly; _____ monthly; _____ yearly; _____ other

REASON FOR INTEREST: _____ recommendation; _____ newspaper ad; _____ radio spot; _____ direct mail; _____ other

PREFERRED MEDIUM: _____ newspaper; _____ radio; _____ television; _____ cable

WHICH: _____ newspaper; _____ radio station(s); _____ television station(s); _____ cable channel(s)

TIME OF DAY/EVENING/NIGHT MOST FREQUENTLY SPENT LISTENING TO PREFERRED MEDIUM: _____ 6:00–8:00 A.M.; _____ 8:00–noon; _____ early afternoon; _____ 3:00–6:00 P.M. NEWS HOURS: _____ daytime; _____ 7:00–11:00 P.M.; _____ midnight and later.

Choosing the Right Media Mix

If you've already put together your publicity media list, now is the time to go back and double-check it against the information gathered in the preceding questionnaire, so that the media you chose will, in fact, reach your carefully profiled consumers.

If you haven't yet assembled the list, keep the profile of your "target" individual at hand at all times while developing the list and whenever it's altered for any reason.

5

Media Relations

*How and why you need to get along
with the news media*

Bad Publicity . . . . It's Reversible

"Wooing the press is an exercise roughly akin to picnicking with a tiger. You might enjoy the meal, but the tiger always eats last."

Maureen Dowd said it in *The New York Times Magazine*, and she knows whereof she speaks.

No business, no nonprofit group, large or small, expects to be the subject of bad news. But it can happen to any organization, no matter how big or small. The secret to not being eaten by the tiger and to handling the situation with a minimum amount of damage lies in being prepared "just in case," and in understanding how to turn bad effects around.

So don't hit the snooze button. Call this your wake-up call, and let's look at how and why you need to get along with the news media. And why just a little advance preparation can be so useful.

First—a couple of instances.

Nothing Succeeds Like Access

Granted, small government isn't small business, but we can definitely learn from their stumbles. Take, for example, what happened when a mayor of York, Pennsylvania, on the day after he took office, ordered city employees not to talk to the press. Later he said he was fed up with leaks and concerned that holdovers from the previous administration would gossip about him and his staff.

Not only did he ignore a state law that gives public access to meetings and records—something private business doesn't have to contend with—but he apparently didn't think leaks would continue under his gag order. You undoubtedly can imagine the press's reaction to his attempts to bottle up the news.

In contrast, the town of Orangetown, New York, built bridges of goodwill with the press. Its officials awarded certificates of merit to the publisher, managing editor, and city editor of the local weekly newspaper, for the paper's investigative reporting. One would think this is a natural thing to do, but *Editor & Publisher* magazine said, "The town of Orangetown has done something unique." And the *E&P* report went on to say that undoubtedly there are many communities "where the local populace and their elected officials appreciate the efforts of their local newspapers but have never thought of how to put it into words."

It doesn't take a lot of smarts to learn from these examples; no one wants doors slammed in his face, and everyone appreciates appropriate recognition—especially media people.

Good (and Bad) Media Relations

Some people seem to be born knowing how to get along with the news media: Walter Cronkite, Ronald Reagan (while he was in office), Barbara Bush, and Olympic Medal winner Nancy Kerrigan are only a few.

There are others, unfortunately, who apparently still haven't learned their lessons even after reaping the biggest crop of bad press in years. You would expect the top executives at Exxon Corporation, who made such a botch of public and media relations during the 1989 oil spill, to have learned from their experience. Not so. The National Wildlife Federation probably should have nicknamed it the bad-press-a-thon. When the federation said it planned to hold a news conference in a space adjacent to the location where Exxon was to hold its annual meeting, to release a "citizen's commission report on the impact of the [Exxon Valdez] oil spill on Alaskan communities," it was "thwarted" by the giant oil company. Exxon rather suddenly and unexpectedly expanded its meeting space to include all available space, including the area in which the federation planned to hold its news conference. Obviously, the move didn't go unnoticed by the media, nor did it stop the federation from making its report.

Even if you're the largest corporation in the universe, it's not exactly smart to try to muzzle people who buy ink by the ton and can talk to almost anyone, anywhere. Not only did the report get out, but undoubtedly more people learned about it than would have if Exxon hadn't tried to deny the group space.

As Justice Brandeis said, "Sunlight is the best disinfectant."

Then There's Jerry Jones

You'd certainly think that Jerry Jones—the "other man from Arkansas"—who skyrocketed onto the news scene when he purchased a football team that the people of Dallas and a goodly portion of the country had cherished for years as "America's Team," would have learned by now how to get along with the press.

After he had made a number of very large foot-in-mouth goofs, *The Dallas Morning News* went public with a prominently featured story that offered him "a little constructive criticism on your public relations skills—or lack thereof." The article gave "tips" from prominent public relations experts and image consultants: "We want to like you, Mr. Jones. . . . When you smacked down a few million dollars for our football team, you bought not only a bunch of big, sweaty guys, but also an important place in our community. We'd really rather like you than not.

"But gee, Mr. Jones, you're making it awfully hard."

That was back in 1989. So you'd bet lunch, after that kind of public advice—that by 1994 Mr. Jones would have learned the lessons the press tried so hard—and so publicly—to teach him. But no . . .

In March 1994, *The Dallas Morning News* carried a banner headline—one that ran across the entire width of the page—that literally shouted, "PR experts to Jones: Put team first, ego second." The story stated that "more reporters cover the Dallas Cowboys than the White House" and went on to suggest that Jones's best approach would be "to respond to some of the concerns and criticisms with conviction and sincerity, rather than to continue to project an image of it being his club and his privilege to do what he wants."

In contrast, less than a month later *The News* published another story under a smaller headline: "Blockbuster handles crisis well, experts say":

> *"Blockbuster Entertainment Corp. has responded to crisis in almost textbook fashion after the tragic slaying of two Dallas video store employees, experts said Wednesday."*

"No one in the community at large can blame Blockbuster or think they did anything wrong," a crisis communications specialist was quoted as saying. And the expert went on to say, "Every business should have a crisis plan. If you're a retail store, you might be robbed. If you're a manufacturing company you might have a recall. You need to have a team in place to react."

This chapter is here to convince you that the basic principles of getting along with the news media are not really so difficult to follow.

Advice on Handling Bad Press

There is no guarantee that everything ever written about your organization will be favorable. So what do you do when the publicity your organization is receiving isn't the kind you're proud to paste in a scrapbook? When this happens, take your media "black eyes," work all the harder to keep further unfavorable situations from developing, and develop a plan for handling any future difficulty.

When receiving telephone inquiries from reporters concerning controversial or otherwise difficult subjects, it sometimes pays to promise to call back in a few minutes and to use those minutes to develop an unmistakably clear reply. This may avoid misunderstandings, for although *you* know what you are talking about, not everyone understands terms and situations that are natural to you.

If you expect to be able to give the reporter the answers to his or her questions later, say so. When the time arrives, it is good business to make certain that you do answer those questions in a straightforward manner and that you don't volunteer the information to the reporter's competitors.

The more difficult the story, the more important it is to talk to the reporter in person, if possible. You might wish to write out a short statement and read it— or even better, fax it—to the reporter to avoid mistakes. Naturally, there is never a reason or an excuse for coloring or stretching the facts. A good reporter recognizes a "curve." Trite as it sounds, honesty is the best policy.

About the only circumstances that call for an official, formal reaction are when there are errors or gross misrepresentations of the facts. Here a letter to the editor is in order, stating the facts and making any necessary corrections. Ask for a clarifying article or retraction; do not demand it. Mistakes do happen, and if the *editor* feels the mistake warrants a correction, he or she will have it made.

The "Know-Who" Factor

In publicity, it is not always what you know; it is often *who* in media knows you! It is important to have at least a speaking acquaintance with the people you hope will use your releases. More important, these people should know you, know your integrity, and have faith in the integrity of the information you give them.

The editor and other people who work on a newspaper are no different from those who staff any business, except that they are usually more pressured. They live by deadlines that require them to write, edit, and print enough material to fill, on average, a book of 100,000-plus words . . . a book the size of the one you're reading right now. And they must do it all in only a few hours! They repeat this unbelievable task every day, day in and day out. Newspaper people deserve your respect for their abilities and for the demands on their time, and they will appreciate your brevity, but not your curtness.

They also will appreciate your gaining an understanding of how they work and the standards they must meet. (Chapter 19 gives an in-depth view of newspapers, that can help you gain such an understanding, which will make your meetings with newspaper people easier and better.)

Benefits of a Media Partnership

It is essential that you learn how an affiliation with the media works. And you may have to know it well enough to teach others in your organization. Such a partnership can provide vital benefits, from which heads of for-profit and nonprofit organizations can build good relationships with the media. As the head of your organization, you can do the following:

- Build confidence in your organization's integrity.
- Build a recognition factor so that your press releases—on your organization's letterhead and with your name as contact—will be given the attention not given to unknown organizations and their executives.
- Establish a personal relationship; this can show big returns if a not-so-positive happening occurs, or your business's image or reputation takes a wrong turn, and you wish to provide your viewpoint. If an editor or a reporter knows you in a positive way, even if only casually, he or she will *listen* to what you have to say. This may mean the difference in the media's being able and willing to present your side of what might otherwise be an unbalanced report leaning heavily to the negative. Getting to know news media people can be a tangible investment in your organization's future.

Rules for Establishing a Good Relationship with Newspeople

Although getting along well with reporters and editors is the very foundation of a productive publicity program, the entire subject can be covered in three short sentences:

- Know your organization; really know it.
- Do the publicity job efficiently, reliably, and credibly.
- Make the reporter's or the editor's job as easy as possible.

Having a great personality and other attributes can be helpful, but only the three things listed here really count.

To develop good relations with the news media, it is prudent first to accept the fact that you are helping newspapers and radio and television stations to do their jobs, which is to tell their readers, listeners, and viewers as much as possible of what is going on in the world. News media, particularly understaffed press associations, can't do a full reporting job without the help of publicity practitioners.

Six "Commandments" for Good Media Relations

Good media relations are built on responsibility and regard for the truth, not on misrepresentation. A professional press agent's six "commandments" for achieving good media relations are as follows:

1. *Integrity*. Thou shalt not prevaricate, nor shalt thou exaggerate.
2. *Immediacy*. Thou shalt come clean quick.
3. *Accessibility*. Thou shalt not build walls.
4. *Deadlines*. Thou shalt not procrastinate.
5. *Familiarity*. Thou shalt do thy homework.
6. *Honesty*. Thou shalt learn to say, "I don't know."

Integrity

The biggest thing you can have going for you is integrity. If the news media begin to question the reliability of a source, the person handling that publicity is better off selling used cars. Keep to the unvarnished truth. Tell it like it is. It works wonders.

The first "commandment" is validated by Jan W. Leemhorst, a Los Angeles public relations man who, in an article in the *Los Angeles Times*, gave the following advice and counsel to Richard M. Nixon during one of Nixon's times of strife.

Because truth is the key to good public relations as much as to good news reporting, there is no conflict between them; because public relations means easy access to certain information, it should lead rather than follow the news if it is properly practiced. When the news media consistently come up with startling disclosures, it is a certain sign that public relations has been mishandled.

(It's too bad the PR people in the White House these days aren't acquainted with Mr. Leemhorst.)

Another reporter, writing in the *Santa Monica* (California) *Outlook*, put it a little more directly. "[Covering the education beat] has taught me to respect those who neither hide from nor even attempt to fight for stories which mislead the public by sugar-coating difficult issues."

Immediacy

This is a critical rule: When there's a problem, admit it immediately.

The Associated Press described how Salomon, Inc. made a snowballing scandal worse. As AP described it, "The company ignored a critical rule: Come clean quick." The chairman of one of the nation's largest financial public relations firms at the time said, "They violated every cardinal rule of good, savvy public relations damage control."

The problem came about when Salomon, the largest dealer in the $2.2 trillion government securities market, publicly admitted that in several instances it bought more than the legal limit of Treasury auctions and withheld the wrongdoings from the government.

The criticism came because of the firm's mode of disclosure—a brief admission of wrongdoing, followed days later by a far broader confession of startling violations—unnecessarily worsened by an already damaged image, according to AP. To top it off, Salomon did not make its leading executives accessible to the press, but managed to salvage that blunder partly by announcing the resignation of top executives implicated in the scandal and naming interim successors.

How Much Information?   There is a murky area concerning what a business is obligated to tell. For instance, when Norman Brinker, chairman and chief executive officer of Brinker International Inc., was injured in a polo accident, there were questions about the depth of details that should have been revealed about his injury. There is, however, an important difference between Brinker International and the average small business—Brinker is a restaurant company that is a stock market favorite. The actual company press release, that was distributed by PR Newswire is as follows:

> *DALLAS, Jan. 22—Norman E. Brinker, chairman and chief executive officer of Brinker International Inc. (NYSE:EAT), was involved in a polo accident at the Palm Beach Polo Club in Florida on Thursday, Jan. 23, 1993. Exact details of the incident are not yet known.*
>
> *Brinker is in the hospital where he is being treated for his injuries. His vital signs are stable and the prognosis appears to be favorable.*

According to *The Dallas Morning News*, experts maintain that securities laws state that a company must keep shareholders informed "in a timely manner" of events "material" to its future. What the laws don't do, they add, is spell out precisely what that means.

The question is a particularly hazy one when the issue is the health of a chief executive. "There's no hard and fast requirement on how and when to disclose information regarding the health of an executive," said a securities lawyer quoted in *The News*.

Whether the company is small or traded on the NYSE, there's little doubt that a diligent press will dig out any "juicy" information that is being withheld. The "spin" put on it under these circumstances will then be seen in a much more negative light than when top executives promptly appear and provide straightforward answers to difficult questions.

And Speaking of Spin. . . .   There are "spin doctors"—public relations experts who specialize in crisis communications—available to help, should bad press get beyond your ability to handle it. The cost can be high, but a greater price may be that the damage becomes so extensive that recovery is at risk.

Johnny Hart doesn't think of spin doctors in quite the serious way most people do. In his "B.C." cartoon one of his characters has come to the "Show Me" rock for some advice. He asks, "Show me a spin doctor . . ." The consultant answers, "And I'll show you a Ph.D. wearing a propeller beanie." Oh well, it's good to know there's a light side about such a difficult job.

Accessibility

Salomon, Inc. was strongly criticized for not making executives available to the press. To make matters worse, it didn't even make its press representative available.

The Dallas Morning News columnist Larry Powell gives good advice on "how to handle newshounds." He advises football players, "If your team has had a bad day, don't lock yourself in the restroom. (Just because you won't come out of the washroom, it doesn't mean that you won't eventually have to comment on that indictment.)"

This third commandment is directed primarily to staff acting on behalf of an organization. If you are the head of the organization, there is an important message here for you too.

A dangerous trap you can fall into is thinking you are the sole source of information for your organization. If you begin to build walls to prevent media people from reaching other news sources within your organization, you can seriously restrict your publicity efforts. Any publicity representative worth his or her salt serves as a bridge between the media and the *best* sources of information with his or her organization.

As the publicity representative for your company, whether you are staff or chief, you are the "advance man/woman." When circumstances are appropriate and, definitely, when requests come from members of the media, be an easy bridge to facilitate access for the media to suitable members of your organization.

It is a wise move for the top echelon of any organization to be in touch with media people, because the public and the media are people—and people respond to people. The public's perception of a business is formed by the personalities of the people they identify with that business. Being in touch also can be a definite plus if the media ever decide to report a problem concerning your organization.

Thomas Griffith, a former editor for *Life* magazine, writer for *Time* and *Fortune* magazines, and author of *How True: A Skeptic's Guide to Believing the News*, explains further:

> Businessmen, who find their own activities under attack these days, seem increasingly inclined to take a dour view of the press—the agency through which those attacks are mainly registered. . . . And so they tend to be skeptical, wary, and critical of the press, ill at ease and generally defensive in their own encounters with it. Unfortunately, this posture only makes things worse. In their own interests, businessmen need to come to terms with the press.

Deadlines

Learn the deadlines of each of the media, and develop a newsperson's sense of urgency about meeting those deadlines. Remember, it's not just their deadline, it's yours, too. There is only one consequence of procrastination in getting your news to them within the confines of their deadlines: the death of that news.

Yesterday's news, the saying goes, is history. History—except as feature material—has no place in a news release. It is your responsibility to get your news to the media before the news happens, if possible, and *immediately* upon its happening if you are unable to give advance notice.

Familiarity

Know your organization and know the people in it. Again, this is a commandment directed mainly to staffers or employees, because the head of an organization knows it intimately and, in most cases, not only knows his or her people, but knows *about* them.

News reporting and public relations are both "people" businesses: People talking to people make the news. In every group there are people who freeze up at the thought of talking to a reporter. Know who they are and hide them in a closet. Send them to Siberia. Put the knowledgeable and articulate people on display.

Honesty

It's tough on the ego to have a reporter ask a nice, simple question and to draw a complete blank in response. Go ahead and make an educated guess, but it's six to five you will be wrong. A couple of bad guesses, and you've dug yourself a shovelful of trouble. Just say, I don't know. Then get the answer—quickly.

Although you may be the owner or head of an organization you may not always have all the answers. You do have advantages over staffers, however. You can ask for information from a vice president, a department head, or any employee for that matter, and you get it, pronto. It's not always that easy for those holding lesser ranks.

Even a "First Publicity Representative," former President Lyndon B. Johnson's press secretary, George Reedy (somewhat comparable to a vice president of Public Relations in a very large corporation) is on record with that very complaint. "There were times," he said, "when I just couldn't get any information out of the White House. But I kidded no one. If I didn't know, I said I didn't know. I was never asked by the President to lie, and I wouldn't have. I would have quit first."

If you experience such difficulties, keep trying; or try another direction, another "tack," another information source. As a last resort, do as George Reedy did. Just say, "I don't know."

The Importance of Sincerity

When Jerry Jones became owner of the Dallas Cowboys, he had a variety of media troubles that usually only the uninitiated come by. "My gut reaction to the man is that he needs more sincerity," said an image consultant, speaking to a reporter. "There seems to be a plastered smile on his face."

The consultant advised, "Don't forget, Mr. Jones, you've taken stoneface Tom Landry's place in the public eye. He didn't smile often, but when he did—by God—you knew he meant it."

The message here is: be pleasant, but be sincere. Be honest about the content of your releases, but be honest about yourself too.

Emotional Restraint

Sports isn't business per se—and the NFL's back-to-back Superbowl winning Dallas Cowboys certainly isn't a small business. But the same publicity and public relations rules apply, and a lesson comes through from Jerry Jones's ongoing stumbles with the media. *The Dallas Morning News* columnist Blackie Sherrod puts it into perspective by comparing differences in the way that Jones and a previous Dallas Cowboys team owner dealt with the press:

> *Tex [Schramm] treated each utterance with the care of a mother driving a station wagon with baby in the front seat, ever on the lookout for chugholes. Tex is a natural master of semantics, omitting a word here, changing a verb there, which might—under careful scrutiny—alter the meaning or afford protection in case the statement was later questioned.*

Jones is—or was—a blurter. . . . He rushed in on his new Christmas bicycle, spouting enthusiasm, running from post to post like an eager puppy. Perhaps he didn't realize that in his new role, in his new critical spotlight, every word or phrase would be rushed off to the microscope, there to be dissected and searched for meaningful intent or philosophy. This trap has caught more than one successful businessman thrust into media glare.

That's the lesson. When you have personal contact with the press, slow down your enthusiasm enough so that you don't give the impression of an eager puppy when you make an announcement about an exciting company development. And if you are giving a reaction to negative publicity, keep your thinking cool so that you can watch your words in case a reporter does rush them off to be dissected for meaning or philosophy.

(An update more than five years after Jones bought the football team indicates that he's still a blurter, which keeps him in an ongoing duel with reporters. But he's proved he is a businessman who has transformed a team that lost $10 million in 1988 into what is probably the most profitable franchise in the NFL.)

Telephone Calls from Reporters

Working with the media is a two-way street. A reporter may contact you in response to a news release or for information regarding an unrelated story. When you do get such a call, find out who is calling and what news organization the individual represents. Find out what the specific questions are and how the information is to be used. This will help you frame an answer to best suit the reporter's (and your) purpose. Tell the reporter you will get back to him or her "ASAP"—as soon as possible.

A Scripps-Howard News Service story explains: "Because so much rides on anything they say to the media, PR people like to double- and triple-check the facts before giving an answer for the record." The story continues, "A PR man who left his newspaper job a while back for the awesome responsibility of filing a larger tax return, likes to tell this one: 'How many PR people does it take to change a light bulb? Answer: I don't know. Can I get back to you on that?' " The humor of the story tends to cover up what really is a backhanded compliment to publicity and public relations representatives who insist on being accurate and an acknowledgment of how hard and how often they try.

Answer only the questions being asked. Decide after the questioning whether you want to go beyond the information that was asked for. There might be an opportunity to make the story more positive from your standpoint. If you do not have the information at hand, tell the reporter you will call back. Find out when the reporter's deadline is and get back to him or her before that time.

Imprudent or Evasive Answers

According to Joyce Haber, writing in the *Los Angeles Times*, "[The late] actor Lorne Greene once said publicly, much to his credit: 'There are no indiscreet questions by reporters. There are only indiscreet answers.' " An old saying puts it another way: Many things are opened by mistake, but none as often as the mouth!

Know well the answers you wish to give—or ask for time to get them. Answering questions you are not equipped to answer only leads to trouble. Don't guess; call back. Conversely, to avoid answering a question that a reporter knows you are capable of answering also leads to trouble. It is damaging to claim ignorance. To say, "No comment," is also harmful. If you wish to avoid a question, simply say that you believe a response at this time would be inappropriate.

No Comment!

Remember the problems the mayor of York, Pennsylvania, created when he "gagged" his people. Reporters know—and detest—the "No comment" statement probably more than anyone else. Would you believe, then, that some newspapers are doing it too?

Editor & Publisher magazine, *the* journal of the newspaper trade, published a recent editorial commenting on the fact that when its staff members need answers from some newspapers, they are told they must talk to the company spokesman "who will speak to the person you are now on the phone with and then call you back with that person's comment."

E&P then asks, "If the person who is deferring to the spokesman is not able to provide necessary information, should not the spokesman always be available to do so?

"It's very frustrating that news organizations that expect their reporters to go out and gather the news—and complain when the reporters are stonewalled—sometimes do the very same thing."

"There's nothing more frustrating than having an editor tell a reporter [the editor] cannot comment, that [the reporter] should speak with the spokesman, only to have the spokesman call back a day later (because he was in a meeting) to tell the reporter that he has no comment."

The fact that even newspapers are committing this unforgivable error doesn't make the slightest change in the rules *you* must follow in order to get along with media reporters. Perhaps it does offer a little satisfaction, though, to know that reporters are experiencing the same frustration from their own kind—and perhaps top level newspaper people will do something about it.

Reporters will not accept evasive answers from anyone. In today's climate, when the public hears such a report they balk—and walk. And the news media know it.

Most newspeople declare that the more unnecessary obstacles are placed in their way, the harder they will work to get their story, for getting it becomes a point of honor. They will almost always manage to print something on the subject, although such stories are bound to contain a high ratio of inaccuracies if the actual facts are denied to reporters by the very persons who are in a position to know the facts.

"Off-the-Record" Remarks

Tom Wilson usually sizes up situations pretty well. In one of his cartoons, Ziggy is sitting in front of his television listening to a news report: ". . . Off the record, unnamed government sources alluded to unsubstantiated innuendos about alleged indiscretions and insinuated that they are rumored not to be without basis for further speculation . . ."

Regardless of all that has been said and written on the subject, the phrase "off the record" is not universally understood. Some media people interpret this to mean that the information may be published if it is not attributed to its source; others interpret it to mean the information cannot be published at all. If you encounter such a situation, it is wise to specify that what you say is not for publication. This may avoid embarrassing misunderstandings.

(Too bad Newt Gingrich's mom hadn't been coached to tell CBS' Connie Chung that her whispers regarding what her son said about the First Lady were "not for publication"—or in that case, "not for broadcast." It's an incident that indicates good reason to coach your own staff—everyone who comes in contact with media people—how they should reply if ever they are asked for inappropriate or confidential information.)

It is a simple fact that reporters and their bosses don't like red tape, evasive answers, or standoff treatment. If they get such responses, what might have been a favorable story may never be written—or a misunderstood "off the record" reply turned into the bad press story of the week.

Let the Story Die!

So often, well-meaning publicity representatives feel compelled to issue information about something they believe will offset a previous "bad news" story after it already has faded from people's memories. Curb the inclination. The best strategy, once negative press is behind you, is to let it remain comatose. (You can't count it really dead, ever. The press have "morgues" from which every story ever presented can be resurrected to use with any future news happening.)

Your Role with the Media

The following points must be reemphasized. Your role with the news media is as follows:

- To be helpful
- To be obliging
- To be honest
- To avoid suppressing the news

The best reaction to criticism is to consider it. It might be valuable. If you are tempted to get into a battle with the media, remember, they always fire the last shot. Just continue working with them in the spirit of a free press.

The bottom line in getting along with the news media is really nothing more than knowing how to get along with the *public*: that's good publicity!

6

Publicity Releases

*What you need to know to
successfully write a straight-news
publicity release*

For Shade-Tree Mechanics

To be the owner of a small business or head of a nonprofit, you not only bear the responsibilities of being the chief, you have to be the "shade-tree mechanic" who does (or, at least, can do) most everything yourself. Already you are chief financial officer and payroll clerk, salesperson and stock clerk, plus doing a hundred or so other jobs.

Now it's time to learn a new skill. As the new publicity director for your organization, you're also about to become the mechanic who writes the releases. (Or at least, learns how, so you can step in if your assigned staffer or volunteer doesn't show up for work.)

As we count down to the year 2000, facing all the mind-bending technologies of our time, there are changes that dictate new ways publicity is to be handled, produced, and presented. One of the biggest changes is in the formats for publicity releases—such as for video and radio news releases. (We'll tackle VNRs and RNRs in Chapter 16.)

The basics of gathering information and writing news releases for all media are, however, fundamentally the same. The news itself is pretty much the same whether it's presented in the extended version that newspapers can use, or in the headline form that is necessary for broadcast because of its time constrictions, and whether it's typed on paper, or satellited, or on tape.

Shocking!

If ever you could visit an editor at any medium shortly after his or her day's mail arrives and have an opportunity to look through it, you'd learn more in just a few minutes than this entire chapter can tell you.

It's hard to imagine where a majority of people's common sense goes when they decide to send press releases or publicity information they hope will turn into published or broadcasted news.

"Some press releases, to put it as gently as possible, were laughable," says Rick Lanning, a writer for such newspapers as the *Phoenix Gazette* and the *Los Angeles Times*. "Each day," he says, in *Supervision* magazine, "I was inundated by press releases and letters from businesses, large and small, and community leaders who wanted publicity."

Try to put yourself in an editor's chair as you imagine this:

- What if every day—before you can even begin to perform your job—you must go through a three- to five-inch stack of *opened, laid-out-flat* so-called news releases? That's *in addition* to reading the stories turned in by your reporters and reading and selecting from all the wire service stories that come across your desk.
- What if 90 to 95 percent of that mail was in some format that no more fits your use requirements than if it were presented as a jigsaw puzzle?

That's exactly the position editors and reporters are put in—every day!

Believe it or not, a jigsaw puzzle was the form one organization used to present its news to a national television network affiliate in a major metropolitan area! An editor or reporter would have to take time to assemble the pieces even to find out who sent the release, let alone to learn what the news it contained was about. The thinking behind such a dumb deed undoubtedly was that the uniqueness of the format would attract the editor's attention. It did. She's never stopped talking about it, but to this day doesn't know who the sender was. In fairness, let's give the sender an "A" for creativity. Obviously, the release wasn't used, so that sender must accept an "F" for goal achievement.

Editors are not renowned for having better eyesight than the rest of the population. Yet in another case, a U.S. government agency sent its news information on a 4- by 6-inch, 19-cent postcard. The type was so small that the $2^1/2$- by 5-inch space allotted to the message contained 19 lines of type—209 words. That's 100 to 150 more words than are on a full page of a suitably structured news release presented on paper.

Another release, also from a government agency, was 62 stapled pages long! Aside from mentioning that newspeople hate stapled news stories, need anything more be said?

But probably the worst examples were several *mimeographed* copies—produced by an age-old process, the machines for which haven't been sold for decades. All were either so faint they couldn't be read, had streaks of unprinted words running from top to bottom, and were on mimeograph paper that tears easily and *never* gives good images. It's embarrassing to say that one of these releases carried the logo of a so-called PR professional.

A business writer wondered to what extent media are being deluged with information so she saved all releases, press kits, boxes, and new products received in a one-month period.

"The result," writes Carla Marinucci in the *San Francisco Examiner* is "a Mount Everest of items: 109 pounds of releases, videotapes, glossy magazines, posters, expensive glossy folders and plastic foam packing materials."

"And business writers don't even receive the brunt of such output," says

Marinucci. "Fashion writers, food writers and columnists are on even more mailing lists and get still more mail."

She goes on to complain that "much of it is exceptionally wasteful, such as the 4- by 4-foot glossy cardboard pizza box, costing nearly $5 to mail, containing packages of Keebler pizza chips (to announce a new pizza flavor)."

Substitute common sense for the extra cents it costs to get this kind of "junk" to your media list. You'll not only win friends and influence media people, you'll win respect that can mean a greater return on your publicity efforts.

TV News Is Abbreviated News

Instant and continuous television news coverage has changed and upset the way news is presented in other media. There is concern among print journalists and some readers that TV reporting may have a negative effect on other reporting. A "Letter to the Editor" in *The Dallas Morning News* spelled out a reader's concerns.

> *On network news, in a typical 10- or 20-second story, they showed Sen. Harry Reid, D.- Nev., telling Mr. [Ross] Perot, "Let me give you a little advice . . . you should start checking your facts a little more and stop listening to the applause as much." That ended the broadcast journalists' story—apparently a successful put-down by the senator.*
>
> *But in [a newspaper story] we learn that Mr. Perot responded by asking Sen. Reid a series of questions forcing him to concede "that the 1990 budget summit generated $1.83 in increased spending for every dollar of new taxes."*
>
> *Unfortunately, too many Americans recline their rocker[s] and listen to greatly abbreviated . . . bits of news stories rather than take the trouble to read what it's really all about.*

Easier-to-Read Writing Is Mandatory

Lower reading abilities and lowered appetites for reading among the public also have caused changes. As the public reads less, and fewer are able to read adeptly, newspapers in particular are turning to easier-to-read writing. That means your release better not have long sentences and use big words, and its content better not be as dull as a 78 RPM played at 33^1/3. Today, print news has become more conversational in tone and much more lighthearted when lightness is appropriate. Newspapers in particular have been forced to repackage to serve both "scanners" and readers.

Local Issues Are Increasing in Importance

The focus today is much greater on the local aspects of stories. Perhaps the word *local* should become the most important word in your publicity vocabulary.

Many editors feel that emphasis on local angles helps newspapers to separate themselves from other media—particularly the electronic media—yet allows them to remain relevant to readers. This was made evident at a recent National Conference of Editorial Writers when there was acknowledgment that a number of newspapers now pay for local material for their editorial and Op Ed pages. And the amount they're willing to pay is higher than that paid for syndicated material, proving that pleasing readers is more important than saving dollars. Remember this every time you sit down at a keyboard to write a straight-news story or a news feature. Do everything you can to include a local angle.

Dimension Has Become a Factor

No longer are readers—and therefore editors—satisfied with one-dimentional reporting. *Los Angeles Times* editor Shelby Coffey III says, "In terms of news, newspapers owe readers a clear look at what's most important, what's most fascinating, what's changed, both sudden and longer term."

It should be noted that even though newspapers are expanding the depth of their news coverage, press releases should remain compact and no longer than one to two pages. Additional information to expand a story can accompany releases in the form of a fact sheet or press kit, as well as a notation that more information is available, with a name and telephone number where it can be acquired.

Because content now calls for broader information, interviewing has become more important to a good story. It will pay you—in terms of releases that are used—to add this technique to your reporting skills. (Interviewing is discussed later in this chapter.) But emphasis on greater depth in reporting does *not* mean writing has become "wordy." Crisp English, tightly written without a wasted word, is still demanded by editors at the largest to the smallest newspapers. The demand is for more information—not more words.

Print Media Are Repackaging Themselves

Even though today's stories tend to contain more information and are sometimes longer and more detailed, readers haven't changed in their demands for nonscholarly writing. They don't have time to read much that isn't easy reading, and they don't want to have to make a *study* of reading a newspaper.

These trends are showing up in magazines too. Rance Crain, writing in *Advertising Age*, says that no medium has a tougher job than the newsweeklies. *Time* magazine was invented when daily newspapers reported the news, he says, and *Time*'s genius was to tell readers what the news meant.

"But now, because of Cable News Network, local television news, network television news and all-news radio, newspapers have been forced to become much more analytical. They've invaded the turf of newsweeklies, forcing them to go on to the next plateau," Crain says.

What that plateau is or will become has not been determined at the time this book goes to press. In the parlance of newscasting, "Stay tuned for developments in this breaking story."

An example of these immense changes is evident in a business magazine that came on the market in 1993, combining the managerial insights of the *Harvard Business Review* with the writing and jazzy graphics of *Rolling Stone*. *The New York Times* reports that the publication—called *Fast Company*—"is aimed at a new generation of business people in what the editors call the new economy."

One thing more before we go on—we have to acknowledge that writing isn't always easy. David Holahan, in a feature story in *The New York Times*, states unequivocally that writing is hard. He quotes Red Smith, another writer, as saying, "There is nothing to it. Just sit down and open a vein." Then Holahan adds, "The gentlemanly Smith was too polite to add: If there is any blood left after the creation it will be shed when the editing is done."

Writing takes effort, but the tricks of the trade spelled out in this chapter (and coaching in copycatting in Chapter 8) are meant to make writing news releases relatively easy.

Focused Writing

Because the reader wants to know immediately what a news story is about, the summary of the story is placed at its beginning rather than at its end, where our grade-school teachers taught us to summarize a story. Thus, the reader can get the gist immediately, decide whether he or she wishes to read the rest, and, if so, hurry on through the entire story—all because of the unique style in which newspaper news stories are written.

E. B. White's "Reminders"

No one wrote better rules for newswriting than E. B. White, coauthor with William Strunk, Jr., of *The Elements of Style*. White calls the rules "reminders," and they appear in a chapter in the book that writers of every type enthusiastically testify is one of the most powerful little books around. You will do well to keep it alongside your typewriter or computer at all times.

Some of E. B. White's "reminders" are:

- Write with nouns and verbs, not with adjectives and adverbs; in general, it is nouns and verbs, not their assistants, that give good writing its toughness and color.
- Avoid the use of qualifiers (e.g., *rather, very, little, pretty*, etc.).
- Do not explain too much (e.g., "he said consolingly," "she replied grudgingly," etc.). Let the conversation itself disclose the speaker's manner or condition.
- Avoid fancy words—the elaborate, the pretentious, the coy, and the cute (e.g., *beauteous, curvaceous, discombobulate, tummy*).
- Be clear. When you become hopelessly mired in a sentence, start fresh.
- Revise and rewrite. It is no sign of weakness or defeat if your manuscript ends up in need of major surgery. This is a common occurrence in all writing and happens to the best of writers.

Another book that is literally priceless (because it is not available to the general public) is *Learning in the Newsroom*. It was published by the American Newspaper Publishers Association (now the Newspaper Association of America) Foundation and was compiled and edited by John L. Dougherty, managing editor of the Rochester (New York) *Times-Union*. Many newsroom supervisors have used it, and undoubtedly still do, as a valued manual for neophyte reporters. The writing rules from the book, mentioned in this chapter, are an edited version in the interest of space.

The *Kansas City Star*'s Condensed Rules

An old *Kansas City Star* style sheet gives much of the same advice as E. B. White's "reminders," but says it more concisely:

- Use short sentences.
- Use short first paragraphs.
- Use vigorous English.
- Be positive, not negative.

Ernest Hemingway used this style sheet when he was a cub reporter for the *Star*. Hemingway said, "Those rules were the best I ever had for the business of writing."

Mark Twain's Rules

Mark Twain set down his own rules for writing. They are still appropriate today.

- Eschew surplusage.
- Say what you propose to say, don't merely come near it.
- Use the right word, not its second cousin.
- Don't omit necessary details.
- Avoid slovenliness of form.
- Use good grammar.
- Employ a simple and straightforward style.

Twain started his writing career as a newspaperman for a San Francisco paper, *The Alta Californian*. In the early 1860s he was city editor of Nevada's *Territorial Enterprise*.

Ten Steps for Writing a Newspaper News Release

Is that blank screen or plain, white, empty piece of paper staring back at you? Are you ready and willing to write your first news release, but still unsure how?

"There are shelves full of books on writing. But often you will experience, even after having read volumes, a terrible empty feeling when you sit down to a blank sheet of paper to write a story." Those lines also are from *Learning in the Newsroom*, the newsroom manual for beginning reporters, most of whom have the advantage of being journalism graduates. This empty feeling is recognized by anyone who writes. Don't let a blank computer screen or a bare sheet of paper defeat you. What to do? Just use these ten steps (which are explained in the sections that follow) to help you overcome your writer's block.

1. *Focus and clarity*. Know what you want to say.
2. *The lead paragraph*. Structure your story.
3. *News story body*. Flesh out the details.
4. *Imitation*. Follow the style and construction of existing articles.
5. *Completeness*. Cover all of the facts.
6. *Editorializing*. Don't give your opinion.
7. *Names*. Use proper style for spelling out of names.
8. *Closing*. Add a final paragraph.

9. *Editing.* Review your copy twice, then review it again.
10. *Accuracy and simplicity.* Strive for a perfect news release.

Newswriting Rules

As in playing bridge, Monopoly, or any game, writing a news release is relatively easy and a lot more fun when you *know the rules.* This chapter concentrates on the basics of writing news releases and what goes into them. Call it the maternity ward—where news releases are born.

Rule 1—Focus and Clarity

"Be sure you have an idea of what it is you want to say. Often when a reporter asks a colleague for help with a lead paragraph," advises *Learning in the Newsroom,*" he finds that he doesn't really know what it is he is writing about, and as soon as he discovers what it is, the lead comes easily and naturally."

Outlines.   Former Associated Press reporter, two-time Pulitzer Prize winner, and book author Don Whitehead writes about his way of organizing a news story in *Reporting/Writing from Front Row Seats.* He says, "Some reporters have the ability to organize a story in their minds merely from reading their notes. But my own method—in writing a news story or a book—is to make an outline of the major points of the story and the sequence in which I wish to present them."

The safest way to be sure of exactly what your story should include is to make an outline of the major points of the story and the order in which you will present them, from most important to least important.

The following is one example of an outline:

1. John Jones is named CEO of _____ (include company name and identification).
2. Jones succeeds Joe Smith, who resigned in February.
3. Jones joins Bill Adams, company chairman.
4. Jones's previous experience.
5. Quotes from Adams regarding Jones's appointment.
6. Quotes from Jones about his plans for employees and the direction in which he expects to take the company.
7. Information about the company and anything it is known for.
8. Beginning date of Jones's employment.

Another sample outline is as follows:

1. Brown will discuss why worker skills are declining.
2. At group meeting of _____ (briefly identify group).
3. Date and place of meeting.
4. Identify speaker and cite prominence.
5. Expand on topic to be discussed and purposes.
6. Include pertinent identifying information about sponsoring group.
7. Luncheon reservations are necessary and can be made by calling Jane Johnson at 000-1111, Ext. 123.

Interviews—The Bedrock of Journalism.   Interviews help give focus and clarity to a story. Sometimes it is necessary to gather information for your news release, and you may need an interview with one or more individuals. The interview, a primary information-gathering technique of reporters and publicists, supplies quotes that embellish a story—it is the bedrock of journalism. An interview can add a human element where otherwise there is none. Include this technique in your growing storehouse of "know-how" information.

Jane Ardmore, a distinguished Los Angeles-based journalist, put together steps for conducting successful interviews, and she tells a story that got her a blank.

An interview is not a series of questions: it is conversation, and you are going to get from it what you bring to it. Like friendship. The better informed you are, the more intelligence, sensitivity, and understanding you have, the better friend you'll be. Ditto the interviewer. Super ditto. For in friendship you get to know a person little by little, marvelous bits and pieces which gradually illuminate a human being. In an interview that illumination must be accelerated; there is a circumscribed amount of time. Your success hinges largely on the ability to communicate, and quickly.

Do Your Homework.   "My first national magazine assignment," Ardmore says, "involved that regal old lady [of stage and screen], Ethel Barrymore, and I never got to her because . . . the day before, another young newspaper reporter was ushered in. She fumbled about, then for openers tried, 'Miss Barrymore, of course, you've never been married.' At which Miss B drew herself up and boomed, 'My dear young woman, everyone *knows* I have been married.' The reporter then stammered, 'But . . . but . . . of course you've never had children.' 'Young woman, everyone *knows* I have had children,' said Miss Barrymore and therewith swept from the room and cancelled all subsequent interviews, including mine."

From that we learn: there are four steps to a successful interview.

1. *Preparation.* Learn as much as possible about the people you are going to interview. Don't embarrass them or yourself by asking obvious questions (where they were born, where they went to school, marriages, divorces, children's names and ages, career data).

   If you are interviewing on some specific subject, such as the person's work with retarded children or participation in the development or marketing of a new service, learn as much as you can about the subject.

2. *Communication.* Whatever the goal of the interview, start with some area of interest that will put your subject at ease, not on the defensive. "Interviewing Jane Fonda, you might expect a brash barbarella," Ardmore said. "In the first few moments—our conversation started with the adjustments of an American girl transplanted to rural France—I realized she was highly sensitive and deeply vulnerable. What I'd come to ask was how had a baby changed her life; once I perceived what a feeling person she is, it was easy."

Which brings us to:

3. *Perception.* You must keep alert, keep flexible; in short, *listen*. In interviews, as in life, people so often ask a question and never listen to the answer. Listen—and don't be afraid to take notes. No pro relies on memory

alone, and no one worth interviewing wants to be misquoted. Unless you have the material written down, it's going to be difficult to:

4. **Project** that interview into a story. You may come away with feelings and awareness, but without notes and quotes, those impressions are likely to be flabby. What you want is to come away from your interview with a story worthy of all that preparation, communication, and perception: "The facts, ma'am."

Listen Through Dead Air.   *Let the interviewee talk!* You don't learn much when you talk. You really learn when you listen, and you may be astonished at the incredible things you'll learn when you listen through seconds of "dead air." This is a tactic used by professional journalists.

People who are not trained interviewers often have difficulty waiting for answers to their questions. A pause following an answer becomes an uncomfortable moment for both participants. Such a pause by the questioner, following the answer to a question, however, may bring forth answers the interviewee never intended to give—deep down answers—because he or she feels compelled to fill the silence with words. The best policy is: *Let the person talk—and then wait for all of the answer.*

On the Other Side of the Interview Table.   Perhaps you've experienced being interviewed and found it not to be the greatest event of your life. Or perhaps you anticipate a day when a newsperson will call to talk about an aspect of your organization. While we're on the subject of interviews, let's look at what produces the best results in terms of publicity when you're sitting in the interviewee's chair.

Christine Brand Naylor is a vice president of a strategic communications firm with offices in Washington, D.C., and New York. She told *Bottomline* magazine that when being interviewed, "questions are less important than your answers, because only your answers will reach the public."

She also advises you to keep in mind that the reporter isn't the audience. "The reporter is merely the conduit to the public that reads the words or listens to the broadcast. No matter how negative a question is, and no matter how hostile and cynical a reporter may be, it is important not to lose sight of your objective and messages," she says.

Here are Naylor's suggestions for the times you're the interviewee instead of the interviewer:

- Stick to what you know. Don't speak for others.
- Refer reporters to appropriate experts or materials for additional information.
- Find out as much as possible about the subject matter before the interview.
- Be prepared to answer sensitive questions and offer solutions to potential problems.
- Don't make offhand remarks. Reporters remember every word, even after the tape or the microphone is off.
- Be prepared to offer examples or anecdotes to illustrate your points, but remember that they might be edited or taken out of context.
- Avoid jargon.

- Remember the local angle at all times.
- Never say, "That was NOT for publication," or request anonymity after the fact. Such a statement will probably irritate the reporter, who has no obligation to honor such requests. Even if there are prior agreements, be prepared to see whatever you have said in print or on the air, especially if your information is newsworthy.

Now you know how to *be interviewed*. Perhaps the tips will also help you as the one doing the interviewing.

The GOSS Interview Formula.   Unlike a living room conversation, an interview must have flow, direction, and intensity. A journalism professor, LaRue W. Gilleland, devised a simple formula for asking effective interview questions. His students named the formula Gilleland's GOSS Formula because the acronym GOSS—from the key words *goal, obstacle, solution,* and *start*—provides a memory-jogging device. It reminds the interviewer to ask questions similar to the following:

- *Goal-revealing questions.* What are you trying to accomplish? What's the real purpose of your organization?
- *Obstacle-revealing questions.* What problems did you face? What stands in your way now?
- *Solution-revealing questions.* How did you handle the problem? What plan do you have for resolving the conflict?
- *Start-revealing questions.* When did the program have its beginning? Whose idea was it?

Rule 2—Lead Paragraphs

> *I keep six honest serving men*
> *(They taught me all I knew);*
> *Their names are What and Why and When*
> *And How and Where and Who.*
>
> —*"The Elephant's Child,"* Just So Stories, by Rudyard Kipling

Call in your "six honest serving men"—the five Ws and, if appropriate, the H. The most common straight-news lead paragraphs use them, with *What, When,* and *Who,* the Ws with the highest priority, included in the first sentence. If it's *local* news, *Where* is also given a top ranking.

In general, the structure of a news story is opposite to that of other literary forms. In a straight-news release, it's what's up top that counts! There is no buildup to a climax; you must boil the story down to its principal facts and lay them all out in the lead paragraphs.

Story Summarization.   Your opening summary paragraphs contain answers to questions readers want to know:

- *Who(m)* is the story about?
- *What* happened?
- *When* did it happen?

- *Where* did it happen?
- *Why* did it happen?
- *How* did it happen?

It is sometimes, but not always, necessary to answer the final item—how it happened. Write the answers to these questions from the facts of each specific news story as part of your outline for a release.

An Example of a "5 W" News Story.   Rick Lanning, writing in *Supervision* magazine, addresses small business people: "[Perhaps you may be] deciding to open a new business or expand your old business. Or maybe you're adding a new product line or service to an existing firm. Or you've hired a new manager, department head or employee.

"Each of these events," says Lanning, who has been an editor and now is a PR consultant, "properly presented in a press release, can answer those five Ws."

"Here is how such a press release might read." Put in the name of your company where appropriate:

FOR IMMEDIATE RELEASE:

Green's Hardware, which first opened its doors in Fair Hope City Oct. 1, 1902, will ring up its final sale at 112 Main Street Friday. Owner Harry Green announced today he is moving his operation into a facility nearly double the size of the old store at the new Brighton Shopping Center.

"I hated to leave the old place," said Green, 67. "My father started it and it's served our customers well. But increased demand for our products and services and a desire to better serve our customers make it necessary for the company to have more floor space. We're looking forward to reopening for business on Monday, April 22, and we hope all our old customers will be there for the grand opening."

What . . . Where . . . Who . . . Why . . . and When—all are answered in the preceding example. (More examples are included in Chapter 8 on copycatting.)

"Blind Leads."   Jack Hart, the writing coach at *The Oregonian* newspaper, puts helpful information into a column for *Editor & Publisher*. He says blind leads are "absolutely central to straight news reporting, because they're the most immediate way of answering the question central to every straight news story: 'What's this about?' "

Skilled reporters and publicity writers use them. Your writing will look a lot more professional if *you* use them, too.

A blind lead is a short, punchy form that makes for high readability because it doesn't dump everything right out in the first graf.

Here are Hart's examples: first, an "all-too-typical version of a lead suffocated by excessive detail," followed by "one possibility for a blind version."

The typical lead:

Officials of the city and the Gladstone School District are breathing sighs of relief following the Clackamas County Housing Authority's decision to pull out of a plan

*to build an apartment complex for moderate-income people on 11 acres of land
between Southeast Oatfield and Webster Roads."*

The blind lead:

*Several officials have applauded the county's decision to scrap plans for a subsidized
housing complex."*

As Hart explains, "Blind leads are a way of showing readers the forest before
plunging into the trees. . . . They hold back on the details so that the central theme
of the story can emerge clearly, free of all the clutter that might otherwise over-
whelm it."

You may want to watch for blind lead stories, which are becoming a way of
doing it for great numbers of newspapers, and add them to your copycat files.

More Copy Writing Guidance.   Try to work the name of your organization high
up in the lead so it cannot easily be cut without destroying the meaning of the
story. Set down your facts, one by one, for the first paragrph.

If the lead paragraph runs longer than about 50 or 60 words, distribute the five
Ws, and the H if used, in two paragraphs. Actually, 50 words may be too much for
a lead graf. Take notice as you read newspapers. The most popular papers have
changed the way leads are written, concentrating on the use of blind leads and
keeping them to 15 to 20 words. But the statement made in those 15 or 20 words
is usually an eye catcher, a thought provoker, or a teaser that is meant to plummet
you into the next graf.

Lead Content.   Capture the essence of your story in the lead paragraphs. The art
of writing a news story demands that the writer tell something of value to the
reader, that this something be told quickly, and that it always be told honestly.

"Whatever you write, have consideration for your reader. He has little time.
You have to tempt him. Make it worthwhile," advises Peter Arnett, a Pulitzer Prize-
winning Associated Press correspondent. He might also have added: And he has
little inclination to read; he'd rather watch a newscast.

Remember that your lead paragraphs are a summary of the entire story. The
reader should be able to stop immediately after having read your lead and know
that he or she has captured the significance and the nature of the entire story. He
can read on for the details.

Your lead should convince the editor either to use your story or to send a reporter
to cover it. In other words, the lead should hook the reader, particularly if that
reader is the editor of the newspaper you want to use your story. (Sample leads are
shown as part of the sample news releases in "A Copycatter's Primer," Chapter 8.)

Rule 3—News Story Body

Have you noticed how the word *story* accompanies the word *news*? Your release is
a news story, so don't underplay or forget the importance of the word. People don't
want a list of facts, they want a *story*.

After your lead paragraph or paragraphs, flesh out the details of each of the five Ws—what, when, who, where, and why. The *body* of a news release explains in more detail the facts covered in the lead, and each paragraph diminishes in importance to the end of the story.

Inverted Pyramid.   The structure of a news story is an *inverted pyramid*—an upside-down presentation of important information. This inverted pyramid technique is used so that editors can lop off final paragraphs to fit space limitations without cutting important information. (In Chapter 2, both a short news story and a long news story are diagrammed in the inverted pyramid style.)

The Pyramid and the Telegraph.   Did you ever wonder how this completely unique foundation of American reporting came about? Technology was the culprit. Early reporting was wordy and disorganized until the advent of the telegraph. Telegraphing news was highly desirable, but it was also costly and often unreliable. So editors demanded that the basic facts be sent first, just in case the rest of the story was lost in transmission. And, of course, publishers—those watchdogs of the budget—recognized and welcomed the savings that resulted from sending shorter stories.

Use your organization's name several times throughout the body of your release, always in a manner that makes its use relevant to the rest of the story.

The Importance of "Who."   Don't downplay the importance of "who" in a news story. Remember, the editor likes names, because people like to read about people and because names sell extra newspapers. So it's well worth the effort that may be required to submit *all* the names of members, delegates, officers, guests, and/or other people involved in your story. Of course, you're not expected to fit all the names into lead grafs, just the most important one or two. More names may be added later in the body of the story. If you doubt that they all belong in the story, use only those names you are sure are appropriate and attach a list (with a paper clip, not a staple) of the remainder to the final copy of the release.

If your release will, in any way, elicit a public response or a desire by readers for more information, be sure to include a final line that will preclude calls to the newspaper (e.g., "For further information, call [give an authorized name and phone number]").

Good Reporters Are "Whys" Guys.   "Why" is an important "W" too. To turn out a good news story—one that will be used—the answers to whys are basic.

Newspaper Style Sheets.   The glossary tells you that *style* is a newspaper's rules on writing, spelling, and so on. One of the style rules (that all newspapers follow) is to use figures for dates, times, street numbers, and sums of money, *except* when beginning a sentence. Whenever possible, avoid starting a sentence with a number, but if it is necessary, spell out the numbers that fall first in the sentence, and spell out numbers one through nine and use figures for 10 and up for numbers within a sentence. For other rules of style, refer to the *stylebook* or *style sheet* used by a particular newspaper to which you are sending a release.

Two stylebooks that are popular with newspapers that don't publish their own style sheets are published by The Associated Press and United Press International. (Ordering information and descriptions of the two stylebooks are provided in Appendix D.) If you are in doubt, call the copy desk during off-deadline time. Someone there can give you the name of the stylebook used by the newspaper for which you are writing.

Rule 4—Imitation

With a minimum of effort and training, imitation can help you develop skill in presenting your news story. (Chapter 8 gives you the basics of "copycatting.") Follow the style and construction of articles that already have appeared in your newspaper. Keep your sentence structure simple and your information direct. Don't expect the editor to rewrite, although most of the time he or she will assign a rewrite—for the newspaper's purpose, though, not to clean up your writing.

Schoolbook Rules.   As you study your copycat samples and examples from newspapers and the professional examples in Chapter 8, take note that many schoolbook writing rules are broken by practical reporters, editors, and professional publicists. You will want to break the same rules they do.

Certain rules are broken because newspeople know that their product—the newspaper—must sell, and in order to sell, the style and writing must be alive and kicking. When breaking these rules, do it for the same reasons, and the recipients of your releases will love you for it.

A classic example of a schoolbook rule regularly broken in newswriting is this: A single paragraph must contain a single idea or thought. In newswriting, one thought may be extended over several paragraphs (called *grafs* by newspeople). This keeps paragraphs short and easy to read.

Another rule often broken is the introduction of a new thought in the last sentence of one paragraph to catch the reader's interest and carry him or her into the following paragraph.

Rule 5—Completeness

Don't assume the reader (or the editor, for that matter) has any background knowledge about the subject of your release. It is far easier for an editor to cut unneeded details than to dig them up to include in a story. Chances are high that the editor won't bother.

You also can submit a fact sheet or a press kit with your story. (What to include in a fact sheet and press kit and how to tailor them to your specific purposes are discussed in Chapter 11.) Attaching a previously prepared fact sheet or a much more complete collection of information in the form of a press kit may be an excellent method for presenting background and details. Either one may provide the editor or reporter with a better understanding of the content of your news release and be the added incentive for him or her to assign additional space for the story.

Rule 6—Editorializing

Don't editorialize the facts in a news release; don't pass off your opinions or beliefs as facts. However, you can add "meat" to a news release when you present another person's opinion in quotes. The quote must be word for word, not your interpretation. It must be relevant, and it must be fully attributed (the source's name and title or other pertinent information).

Attribution.   With regard to attribution, it has become increasingly important to give the name of an information source, rather than to use a phrase such as "sources said." David S. Broder, author of *Behind the Front Page: A Candid Look at How the News Is Made*, assigns blame to the press itself for the public's loss of faith in the truth of information attributed to unnamed sources. One of several examples he gives is the famous falsehood presented by Janet Cooke in *The Washington Post* about an eight-year-old heroin addict. Broder states that overuse of the phrase "sources said" worsens the credibility problem. The more the phrase is used, the less readers trust a story. Using an eye-catching, stimulating quote that is fully attributed, however, can be a very effective way to begin a news release. Using quotes throughout the story is good journalism.

Words That Express Your Opinion.   To avoid editorializing, watch the words you use. John L. Dougherty was an editor at the Rochester (New York) *Times-Union* at the time he compiled and edited *Learning in the Newsroom*. In one of Dougherty's earlier news stories, he wrote about the quarterly report of the old Boston Elevated System, which had a nearly unbroken record of deficits but was at the moment in the black. In the article, he stated, "The Boston Elevated had a remarkable record for January—it showed a profit." He relates his experience concerning the article:

> The old night editor brought my copy back. He knew I was green. In a kindly way, he spelled out the trouble. "Remarkable is not a reporting word," he said. "We just tell the facts. Tell the story so that the reader will say, 'That's remarkable.' "

Editorial "We."   In straight-news releases or in reporting, the first-person pronoun "I" is never used. In a letter to the editor to the *Los Angeles Times*, recognition of the universal acceptance of the editorial "we" is given:

> The President and the Governor always refer to themselves as "we" when they really mean "I." Only two groups of people are entitled to refer to themselves as "we"—the editors of newspapers and fellows with tapeworms.

There's a theory, purely facetious, about why newspapers use the editorial "we": so the person who doesn't like what's printed will think that there are too many to lick!

Rule 7—Names

Always spell out the name of your organization in the first use, then follow the name with the accepted initials in parentheses—if the organization is well known by its initials [e.g., General Electric (GE), Platt Accountants Service, Inc. (PASI), or The Resource Assistance Center (TRAC)]. After the first, spelled-out use of the name, use of the acronym throughout is acceptable. Some newspapers now eliminate the parenthetical use of acronyms following the first use of the full name; others follow the older style. Be safe and add it—it's easier for editors to cut than to add.

When using people's names, follow the publication's style when you know it. It is common practice to use each person's full name—for instance, Mary J. Jones (with her title or other identifier)—when the name is first used in the story. Further references then use only the last name (e.g., "Jones will take office at the next . . .").

Ms. Nomers.   There are, however, exceptions. *The Wall Street Journal, The Dallas Morning News*, and a few other newspapers, after the initial use of the name use the abbreviations Mr., Mrs., or Ms. along with the last name throughout the rest of the story. In addition, some newspapers always use Ms. (instead of Mrs. or Miss) with all women's names. It's safe to list female names as Ms. The majority of newspapers, however, after the first use of a full name, subsequently use only a person's last name in the story, regardless of whether the person is a man or a woman.

Rule 8—Closing

To complete your news release, add a final, standard closing paragraph that succinctly describes the function, purpose, mission, operation, services, or work of your company or group. Expect this last paragraph to be cut, but occasionally an editor's need to fill news hole space will permit use of the closing graf.

To save time keep on hand a previously prepared paragraph. Your model graf can be extensive and can contain more information than is appropriate for the release you are currently writing. It is easier to edit a standard graf to fit each circumstance rather than to create a new one for each release.

Rule 9—Editing

Look for ways to make the writing more intelligible and brief. Hunt out and change words that aren't precisely what you mean. Mark Twain expressed it this way: "The difference between the right word and the almost right word is the difference between lightning and the lightning bug."

Excessive Wordiness.   Good journalistic writing is vivid, clear, concise, and simple. *Write tight* and *keep it short* are expressions every newspaper reporter hears over and over again, meaning that all the flab around the midsection of a story and, particularly, in the lead must be eliminated.

Obese flab to the nth degree is demonstrated in a paragraph that appeared in a U.S. Department of Labor publication. It surely was not written by a trained newswriter:

> *The occupational incidence of the demand change is unlikely to coincide with the occupational profile of those registered at the employment office.*

Translation: The jobs may not fit the people.

Rule 10—Accuracy and Simplicity

Accuracy, clarity, simplicity, and objectivity are essential in writing news releases. And perhaps most important of all is *clarity* in your writing. Remember Mark Twain's rule: "Say what you propose to say, don't merely come near it."

An amusing statement familiar to many people (and edited slightly here so that it can be a gentle reminder to write clearly) is as follows: "I know you believe you understand what you think I wrote, but I am not sure you realize what you read is not what I meant."

Even as an extremely busy businessperson with little extra time, you still have an advantage—you are not a reporter on deadline with no time to rewrite. Do write a draft. You may make several drafts before you have copy ready for release. Don't be concerned with the mechanics or the final format at this time. Just get the words down. If you think better in longhand, that's fine. It is only the final copy that must be typed.

Grammatical Correctness.   Try to make every news release you send to an editor as accurate and impartial as a news story prepared by one of his or her own reporters.

California Publisher magazine listed the following grammar "unrules." Call this list your "chuckle check"!

1. Don't use no double negative.
2. Make each pronoun agree with their antecedent.
3. Join clauses good, like a conjunction should.
4. About them sentence fragments.
5. When dangling, watch your participles.
6. Verbs has to agree with their subjects.
7. Just between you and I, case is important too.
8. Don't write run-on sentences they are hard to read.
9. Don't use commas, which aren't necessary.
10. Try to not ever split infinitives.
11. Its important to use your apostrophe's correctly.
12. Proofread your writing to see if you any words out.
13. Correct spelling is esential.

A subscription to *Reader's Digest* could mean a big payoff in terms of honing your grammar. They recently introduced a feature, "Honing Your Verbal Edge," that is a guide to using words correctly—in verbal or written form. It presents word-usage blunders from TV, magazines, and newspapers, and then gives the correct usage. The editors of *Reader's Digest* give an example:

In a press release, a corporate executive insists, "This would have happened irregardless of the Chapter 11 proceedings."

It's this type of little grammar mistakes that hurt the reception your press release receives. Try your best to avoid them.

Final Draft Checklist

Perhaps you've done several drafts. Now the material is as carefully prepared, concisely presented, and clearly written as you can make it. You're ready to commit it to the final, typed release form. But again, wait! You will buy yourself a lot of insurance (that your news release will be used) if you take a few more moments to give it a final test.

- Is this information of interest to a large number of people?
- Does it include names of well-known people?
- Does it have a human-interest angle?
- Does it have a local angle of interest to the readers reached by this particular newspaper?
- Are spelling and grammar 100 percent correct?
- Is it an ad?
- Did you include a headline?

News Release Headlines

The headline you put at the top of your release is for one purpose only—to tell the editor what the story is about and to sell him on reading through it, then using it. It is *not* meant to be used by the newspaper, and it won't be. The headline that actually appears in the newspaper over your news story is the newspaper's sole responsibility. Whether the editor uses your story verbatim or rewrites it totally, the headline will be written by someone at the newspaper. The headline you write for your news release is merely a summary statement and an attention grabber.

Special Constrictions for Headline Writers.   You may find it interesting to know how real newspaper headlines are written. Headline writers have sharp minds, literally, and sharp pencils, figuratively. They produce under confining rules, each of which is an excellent guideline to help you write your summary-release headline:

- Present the most important facts of the story.
- Attract the reader's attention and pique his or her interest.
- Be accurate and brief.
- Use a verb but do not start with one.
- Use present or future tense.
- Use active voice.

A Headline-Imperatives Game.   Headlines that start with verbs are infinitely easier to write, and that is why such a headline occasionally slips by. An editor at a Pennsylvania daily paper liked to play a little game when he found one of these no-noes—the game of answering headlines written in imperative form. Here are some of his gems that appeared in *Editor & Publisher* magazine.

PROPOSE THEORY ON ENIGMA	(You give me the enigma, I'll try it.)
PLAN PARADE ON HALLOWEEN	(I think it would be better if it were planned before Halloween.)

NAB YOUTHS FOR STEALING MOTORCYCLES	(I'm not sure I could catch them.)
FIND MAN GUILTY OF ROBBERY, ASSAULT	(I can't. I wasn't on the jury—and therefore don't know the facts.)
CONFIRM, PROMOTE GENERAL JONES	(This is beyond my province.)
BOMB STRATEGIC BRIDGE	(I did, in that nasty war—let someone else do the dirty work.)
LAUNCH FIRST OF TV SERIES	(Would that I could, then I might make a lot of money and get out of the newsroom.)

Completion

Now, at last, your final draft really is completed. You've checked it several times, and you have edited and reedited until it is as accurate, clear, concise, and carefully written as you can make it. It is ready to be released. (Chapter 9 presents the basic rules for submitting copy to print media—the mechanics that will put it into an acceptable format. Rules for submitting broadcast copy are included in Chapters 15 and 16. Knowing these formats can make a difference in whether the story gets across the editor's desk and into print or is used in a newscast, or whether it is tossed because it looks unprofessional.)

A Pro Tells How to Avoid the "Round File"

A roundup of information on why news people complain about the majority of press releases, and therefore reject them, may be helpful when you sit down to construct your news stories. The information isn't new—it's merely a confirmation worthy of endorsement.

Linda Morton, a public relations instructor at H. H. Herbert School of Journalism and Mass Communication at the University of Oklahoma, believed for years that the press's complaints reflected bias against PR practitioners, rather than weaknesses in their press releases. "But," she says, "after studying releases for a decade, I admit [they] have cause for complaining."

Her research, reported in *Editor & Publisher*, goes back to 1961, and the sum total of complaints remains today:

- Releases too long and cumbersome.
- A photograph not included.
- Not newsworthy.
- Send releases to the same publication too often.
- Make sure that release actually contains an element of news.
- Releases are not localized enough.
- Contain too much puffery.
- Propagandistic and heavily slanted.
- Arrive too late.
- Are poorly written.
- Missing information.

- Read too much like an advertisement.
- Have style or presentational problems.
- Use out-of-date mailing lists.
- Blanket mailings.
- Duplicate information already received.

Morton found from one of her recent studies that readers must be juniors in college to read and understand press releases; that "a reader must have four more years of education to read and understand press releases than (newspaper stories)."

Morton's studies also found that less than 10 percent of releases are localized—not good when the news industry has centered its needs on localization.

Although no studies are available to show percentages, there's another major reason a news release is not used: no space is available, or a breaking story of great importance knocks it off the page. Of course, that's not the fault of the writer; it could happen to a release written by Mr. Pulitzer!

Obituaries

There is one other news release you may need to know how to write—an *obituary*, or *obit*. If someone in your organization dies, you may be the person who sends out the information to business journals and papers or to other special publications.

An obituary is news—straight news. The time factor is important, so you can't procrastinate in sending the information, in a news release or a fact sheet, to appropriate publications. Remember that because this is straight news, there is no place for editorializing. Often the person who has died is of such importance that editorial comment is warranted, but leave that to editorial page writers. Emotional writing has no place here, either. An obituary is a brief, factual news report about what happened and about the accomplishments the person achieved.

Content

The following list gives the appropriate information about an individual to include in an obituary. (If possible, include all of the first five items in the lead.)

- Full name
- Occupation
- Date of death
- Cause of death (if family approves)
- Age
- Date, time, and place of services
- Noteworthy information about the deceased and his or her family
- Short paragraph about education, if appropriate
- Facts about business affiliations, church, and club memberships
- Survivors' names, with spouse leading the list (if a woman, first, maiden, and married name—use "Janet Brown Jones" not "Mrs. John Jones"), followed by children, then parents, siblings, and grandchildren
- Details regarding memorials, if relevant

A Fictitious Sample of an Obituary

FEDERAL HOME BLUEPRINT COMPANY

Street Address
City, State, Zip
Telephone Number

Contact: (Your name)   <u>For Immediate Release</u>

William D. Carpenter, Blueprint
Firm President, Dies

William Daniel Carpenter, president of Federal Home Blueprint Co., died Sunday at Gateway Medical Center. He was 53.

A memorial service will be held at 11 a.m. Wednesday at Interfaith Bible Church. Burial will follow at Sunset Shadows Cemetery.

Mr. Carpenter, a New London Native, attended Norwalk public schools and earned his bachelor's degree in math from Blackman State University in 1959. Four years later he earned a master's degree in business management from BSU.

He began his career with Southwest Engineering Corp. in Norwalk, as an assistant manager of the firm. In 1975 he returned to New London to join Federal Home Blueprint Co., a family-owned business. He became president, following his father's death, and remained in that position until his own death.

Mr. Carpenter was a member of the social fraternity of Phi Phi Phi and the New London Musical Society. He also belonged to several professional organizations and the New London Chamber of Commerce. He served as president of the latter.

He is survived by his wife, Jean Bell Carpenter of New London; a daughter, Maryanne Carpenter Longstreet of Templeton; and a son, William Daniel Carpenter, Jr., also of New London, who assumed the presidency of Federal Home Blueprint Co. upon his father's death.

Memorials may be made to the Blackman State University Cancer Center.

#   #   #

7

Feature-News Stories

*How to write features that can build
an image and possibly present only
one side of the story—yours*

*If the building your
organization is housed
in burns down, that is a
news story. When,
where, and why is reported.*

*How people feel about
the burning is a feature
story.*

*Newspaper features concern
themselves with
anything and everything
that has emotional appeal
for readers.*

All the Write Moves

In today's world, businesses and nonprofits must convince people that what an organization stands for is as important what it sells. What it sells may be a product, a service, or sometimes more important, an image.

Convincing people these days means educating them to believe that what the organization stands for is positive. Publicity feature stories are a good way to build image and an excellent means to present a wholly positive message, because "with a feature you're able to provide the human interest for the reader's heart," as journalist Jules Loh used to say. It also may give readers only one side of a story—the positive side.

A primary purpose of publicity has always been to get messages out. But, oh, how those messages have changed over the years!

National Easter Seal Society, the nonprofit organization that supports Americans with disabilities, provides a good example. In the 75 years since the organization began, its message has gone from highly negative to positive, with outstanding results. The change is most obvious in their posters then and now.

Seventy-five years ago posters posed the question, "What do you say to a kid who can't walk?" Today's posters focus on what Easter Seal does, what its programs are, and they communicate the attitude that a disabled person is a person first, somebody who can contribute, who can be in the mainstream of life.

Mary Lynne Cochrane, the 1958 National Easter Seal Child, says the Society is now focusing on the positive message that all a disabled person really needs is an opportunity to be independent. It wants you to look at someone for his or her abilities, not the disabilities, she says.

In an effort to assist media in helping the Society change negative images to positive, it has published a pamphlet, "Awareness is the First Step Towards Change: Tips for Portraying People with Disabilities in the Media." In it Easter Seal acknowledges that "people working in the media can exert a powerful influence over the way people with disabilities are perceived." Restate that sentence with one change, and it should become your dogma:

> *People working in the media can exert a powerful influence over the way [name your organization] is perceived.*

The Easter Seal brochure gives numerous tips for reporting on and interviewing people with disabilities.

Differences Between Straight News and Feature News

Even though feature stories are considered news—in the newspaper business they're called newsfeatures—they don't follow the structure of straight news reports.

Jules Loh, a renowned reporter, writing in *Reporting/Writing from Front Row Seats*, describes the differences between straight news and newsfeatures this way: "A news story lets the reader know what happened; a feature story tells him what it was like to have been there."

A newspaper *feature story* is at heart a news story. It reports facts—the more the better. It can include opinion—even your own—but always remember that personal opinion isn't fact. It can provide only the positive side of a story—there is no requirement to give "the other side" of the story.

Newspaper news stories must be printed *now*—today. A news story cannot be held over until it is convenient—or until there is space—to print it. It is used immediately, or it is dead. Although a feature story may also inform, expand the facts given in a news story, and offer background information, the timeliness of its information is not vital. Usually, it can be printed a day or two, or even weeks or months, later.

Feature News as Publicity

For the very reason that time is not such a critical factor, feature-news stories are excellent publicity vehicles. If your goal is to keep your organization's name—its *good* name—before the public, in addition to sending out occasional releases of special news items you will want to employ the use of newsfeatures.

Because features are more appealing to readers, publications are depending more and more on them to attract and hold readers. This means that the market for your publicity is greatly expanded, and chances are considerably higher for the use of your publicity features.

Advantages of Feature News

A feature story that shows your organization is made up of real people will do more to create a favorable image than any number of straight news stories. The first letters in the term *publicity features*—*p* and *f*—could stand for two of the most important ingredients in a feature story:

P = People—real people
F = Facts—loads of them

Even when your organization's self-interest is your primary concern, it should be a secondary consideration in writing a feature-news release. Think first of what will be of interest to the public and to the newspaper's readers, or your release will never make the paper.

You may have noticed that Sunday editions of most metropolitan news-papers usually consist largely of feature-news material. Because there's so much advertising in Sunday papers, they are considerably more sizable than weekday editions. Therefore, editors have much greater amounts of space to fill and can do it only by imposing much earlier deadlines for many of the sections—in some cases a week or two in advance—to get them out in time. So features are used. Only the strictly news sections of Sunday papers must adhere to daily deadline schedules. And even in these sections, features are used to fill in last-minute news holes.

In addition to the accomplishment of getting your feature story printed, you may enjoy the purely personal satisfaction rarely enjoyed by publicity practitioners—the pleasure of occasionally seeing your byline in print.

Image Building May Be the Biggest Benefit

Image may appear to be an invisible profit maker that doesn't put detectable amounts of currency in the cash register. It's something that is easily forgotten and more easily left to be built or strengthened *tomorrow!* But as a three-page advertisement for *The Wall Street Journal* said,

> A company [and every nonprofit in existence] would be well-advised to monitor its corporate image almost hourly.
>
> Even in less revolutionary times, the image that customers, prospects, stock-holders, employees and others have of an [organization] is constantly changing. Prudent companies [and nonprofits] diligently track these blips and wiggles, then counter or adjust them with a steady stream of corrective communication, otherwise known as corporate advertising. [Or, better yet—otherwise known as publicity!]

Newsfeatures are a fine avenue—a fine way, a no-cost way—to build or reinforce image.

Image is something best forged in good times. But image building becomes crucial when an organization's name, reputation, or character takes a wrong turn.

The banking industry—savings and loans especially—have been taking it on the chin for a long time. Christine Briand Naylor explains in *Bottomline* magazine, "You know you aren't part of the problem—your financial institution is healthy, your bank officers haven't been indicted for corruption—but you're losing customers and profits are down. 'Why me?' you ask. Because you are part of the savings industry, and neither the media nor your customers take the time to distinguish between you and the Silverados and Centrusts of the world."

She's right. You needn't be part of the problem, whatever your business. But when someone at one YMCA is accused of child molestation, every YMCA in the country takes a blow to its image.

Re-building an image is covered extensively in Chapter 5. The point here is that features are an excellent way to *create* a respected, honest, dependable, honorable, qualified, reliable, trustworthy image. All these are qualities the public looks for—and demands—in organizations with which they do business, or to which they give their money or time.

Image Ratings Have Changed

It used to be that used car salesmen were at the bottom of the "trust" list. And journalists were right there next to them. A recent Harris Poll, reported in *Reader's Digest*, shows some interesting changes:

- Members of Congress have the lowest public trust: 10%.
- Lawyers are rated at 25%.
- Business executives get a 31% positive rating.
- Journalists are respected by 39% of the public.

And whom do we trust most?

- Small business owners are given the highest rating: 64%—because "Americans admire those who create jobs, pay bills, and deliver honest value," the poll claims.

That's gratifying. But even a 64 percent positive rating means that 36 percent of the public has negative perceptions of small business owners.

Advertising is somewhat effective in building image, but publicity—particularly via highly read newsfeatures—is a more trusted way. As the saying goes, the louder a person/organization touts its honesty and integrity—personally or through advertising—the faster people count their spoons!

The "What" of a Newsfeature

Newsfeatures deal with human interest and emotions. They satisfy curiosity or arouse it. They may provide a chuckle. They can give little-known information about famous people or provide news about little-known people who are interesting because of their experiences, jobs, or personalities. Business, management, travel, science, social problems, and practical guidance are a few of the many popular newsfeature topics.

Features have a style of their own. A feature story is like a short story, and we read both for the same reasons—to share the experiences and emotions of other people and to reach out from our own world to someone else's.

The Emotional Appeal of Feature Stories

In order to involve a reader's emotions and develop human interest, a feature story appeals to the five senses: touch, taste, smell, sound, and sight.

Ernest Hemingway described the best feature writing when he said:

> The good and the bad, the ecstasy, the remorse and sorrow, the people and the places and how the weather was. If you can get that so you can give that to people, then you are a writer. [You are the best of feature writers!]

Events and decisions reported in a feature story are not necessarily important in themselves; what is important is the human appeal of the story.

Is Feature Publicity Great or What?

One recent Sunday, one of the largest newspapers in the country gave a full page-and-a-half of nothing but image publicity built out of a few facts gathered from background information, almost as a history, to Dairy Queen. The newspaper was *The Dallas Morning News*, and the headline was "Serving Up That Texas Flavor." The subhead said: "Dairy Queens gain special place in state's small towns."

The story carried a small-town dateline and its three lead grafs bounced you right into the story:

> Rockwall County District Attorney Ray Sumrow strives mightily to keep abreast of community issues.
> That's why he frequents the local Dairy Queen.
> "If you really need to see someone," he said one afternoon as he chased the last drop of ice cream around a banana split bowl, "you can come here and catch `em."

The columns and columns of type went on to mention well-known people who frequent the eatery, and that there are 800 stores in Texas, "the highest concentration of DQs in the world."

The story included quotes that the biggest PR agencies would dance for, such as: [former] "Gov. Ann Richards describes her trademark hairdo as a `Dairy Queen whip.'"

There also were amusing anecdotes to tickle readers' sense of humor, such as this one:

> Two New Yorkers driving through Texas puzzle over the pronunciation of the town of Mexia. When they stop for lunch, the driver asks the waitress, "How do you pronounce the name of this place?"
> The waitress frowns, then says slowly: "Day-ree Kweeen."

So you're thinking—"That's Dairy Queen. They're *big* business. We couldn't get a spread like that for our business (or nonprofit group)."

Oh, yes you can—if you're willing to come up with a good idea and dig out the information. You have to do the work, remembering that editors and reporters are overworked, overbusy, and lazy just like everybody else. And they're always looking for good features.

But what organization needs a page and a half? Go for a much smaller story. And go for smaller stories, more often. One good newsfeature—no matter how big—doesn't remain in readers' minds. It's the drip, drip, drip of periodic stories that eventually breaks through to readers.

Newspapers Love Humor Features

Another restaurant chain bagged page-one publicity with a story about a shortage of okra and the fact that "Grandy's, the home-cooking restaurant chain, finally announced the crisis last month with signs apologizing to customers about the [shortage]."

The headline, "Okra gives cooks the slip," was followed by a subhead that undoubtedly sparked a smile among okra haters: "Shortage of slimy vegetable leaves restaurants in a stew."

The story wasn't all wit and smiles. Like all good features, it contained serious facts about where the vegetable is grown, why it was in short supply, and where locals could find it. It also contained "interesting" information such as:

Last year had 13 full moons . . . , which generally spells trouble for okra. In the last 20 years, the okra crop has been notably short four times, and each happened in a 13-moon year.

Smaller Is Great, Too

A further story giving the kind of coverage that professionals dream of getting for their clients is reproduced in full here, not only to show that "small and serious also work," but to function as a copycat example. The story ran in the business section of *The Dallas Morning News* and included a two-column photo.

CBI Laboratories founder began company in Cape Cod kitchen

Paul Cain started CBI Laboratories in his Cape Cod kitchen in the late 1970s. He sold his botanical-based European-style bath and body formulations to health food stores on Cape Cod from his Volkswagen bus.

He moved his company to Carrollton in 1982 and sold it in December to Thermo-Trex Corp. of San Diego for $9.5 million in cash. Sales are expected to exceed $20 million this year, up from $12 million in 1993. The company has expanded its workforce and is running two 10-hour shifts a day, six days a week.

Dr. Cain learned about plant extract products in the Odin Forest in Germany, where he lived for two years while working on his doctorate from Heidelberg University.

Dr. Cain says the popularity of his products is based on "a lifestyle expression. The feathering-your-nest, aging, baby boomer generation is operating on a tighter budget.

"It seems the nation is enjoying the spa experience at home."

The "How" of a Feature-News Story

There are two ways to get your newsfeature written. The first is to get in touch with a reporter who has covered your organization in the past and try to interest him or her in writing the story. There is great incentive for this option: If the reporter *agrees* to write the story, it means that he or she has cleared it with the editor; odds that the story will run are about as high as they can get. The Dairy Queen story carried a reporter's byline and undoubtedly was handled in this manner.

Using this method, however, also means that the story will have limited circulation; it will run only in that reporter's publication and cannot be circulated to other publicity outlets.

Your second option is the do-it-yourself method. You write it and you submit it. The CBI story did not carry a byline and did not have the "touch" of a reporter's writing style. It reads more like a straight-news story and could be circulated to any number of media. Because it did not have a "time factor," it could be used immediately or held for weeks, even months. Notice, however—it did have a *local* angle: "He moved his company to Carrollton in 1982. . . ."

Whether you enlist a reporter or do it yourself, the greatest part of the work remains for you to do. You must dig out the information for the article and come up with several angles for presenting it.

Feature Syndicates

If you want to give your story a wider circulation than is permitted when it is written by a newspaper's reporter, you should be aware of an available channel.

Some columns in newspapers are *syndicated features*. They may be written by people whose bylines have become known to readers all over the country. Such columns are distributed by a feature service to many newspapers, thereby cutting each newspaper's cost to only a fraction of the full payment to the columnist. Many of these writers look for and appreciate submissions of feature ideas or material. Be alert for such columnists, and add them to your media lists.

The Reporter as Writer

If you elect to work with a reporter, try to choose one who knows your organization and who has worked with you previously.

Send your ideas, written in outline or descriptive form, along with an attached note stating that you will be in touch by telephone to discuss the story-idea with him or her. When you phone, be prepared to emphasize pertinent points or to explore with the reporter other directions in which the story might be directed. Be tactful and courteous, with no hint of demand or insistence. In other words, treat the reporter in a way that will make him or her want to "do business" with you.

You as Writer

If you decide to write the story yourself, be aware that there is no set formula for writing a good newsfeature. There are no rules, as there are for writing straight news. Prize-winning Associated Press European correspondent Hugh Mulligan described the enigma in *Reporting/Writing from Front Row Seats:*

> *When it gets down to actual writing, most of us, even after all these years, still don't know whether to head up the street or down the street. Whether to start with a note or an anecdote; whether to begin with something new and then work into the background or lay down an orderly chronological tale in the manner of a crime story in the British press, which always starts with the constable and his torch going down Grosvenor Road and finding a body.*
>
> *There are no writing cookbooks that can tell you precisely how many quotes and how many anecdotes one must blend and stir to come up with, say a humorous story, compared with an informative piece.*

Tips for the Do-It-Yourself Road

Probably the most valuable tip is this: Write in a conversational style so that your "writing doesn't sound so much like somebody just sat down at a typewriter, but almost as if I've gotten up and called my best friend and said, 'You'll never guess what I saw today,' or 'You'll never guess who I met today.' " Those are newspaper columnist Bob Greene's words in *Handbook of Magazine Article Writing.*

You should know the important differences that set feature newspaper stories apart from straight-news stories. The following are some of those differences:

1. Feature news is *not* written in inverted pyramid style. Because a feature plays up the human side of the news, its style is closer to that of a short story than to that of straight news.
2. The five Ws lead gives way to an opening that, in some way, will arrest the reader's attention.
3. A straight-news story is never written in the first-person singular, but sometimes a feature writer does use the word *I*. In using the first person, however, you must still remain as objective as possible.
4. Feature leads follow no set pattern. You could begin your story with any of the following items:
   - An eye-catching quote, as with a news story, to create interest and spirit
   - An anecdote
   - An arresting short sentence that makes its point quickly
   - A pure description, a word picture
   - A question, also as in straight-news stories
5. Feature writing is similar in many ways to fiction writing, with a strong opening that catches the reader's interest and builds to a strong, often surprising, close.
6. The first responsibility of a newspaper feature story is to provide facts. Jam-pack it with facts, but adorn them, dress them up, make them appealing and attractive with very alive, three-dimensional people. Make the facts come to life with the real experiences of real people.

Remember your memory joggers—*P* and *F*—which stand for *people* and *facts* and for your ultimate goal, a *publicity feature*.

Reader Attention

Hugh Mulligan said there is no set pattern for beginning a feature story. But there is one "decree": The lead must grab the reader's attention. In other words, good feature writers "bait their hooks" in their leads, then follow up with the facts (the five Ws) later throughout the story.

As Jack Hart advises reporters in *Editor & Publisher*, "Whatever path you take, you probably won't pull many readers along unless you get moving. Step right out. Grab readers with a concrete noun and yank hard with a strong, transitive verb. Then hang on tight and keep pulling."

Don't—repeat, *don't*—take a bland, offend-no-one approach. Hit the ground running, bouncing, falling, jumping with excitement, striding.

As with news stories, remember to work in your organization's name early in the story and wherever and as often as is appropriate, so that you will achieve your publicity objective. However, do not mention the name so often that an editor will see the story as pure advertising that should be accompanied by a check or money order and directed to the advertising department.

In a straight-news story, you *must* be objective. You may not insert your opinion into such a release (although you may quote a person who just happens to express your opinion). As a newspaper feature writer, you may offer a decided point of view, and you may present only one side of a story. There is no requirement that the feature must be objective. And you do not have to strive for that lean, concise writing style that marks a straight-news story. A feature story's chief purpose is to entertain or instruct; so, like a short story, it must read smoothly, build in intensity, and carry the reader along right to an end that is a climax.

Tips for Using Adjectives

The late Frederick Othman of United Press International shared his knowledge of newswriting back in 1945. It stands as true today as it did then:

> When you use an adjective, use a concrete one. "Beautiful," "ugly," "very" mean little. If a girl looks like Lana Turner that means plenty and there's no reason why you shouldn't say so. If a gent wears a dark brown coat, say it's chocolate-colored. Not only is that descriptive, but it gets food into the story. Any word connoting food adds interest value.

The late Saul Pett of *APNewsfeatures* adds this:

> The reader wants to know more about a man's personality than that he is "mild-mannered," "quiet," or "unassuming." Willie Sutton, the bank robber, was mild-mannered, quiet, unassuming. So was Dr. Albert Schweitzer.
>
> > He was "forceful." How? Who says so?
> > She was "charming." To whom? How?

She was "chic." How? Describe.
She was "gracious." How, please?

Rewrites

You may find that even with all these tips and techniques about what a feature is and how to write it, the story just isn't coming together (and it happens to the best writers in the business). When this happens, stop and start again. Learn to stop fighting to make it come together early on. Chances are high that, when you begin to write it again, it will jell nicely and quickly.

Accuracy Check

When you've finished your final draft, you will want to hone your copy to a fine point. Just as with any information you send to news media, be sure of your facts and figures. Take care that names are spelled correctly and that all quotes are accurate. Be sure that your feature story is neatly typed, using the same mechanical rules for setting up the pages in a straight-news release (see Chapter 9), except for one. Because this is a feature, timeliness is not critical. Therefore, don't indicate immediacy in the release timing line. Use "For Release at Your Convenience" rather than "For Immediate Release."

Editor's Standards

The points by which an editor judges and ultimately uses your publicity feature article include the following:

- Interest value. If you are deeply interested in the subject, chances are that your interest will show through and intrigue the reader.
- Exact facts. The more the better, but be sure they are *interesting* facts, or facts presented in an interesting way. Statistics are facts, but seldom are they interesting until you give them some perspective.
- Strong, moving verbs. Use as many as you can, and cut down on adjectives.
- Adherence to basic newspaper style and writing rules.
- Anecdotes. Use several of those lively little stories, often of an amusing nature, that help to flesh out a fact, an incident, or a personality.

Sources of Feature Material

An alert person with a sense of news value and an understanding of how to write in an interesting manner finds feature stories everywhere. Spotting stories is elementary once you are tuned in to look for them and to know what to look for.

Businesses are rich sources for feature stories. Among other things, you can write about the business's employees, customers, services, or products.

The history of an organization is excellent material. You can trace its growth, but it must read like a story. Use quotes and anecdotes; make it come alive through the people who have been involved with it throughout the years.

Biographical material is also a source. In such a feature you can emphasize a person's character, activities, and achievements with the organization. The subject could be an important officer or manager—or a little-known employee, volunteer, or customer.

"How-to" information is high on the list of readers' choices. As the words imply, the article gives advice to the reader based on how your organization or someone associated with it overcame an obstacle, achieved a goal, or handled a problem. Or it can give the reader information he or she can use. The information must be factorial and accurate. No fiction here.

Background-news features enlarge on a straight-news event. Suppose, for instance, your group staged an event (a lecture by a prominent speaker, a fund-raiser for a community project, a workshop, or a seminar). You can find great feature material about the background and business life of the speaker, about previous work with a community group and how your people have assisted it in the past, or about an unknown but humorous incident that happened before or during the event.

Isn't High Tech Wonderful?

Hi tech dominates our lives and follows us everywhere—even into the dentist's office, where lasers have taken the pain out of the drill.

Strictly for your information and to show the degree to which hi tech has invaded our lives, here are some stats: When cellular phones were introduced, AT&T forecast that by the year 2000 there would be 200,000 of them in use. To date there are more than 60 million!

Unless your business or nonprofit organization is based on another planet, you're using some forms of new technology—computers, CD-ROMs, cellular phones, fax machines, on-line services, or something else that wasn't around a few years back.

It's safe to say that at some point in your installation of one of these gee-whiz technologies, you ran into problems or dilemmas or obstacles, or perhaps simply questions. All of these, too, are meat for newsfeatures. Think about the consternation you felt and how you overcame it, then tell your story.

As an example, shopping for a computer can be a trip to another land where English hasn't been spoken since computers were invented. Your solutions to dealing with techno-gobbledygook can deeply touch human emotions in many readers who have had similar experiences. It also can tickle funny bones if you give it a light touch, and editors love this kind of story because such experiences affect so many of their readers.

Or you might write an assessment—yours or that of someone connected with your organization—of whether this or that technology is making our lives better, easier, safer, and cheaper in ways we've come to take for granted.

Perhaps you could write a feature showing comparisons of costs—for instance, if you send a letter across country by mail it's 32 cents and five days—if you're lucky. But send it by fax and it takes less than a minute to get there, at a cost of 20 cents or so.

"Fillers"

There is no need for a feature to be long. The most widely read stories in any newspaper are the one- or two-paragraph human-interest *fillers*.

Many major metro dailies don't use fillers much any more, because high technology makes layout a fairly exact science. But smaller papers and weeklies still use them by the dozen and it's safe to say that they never have enough *good* ones. A filler's only purpose is to fill a hole—and perhaps prompt a smile or a nod from the reader.

If yours is a serious, ongoing publicity program looking for additional means to get your organization's name before the public, don't overlook fillers. Some of the most productive publicity comes from fillers. Longer news stories and full-length features are a publicist's dream come true, but with today's hectic life-styles, how many people actually read through those longer articles? Fillers—showing that the people in your organization are real and human—are also priceless because they are so well read.

What a Filler Is

A filler is a very short, interesting, and perhaps humorous news item that an editor can use to fill space below or between longer articles. Its chances of being used are far greater than those of straight or longer feature-news stories, because there never seem to be enough fillers when an editor puts a page together. If it includes a chuckle, the odds for its being used increase even more.

An example of a filler comes from the Associated Press, repeated by Singer Education & Training Products in a sound filmstrip:

Operations at the Cat's Paw shoe heel plant were brought to a sudden halt Wednesday night by an alley cat.

The feline's nine lives ended in a 13,000-volt flash when it fell from a ledge into the plant's circuit breakers, knocking out power for two work shifts.

Filler Up

It was a tiny filler item in *The Wall Street Journal* that alerted ABC's "Good Morning America" to a social assistance program and resulted in a full GMA program highlight segment. The information was about North Adams State College, a public liberal arts college in Massachusetts, and how it helps the unemployed to upgrade their skills by filling empty seats in already scheduled classes—at no cost to the college. Can you imagine what a full 60- second *commercial* on "Good Morning America" would have cost North Adams State, as compared with the literally free publicity given to the college and its program? And no 60-second commercial is able to present the detail—with the authority and influence—that the 7-to-10 minute segment did.

Letters to the Editor

Every person who advises and instructs about garnering publicity warns his or her students to leave editorials alone. Editorials are the province of the newspaper itself to express the paper's own thinking and recommendations. Yet one of the easier forms for getting a name before the public (and of reaping the fruits of publicity) is actually a kind of editorial: a letter to the editor, published alongside the newspaper's editorial column or on the *op-ed* page. Call it a do-it-yourself editorial.

Research shows that letters from readers are widely read and that they are excellent devices for commenting on some item in the news or for making a point. There is higher readership of letters than of guest editorials or guest opinion columns.

Keep your letters short and to the point, and address them to the attention of the editor. They should be clear, concise, and well written. They should not be small-minded personal tirades or recitations of petty issues or opinions.

The most effective letters to the editor are written by respected, well-known local leaders. If you do not want to sign such a letter, enlist the help of someone who is well known in your organization or someone whose title demands respect.

Remember, of course, to work your organization's name into the text of the letter.

The Formula

A simple formula for writing one of these do-it-yourself editorials—a letter to the editor—is as follows:

- State your opinion.
- Give facts to support it.
- Suggest some action.

For example, present a fact showing a need for attention. Give two, three, four, or more facts with supporting evidence. Finally, restate your opinion and the action you suggest; or state the intended conclusion you hope the reader has reached, and suggest some type of action.

Gene Bullard's Rules

After 30 years of writing letters to the editor—and getting a goodly number published—Gene Bullard knows a thing or two about what gets an editor's attention. He says, in *The Dallas Morning News*, "I learned how *not* to get published by reading the letters for years and years. You write a letter too long, your letter is not well constructed, your letter is not fair—especially if it's mean-spirited in opposition to the publication. Like, 'You've got a dumb, conservative paper.'" Bullard also says he has figured out that it can't hurt to include a clever line or two for the editors to pull out as a headline.

The First Op-Ed Page

In a letter to the editor, signed by Charles M. Antin, *The New York Times* was gently chided for giving the impression that it had created the first op-ed page. The writer explained that "the idea was conceived by Herbert Bayard Swope, an editor at *The World* newspaper in the 1920s, who used the name Op. Ed." The writer then quotes Swope, writing to newspaperman Gene Fowler, from *The World of Swope* by E. J. Kahn, Jr.:

> *For a long time while I was on the outside, and later when I was the City Editor, I would notice, from time to time, that the opinion stories which had crept in, in spite of our hard and fast principle of having little or no opinion in our news columns, had been dominantly interesting . . . nothing is more interesting than opinion when opinion is interesting, so I devised a method of cleaning off the page opposite the editorial, which became the most important in America . . . and thereupon I decided to print opinions, ignoring facts.*

The only difference from op-ed pages then and now, says the letter writer, is that Swope did not print unsolicited letters from the general public; instead, he rounded up big names to write the letters.

Rewards for Bad Writing

Now, after all your efforts—and success—in turning out a top-rated feature story, it's fun to know that there is an annual contest that recognizes *bad writing*! It's the Bulwer-Lytton Fiction Contest, founded by Scott Rice, an English professor at San Jose State University. The contest is named for Edward George Earle Bulwer-Lytton, a contemporary of Charles Dickens, who began an 1830 novel with the phrase, "It was a dark and stormy night . . ." which today is Snoopy's favorite line when he sits down atop his doghouse to write some of his forgettable prose.

A recent year's winning entry began, "The notes blatted skyward as the sun rose over the Canada geese, feathered rumps mooning the day, webbed appendages frantically pedaling unseen bicycles in their search for sustenance, driven by cruel Nature's Maxim, 'ya wanna eat, ya gotta work,' and at last I knew Pittsburgh." Another winner, in the Purple Prose category, began, "The sun rose slowly, like a fiery furball coughed up uneasily onto a sky-blue carpet by a giant unseen cat."

Somehow, we can now better understand all those admonitions about cutting down on the use of adjectives, about using strong, moving verbs, and loading the piece with facts.

8

A Copycatter's Primer

*Your "Lessen Plan" for making
publicity release writing easier*

Make It Your Cache Register

A Copycat Kit is your idea factory. It's where you can stockpile and store an unlimited supply of information to stimulate thinking about potential publicity news releases or feature stories. It can even be a cupboard of ideas to kick off productive publicity brainstorming sessions. But its most important function is to serve as your easy-as-fill-in-the-blanks hard-copy examples of how to write publicity releases.

If you followed the advice in Chapter 1, you now have the beginnings of your copycatter's kit—a collection of news stories and features that range from simple announcements about executives and new board members to technologies that affect your company, industry, or area of nonprofit support.

Copycatting is really no different from what is done in the fashion business. As James Brady says in *Advertising Age*, "Designers don't create in a vacuum; they sniff the air."

So let's start sniffing!

Copycat Kit Mechanics

Get out your collection of news and features and obtain a notebook large enough to accommodate four separate sections with expanding collections in each section.

Section 1: Examples of newspaper, magazine, and/or trade journal news stories

Section 2: Dated copies of your news releases

Section 3: Dated copies of news stories or features published as a result of your releases

Section 4: Your media release list—the media to which you send publicity releases

Section 1. Cut out the stories you've gathered and paste them into Section 1 of the notebook—one to a page—with the publication's name and date of publication. Separate the stories by types: new personnel announcements, grants awards, planned moves, award recognitions, image builders, mergers, feature news, new locations, and so forth.

Section 2. This is the section where you will file *dated* copies of your news releases. All releases carry information about release dates, such as "For immediate release," "For release January 2," or "Release at your convenience," but your *file* copy should add the date when it was mailed or delivered so that you can compare this added date on your file copy with the date the release was actually used in the media to which it was sent.

Section 3.   This section will include file copies of the stories published as a result of your releases, along with the names of the publications that printed them and the dates they appeared.

Section 4.   This is your media list, which you compiled in Chapter 4. It will be as big or as small as your needs require. If you plan to send only to a local newspaper, the list will be short. But even a one-publication list requires names of the various editors and reporters—*correctly spelled*—to whom you will send a variety of straight news or feature stories. Include each person's title, the section each edits, and any direct-dial telephone numbers, along with the newspaper's address and telephone and fax numbers. Larger lists can be compiled from current editions of either *Editor & Publisher International Year Book* or *Bacon's Publicity Checker*. These resources include names and titles of editors at each publication and are probably available at your local library. However, people change jobs, and even the most recent edition may not list current editors. It will pay you to check each newspaper by telephone every few months as to the names of the current editors, because editors—like everyone else—react much more favorably to anything directed to them rather than to persons they replaced months back. And nothing spells inefficiency more than a release to someone who left the publication a couple of years ago.

Alongside each listing make notes about the types of material preferred, deadline timings, and the day(s) of the week the newspaper is published if it's other than a daily. Also include the amount of lead time required if stories are for Sunday editions (some newspapers have much longer lead times for Sunday editions, and deadlines often vary from paper to paper).

Copycat Benefits

Think of your Copycat Kit as your "lessen plan." It will lessen your learning time and make learning easier. Copycatting can be the secret to a beginning publicity writer's success—your "superstart" program.

Once established, your Copycat Kit—in notebook form—becomes a handbook on how to write releases. Later, comparisons of your releases with the printed results show changes editors made in your copy. These changes are unspoken instructions about ways you can improve your future releases to better comply with style and content requirements of each editor and each newspaper.

The notebook also becomes a written record—a history—with dates of the events and developments that made news for your company or nonprofit group. Equally important, it will become the guide for a successor or for anyone you assign to do the job.

There is another important benefit that you will come to recognize and want to prepare for now: *Printed* publicity about your organization and the people associated with it can be quoted or reproduced in ads and used as direct mail pieces. This not only impresses customers—or prospective donors to a nonprofit—but it is one of the least expensive forms of advertising. (For this use, keep a second original copy of the *entire page* on which the story appeared, in a separate envelope or container where it will be protected from yellowing, tearing, or marking.)

Perhaps the biggest benefit of all is a personal one: the practice of writing makes a better writer—an important qualification for business success. A word of encouragement is offered by David Ogilvy, who said, "Good writing is not a natural gift. You have to LEARN to write well." In other words, writing isn't a talent or an inherited ability. It's a skill. You don't just do it, you *learn* to do it—and the more you do it the better you get at it. Anyone, everyone, can learn to write well. Copycatting just makes the learning a little easier and perhaps a little faster.

Copycatting Should Raise Your Use Rates

New studies show that only 3 to 8 percent of all press releases are actually printed. Don't let that paralyze your efforts, however. If you could see the dreadful examples that virtually flood newsrooms all across the country, you might wonder how even that number get used. That's why in broadcasting newsrooms they're called "junk mail."

In this chapter we tap into the knowledge, training, and experience of a few publicity professionals across the country. We don't have a statistical report of how many media uses there were of the professionally prepared releases reproduced in this book, but we do know the rates are up there in the top range.

In addition to using these professionals' releases to understand copycatting and to raise your chances of having your efforts pay off, they also should be used to stimulate your thinking about potential publicity stories that *you* can develop. Reproductions of the releases as the agencies produced them also show you a variety of effective logos and formats to give you some ideas about how to produce your own. Once you've decided on a logo and format for your releases, however, stay with it to build recognition among recipients.

First, let's begin by setting down some basics about copycatting.

Setting the Framework for Copycatting

First and most important: Copycatting is *not* copying; it's not plagiarizing. Don't copy the words, particularly if your model is an actual publication, rather than the professionals' models used in this book. Just copy the "pattern" and the ideas.

Pattern? Yes, there is a pattern to news stories; it's fully explained and summarized in Chapter 6 in "Ten Steps for Writing a Newspaper News Release." You may want to go back and reread that chapter to refresh your memory.

The two most important parts of the "pattern" are the lead paragraphs and the headline. Both are written to catch the attention of the editor to whom you will send the release. The headline is strictly for the benefit of the editor, to summarize the main point in the story that follows. The lead grafs also are to grab his or her attention, but they must be written to capture the attention of the readers, or the editor won't be even remotely interested.

The body, or text, consists of fleshed-out details presented in the lead in diminishing significance. If you're foggy about this, go back and review the information in Chapter 6.

The close is a final graf about your organization, which you hope an editor will have space to include.

Let's turn to the pros now and see how they do it—and how you can hitchhike on their knowledge, training, and experience to build publicity releases that beat the use stats.

New Staff, Executive Named

Possibly the most common news story among businesses of all sizes is the announcement of executive or staff changes.

Two examples—one from *Fineman Associates Public Relations*, based in *San Francisco* (Figure 8.1), and the other from *Communications Concepts Unlimited (CCU)*, *Racine, Wisconsin* (Figure 8.2)—show a lead graf of only one sentence. The first is the announcement of a single appointment, whereas the other reports four changes.

The Fineman release follows this structure:

- Lead graf—The statement that an individual has been named to a position within a company, with a concise description of its function and geographical location.
- 2nd graf—The new exec's former affiliations and achievements.
- 3rd graf—The task/role the new executive will perform in his new position.
- 4th graf—Additional information about his previous achievements and education.
- 5th graf—Two succinct sentences that name some of the company's clients and its other locations.

All information is presented on one page.

In both stories the leads are simple and concise.

The CCU release (Figure 8.2) is structured as follows:

- Lead—A sentence stating that the company has made three additions and one promotion.
- 2nd graf—The names and assignments for two of the three new personnel.
- 3rd graf—Background and qualifications for one of the two additions named in the second paragraph.
- 4th graf—Background and qualifications for the other person named in the second paragraph.
- 5th graf—The third new staff member is named, along with her previous experience and new responsibilities—all in three sentences.
- 6th graf—Information about the person within the organization who has been promoted is presented, along with his new responsibilities, previous education, and prior employment.
- A one-sentence description of CCU's functions as well as its founding date, which tends to amplify the image of reliability and stability for the agency.

The release runs to two pages, but it includes substantial data about four people.

FIGURE 8.1   Bacon Universal News Release

901 BATTERY STREET
SUITE 308
SAN FRANCISCO
CALIFORNIA
94111

415 391.4744
415 391.8731 FAX

FINEMAN ASSOCIATES   PUBLIC RELATIONS

★ N E W S   R E L E A S E

November 9 ,1992   **FOR IMMEDIATE RELEASE**

FOR: BACON UNIVERSAL

CONTACT: Michael Fineman
                    Fineman Associates
                    (415) 391-4744

MIKE MURNIN TO HEAD HAWAII-BASED EQUIPMENT DISTRIBUTOR BACON UNIVERSAL

HONOLULU -- Mike Murnin, 46, has been named president and chief executive officer of Bacon
Universal, it was announced today by the Hawaii-based equipment dealer.

Murnin had been the vice president of sales and marketing for UpRight Inc., a leading aerial work
platform manufacturer and sister subsidiary company of Bacon (both subsidiaries of UpRight
International, Ltd.). Murnin has been credited by UpRight with increasing the number of its U.S. outlets
by 35% and significantly helping the company expand into the Japanese and other Pacific Rim
marketplaces.

Murnin's role at Bacon will be to increase revenues through an accelerated diversification into Hawaii's
industrial markets. He is also expected to consolidate Bacon's traditionally strong position in the state's
construction market. Additionally, Murnin will oversee Bacon's relocation to new headquarters, now
under construction just outside Honolulu, in 1993.

Prior to joining UpRight in 1988, Murnin was the general manager for Golden Bay Equipment Company
of San Francisco, a heavy equipment distributorship which represented several major manufacturers in
Northern California including Komatsu. A 1971 marketing graduate of the University of Southern Illinois,
Murnin was also general manager of Bi-State Equipment Company in St. Louis. His first job out of
college was in the heavy equipment industry where he spent over five years with Caterpillar.

Bacon Universal represents major manufacturers such as Komatsu Dresser, Ford, Gehl, UpRight, Tadano
and Multiquip in Hawaii. The company has four additional branches throughout the Hawaiian Islands as
well as operations in Guam.

-30-

FIGURE 8.2   Communications Concepts Unlimited/CCU, Inc.

CCU, Inc.
Communication Concepts Unlimited
927 Main Street
Racine, Wisconsin 53403-1524
Phone 414 633 4500
Fax 414 633 0249

For immediate release   For more information contact
                                                 Gabriella S. Klein
                                                 (414) 633-4500

**STAFF ADDITIONS, PROMOTION
ANNOUNCED AT CCU, INC.**

RACINE, Wis. (Nov. 3, 1993) – Communication Concepts Unlimited (CCU, Inc.) has announced three staff additions and one staff promotion.

Joining the firm, located at 927 Main St., are project managers Gregory B. Bell and Linda K. (Peterson) Longton. Both will manage client projects with local, regional and national companies and organizations using the communication and marketing services provided by CCU.

Bell, who has 19 years of experience in the communication and marketing fields, spent six years as director of communications for the Catholic Archdiocese of Milwaukee. He is accredited by the Public Relations Society of America and a member of the Wisconsin chapter PRSA board of directors. A graduate of Northern Michigan University, he also has done graduate study at Loyola University and Keller Graduate School of Management.

-more-

FIGURE 8.2   *(continued)*

---

add 1 - CCU staff additions

Longton has more than eight years of working knowledge in the communication field. For the past four years she was editor of Equipment Today magazine, which serves the construction equipment industry. Prior to that, she spent three years as associate editor for Equipment Today and one year for Rental magazine. All are published by Johnson Hill Press, Fort Atkinson, Wis., where Longton began her career as an account coordinator. Longton holds her bachelor of arts degree in English from the University of Wisconsin-Whitewater.

Debra Klopstein is a new account services associate for CCU. Her prior experience includes Acme Bookkeeping Service. In her new position, she is responsible for providing client support services and administration.

Don Schauf, who joined CCU in 1988 as a project manager, has been promoted to director of graphic design and production services. In this position he is responsible for overseeing the firm's graphic design activities and for supervising project implementation. A graduate of the University of Wisconsin-Milwaukee, Schauf previously was manager of design and electronic publishing at CCU. Prior to joining the company, he spent four years as a reporter for the Journal Times in Racine.

CCU was established in 1983 to provide creative, dynamic support for the planning and implementation of business-to-business communication, consumer awareness campaigns, employee information programs, issues management and community relations programs.

-30-

News of Awards and Honors

Three public relations agencies make awards announcements—two on behalf of clients (Figures 8.3 and 8.4) and the third to achieve publicity for itself (Figure 8.5). *Edelman Public Relations Worldwide, Dallas, Texas,* offers an announcement of an award given by ARC, a national nonprofit organization on mental retardation, and its winner, although nowhere does Edelman Public Relations' name, address, or phone number appear on the release. The release bears the client's logo, address, and names of two ARC contacts. Its structure is as follows:

FIGURE 8.3   Edelman PR Worldwide/ARC Release

The
Arc

National Headquarters
500 E. Border Street, Suite 300
Arlington, Texas 76010
(817) 261-6003/ FAX (817) 277-3491
TDD (817) 277-0553

News Release

FOR FURTHER INFORMATION CONTACT:
Shannon Couzens (214) 443-7563
Liz Moore (817) 261-6003

Utah "Cowboy" Lassoes National Award:
The Arc Honors Integration Into Community

ARLINGTON, Texas (October 11, 1993) -- Finding Pete Alvey of St. George, Utah at the closing ceremonies of the 44th Annual National Convention of The Arc should not have been difficult. If the man in his trademark "cowboy" outfit was not easily spotted, he could have been sighted receiving The Arc's national Bill Sackter Award.

The Arc, a national organization on mental retardation, bestows the Bill Sackter Award each year to an individual with mental retardation who has left an institution and successfully made the transition to living and working in the community.

Alvey, who claims he has always been a "cowboy", has rustled many obstacles in his life, including mental retardation. Through his accomplishments and volunteer efforts, he has become a pioneer for others with mental retardation.

The award honors its namesake Bill Sackter who spent 44 years in an institution before moving into society. In order to be eligible for this award, an individual must meet the following criteria: 1) Must have been in an institution for a minimum of three years; 2) Must have lived in a community (independently, semi-independently or in a small group home) for a minimum of three years; 3) Must be involved in the community in some activity; 4) Must have shown growth in self-help skills, work skills and in independent living skills; 5) Must demonstrate success in competitive or supported employment.

-more-
a national organization on mental retardation
formerly Association for Retarded Citizens of the United States

- Lead—A two-sentence roundup of information that piques interest about the story that follows.
- 2nd graf—The name of the nonprofit group, its function, and a description of the award.

FIGURE 8.3   *(continued)*

Alvey Release/2

Eight Years In Institution Enough

Alvey meets all of these requirements and then some. He was admitted at the age of eight to the Utah State Developmental Center in American Fork, Utah, and he remained there until removed by an aunt at age 16.

He lived with his aunt in Salt Lake City for 11 years before moving to a group home in St. George sponsored by The Arc. Ten years in the home helped Alvey prepare for life on his own.

"I learned a lot from being there," said Alvey. "They taught me how to budget my money, how to go to the grocery store and buy food, how to pay my rent and how to take care of myself when I got out on my own."

Alvey has steadily progressed over the years to the status he holds today. He has been married for ten years, rents his own three bedroom apartment and works three jobs. Alvey has been employed with St. George Steel for the past eight years, for Denny's restaurant as a security guard and for the City of St. George.

All of this would keep the average person busy, but it is easy to see that Alvey is not your average person. In addition to his employment, Alvey has been active as a board member of the Washington County chapter of The Arc for the past 17 years and serves on the Governor's Council for People with Disabilities. In this position, Alvey has been instrumental in helping pass legislation concerning the education of individuals with disabilities.

Alvey volunteers for the Special Olympics and the Washington County Rodeo and Fair. He says it is his willingness to help others with disabilities that makes him unique.

-more-

- 3rd graf—A little information about the award recipient is presented.
- 4th graf—Extensive information about the award and the person for whom the award was named, plus a list of eligibility requirements.
- Remaining grafs in the three-page release about the recipient and his background, along with some quotes from him, which make reading the announcement more like reading a short story.

FIGURE 8.3 *(continued)*

Alvey Release/3

An Autobiography on the Horizon

"It just makes me feel good that I can help other people with disabilities," said Alvey.

"I wouldn't turn any person away if I knew there was any way that I could help them."

Alvey plans to write his autobiography and already has a publisher in St. George.

"I want to share my life so I can help someone else with a disability get their life together," said Alvey.

Other goals he has set for himself include schooling and adopting a child with a disability.

Alvey received his award on Oct. 9 during the closing ceremonies of The Arc's 1993 National Convention in Providence, R.I.

The Arc is the nation's largest volunteer organization solely devoted to improving the lives of all children and adults with mental retardation and their families. The association also fosters research and education regarding the prevention of mental retardation in infants and young children. Founded in 1950, the organization now has more than 1,200 state and local chapters across the nation.

###

Davis-Hays & Company, Inc., Maywood, New Jersey, presents a press release for its client, United Savings Bank, under a Davis-Hays logo (Figure 8.4). It follows this pattern:

- Lead—The first sentence establishes an ethical principle followed by United Savings, strengthens its image of dependability (owing to its more than 100 years of service), tells of its location in Englewood, New Jersey, plus facts about the upcoming awards.
- Facts about the awards are fleshed out.
- The president of United Bank is quoted about the purposes of the awards.
- Details about selection of winners and where applications may be obtained.
- A contact name and phone number.
- A roundup of information about United Savings Bank.

With all the information this release contains, it runs to only a page and a half.

FIGURE 8.4   Davis-Hays & Co. Inc./United Savings Bank Release

PRESS
RELEASE

FOR IMMEDIATE RELEASE

CONTACT: Rick Brush
(201) 368-2288

United Savings Bank Sponsors Awards
Program for Young Community Leaders

ENGLEWOOD, N.J., March 1, 1994—Giving back to the community has been a guiding principal of United Savings Bank, S.L.A., since it was founded in 1887. This spring, the Englewood, N.J.-based thrift will award six local students who have also demonstrated outstanding commitment to their community.

Now in its second year, the United Savings Community Service Leadership Program provides cash awards to local high school seniors who have made significant contributions to their community through volunteer work, civic responsibilities, etc. The competition is open to community-minded seniors who will graduate this spring from any of the following high schools located in United branch towns: Cresskill High School, Dwight Morrow High School, Leonia High School, Pascack Valley High School, Teaneck High School and Tenafly High School.

"As a corporate citizen, United Savings Bank is proud to reward young leaders who share the same values and sense of community that we have supported for over a century," said John Delaney, president of United. "We are proud to reinvest in those young citizens who contribute greatly to our community."

— continued —

(201) 368-2288 • 930 Spring Valley Road • Maywood • NJ 07607

FIGURE 8.4 *(continued)*

United/Page 2.

      Award winners will be selected by their high schools based upon their community service activities, references and a description of 250 words or less on how their activities have benefited the community. Applications are available at participating high school guidance offices and must be completed by May 6, or by a deadline set by the school.

      For more information, please contact Rick Brush at 201-368-2288.

      Founded in 1887, United Savings Bank, S.L.A., has helped provide financial growth and opportunity for families and businesses for over a century. Today, the greatest portion of the bank's $345 million of assets is invested in residential mortgage and consumer-related loans to thousands of families in Bergen County and surrounding communities.

###

A 4-graf, 1-page release from *Anne Klein & Associates, Mt. Laurel, New Jersey.* (Figure 8.5), tells about two awards won by the agency.

- Lead—Names of the awards, their purposes, and the name and city of the agency-recipient are presented.
- A description of the awards.
- A description of the agency and its size and placement in its geographical area.
- A description of the organization that presented the award.

Expansion Plans and Renovation Announced

Another *Anne Klein & Associates* release tells about expansion plans for a retirement community (Figure 8.6).

- Lead—The bare basics of the plan, its approval, and the amount of space the expansion will occupy.
- 2nd graf—The name of the architectural firm doing the work, with a quote from its project director about the building's historical qualities.
- 3rd graf—More information about the importance of the more-than-130-year-old building and what the expansion calls for.
- 4th graf—Bids and negotiation data, plus projected date for construction to begin.

FIGURE 8.5   Anne Klein & Associates Release

**ANNE KLEIN
& ASSOCIATES**
PUBLIC RELATIONS
COUNSELORS

News Release

Anne Klein & Associates, Inc.
533 Fellowship Road, Suite 250
Mt. Laurel, New Jersey 08054

609-778-0380
Facsimile 609-778-9284
MCI Mail No. 199-9855
Telex No. 650-199-9855

For Immediate Release

Contact: Kathy Loehrig
(609) 778-0380

ANNE KLEIN & ASSOCIATES WINS
TOP HONORS FOR EXCELLENCE IN
PUBLIC RELATIONS PROGRAMS

MT. LAUREL, N.J., May 6 -- Anne Klein & Associates, a Mt. Laurel, N.J., public relations consulting firm, won two awards including "Best of Show," at the 1993 Berny Awards sponsored by the Public Relations Professionals of Southern New Jersey (PRP). The Berny Awards honor excellence in creativity and implementation of public relations programs.

The firm received the "Best of Show" award and first place in the Publicity/Media Relations category for "Own Your Share of America," a campaign designed to encourage individuals to invest in the stock of America's publicly held corporations. Anne Klein & Associates conducted the nationwide publicity program on behalf of the National Association of Investors Corp. (NAIC), a non-profit organization of investment clubs and individual investors.

Anne Klein & Associates is one of the leading independent public relations firms in the Philadelphia region, and is the largest in southern New Jersey.

PRP is a professional organization consisting of public relations practitioners throughout southern New Jersey. The Berny Awards are named after Edward Bernays, a pioneer in the creative practice of public relations.

-30-

May 1993

FIGURE 8.6   Anne Klein & Assoc./Kearsley Release

A Retirement Community Since 1772

2100 North 49th Street
Philadelphia, PA 19131-2698

TELEPHONE: (215) 877-1565

Pamela A. DeLissio, NHA
President

KRS #2

<u>For Immediate Release</u>   <u>Contact</u>: Connie Spencer
                                                                Kearsley
                                                                (215) 877-1565
                                                                   or
                                                                Kathy Loehrig
                                                                Anne Klein & Assoc.
                                                                (609) 778-0380

PHILADELPHIA HISTORICAL COMMISSION APPROVES KEARSLEY'S "CONTINUUM OF CARE"
Expansion of Original Building will Complement 19th Century Architecture

PHILADELPHIA, Pa., Jan. 10 -- The Philadelphia Historical Commission has approved expansion plans at Kearsley, America's first retirement community, for a Continuum of Care program that will add 100,000 square feet to Kearsley's facilities.

MPB Architects of Philadelphia designed the new Kearsley addition, which is intended to complement the community's historically certified original building. "The original building is a four-story stone structure with brick partitions and peaked roofs. It looks like a castle," said Clark Van Sant, project director at MPB Architects. "The addition will have peaked roofs and a stucco exterior to coordinate with the stone exterior of the original," he said.

(more)

MEMBER
American Association of Homes for the Aging
Pennsylvania Association of Non-Profit Homes for the Aging

FIGURE 8.6   *(continued)*

```
Kearsley Approval
Ad 1


     Kearsley's original building dates back to 1861 and was

designed by well-known Philadelphia architect John M. Gries.  The

Historical Commission unanimously approved the plans for the

expansion, which will enable Kearsley to build 84 new nursing

home beds, 60 studio apartments with support services (or

personal care), and new common areas.

     Kearsley and MPB Architects have received construction bids

for the Continuum and will begin negotiations soon.  Construction

is expected to begin in early summer.



                    -30-


     Kearsley is a private, not-for-profit retirement community
for older adults with low incomes.  It is located in the
Wynnefield area of Philadelphia and currently provides housing,
nursing care and specialized services to more than 100 men and
women age 62 years and older.

January 1994
```

- A final, single-spaced paragraph containing information about the non-profit group is added as a "postscript," rather than as a part of the release.

Edelman Public Relations Worldwide composes a release about a renovation that is expected to boost business and reveal a motel's new image (Figure 8.7).

- Lead—A tightly written lead sentence includes facts about completion of a local motel's renovation as part of the many-million-dollar national chain's attempt to attract new customers. ("Local" is a key factor in this release, undoubtedly meant to grab the attention of editors in the immediate area.)
- 2nd graf—A description of the architectural scheme, its new landscaping and signage; the official "unveiling" dates, times, and address.
- A single sentence about employees' completion of training, which is meant to heighten a company goal to provide a kind and level of service the public always wants and considers a benefit.
- The purposes for the redesign are given, along with a notation that increased occupancies have occurred elsewhere where renovations have been completed.
- A quote from the local manager speaks of employees' pride and excitement about the changes.

FIGURE 8.7   Edelman PR Worldwide/LaQuinta Release

La Quinta Inns, Inc.
112 E. Pecan Street
P.O. Box 2636
San Antonio, Texas 78299-2636
210-302-6000

FOR IMMEDIATE RELEASE

Contact: Ann Marie Peters/Allison Ellis
                Edelman Public Relations
                3131 Turtle Creek Blvd., Ste. 500
                Dallas, TX 75219
                (214) 520-3555

NEW LOOK COMPLETED: WACO LA QUINTA INN
UNVEILS NEW IMAGE

Increased Curb Appeal Designed to Boost Occupancy, Attract New Customers

----

WACO, Texas (March 16, 1994) -- Waco's La Quinta Inn has completed extensive

renovations as part of the company's national $55-60 million reimaging campaign, expected

to be completed at all of La Quinta's more than 215 inns nationwide by June.

The inn's new Santa Fe look -- which includes a new exterior color scheme and

redesign of the entrances and lobby, as well as enhanced landscaping and new signage -- will

be officially unveiled Thurs., March 17, 1994 at two open house receptions (11:30 a.m. -

1:00 p.m.; 4 p.m.- 8 p.m.) at the La Quinta property (1110 South 9th Street).

Also, the inn's employees have completed training to fill La Quinta's goal to provide

personal, home-like guest relations and service.

-- more --

FIGURE 8.7   *(continued)*

LA QUINTA RENOVATIONS/Page 2

The contemporary design was created to update and freshen La Quinta's image and build its business. In fact, the company has recorded significantly increased occupancies at its hotels in markets where reimaging has already been completed.

"The improvements at our inn and involvement with La Quinta's transition to a new image nationally have given a real sense of pride to our employees here," said Robert Southwood, who manages the Waco La Quinta Inn. "These changes mean improvement for the Waco property and La Quinta as a whole and we're excited to be a part of it."

John Kaegi, senior vice president of marketing for La Quinta, added, "We are proud of this property's new contemporary look and we are confident that our chain's reputation and updated image will contribute to an improved performance and a stronger presence for La Quinta Inns in the Waco area."

Renovations at the La Quinta Inn were handled by Dallas, Texas-based Tony Crawford Contracting.

San Antonio-based La Quinta can be found in 29 states and employs more than 6,000 people.

--30--

- Another quote, from a senior VP of marketing, speaks of reputation and image and how they will make for a stronger local presence.
- Name of the contractor and its location.
- A statement about the number of locations and employees in the national organization.

Again, use of local names brings the story home to local readers, while the national affiliation is maintained.

FIGURE 8.8   Fineman Associates/Swander, Pace & Co. Release

901 BATTERY STREET
SUITE 308
SAN FRANCISCO
CALIFORNIA
94111

415 391.4744
415 391.8731 FAX

★ N E W S R E L E A S E

FINEMAN ASSOCIATES PUBLIC RELATIONS

DATE: October 2, 1991   FOR IMMEDIATE RELEASE

FOR: SWANDER, PACE & CO.

CONTACT: Michael Fineman or Barbara Feder
             Fineman Associates
             (415)391-4744

KEEPING MARGINAL PRODUCTS ON THE MARKET CAN COST MUCH MORE THAN YOU THINK

<u>Leading management consultant provides tips for separating "winners" from "losers" to avoid hidden cash drain</u>

If companies realized the immense cash drain of their problem products, they would quickly move to restructure or shut down large portions of their operations, asserts Dan Swander, founder and director of management consulting firm Swander, Pace & Company, in a recent front-page article in the management publication <u>Boardroom Reports</u>.

Most companies, however, delay necessary cost-cutting actions because they fail to measure the true costs involved with keeping marginally profitable products or services on the market, Swander contended. These companies reason that a small profit is better than no profit at all.

But, Swander said, there are many hidden costs in addition to the obvious ones of production, personnel and marketing. These include wasted clerical and accounting hours; the high costs of inventory maintenance; a drain on salesforce time; and incalculable lost opportunities for developing and enhancing other top-selling products.

Swander identifies a process for sharpening a company's focus on its core business to improve overall performance.

The first step, he says, is to identify the company's most lucrative products and most profitable customers. Typically, this reflects the old maxim that 20 per cent of a company's products produce 80 percent of its profits, and 20 percent of its customers produce 80 percent of the sales.

"This doesn't necessarily mean that 80 percent of the company's products must be eliminated," said Swander. "But it does mean that <u>some</u> of those products probably should be. The real question is which ones ... and how."

- more -

Using Publicity to Get Publicity

To garner publicity for a client, *Fineman Associates* combines components to attract and engage the attention and interest of editors: tips for avoiding a common business problem presented by a qualified business person, and the stature of a prominent national publication in which the information was presented (Figure 8.8).

FIGURE 8.8   *(continued)*

2-2-2-2-2
KEEPING MARGINAL PRODUCTS ON THE MARKET CAN COST MUCH MORE THAN YOU THINK

According to Swander, the company's accounting department should calculate the profit/loss from each product using its actual -- as well as less obvious -- costs.

"By identifying those products produced to serve top customers -- and those which are more expensive to deliver and to service -- managers can determine how much the company can save by ... eliminating the worst performers," Swander wrote. "The key to success, of course, is that [the company] follows through by cutting all related fixed and indirect costs."

The next step is to look to customers in deciding whether to eliminate some products or to modify the ones that lose money. "With input from the marketing and sales departments, investigate how problem products can be turned into moneymakers," Swander advised.

According to Swander, "turnaround" options include:

- **Raising prices.** Companies can profitably sell at a lower volume -- providing that they eliminate the fixed and indirect costs as volume declines;
- **Improving the product** in ways that benefit the ultimate user; and
- **Adding value**, e.g. buy-one-get-one-free offers.

It is a mistake, Swander contends, to keep marginal products on the market in the belief that a wider product line enhances the company's image. "If a losing product can't be changed into a winner, eliminate it. In reality, weak items kept to bolster product lines almost never benefit corporate image. They may actually detract from it in today's climate of specialization and focus on quality and service."

With offices in both San Francisco and Ann Arbor, Michigan, Swander, Pace & Co. is a leading management consulting firm serving the apparel, retailing, food and other consumer industries. The firm, which counts among its clients both Fortune 100 companies and start-up ventures, consults to top management on strategy development, mergers and acquisitions, market assessment and marketing planning, sales force effectiveness, customer service, operations, distribution and organization.

-30-

Business pages in newspapers and business publications are always receptive to information that will benefit their readers.

The entire release, covering two pages, explains the problem—cash drain by problem products, recommendations for overcoming the problem, along with reasons for the tips and steps to accomplish the goal.

There are quotes that enliven the writing, bulleted "turnaround options" that catch a reader's eye, and a final paragraph that describes the company's qualifications and background.

FIGURE 8.9   Edelman PR Worldwide/Butterball Release

FOR IMMEDIATE RELEASE

CONTACT: Patty Sullivan, Kristi Anderson
Edelman Public Relations
3131 Turtle Creek Blvd., Ste. 500
Dallas, TX 75219
214/520-3555

EXTRA! EXTRA! TENDER & JUICY!

Butterball Fresh Chicken Introduces Full Product Line In Phoenix

While the rest of the country has to settle for bland, ordinary chicken, Butterball Fresh Chicken introduces its full "Extra Tender & Juicy" fresh chicken product line to Phoenix, one of only six new Butterball Fresh Chicken markets to experience premium quality chicken by Butterball -- one of the most well-known names in poultry.

The addition of Bone-In Prime Parts completes Butterball Fresh Chicken's 21-product line and provides consumers with new alternatives to help make the most ordinary meal *extra*ordinary.

Butterball Fresh Chicken reveals it's the **natural baste** that brings an extra tender and juicy taste to its fresh chicken product lines. Whatever the variety -- Boneless/Skinless, Skinless, Bone-In Prime Parts, Family Pack, or the Whole Chicken -- Butterball Fresh Chicken uses only specially selected, Grade A chicken to produce premium quality and taste, any way you slice it.

- more -

New Product Releases

Edelman Public Relations Worldwide gives us examples of new product releases for Butterball Fresh Chicken (Figure 8.9) and Zooth, Inc. (Figure 8.10).

The first, for Butterball (Figure 8.9), is a two-page release that tells readers

FIGURE 8.9   *(continued)*

Butterball Fresh Chicken/2

And for today's health-conscious shoppers, Butterball hand-trims each product for extra leanness and then rushes it to your store fresh, never frozen.

Butterball's packaging also is designed with consumers' ease in mind -- hungry shoppers actually can see the chicken before they take it home. Butterball's Clysar packaging uses a special vacuum-sealing process to lock in flavor and freshness, prevent messy leaks and allow for total product visibility.

Butterball's Bone-In Prime Parts chicken line includes: Split Breasts, Drumsticks, Wings, Drummettes, Thighs, and Best of the Fryer (3 Split Breasts with Ribs, 3 Drumsticks, 3 Thighs).

And here's the best news of all. With suggested retail prices ranging from $1.15 - $4.29 per pound for its various chicken products, you can eat chicken every night of the week.

So, don't "chicken out" when faced with the prospect of cooking another dry, boring chicken for dinner. Whatever your mood, whatever's in the pantry, you'll find plenty of Butterball Fresh Chicken "Extra Tender & Juicy" products to suit your family's tastes and make your chicken the talk of the table.

Butterball Fresh Chicken is available at Phoenix ABCO, Albertsons, Bashes, Fry's, and Smitty's stores.

Butterball Fresh Chicken is a product of ConAgra Broiler Company. Headquartered in El Dorado, Arkansas, ConAgra Broiler Co. is an independent operating company of ConAgra Incorporated.

- 30 -

Black-and-white, 5" x 7" Butterball Fresh Chicken product photos available on request.

about the introduction of a new chicken product line in Phoenix, and that Phoenix is one of Butterball's six new markets. An added line also alerts editors that "Black-and-white, 5" × 7" Butterball Fresh Chicken product photos [are] available on request."

The Butterball headline and subhead notifies Phoenix editors that this is a *local* story and that a new "full product line" is being introduced.

The focus of the entire story is on benefits of the product to buyers, using words that tend to play to a person's sense of taste. It also plays to the health- and money-consciousness of readers, and then tells them where the product can be purchased.

Its final paragraph gives information about the company and where it is headquartered.

FIGURE 8.10   Edelman PR Worldwide/Zooth Release

FOR IMMEDIATE RELEASE

CONTACT: Patty Sullivan, Kristi Anderson
             Edelman Public Relations Worldwide
             3131 Turtle Creek Blvd., Ste. 500
             Dallas, TX 75219
             214/520-3555

ALLIGATOR BRUSH TEACHES TOTS ABOUT DENTAL CARE

New Toothbrush for Pint-Size Gator Fans Hits Florida Stores

Parents, Gator fans and alligator wrestlers take note: Now anyone can have a brush with an alligator, right in their very own bathroom.

Any parent will tell you that getting children to brush their teeth regularly is a real struggle. Until now.

Amos Alligator -- a just-for-kids, three-dimensional toothbrush and holder in one -- has hit Florida stores.

Designed to make brushing fun for children, the toothbrush features soft, rounded, polished bristles and a sculpted handle easy for small hands to grip. Each package offers tips on proper brushing and step-by-step instructional illustrations children can follow.

Made by Zooth Inc., creators of the Zoothbrush® Collectibles line of children's toothbrushes, Amos Alligator retails for $3.99. It is available at 500 Circle K locations in 50 Florida communities, along with department, drug, discount and grocery stores statewide.

Established in 1991 by founder and president Susan Harrison, Zooth Inc. is based in Wichita Falls, Texas. Zooth products are sold in 42 states and 10 countries.

- 30 -

* **Product, color slides and B/W photographs are available upon request.**

The second Edelman release (Figure 8.10) is about a new toothbrush for children. But the one-page, 6-graf, 10-sentence release is accompanied by a backgrounder (Figure 8.11) and a fact sheet (Figure 8.12) that otherwise might be part of a press kit. (See Chapter 11 for detailed information about press kits.) An

FIGURE 8.11   Edelman PR Worldwide/Zooth/Backgrounder for Editors

BACKGROUND FOR EDITORS

CONTACT: Patty Sullivan, Kristi Anderson
Edelman Public Relations Worldwide
3131 Turtle Creek Blvd.
Dallas, TX 75219
214/520-3555

ZOOTH, INC CAPTIVATES CHILDREN
AND DEVELOPS HABITS

Most parents would agree getting young children to brush their teeth regularly and eat well can be an exhausting struggle. Coaxing, promises and rewards lose their appeal. And explaining the importance of dental care and nutrition doesn't quite capture a youngster's attention and concern. Until now.

Zooth, Inc., creators of the Zoothbrush Collectibles™ and Zootensil™ Collectibles line of childrens' toothbrushes and eating utensils, has the tools for making life's daily necessities fun for children and parents.

"It's tough trying to teach children to brush their teeth regularly. I know, I've tried with my nephew," said Susan Harrison, founder and president of Zooth, Inc. "I believed if this 'necessity' was made fun and easy for kids, they would be more disposed to making brushing a daily routine. Until Zoothbrush® Collectibles, there was virtually nothing available to young children that made brushing entertaining and manageable."

Zoothbrushes are specifically designed to excite children through positive character association. Zoothbrushes are three-dimensional, made in the shapes of zoo animals children can easily remember, "Amos Alligator™," "Eloise Elephant™," and "Tom Tiger™." Each Zoothbrush is designed with soft, rounded, polished bristles and sculpted handles easy for small hands to grip. Because parents are often the "brusher," Zoothbrush handles are wide

- more -

FIGURE 8.11   *(continued)*

ZOOTH, INC./2

enough for an adult to comfortably hold and maneuver in a small mouth. Zoothbrush .
packaging features tips on brushing and easy step-by-step instructional diagrams children can
follow.

According to the American Dental Association, it is never too early to begin taking
care of a child's teeth. Showing children how to properly care for their teeth at an early age
may eliminate potential problems in the future.

To instill the need for daily brushing, Zoothbrushes also are available with
"Zoothtooth," an educational read and learn book. The four-color, animated storybook
reinforces the value of brushing through the main character Marvin and his adventures in the
Land of Zooth.

"Motivating kids to brush sometimes requires additional and engaging tools," noted
Harrison. "Story books, and 'Zoothtooth,' are tangibles that capture a child's attention and
bring messages to life in a manner they can relate to. Plus, 'Zoothtooth' is written in
rhyme, which is appealing to kids," said Harrison.

In addition to Zoothbrush Collectibles™, Zooth also manufactures Sportsbrush/tm
Collection™, a line of brushes made in sports characters, including a cheerleader, baseball,
basketball and football players. Sportsbrush brushes and holders are sold as one unit that can
be mounted on a wall or mirror and have replacement brushes available in each Sportsbrush™
character.

"Dentists recommend replacing toothbrushes every three to four months," said
Harrison. "This could become costly, particularly with specialty products. To avoid this,
we've created Sportsbrush replacement brushes that allow parents to follow dentists
recommendation without replacing the holder."

Zootensils and Zootrition

As encouraging brushing and teaching correct techniques can be an exercise in
patience and persistence for parents, so too can the process of nuturing healthy eating.

"When toddlers begin eating table food, they also begin wanting to hold the utensils
on their own, like cups and spoons," said Harrison. "Traditionally, they've learned to eat by
using adult-sized flatware or miniature versions, which still are made for adult hands, not a

- more -

added line also tells editors that "Product, color slides and B/W photographs are
available upon request." Altogether, there is plenty of information so that a reporter can expand the story to give product prices, where it is distributed, history
of the company, and the names and descriptions of sister products.

In other words, the compact story can be used when a newspaper's space is
tight, or expanded when an editor must fill space.

FIGURE 8.11 *(continued)*

ZOOTH, INC./3

toddler's. Zootensils fill the need for toddler-size flatware because they're made to fit small
hands for easy handling."

The Zootensil™ Collectibles are made in the same Zooth animals -- Amos Alligator™,
Eloise Elephant™ and Tom Tiger™. Zootensils also offer the "Zootrition Story," storybook
that explains the importance of eating well and ways to make it fun.

Established in 1991, Zooth, Inc. manufactures and distributes Zoothbrush™
Collectibles, Zoothtooth™ Storybook, Zootensil™ Collectibles, Zootrition™ Storybook, and the
Sportbrush™ Collection and Holders.

Based in Wichita Falls, Texas, Zooth products are sold nationally and internationally
in department, drug, grocery stores, discount retail chains and military outlets in 42 U.S.
states, Canada, Chile, Guatamala, Jordan, Libya, Mexico, Nigeria, Puerto Rico and Seria
and Spain.

- 30 -

FIGURE 8.12　Edelman PR Worldwide/Zooth Fact Sheet

ZOOTH, INC.
FACT SHEET

History:　Founded in 1991 by Susan Harrison, Zooth, Inc. designs and distributes childrens' early dental care and mealtime products to retailers, supermarkets, and discount, department and drug store chains nationally and internationally. The Texas-based company is the first in the health and beauty aids category to manufacture and market child-sized toothbrushes, forks and spoons in the shapes of zoo animals and sports characters.

Product Description:　Zoothbrush™ Collectibles and Zootensil™ Collectibles are easy-to-grip, three-dimensional toothbrushes and mealtime utensils designed to make proper dental care and good nutrition fun for children ages two to 10.

Zoothbrushes and Zootensils also are optionally sold with Zoothtooth™ and Zootrition™ Storybooks. The twenty-page, educational storybooks are illustrated in four-color and written in rhyming couplets to capture youngsters' attention. Each book's storyline uses positive play values to teach children that brushing and good nutrition can be fun. Zoothbrushes™ and Zootensils™ are also sold separately to allow for collecting and replacement.

Product Line:　**Zoothbrushes™/Zoothtooth™ Storybook**
　　Tom Tiger™, Eloise Elephant™ and Amos Alligator™
Zootensil™ Collectibles Forks and Spoons/Zootrition™ Storybook
　　Tom Tiger™, Eloise Elephant™ and Amos Alligator™
Sportsbrush™ Collection and Holders
　　Cheerleader, baseball, basketball and football players mount to a bathroom mirror or wall to hold its matching Sportsbrush™ (pom-pom, baseball, basketball and football). (Sportsbrushes™ and holders are also available in African-American sports characters.)

Prices:　$1.39 - $3.99

Revenues:　$600,000

No. of Employees:　Nine

Distribution:　Zooth products are distributed nationally in 42 U.S. states and internationally in Canada, Chili, Guatemala, Jordan, Libya, Mexico, Nigeria, Puerto Rico, Syria and Spain.

Key retail accounts include: Eckerd Drug; Nordstrom's; Service Merchandise; Target; Toys-R-Us; Wal-Mart.

Headquarters:　4163 W. Airport Drive
Wichita Falls, TX　76305
(817)855-9035

FIGURE 8.13   Fineman Associates/Hudson Soft USA-Jan. 6-Release

901 BATTERY STREET
SUITE 308
SAN FRANCISCO
CALIFORNIA
94111

415 391 4744
415 391.8731 FAX

★ N E W S   R E L E A S E

FINEMAN ASSOCIATES   PUBLIC RELATIONS

January 6, 1992   FOR IMMEDIATE RELEASE

FOR: HUDSON SOFT USA, INC.

CONTACT: Michael Fineman or Barbara Feder
            Fineman Associates
            (415) 391-4744

NINTENDO GAME DEVELOPER ANNOUNCES CAMPAIGN TO LIMIT TIME KIDS SPEND ON VIDEO
GAMES

"Responsible Play" Sales Materials to be Unveiled at January 9-11 Consumer
Electronics Show in Las Vegas

South San Francisco, Calif. -- Video game developer Hudson Soft USA, a
Nintendo licensee, announced today that it will produce materials advising its
young customers to limit the time they spend playing video games.

"We want to get a message out to kids that video games are just one of life's
pleasures and that there are other important and fun things they should
investigate," said Hudson Soft USA Marketing Manager Kevin Sullivan.

"Though much has been said about the mesmerizing nature of video games, no
game manufacturer has taken the initiative to remind its young customers to
play responsibly and balance video games with other activities," said
Sullivan. Hudson Soft has decided to take that leadership position and calls
on other game manufacturers to follow suit."

The company's point-of-purchase materials, which will be displayed in retail
outlets throughout the U.S., will carry illustrations of Master Higgins™, a
character in several Hudson Soft games, who is pictured saying: "Play video
games responsibly. Spend time on school, fitness and family too; there's a
whole world to explore."

As part of the program, Hudson Soft USA will establish a phone support line
and provide a pamphlet entitled "Master Higgins™ 10 Tips for Responsible Play"
(a guide describing ways to diplomatically regulate video play) for parents

- more -

Two Releases for the Same Subject

Fineman Associates offers two releases that basically report the same news. The release dates show they were circulated six months apart—in January (Figure 8.13) and in June (Figure 8.14).

The first—a two-pager (Figure 8.13)—is a simple report that a video game developer plans to produce materials that tell youngsters to limit the time they spend playing video games.

FIGURE 8.13 *(continued)*

2-2-2-2-2
<u>HUDSON SOFT USA ANNOUNCES AWARENESS CAMPAIGN FOR SENSIBLE VIDEO GAME PLAY</u>

who feel their children spend too much time playing video games.

For young gamers who volunteer to limit their video game play, Hudson Soft USA
will offer membership in a special club which includes a free quarterly
newsletter and membership card.

Mock-ups of the point-of-purchase displays will be unveiled at the Hudson Soft
booth at the Consumer Electronics Show in Las Vegas on January 9 and will be
launched in June.

According to Hudson Soft USA Executive Vice President Bernie Yamada, the
American "Responsible Play" campaign is part of the company's longtime
commitment to parents of gamers. The campaign was first launched in Japan in
1987 when Hudson Soft and Japanese video game celebrity Takahashi Toshiyuki
traveled the country in a whistle-stop train tour to bring a message of
sensible video game play to Japanese children and their parents and teachers.

Takahashi, 31, a Hudson Soft employee, children's television host and comic
book hero in Japan, was the model for the Master Higgins™ character featured
in the popular *Adventure Island* game series. Takahashi and Hudson Soft
executives will be at the CES Show to bring the message to the consumer
electronics industry.

South San Francisco-based Hudson Soft USA, Inc. is the U.S. subsidiary of
software and game publisher Hudson Soft Co. Ltd. of Sapporo, Japan. The
parent company was the first developer to be licensed for Nintendo's 8-bit NES
system. Hudson Soft games include *Adventure Island*, *Bill Laimbeer's Combat
Basketball*, *Atomic Punk* and *Jackie Chan's Action Kung Fu*.

- 30 -

FIGURE 8.14   Fineman Associates/June 1 Hudson Soft USA Release

901 BATTERY STREET
SUITE 308
SAN FRANCISCO
CALIFORNIA
94111

415 391 4744
415 391 8731 FAX

★ N E W S   R E L E A S E

June 1, 1992

FOR IMMEDIATE RELEASE

FOR: HUDSON SOFT USA, INC.

CONTACT: Michael Fineman or Barbara Feder
            Fineman Associates
            (415) 391-4744

VIDEO GAME-MAKER SHOWS PARENTS HOW TO LIMIT TIME KIDS SPEND AT SCREEN

SOUTH SAN FRANCISCO, Calif. -- Video game-maker Hudson Soft USA will begin distributing a booklet today advising parents how to limit the amount of time their children spend playing video games.

The booklet is part of the company's new "Responsible Play" campaign which is being launched to help prevent excessive use of video games. The campaign also includes point-of-purchase displays, an informational hotline, a newsletter and a membership club, all to be launched in June.

"The Ten Tips for Responsible Play booklet is intended to help parents regulate their children's video game play without alienating them," said company marketing manager Kevin Sullivan. "We're happy that kids love our games, but we don't want them to overdo a good thing and neglect their school work, sports and family life."

Booklets will soon be available at participating video game retailers and can be obtained now by writing to Hudson Soft USA at 400 Oyster Point Blvd., Suite 515, South San Francisco, California, 94080 or calling the company's consumer hotline: 415/495-HINT.

Hudson Soft USA, Inc. is the U.S. subsidiary of Hudson Soft Co., Ltd., a 300-employee manufacturer of business and entertainment software headquartered in Sapporo, Japan. Hudson Soft Co., Ltd. was the first developer to be licensed for Nintendo's 8-bit NES system. Hudson Soft games popular in the U.S. include the *Adventure Island* series, *Bill Laimbeer's Combat Basketball*, *Atomic Punk*, and *Jackie Chan's Action Kung Fu.*

-30-

[EDITORS: TEN TIPS ARE ATTACHED]

(sidebar, vertical text) FINEMAN ASSOCIATES   PUBLIC RELATIONS

The second—a one-page release (Figure 8.14)—includes a two-page attachment that lists "ten tips for responsible play." The second, very concise, news story can be used when there is a shortage of space, or the tips (Figure 8.15) may be added when space permits, perhaps as a sidebar, or when editors want to add solid how-to information for their readers.

Both releases include quotes, and both end with a graf about the company. The second release counts on the "tips" attachment to give substance to the story, whereas the lengthier first release provides information about how and by whom the campaign was begun and more about the company's commitment to the parents of "gamers."

FIGURE 8.15   Fineman Associates/Hudson Soft 10 Tips

-- ATTACHMENT --

HUDSON SOFT USA'S TEN TIPS FOR RESPONSIBLE PLAY

1.   <u>Be firm in setting limits</u>. Don't be afraid to set reasonable game playing limits. Discuss with your children when and for how long they may play their video games -- and tell them why.

   Explain that your limits are not a punishment, but are "house rules" that will promote better play. After all, expert game players stay focused and avoid burnout through limiting playing time: they know from experience that *short* game sessions make the *best* game sessions.

2.   <u>Set a time for game playing</u>. Having a set time when it's okay to play video games can help motivate your children to accomplish their other responsibilities -- homework and chores, for example -- before the scheduled "game session."

3.   <u>Avoid banning video games from the home</u>. Kids will always be able to find other places to play -- if not at your home, then at a friend's house or at an arcade where you have no control. Instead, make it more desirable, less expensive and more convenient for your children to play at home -- despite the rules you establish.

4.   <u>Make extended video game play time a reward for good behavior</u>, for chores accomplished, school goals achieved, or a good deed done. Ideally, these should be the only occasions when you depart from your agreed-upon time limit.

5.   <u>Learn about the games your children play</u>. Let your children teach <u>you</u> something for a change. They will enjoy relating their activities to you. You may even enjoy playing the games yourself!

6.   <u>Find the moral in the mania</u>. Talk to your children about the themes in their favorite games. Help your children figure out the "moral of the story" implicit in the games they play and how certain game situations can apply in real life.

7.   <u>Encourage shared game play</u>. These days, many games are designed to be played by two or more players. So, make video game play a social event. Encourage your children to play with other family members and to invite their friends to play at your home.

-more-

FIGURE 8.15   *(continued)*

2-2-2-2-2

<u>HUDSON SOFT USA'S TEN TIPS FOR RESPONSIBLE PLAY</u>

8.   <u>Encourage your children to take breaks</u>. To prevent your children from becoming "glued" to a game, interrupt them with something nice -- a healthful snack, for example -- for which they must temporarily leave the game.

9.   <u>Become involved in the game-buying process</u>. Once you know the games and your children's tastes, you can better discuss game purchases with them. You will be in a better position to explain why you oppose the selection of some games.

10.   <u>Fill the void</u>. It is not enough to merely limit the amount of time your children spend playing video games. Encourage them to fill their free time with other pursuits -- outdoor sports, reading, family activities, hobbies...as Master Higgins says, there's a whole world to explore!

                                        ###

CONTACT: Michael Fineman or Barbara Feder
            Fineman Associates
            (415) 391-4744

June 1, 1992

Teaming Up Often Produces Big Results

Often one of the best publicity producers is generated when a for-profit business teams up with a nonprofit to sponsor a fund-raising event.

Although the next press release, from *Davis-Hays & Company*, is a solicitation for donations for a nonprofit group (Figure 8.16), it also seeks publicity on behalf of a commercial business. It undoubtedly received excellent support from editors because the appeal is for a highly worthy cause, and it plays to readers' emotions by recognizing that large numbers of residents live in poverty and find that the "holiday season can be an especially cold and hungry time." Take note of how the quote by the bank's president is aimed to the *local* concerns of *local* people. The two-pager managed six mentions of United Bank, sponsor of the food drive.

FIGURE 8.16   Davis-Hays/United Bank Food Drive Release

PRESS
RELEASE

FOR IMMEDIATE RELEASE

CONTACT: Rick Brush
(201) 368-2288

<u>United Savings Bank Sponsors
Community Food Drive</u>

ENGLEWOOD, N.J., October 26, 1993 — For the nearly 800,000 New Jersey residents living in poverty, the holiday season can be an especially cold and hungry time. But United Savings Bank, S.L.A., of Englewood, is working to make the coming months a little warmer for families in the area, by sponsoring a holiday food drive in conjunction with the Office of Concern at Holy Trinity Church in Englewood.

During November and December, United Savings welcomes customers and other members of the community to bring food donations to any of the bank's eight branches, located in Englewood, Tenafly, Cresskill, Leonia, Teaneck and Hillsdale. Items most urgently needed this holiday season include canned juices and vegetables, cold cereal, syrup, pancake and cake mixes. Cash donations to the Office of Concern are also encouraged.

"The depressed economic conditions over the past few years have had a dramatic effect on many people in this area, resulting in an overwhelming increase in the need for food assistance," said John Delaney, president of United Savings. "If we all pitch in, we can make an enormous impact on the lives of those neighbors who need our help most."

– continued –

(201) 368-2288 • 930 Spring Valley Road • Maywood • NJ 07607

FIGURE 8.16   *(continued)*

United Savings Sponsors Food Drive/p. 2

In New Jersey, where the unemployment rate is more than 7 percent, close to 10 percent of the total population—the highest level since 1982—live below the poverty level. In Bergen County alone, the number of children receiving food stamps increased from 5,070 to 6,586 over the past two years, according to the Bergen County Board of Social Services.

"As the number of hungry people rises, donations to shelters, soup kitchens and food banks have become even more critical," said Bill Atkins, director of development at the Office of Concern. "Without help from concerned citizens and community businesses like United Savings Bank, we would not be able to keep up with increased demand for food and other services."

In 1992, the Office of Concern collected and distributed food for about 30,000 individual meals, 2,000 Thanksgiving and holiday meals, and 3,500 meals for homeless shelters and elder-care facilities. In addition, the agency provided toys for children as well as immigration assistance to the needy.

For more information on the food drive, or for the address of the United Savings branch nearest you, call Rick Brush at 201-368-2288.

Founded in 1887, United Savings Bank, S.L.A., has helped provide financial growth and opportunity for families and businesses in New Jersey's Northern Valley region for over a century. Today, the greatest portion of the bank's $345 million of assets is invested in residential mortgage and consumer-related loans to thousands of families in Bergen County and surrounding communities.

###

A Fill-in-the-Blanks Appeal

The *Davis-Hays & Company, Inc.* release shown in Figure 8.16 is an excellent illustration of a fill-in-the-blanks example for copycatters. The lead for your copycat version might read as follows:

For nearly _____ (number) local citizens living in poverty, this is a particularly trying time. But _____ (nonprofit name) is working to _____ (goal). The organization is sponsoring a _____ drive.

Donations of _____ may be dropped off at _____. Cash donations may be mailed to _____.

(A quote from the chairman of the board of directors or a prominent local person regarding the effects the donations will have or have had in the past.)

(Some figures to support the need for the drive, citing the source of the data.)

(Another quote from someone who has seen the benefits from a previous drive, or from a person who has formerly received assistance.)

(Some solid data about past accomplishments by the nonprofit group.)

For more information about the _____ drive, or for locations near you where _____ may be dropped off, call _____ at _____(phone number).

A paragraph giving historical information about the organization and/or the names of local people who are active in the group, and the area served by the organization.

Releases Report Formation of a New System, Company

The following two releases, of two pages each, report the formation of a new system and a new company. Demand Side Management system (Figure 8.17) was developed when a telecommunications company and an electric utility made an agreement. NZ Productions (Figure 8.18) was created when two people combined talents and abilities. Both releases, produced by *Fineman Associates Public Relations* are excellent copycatting guides.

FIGURE 8.17   Fineman Associates/First Pacific Networks Release

901 BATTERY STREET
SUITE 308
SAN FRANCISCO
CALIFORNIA
94111

415 391.4744
415 391.8731 FAX

★ **N E W S   R E L E A S E**

August 1, 1991

FOR IMMEDIATE RELEASE

FOR: FIRST PACIFIC NETWORKS INC.

CONTACT: Michael Fineman or Carole van Grondelle
            415/391-4744

SILICON VALLEY'S FIRST PACIFIC NETWORKS SECURES $14 MILLION IN AGREEMENT WITH ELECTRIC UTILITY GIANT ENTERGY CORPORATION'S SUBSIDIARY ELECTEC, INC.

Sunnyvale, Calif.-based telecommunications company First Pacific Networks Inc. (FPN) has secured a $14 million agreement with electric utility giant Entergy Corporation. Under the terms of the agreement, the two companies will develop an advanced customer-controlled Demand Side Management (DSM) system that could have major long-term conservation effects on national power usage and the environment.

The terms include the sale of a 9.95 percent equity interest in FPN for $3.5 million and a collaborative agreement with Entergy subsidiary Electec, Inc. to utilize FPN's unique Personal Xchange ("PX™") System in the development of "PowerView," a customer-controlled utility management system.

Entergy also paid FPN $8.5 million for the exclusive (except for FPN) licensing rights to market such applications to utilities. FPN will be the principal marketer and negotiator for utility licenses. Electec pledged a further $2 million for research, development and field trial costs. Securities and Exchange Commission approval has been granted, and the first field trial using FPN technology and fiber-optic cabling will begin in September.

"For FPN, this new funding represents a major step forward as well as an important endorsement from one of the top 100 companies in the United States," said FPN Executive Vice President Donald Marquart. "Entergy's collaboration with us in the development of a PX™-based energy management system maximizes our respective strengths for application in the electric utility industry."

"A primary consumer benefit of DSM would be the more efficient use of energy through a practice known as load management -- but with the consumer as the

- more -

FIGURE 8.17   *(continued)*

2-2-2-2-2
<u>FPN SIGNS $14 MILLION AGREEMENT WITH ELECTEC</u>

controlling party instead of the utility," said Entergy Vice-President, Strategic Planning, Michael Niggli.

Conventional load management programs, according to Niggli, are strictly limited in their capabilities. The proposed Entergy/FPN system, he said, is much more comprehensive in its potential applications. Attractive features include its cost effectiveness and its innovation in allowing consumers to make informed electrical usage decisions.

The PX™ System was developed as a "last mile" solution for transmission of digital telephone, entertainment CATV and high-speed computer services on a single cable.

"The PX™ System will be adapted to create a Customer-Controlled Load Management and Automated Feedback System (CCLM/AFS) for electric utilities," said Niggli. "This application of a modified PX™ System is intended to promote more efficient use of energy by providing consumers with expanded energy usage information and enhancing communication between consumers and the utility company. For the first time, a comprehensive DSM system can be deployed using either fiber-optic, coax or potentially wireless configurations at a significantly lower cost than the expense of constructing power plants."

Entergy Corporation is a $15 billion-asset, publicly-traded electric utility, servicing over 1.7 million customers. Its other subsidiaries include Arkansas Power & Light, Mississippi Power & Light, Louisiana Power & Light and New Orleans Public Services, Inc.

First Pacific Networks, established in 1988, provides sophisticated multi-media networking products for the domestic and international business systems marketplace and fully distributed digital telephony switching for telephone services on CATV systems in foreign markets.

- 30 -

FIGURE 8.18   Fineman Associates/NZ Productions Release

FINEMAN ASSOCIATES
PUBLIC RELATIONS
901 Battery, Ste. 308, San Francisco, CA 94111
Phone (415) 391-4744 • FAX (415) 394-7158

NEWS RELEASE   *NEWS RELEASE*   *NEWS RELEASE*   *NEWS RELEASE*
April 5, 1989   FOR IMMEDIATE RELEASE

FOR: NZ PRODUCTIONS

CONTACT: Michael Fineman
          Fineman Associates
          (415) 391-4744

**AWARD-WINNING FEATURE FILMMAKER ROB NILSSON JOINS AWARD-WINNING
CORPORATE PRODUCER WARREN ZARETSKY TO FORM PRODUCTION COMPANY**

Director and Cannes Film Festival award-winner Rob Nilsson, 44, has teamed
with veteran corporate strategist and communications producer Warren
Zaretsky, 43, to form NZ Productions in Mill Valley, Calif.

The new company is a unique alliance of Nilsson's 18 years of documentary and
feature filmmaking and Zaretsky's 15 years of experience producing film,
video and live communications programs for AT&T, Bell Labs, Chase Manhattan
Bank, Coca Cola, Kodak, Gillette, IBM, Panasonic, Xerox and others.

NZ Productions will produce internal and external company communications
programs: corporate profiles, strategic marketing campaigns, product
introductions, sales promotions, tradeshow presentations, and investor and
employee information. According to Zaretsky, NZ Productions was created to
address a growing demand in American business for substance over style and
content over form.

"Most of today's corporate and commercial messages are filled with
disembodied pretty pictures and meaningless buzzwords," said Zaretsky. "We
see a trend in business for more straight-forward, reality-based
communications that command people's attention and inspire their trust.
Customers, employees and stockholders do business with people, not symbols.
With Rob on board, our creative proposition is the ability to help
corporations project a more human face."

-more-

FIGURE 8.18   *(continued)*

2-2-2-2-2
<u>NILSSON JOINS ZARETSKY TO FORM NZ PRODUCTIONS</u>

Nilsson has received international, critical acclaim for his realistic and
impassioned, "direct action" filmmaking. Zaretsky described the approach as
one which assumes "the most powerful messages come from the pursuit of
emotional truth." Nilsson's feature films include Northern Lights, Signal 7,
On The Edge, and Heat and Sunlight.

As a corporate producer, Zaretsky's track record in creating successful,
results-oriented programs for blue-chip clients includes awards from the
International Film & TV Festival of New York, Houston Film Festival,
Advertising Club of New York and the Ad Club of San Francisco's Visual
Communications Showcase. Prior to forming his own production company,
Zaretsky served as director of marketing for Berkey Photo, a $200 million
consumer and industrial marketing company, and as a national sales manager
and product manager for GAF Corporation.

Nilsson, a Bay Area native from Mill Valley, Calif., has a Bachelor of Arts
degree from Harvard. Zaretsky, a native of New York City, holds a Bachelor
of Arts from Wayne State College and a Master of Arts from Los Angeles State.
Nilsson resides in Sausalito, Calif., and Zaretsky resides in Mill Valley,
Calif.

NZ Productions clients include: Apple Computer, Computer Curriculum
Corporation, Electric Power Research Institute (EPRI), MWW (Canada), Revlon,
and Teradyne EDA. For more information, call (415) 383-4647.

-30-

Giving Advice/Help to Acquire Publicity and Build Image

Nowhere on or in the following news release from *Deen & Black Public Relations,
Sacramento, California* (Figure 8.19), is there an indication that it is prepared and
distributed by a professional publicity agency. (Actually, the first "contact" listed
is an agency representative and the phone number is that of the agency.)

The release relies on a tactic that pays off when other efforts may not. It offers
information and sound advice for readers. The Do's and Don'ts listed are the kinds
of facts readers are very likely to clip and post as reminders, which adds up to
ongoing publicity for the organization—in this case the *California Landscape Contractors Association*—that is read and reread often.

FIGURE 8.19   Deen & Black/CA Landscape Contractors Assoc. Release

TONY BERTOTTI
Chairman of the Board
A. Bertotti Landscaping Inc.
Novato
(415) 897-8517
FAX: (415) 897-7314

JON EWING
President
Landtrends
San Diego
(619) 453-1755
FAX: (619) 453-7197

JIM EVERETT
Vice President
Everett Landscape
Woodside
(415) 363-0461
FAX: (415) 363-1236

KEN CROWL
Vice President
Riverside Landscape
and Irrigation
Riverside
(714) 687-4242
FAX: (714) 687-4274

RICHARD JARK
Vice President
South Coast Landscaping
Los Alamitos
(310) 596-6666
FAX: (310) 431-6386

ROBERT BATTINICH
Vice President
Battinich Tree & Landscape
Castro Valley
(510) 538-0766

RICK NEUGEBAUER
Vice President
Neugebauer & Associates
San Bernardino
(714) 381-5889
FAX: (714) 381-3308

JOHN REDMOND
Treasurer
Cypress Landscape Inc.
Fairfield
(707) 425-3338
FAX: (707) 428-1280

THOM MAXWELL MILLER
Secretary
Ecosystems Imagery Inc.
Encinitas
(619) 436-2094
FAX: (619) 436-4010

FRED HANKER
Associate Member
Representative
Delta Bluegrass Company
Stockton
(209) 464-8355
FAX: (209) 464-1701

SHARON McGUIRE
Executive Director

CALIFORNIA LANDSCAPE CONTRACTORS ASSOCIATION

Contact: Jennifer Bulotti, 916/444-8014
           Marc Gerig, 916/448-2522   November 19, 1993

LANDSCAPERS SEND URGENT MESSAGE TO CALIFORNIA PROPERTY OWNERS

PREVENT URBAN WILDFIRES

SACRAMENTO — As Southern California fires rage through Ventura, Los Angeles, San Bernardino, Riverside, Orange, and San Diego Counties, property owners are urged to take certain fire-preventative measures to protect their homes against potential disasters — according to the California Landscape Contractors Association (CLCA).

"Despite plentiful winter and spring rains, the high propensity for fires this time of year and the Santa Ana winds have combined to make urban Southern California a potential tinderbox," says Rich Jark, vice president of CLCA. "The conditions may seem friendly, but the threat of wildfire still exists just about anywhere in California."

CLCA currently plays an instrumental role in "Project Firescape" — a fire prevention program sparked by the 1991 Oakland fires. Through Project Firescape, CLCA develops "fire-resistant" gardens throughout the Bay area to demonstrate that landscaping need not invite disaster during high fire season.

According to Jark, the most common mistakes include allowing dead tree limbs or underbrush to accumulate and planting highly flammable trees such as eucalyptus, pine, or juniper near building structures.

"That's what's happening in Southern California," says Jark, referring to the wildfires that have destroyed over 600 structures and nearly 200,000 acres. "Our hope is that communities in high risk areas recognize and address the dangers that lie right outside their front door."

MORE...

California Landscape
Contractors Association, Inc.
2021 N Street, Suite 300
Sacramento, CA 95814
(916) 448-CLCA
FAX: (916) 446-7692

FIGURE 8.19   *(continued)*

2-2-2

Jark warns against using plant selection as a sole fire-prevention strategy, because no greenery is "fireproof." The CLCA's fire-resistant strategy includes a combination of plant selection and placement, maintenance, and water-efficient techniques.

Here are some suggestions on how to make home landscaping more resistant to wildfires:

DO:

• use masonry walls, patios, walkways, and pools to create a safety barrier close to structures

• plant trees and shrubbery far enough apart so their crowns will not touch when vegetation reaches maturity

• prune low-growing, deep-rooted ground covers close to structures on hillsides

• use timers on automatic sprinkler systems for consistent irrigation and water conservation

• urge neighborhood cooperation to develop area-wide landscaping that inhibits flames from spreading

• keep roof and gutters clean by removing pine needles, leaves, and other debris

DON'T:

• landscape shrubbery and adjacent trees in a "fire ladder" that allows flames to quickly jump from ground level to height

• plant highly flammable trees such as eucalyptus, pine and juniper, avoid shrubbery such as chamis, red shanks and coyote brush

• build narrow archways or passageways, or plant trees in a manner that restricts access to fire-fighting equipment.

• stack woodpiles against residence walls

• allow dead tree limbs or underbrush to accumulate within 30 feet of your home

• water too frequently if a natural area tends to dry out late in the season. Irrigate at intervals of several weeks or use drip irrigation

For more information, contact CLCA headquarters at 916/448-2522. CLCA is the nation's oldest and largest organization of licensed landscape contractors and their suppliers.

\# \# \#

Moreover, publicity containing advice and information for businesspeople is often used by editors who get a deluge of the kinds of releases they cannot use—"junk mail," as they call it.

Another tactic shown here that can be effective is the listing of organization associates with their titles and their companies' names, addresses, phone, and fax numbers as part of the letterhead. For a reporter who wants to expand a story, this is, in effect, a list of 10 people he or she can call for an interview or for additional information.

FIGURE 8.20   *The Dallas Morning News*/Oak Lawn Community Services

Gay support agency moves to bigger site

Oak Lawn Community Services plans reception

By Frank Trejo
Staff Writer of The Dallas Morning News

A longtime Oak Lawn social service agency has found a new home.

Oak Lawn Community Services, located on Fairmount Street for several years, recently moved to larger facilities at 4300 MacArthur Ave., near Lemmon Avenue and the Dallas North Tollway.

The agency will have an open house and reception from 4 to 7 p.m. Thursday to honor its volunteers and donors.

"We see this as a real positive move for us," said Evilu Pridgeon, director of marketing for the agency. "In addition to having more room, this new building is even more professional for us."

Oak Lawn Community Services, which opened 12 years ago, is a service agency primarily for gay men and lesbians.

"But we certainly don't discriminate against anybody," Ms. Pridgeon said.

The organization provides mental health services, including counseling, support groups and educa-

> "In addition to having more room, this new building is even more professional for us."
> — Evilu Pridgeon,
> Oak Lawn
> Community Services

tion, and comprehensive services for people with AIDS or HIV. The agency has about 1,000 clients.

Its AIDS programs include the Buddy Project, which provides one-on-one assistance for people with AIDS, an AIDS hotline and the Daire Center, a daytime activity center for people with AIDS.

The organization also provides services to help people deal with relationships, homosexuality, incest recovery and chemical dependency.

The agency also includes the Candy Marcum Institute for Women's Studies, which concentrates on women's programs and issues.

Copycatting a Newspaper Article

There are a few things to note in a story that appeared in *The Dallas Morning News* (Figure 8.20):

- We can't say it too often, quotes are important—in this case, important enough to be lifted and used as a space filer for the story. Whenever possible, include one or two quotes in a news release, and add extra quotes as a separate attachment or part of an enclosed press kit if what is said is pertinent and interesting or the persons making the statements are well known.

- Relocation by a company or nonprofit group isn't the most exciting news to come down the pike. But the short one-sentence first graf takes the reader by the hand and gently leads him into a paragraph that actually is the real lead to the story. It's a friendly kind of introduction to the facts.
- The last graf about an organization is usually cut because of space limitations, but in this case it—or at least part of it—was used to fill the boxed space.

Familiarity Breeds Affection

There you have it! A number of examples that repeatedly demonstrate the principles of producing publicity copy. It's difficult to think of a subject that won't lure some editors to use publicity about it *if* the subject is presented in an interesting, useful manner—interesting and useful to the editors' readers, not just to you.

Read and reread, use and reuse the collection of professionally produced releases in this chapter. To coin a cliché, familiarity breeds affection, and the more often you read and copycat, the easier the job becomes.

9

Copy Preparation for Hard-Copy News Releases

How to accomplish the nuts-and-bolts mechanics of news release copy for print media, with some tips about media relations

It's Not Obsolete . . . Yet!

This chapter is useful only as long as old technologies exist. Soon the information in it will be obsolete! As newspapers reformat themselves, they will require news releases and press kits—anything currently presented in hard-copy form—to be offered in new formats.

It is fact that more and more newspapers are exploring ways to climb aboard the high-tech train. Among others, Hearst Corporation has established a division it calls the New Media and Technology Group, with a goal to find ways to adapt Hearst's media and entertainment properties to emerging electronic delivery systems and interactive technologies.

Many believe that the new newspaper will be tailored to individuals' interests and could be presented in a variety of forms, such as on a personal computer screen, in a PC printout, on the TV screen, by audio, or in a flat, electronic, tabloid-size, hand-held tablet that a person can take along in the car or wherever he or she desires. There's also serious speculation that color pages will soon emerge from newspaper pages faxed through high-speed machines.

No one model, no one style has yet surfaced as *the* model, *the* one design, for the future. But as surely as you're reading these words, there will be changes, or newspapers will be obsolete. And you can be equally sure that newspapers will not allow that to happen.

The old way, the hard-copy way, of presenting news releases for use by television and radio stations is already in a near-death state. In Chapter 16 you'll master new ways, using VNRs, RNRs, and video press kits, to meet the demands of broadcast media.

Actually, Ink-on-Paper May Stay Around a While

There is a substantial group of knowledgeable prognosticators who believe that hard-copy newspapers will stick around for a *long* while, *but* that the daily news product will be *supplemented* by new technology such as fax, audiotext, and video-text.

A story in *The New York Times* offers a report indicating that futurists are praising the enduring power of the written word. The article tells of a new magazine, named *Wired*, that is "dedicated to the 'Digital Generation,' which reports on the communications revolution 'whipping through our lives like a Bengali typhoon' and creating 'social changes so profound that their only parallel is probably the discovery of fire.' "

Those words were in the magazine's debut edition. But then, in its second issue a headline announced a "hot new medium"—known as "text." The writer acknowledged that the written word remains and, in fact, is "flourishing like kudzu vines at the boundaries of the digital revolution." (Kudzu has taken over miles and miles of terrain in the South because it grows so relentlessly.)

"There's nothing that comes close to the user-friendliness of paper," the editor of *Wired* wrote. "Paper is completely random-access; it's high-resolution; it's portable; it's almost interactive in the way it gives you the ability to determine the pace, to go backward or forward. Paper is still the best way of delivering high thought content."

"Reading," the magazine went on to say, "is still fashionable and trendy enough to be called an interactive medium" and "after trying to read the magazine on their computer screens, even the most devoted computer users express a preference for the nonwired version of *Wired*."

However, Knight-Ridder's Roger Fidler, as we reported in Chapter 1, believes that "our dependence [on paper] is going to decline rapidly after the turn of the century." He predicts electronic publishing will become prevalent over print publishing within two or three decades.

Confusion "Rains"

Confused about the life-expectancy of newspapers on paper? At this moment, the confusion is widespread. Make your own conclusion.

What is obvious, however, is that publicity practitioners must understand, be able to use and circulate information in the present format, and be geared to tackle upcoming format requirements. For the time being, hard-copy releases are alive and well for distribution to a majority of newspapers.

The Upside of the New Design

Since Knight-Ridder's *The Boca Raton* (Florida) *News* underwent a radical redesign in 1990, about three-fourths of the chain's 29 newspapers have also undertaken new ways to "put the paper together," says Knight-Ridder's Vice President/News Bill Baker.

The San Jose Mercury News, another Knight-Ridder paper and a forerunner in a number of major changes, used as its redesign rationale: "If you make it easier to read, they will come." Reader response among all Knight-Ridder papers is positive:

The number of those who are extremely or very satisfied jumped from 37 percent in 1989 to 59 percent in 1991.

A word of advice: Embrace Knight-Ridder's rationale as your own—if you make your releases easier to read, they will use them."

Keep all this in mind as you prepare and distribute your releases. Among most newspapers the new look includes shorter stories and a more graphic presentation of information, which may involve more use of color and graphs.

There's a reason for emphasizing the ways newspapers are changing. You must recognize and accept the changes and be sure they are part of your thinking as you assemble and distribute your releases.

Insatiable Appetite for News

New technologies have expanded all media's need for news, and press releases are the simplest—and least costly—means of getting it. "Press releases greatly influence the content of the news, although not all of the releases are published," *Public Relations Review* found when the trade journal explored the subject. The explanation given was that "the reporter cannot depend on legwork alone to satisfy his paper's insatiable demand for news. He looks to [other] channels to provide him with newsworthy material day after day."

The magazine also found that the size of the newspaper does not restrict this need for news. Its study showed that "the seven newspapers [surveyed] with circulations of 100,000 and above were about as likely to use the releases in all categories as were approximately 88 newspapers with circulations of 99,999 and below."

Factors Determining News Release Use

The following are the factors that determine news release use. Set these in gold alongside your keyboard:

1. Newsworthiness of the material
2. The inclusion of a local angle
3. The association of the source with a reputable institution or agency
4. Previous level and quality of output
5. Trustworthiness and authoritativeness

That last factor should not be last in importance. The report concludes that success rates depend largely on media's confidence in the sources (also indicated in factor 3). Media recognize that "releases are not always balanced [they provide only the sender's side of an issue], but they [must] know that they are factual, newsworthy, and accurate."

In other words, it pays bigtime to work continually to prove and improve your trustworthiness and dependability.

Timeliness, E-Mail, and Fax Are Major Factors

Another point made by the report is, "No matter what their size, newspapers were swayed by considerations of timeliness in their response to press releases. Articles were published quickly; more than half appeared within three days of release."

Timeliness is a major factor in determining whether a release is used. Promptness as a decree has rocketed since newspapers finally recognized that their audience is increasingly satisfied with television's and cable's abbreviated but *immediate* news reports. And because the post office cannot provide same-day delivery of regular mail, the article states, "to insure promptness in delivery, many releases are sent by fax and E-Mail, a process by which the releases are fed directly into the computer network of major newspapers."

As a Matter of Fax

Personal computers, word processing programs, mail-merge programs, data bases, scanners, facsimile machines, and other such tools are a publicist's dream come true, says Tom Steinert-Threlkeld, technology reporter and expert for *The Dallas Morning News*.

"Mail by definition is no longer news. It takes at least two or three days to get here. Even overnight express is at least yesterday's news. If it doesn't come by fax or electronic mail, it's not today's news," he says.

But then, in what appears to be total frustration, he says that he is establishing a new set of ground rules that turn back time, as a blocking device to the deluge of releases he gets. He says that the mail that absolutely will get opened:

- Comes in a standard No. 10 business envelope
- Has his name and address handwritten on the front

Anything else, he says, is at risk of going straight into the circular file, and he points out that even typed addresses can be automated.

Another reporter says the use of faxes is harassment, and that a seven-day waiting period should be imposed before a faxing license is granted!

You may gather that newspeople are not the least impressed by, and only mildly receptive to, releases that are delivered by fax *unless* the news really is "hot." (In the exploration and listing of media for distribution of releases that you did in Chapter 4, you found that not very many newspapers list their fax numbers, which is about as strong a statement as possible about their resistance to receiving information via fax.)

Some newspeople and professional publicists emphasize that faxes should be sent *only* if the reporter requests it.

Mechanics of Preparing Hard-Copy Releases

Professional Appearance

The first and major step a news editor takes to quickly reduce the flood of incoming information is to eliminate as many publicity releases as possible. That first run-by is based on appearance alone: difficult-to-read typefaces, sloppy typing, overused typewriter or printer ribbons, handwritten copy, and anything else that shouts "unprofessional." The editor or reporter simply does not have time to read them all.

Even though newspapers have far more space to give to news than broadcast media have, competition for space is intense. And with the infinite numbers of other things that can happen to kill your news story, it is essential that your news releases have a professional appearance.

Appearance also is important because it affects an editor's reaction to the *content* of your release. Its look is unspoken testimony to the care and concern given to your preparation of the story. Equally harmful, a sloppy, carelessly prepared release tends to create an impression of incompetence of the entire organization. By comparison, a professional-looking release reflects well on you and on your organization.

The bottom line is that you are expected to be an expert in producing technically and mechanically correct releases, no matter how little experience you have in producing publicity.

Because the biggest portion of publicity *at this moment in the technological revolution* still is written copy, this chapter takes you step by step through the processes of generating professional *hard-copy* news releases. You may not be an old hand at writing news, but if your release is typed and neatly presented, follows accepted format, has an interest-arousing headline, and is easy to read, it will stand a far greater chance of being used. In other words, make sure your release is user-friendly!

Appearance Guidelines

Points to remember are listed here.

- Neatness counts. *No typos, misspellings, or cross-outs.* No excuses, please! If your typewriter or computer is in the shop for repairs, that's your problem. Borrow or rent one. The editor doesn't want to hear your apologies any more than you would care to read a line in the newspaper saying, "Sorry, this story in today's paper is handwritten because our equipment is being repaired." If you use a computer or word processor, be sure your printer is set for letter-quality type and has a new ribbon, or is a laser printer.
- Do not use "exotic" typefaces. Script and italics are harder to read—and to edit—so an editor is more likely to toss such copy when his or her time is critically limited.
- Use business-size, 8 ½- by 11-inch paper. Do not use onionskin, colored, or erasable paper.
- Keep handy a current directory or list of officers, board members, executives, and employees. If you represent a club, include members or volunteers. Use the directory to check spelling and residence locality and to have addresses and phone numbers handy should a reporter or editor call to request interviews or to follow up on an angle of your release.

Tools of the Trade

The following are items to keep close by for quick reference:

- A good dictionary, for word spellings and meanings. (Sometimes even your computer's thesaurus or dictionary doesn't include a word for which you need a synonym or correct spelling.)
- *The Associated Press Stylebook and Libel Manual, The United Press Interna-*

tional Stylebook, or the individual style sheets from newspapers you service. Use these to check on whether to abbreviate or spell out such things as the name of a state, an avenue, or a street; how to present figures; when to capitalize a word; and how to punctuate.

- *The Elements of Style.* This will serve as a guide to correct language usage.

See Appendix D for a more complete description of each manual and for ordering information.

Preparation of News-Release Copy

The following are guidelines and instructions for preparing your news releases in a hard-copy form. (Instruction for prepared news releases on video and audio tape is covered in Chapter 16.) The format guidelines, listed first, give general information and tips; the format instructions present specific steps in the actual typing of the copy.

Format Guidelines

Your typewriter, word processor, or computer/printer must be in first-class shape, and your typing must be neat and accurate.

In Chapter 8 there are numerous reproductions of professional publicists' news releases. Study them and, in accordance with the copycatting principles recommended in the chapter, adopt and adapt whatever techniques fit your purposes and desires. The following are further guidelines for preparing your final copy.

- Type the release on your organization's letterhead. If there is no official stationery, it is not difficult to create your own. Computer users, with scanners, know how to reproduce their logo and incorporate it as part of their news release letterhead.

  Or, using white bond paper, paste the logo of your organization, with address and phone and fax numbers, at the top. Some releases include the words, *News, News Release,* or *Press Release* printed at or near the top of the page, but this is not a requirement. Take your paper to a quick-print shop and reproduce as many copies as you will need. (A word of caution: Be sure the copy machine has adequate toner to give top-quality reproductions.)

  You also can use plain white, $8^1/2$- by 11-inch paper and type all the necessary information onto it.

- Type on only one side of the paper.

- Leave ample margins. Leave $1^1/2$ inches for each side and bottom margin. (If your release is used, copy editors will use the blank spaces for notations.)

- If possible, give each newspaper in the same geographical area a release with a different lead.

  Each paper will be more likely to use your copy if there is a local angle in the lead and if local names are used.

- *Never* end a page so that a part of a sentence or a single word ends the page or heads the next page. These are called *widows* and *orphans*, and allowing one to slip through does not give a professional appearance.

Try not to break a paragraph: if an entire paragraph will not fit at the end of a page, start it at the beginning of a new page. If this leaves an unattractive amount of space along the bottom margin, drop the entire news story copy (beneath the summary headline) to compensate. (This latter technique merely provides more space for editors' notes and their own headlines.)

- If the story requires more than two typed pages, read it over carefully and do a little more editing. Writing concisely, in a simple and understandable style, takes effort and time. Thoreau is often quoted as having said, "Not that the story need be long, but it will take a long while to make it short." Benjamin Franklin said it a little differently (in a letter to a friend): "If I had more time, I'd write a shorter letter."

- If editing the story down to two pages requires leaving out information you believe would add to the story and that an editor would possibly use, include the extra information in the form of an attached fact sheet or backgrounder, or in an accompanying press kit.

- If you are sending more than one copy, run off the copies on your printer, or have good, clear, sharp original copies commercially made, or reproduce them with a top-grade copy machine.

- Use paper clips to fasten the pages together. *Do not use staples*. You have no idea how many editors and reporters deeply resent the daily finger tears they receive from handling stapled materials—and that's no way to foster a friendly, accommodating attitude.

- Be sure to keep a dated copy in your files.

Format Instructions

The following instructions can help you type your release in the proper format. Use Figure 9.1 as a guide.

Instructions 1 through 6 pertain only to information that must be included above the news release body text. Instructions 7 through 10 apply to the format for the lead and body copy of your release.

1. If you are not using letterhead or "instantly created letterhead," type and center (at the top of the page) the following information about your organization:
   - Name
   - Address
   - Telephone and fax numbers
2. Type the contact information. Immediately below the letterhead or typed organization heading, at the left margin, skip a line or two and type the contact information. Align it at the left margin, and align each contact's telephone number under the respective name.
   - Type the word "Contacts," then your name, then space down one line.
   - Type your telephone number (if it is different from the one listed in

FIGURE 9.1   Sample Format for a Newspaper Release
(When no letter head is available, use plain white business-size paper.)

PLATT SERVICES, INC.

1234 West First Road
Abbotsville, Rhode Island, 85123
123/456-7890

Contacts: Jane Jones
123/666-7878

For Immediate Release

Stephen Sullivan
123/456-7890

**Tax accounting firm adds new service for
nonprofits; can be boon to local economy**

ABBOTSVILLE, R.I. — Platt Services Inc., a company previously known

only for its accounting and tax functions, is introducing an added service

that will search out grants donors and prepare proposals for area nonprofit

organizations.

The service is believed to be a first, says Gerald G. Gannon, owner

of Platt Services. "Now that government grant dollars have been slashed

so drastically, nonprofit groups must compete for private dollars, and many

don't have the expertise and experience required to produce these high-

stakes grants proposals."

— more —

FIGURE 9.1   *(continued)*

Platt offers new service for nonprofits—2-2-2

According to Gannon, Platt's new service covers researching foundation and corporate funding sources that are receptive to individual nonprofit's special services; gathering supporting data and documents; then writing a proposal that is well conceived and well documented and presents the group's special needs in an appealing, attractive and appropriate manner.

"The goal of this new service," states Gannon, "is to increase funding to Abbotsville-area nonprofits, thereby increasing the level of services at a time when needs are dramatically increasing yet funding is being slashed to the bone."

It is not generally recognized, says Gannon, that increased grants monies coming to local nonprofit groups can be a substantial stimulus to the local economy. There is, he says, a three-time turnover of the monies before they leave the area.

Platt Services, Inc. was established in 1977 in Groveton, N.J. and moved to Abbotsville in 1983. It serves clients within a four-county area.

— more —

FIGURE 9.1   *(continued)*

Platt offers new service for nonprofits—3-3-3

Nonprofit groups interested in this service should contact Ms.

Joanna Johnson, who heads up the function for Platt Services, at

123/456-7890.

# # #

the letterhead logo, or if it is a direct-dial number), then space down
two lines.
- Type the name of an alternate contact: a responsible, knowledgeable
executive or staff member, then space down one line.
- Type the alternate contact's telephone number.
3. Summary headline. Space down two lines and insert, flush left under the
contact information, a summary headline. If the headline runs to two lines,
space down only one line for the second line of the headline. This headline summarizes the story for the editor, with the purpose of attracting and
enticing him or her to read it.
   A head that would definitely attract any editor's eye showed up in
Johnny Hart's "B.C." cartoon strip. First panel: An editor, complete with
eyeshade, stands at *"The Daily Mud* rock" and yells to a counterpart, "I
need a headline for this story." He's asked, "What's it about?" Second panel:
The editor answers, "Naked people qualifying to run in the marathon."
Third panel: "How 'bout 'All the nudes that's fit to sprint'?"
4. Type the release timing line. This information will go on the upper right-
hand side of the paper, below the organization's letterhead and opposite
the contact information.
   Be sure the release information is the same for all newspapers or for
other media to which this specific release goes.
   Use whichever release timing line is appropriate:
- For Immediate Release
- Release at Your Convenience
- For Release on (give a specific release date). Whenever possible, try
to avoid locking an editor into a specific date.
5. Indicate whether the story is an exclusive. An exclusive story should be
prominently marked as such at the top of the copy. Any exclusive must be
honored. Let the editor know by typing the word "EXCLUSIVE" in capital letters above the release timing line. Then, don't give the story to any
other news source. (This means television, cable, and radio too.)
6. Type the mailing date (optional). There are two schools of thought about
whether releases should carry a mailing date. Many professional publicists
do not include a mailing date, because slow delivery can work against the

release's being used. (It may appear to be outdated.) If you choose to include the mailing date, it should be at the top, directly beneath the letterhead logo or organization heading. Whether or not you use it on your news release, be sure that you note the mailing date on your file copy for future reference.

Instructions for News-Release Lead and Body Copy

7. Insert a dateline. Type the dateline flush left (not indented as for all the following paragraphs). The dateline is actually only an identification of the city and state from which the story originates; it usually does not contain a date. There is no need for a dateline on releases that are distributed only to local newspapers.

    The word *dateline* comes from past years when transmission of news was slower (particularly from outside the newspaper's immediate coverage area) and newspapers listed dates along with the city of origin.

    The first paragraph (lead) immediately follows the dateline. Indent each of the following paragraphs of the lead and body copy by five spaces.

8. Indicate whether the story runs more than a page. If the story runs to more than one page, type the following at the bottom center of each page (except the last page):

                        - more -

9. At the top of the second page and on each succeeding page, type a line using a shortened version of your summary headline, and follow it with the page number. Example:

    PASI Staff Appointments - 2-2-2

10. Signify the end of the release copy. At the end of the copy, center and type the following:

                        # # #

    or

                        — 30 —

Copy Preparation Tips

The following pointers are worth noting:

- Never trust your typist—particularly if the typist is you! (People tend to see what they think they wrote when they try to proof their own work.)
    Proofread each page. Typos don't do much for your story in the newspaper, but they often become the laugh of the day in newsrooms around the country. This is one that appeared in the *Fort Worth Star-Telegram:* "At a busy airport terminal, a harried passenger stepped up to the ticket counter and inquired, 'How long a hangover will I have in Chicago?' " Here are some other "slips" from *Reader's Digest:*
    The pilot apparently lost control moments before ouchdown.

An Israeli bus driver suffered minor injuries when his but was hit by a firebomb.

We will widow-shop and exercise.

- Never, *never*, play favorites among newspapers, editors, or columnists. Be impartial when there is more than one paper in an area. Mail or distribute your releases so that each has an equal time break in using them.
- Never, *never*, **never** double-plant. This means, never place the same story with more than one person or section of the same publication.
- Check that all names are proper, given names. Do not use nicknames, even when writing about children.
- Check and recheck spelling of all names in your copy. If the correct spelling is unusual, write "CQ" over the word. Most people—other than child abusers, drug purveyors, and bad-check writers—nearly always like to see their names in print. A newspaper likes to use names because a person whose name appears in the paper (mentioned in a complimentary way and spelled correctly) is likely to buy several copies.
- If you include a date, such as Thursday, October 3, check that Thursday is indeed October 3. Also check that the exact hour for an event is given.
- If you have any question whatsoever about the meaning of a word in your release, look up its meaning and spelling in the dictionary.
- Do not break and hyphenate words at the end of a line. It's not a good policy, and hyphenation errors can be disastrous, as happened in the following instance, told in *Word Perfect 5.0 Desktop Publishing in Style* by Daniel Will-Harris:

Throughout his long career, he was known as the-
rapist of the stars.

"Therapist of the stars" was the original intent of the writer.

- If there is any information in the release that is technical or controversial or that could create a problem for your organization, and if you are an appointee or staffer, get your boss or an officer to initial a file copy of each release. Don't hesitate to check your copy with your sources.
- Address your news release copy to the appropriate editor. Even if you personally deliver it, address it to the proper person so that it can be left if he or she is not available at the time you are there.
- If you include a note, write it on a separate sheet of paper and attach it with a paper clip.
- If you attach a list of names, paste together the pages (if there are more than one) so there is no danger of their getting separated. Then fold the long sheet to match the size of a single sheet and attach it to the release with paper clips.
- Don't expect the editor to rewrite (although he or she probably will).
- Remember the KISS aphorism: Keep It Short, Simple. You will soon perceive that it is much more gratifying to see a brief item in print, with all its essential information intact, than to lament over a beautiful, long story that found its resting place in a wastebasket.

- Better never than late! (Add another "commandment" to those in Chapter 5: "Thou shalt not procrastinate.") Use of your release could hang on its timeliness. Routine material should be in editors' hands at least 24 hours prior to the day of publication. If the release is for use in a Sunday or weekend edition, it must be sent at least one week, possibly two, in advance.

- Be sure to keep a dated copy of your release in your files so that you can answer questions if you are called and so that you can compare the original with the final, printed version and thereby learn from it.

News over the Telephone

You won't have anything going for you if you try to phone in your story. One of the worst ways to get along with newspeople is to ask them to do your job for you. Even if they have the time, phoning in copy substantially increases chances for misunderstandings, misspellings, and possibly the miscarriage of your efforts.

If ever, for any reason, you *must* transmit information over the phone, such as to correct an error noted after sending out a release, or because of a change in date, location, or hours, time the call away from the paper's crucial deadlines. For afternoon or evening papers, call in the afternoon; for morning papers, morning is a better time.

Suppose, however, that all your news releases have been written and sent out. You've followed all the rules; you've mailed or carried in your releases instead of phoning or faxing them. You are proud of the job you've done, but *suddenly*—the event is cancelled! (Or there's a change in speakers or dates.)

What do you do? Very simply, immediately notify the newspaper. This is the time to phone or fax, although a fax may get lost among the torrent of everything that gets faxed to newspapers. If you fax, indicate by name the individual to whom you're directing the information.

If there is no crisis, however, please don't call to find out when your story was or will be used. (Many an editor has had such calls, with the caller saying, "Oh, I don't read your paper. . . ." Even if you don't say exactly that, the implication is there. That is no way to get along with the press.)

Fact Sheets and Backgrounders

If, in the beginning, the writing of a news release baffles and intimidates you, you may wish to send a fact sheet—and perhaps attach a backgrounder—as an alternative to a release. Use a fact sheet only if you wish to count on the editor or a reporter having the time and inclination to write the story from it and any other information you send along.

Chapter 11 discusses the items that should be included in fact sheets and backgrounders and how to prepare them. Note, however, that your odds of achieving a news story from a fact sheet in any given newspaper are substantially reduced, if even for only one reason—the shortage of time and staff to write it.

Clipping Services

Heed the warning given earlier—*do not* ask an editor or a reporter to send you a copy of the news item you sent to him or her. If all of your releases are local, you will be able to watch for and clip publicity stories as they appear.

However, if your media list is not confined to your immediate locale, your organization may wish to subscribe to a clipping service. If there is one in your area, you will find it listed in the Yellow Pages. (The major national clipping bureaus and their addresses are listed in Appendix D.)

10

Publicity Photos

*Why a picture truly is worth hundreds
of news-release words*

The Power of Visual Images

Your eye can't miss the photo of a hen covered with a newspaper to shield her from the elements. The headline "Painting the Town," across the top of the photo that occupied two-thirds of the section's page 1 in *The Dallas Morning News*, can't help but spike your curiosity. What on earth do the two . . . ?

Your eye immediately drops to the story beneath the photo, and the caption's headline—"Volunteers fan out to fix homes, plant gardens, work at zoo"—then on to the photo's caption:

> A hen that wouldn't budge from her nest Saturday is covered with a newspaper to shield her as volunteers paint the home of Jonas Cleveland in east Oak Cliff. The project was part of the Volunteer Center of Dallas County's first community service day.

What the combination of that picture and caption is, is knock-'em-dead publicity for the nonprofit organization and its efforts.

The photo is also a lesson—a lesson in how professional news photographers grab a human-interest angle every chance they get, to seize the eye and interest of readers. Everyone has seen photos of volunteers climbing ladders to paint the homes of the underpriviledged. But a catchy headline—"Painting the Town"—over a photo of a rain-drenched hen with a newspaper sheltering it provided publicity for the nonprofit group's efforts that built image and gained support perhaps even to the extent of future grants approvals, in-kind donations, and hard cash donations.

People use pictures as a necessary reference, and they need that visual reference to many news stories. Kenneth Byerly in *Community Journalism*, quotes an editor of a weekly newspaper: "If names make news, so do faces. . . . And a news photographer uses a camera just as a reporter or publicity writer uses a typewriter."

Someone once kidded that photography is a snap judgment! Don't laugh. That's what this chapter is all about: how to get your publicity photos past the critical eye and the harried snap judgment of an editor.

Instant Impact

A photo often is more valuable than a story in transmitting your message. The greatest advantage of photographs over the printed word is that they make their point in an instant—or prod you to read accompanying information. They illustrate and clarify a news story and often increase the impact. They can create curiosity or pull the reader to a new view of the familiar. They can and should create readership, and that is a responsibility a newspaper doesn't take lightly.

Advantages of the Publicity Photo

Whether a publicity photo is sent as a stand-alone, separate release or as part of your written release, it is important to your publicity efforts for a number of reasons:

- It can graphically describe and show what words cannot.
- It can attract readers' eyes to your news or feature article.
- It cannot be edited, other than by *cropping* (trimming edges to fit space).
- It will seldom be missed by a reader, and your news story—in picture form—can be "read" at a glance.
- It may be run with a publicity "plug" for your organization when an editor has no space for a printed release but is still short of eye-appealing material with which to dress up pages.

Lights! Camera! Reaction!

Before we get into the mechanics of publicity photos, it's important that you know and understand that newspaper photo departments—like other newspaper operations—have moved into the techno-age. For more and more newspapers, particularly the larger ones, the mechanics have changed.

Today there are electronic cameras, digital scanner-transmitters, satellite transmission systems whereby photographers can transmit scanned pictures over portable satellite radiotelephones—without phone or power!—dedicated fiber-optic lines, and newspaper flexo presses that bring both color and black-and-white photo reproduction up to near-magazine-slick-paper quality.

Even "low-tech" cameras now are crafted so that while the photographer composes a shot through the viewfinder, the camera looks back through the viewfinder at the shooter's eye to find the intended target of its autofocus.

Radiotelephone, powered by a car battery and linked to a collapsible antenna, is the means by which photos are transmitted from places without phone service or even electricity. This means a photographer has extraordinary freedom to cover stories even where communications facilities have been knocked out by storm, war, or earthquake.

Generally, image-receiving time has been reduced from 35 seconds to 8 seconds, although the Associated Press can transmit at 56 kilobits per second. But speed is only part of the advantage of digital delivery; the quality of digitally delivered images is the motivation for the changeover.

Beyond technology, "the role of photojournalism has completely changed," states *American Photo*. "It's clear that photojournalism is struggling to define its place in the era of CNN and computer technology."

And beyond photojournalism and photo transmissions, newspapers are using heatset inks and drying ovens that provide the lustrous look of magazine color printing that has never before been captured on porous, spongy, gray newsprint. Old letterpress equipment is being replaced by flexo presses that boast no rub-off of ink or print-through. It's a whole new world!

The essential point of all this—publicity photos must be as good as those available from a medium's own professional photographers.

The Photo Editor's Job

A photo editor is primarily interested in a photo with the following qualities:

- Storytelling ability
- Technical quality of the print
- Complete and accurate caption information

Keep in mind that a photo editor of a newspaper receives hundreds of photos every day. On average, he or she can use only one of every 10 photos that crosses his or her desk. Your job is to see that your photo is good enough to compete for that valuable news space. Where do all the others go? Right! Into the wastebasket. (Don't expect the photos you send to be returned, and do not ask for them.)

Your Job

You don't have to be a photographer in order to submit photos for a news release. You don't even need to know how cameras work. There are some things, however, that you must know about newspaper photos.

First, and probably most important, you are the one who must *plan* the photo. Even when the publication sends its own photographer, it is your job to contact the editor in advance to "sell" the merit of the photo assignment. If you are using your own photographer, don't expect him or her to plan the picture or to know the purpose for the picture. Plan your photos well. When possible, have a conference with the editor and photographer in advance.

Here are some tips on planning your photos:

- Write outlines of the pictures.
- List the props necessary for each.
- Plan each photo so it tells a story, and make a blueprint.
- Be original.

In addition to the preceding points, keep newspaper space limitations in mind. Pictures for a photo *spread*, in which several pictures appear, are almost always taken by the newspaper's own photographers. However, space is so precious that a photo spread is highly unusual and would have to be of an event of major significance—a highly publicized charity event or a social, business, or celebrity event involving nationally or widely known people. Seldom would a for-profit organization qualify for a photo spread. However, sponsorship of a major event often produces caption credits.

Types of Photos

Most local dailies and weeklies with limited photo staffs will expect you to provide all photos. These may include, for instance, a picture of someone selling the tickets to a charity affair; of a presentation to an award winner; or of any other publicity opportunities; or they could be standard head-and-shoulders photos or a *mug shot* (head only) of your organization's newly announced executive or newly selected committee chairperson.

However, your photos could-should have a more original theme, and that calls for you and your people to put on your creative hats and do some brainstorming.

The Right Photographer

Maury Falstein, a newspaper photo editor of *The Chicago Sun-Times* for more than 35 years, described at one of his lectures how an excellent shot was turned into a second-rate shot by a photographer who didn't recognize the human-interest factor or understand its value in newspaper photography:

> *I once watched an emotional tear-jerking reunion take place in Union Station while a photographer waited on the sidelines to set up his picture. Then he posed the new arrival with relatives kissing her on each cheek. Instead of capturing the realism of their event, he played the role of a director restaging life in a stereotyped pattern.*

Technical Aspects

Maury Falstein gave the following advice on the technical aspects of taking pictures.

> *I realize that much thought goes into the planning of a publicity campaign. But when it comes to pictures, too many persons are inclined to let the camera do all the thinking.*
>
> *To get a good news-feature picture, preplanning of the composition and action is more than 75 percent of the job. The technical aspects of photography—the focusing, the exposure, and the lighting—are important, too, but they rate second to the picture message.*

If you don't know a good photographer who is experienced in taking newspaper shots, ask the editor you hope will use the photo. He or she undoubtedly will know several you can hire. And if the editor or reporter recommends a photographer, that means the photog has previously produced pictures the editor liked—and *used!*

Before you retain anyone, though, do a little research. Study the kinds of photos the paper uses; they vary from paper to paper.

Vertical Format

One thing you undoubtedly will notice as you become more aware of publicity photos is that newspaper photos usually fit a vertical format rather than a horizontal one. (TV pictures are always horizontal, however.) Yet most photographers, unless they are trained news photographers, tend to shoot only horizontal pictures, particularly if the purpose of the release is to announce an entirely new board of directors.

If your photo plans call for any kind of a lineup, you should know that such pictures—of a group of people looking into the camera or of someone signing a contract with a lineup standing behind him or her—have been dead for 20 years (unless it's the president of the United States). This kind of photo is sure to be rejected.

As you make your plans, ask yourself, "Is this picture intended for use in a four-column, two-column, or one-column space? Is there room for cropping vertically or horizontally?"

Of course, if you have doubts about whether the newspaper you're shooting for will prefer vertical or horizontal shots, sending both is good insurance.

Compact Shots

An editor can often use a small, close-cropped photo when the available space cannot accommodate a large one. Or the editor might wish to use two small photos in preference to one large, horizontal one. The more adaptable the size, the better. The best photos are so compact that an editor can run them in a three- or four-column space, or reduce them to a one- or two-column size, and still maintain the picture's meaning.

When possible, query the editor in advance, particularly if you anticipate a picture story or if you plan to send more than one shot. And be sure to check the newspaper's photo deadline. Photo deadlines often vary from copy deadlines.

If you have a picture story or if the editor indicates an interest in one, send your photographer to the newspaper and let the editor look at the *contact sheets*. That will allow the editor to make the choices that are difficult for you to make because you can't peek into his or her thinking or get a look at the dummy page layout that must be filled.

Composition and Direction

An assigned newspaper photographer is the best judge of the composition and direction of a photo—whether a shot is good, where and how the person should be posed, and whether the photo is worthy of being used. He or she may even resent your attempts to direct a shot and consider your efforts as meddling.

If, however, the photographer has been hired by you, collaborate with that person. He or she will know best about composition and technique, but if you have studied your outlet and the kinds of photos it prefers, your input will be valuable in decisions about picture content. The photographer should know from you whether the photo is intended for use in four columns, in two columns, or as a mug shot. Discuss with the phtographer whether there will be room for vertical or horizontal cropping.

Backgrounds.   The photographer, whether hired by you or sent from the newspaper, should recognize conflict of backgrounds, but it is your job to envision possible problems before the photographer arrives. Arrange in advance for photo subjects to come dressed according to your background setups. A person in a light outfit should be seen against a dark background; a person in a dark outfit should be seen against a light background. There is little room for anyone dressed in a "busy" print or a large pattern. Large patterns in men's ties do not photograph well either. And "busy" backgrounds are equally difficult for a photographer to work against. Try to choose simple, plain backgrounds.

People being photographed may want to remove eyeglasses so that light from a camera flash won't create reflection.

To protect against such problems, professional publicists often carry their own props to photo sessions—from the right kinds of neckties, to plants and flowers, to a makeup kit for a last minute touchup. You may wish to do the same.

"Deadly Cliché" Photos.   A former picture editor at a major metropolitan daily moaned over what he called "deadly cliché" photos submitted by many publicists. He said these are the two men and a piece of paper award or proclamation pictures, the deadpan plaque presentations, the routine ground-breaking pictures, and the dull luncheon pictures, in which the rolls and water glasses in the foreground have as much animation as the characters seated behind them.

You will need to be original. Otherwise, why waste the time of the photographer and of the people being photographed, and why waste the funds you have budgeted to shoot the photos, when the editor will surely discard a "deadly cliché" photo. Photo editors agree on the following suggestions.

- Be as candid as possible when covering an award presentation. Try to catch the expressions at the original ceremony, if possible, rather than attempt to restage it. Look for an offbeat approach. If an award is being presented for traffic safety, for instance, get the winner in a spot where the background will show a busy traffic pattern.
- Try a new angle. Sometimes a low angle or overhead view will help dramatize a situation.

What these suggestions say is that it is necessary to find situations that evoke some kind of emotional response—that precious ingredient called "human interest"—and then the picture will sell itself to the newspaper. Don't be a lazy planner and let the camera do all the thinking. Preplan each photo.

Equipment.   When you make the picture assignment, you should give the photographer not only the place and time, but also a description of the area in which he or she will be required to shoot so that the proper equipment can be brought. Is it a confined area? The photographer will need wide-angle lenses. Is there ample light, or are lights needed? Remind the photographer that the photos are to be used in a newspaper and state whether they are to be in black and white or in color so that he or she can bring the proper film.

The Day of the Shoot

If you have planned well, there is very little for you to do at the photo session. If the photographer is a staffer from the newspaper, provide him or her with a typewritten sheet giving background information, correct spelling of names and titles, and any other pertinent information to take back to the editor.

Arrangement of Poses

Snoopy puts his spin on making a photo subject look good in a "Peanuts" strip. In the first panel he's focusing his camera and posing his little feathered friend. Second panel, he tells the photo subject, "Okay, say, 'Birdseed.' "

Part of your job is to see that everyone does look good, but your main responsibility is to take care of details:

Have everyone and everything at the site before the photographer arrives. Try to see that the principals in every photograph are as close together as possible, almost crowded. It is well to remember that the fewer people in a picture, the better the picture and the better each person will look. Also, if possible, unless it is a portrait or mug shot, have the principals doing something, not just looking at the camera or at each other. In other words, use action shots, not group portraits. This isn't always easy, but it can and should be done.

Here are a few more tips. Try to avoid pictures of people eating or drinking. Few people look good or have good manners when they're eating.

In case your publicity goal is to alert the public to some new type of equipment, remember that there is nothing more static than a photo of equipment. Include people in the photo, using the equipment or doing something with it.

If you are shooting for more than one newspaper in the same area, arrange different shots for each paper.

Photographic Release Forms

There may be a rare time when you must provide a newspaper with a signed *photo-release form*, or you want one because you plan additional uses for a photo.

Be sure to obtain a release if you have, for instance, hired a model for a shot or included a child in a photo that you hope can be used later in an annual report or in some form other than a straight-news shot. (A standard photo-release form, which may be copied, is included in Appendix A.) Keep the original, signed form for your files, and attach only a reproduction with the photo. (Also included in Appendix A is a copy of instructions to nonphotographer staff members of an advertising and public relations organization. You can adopt these instructions as the standard photo instructions used by your organization.)

That's it—you've done your job. The photographer has taken the pictures and gone. There's nothing more for you to do until he or she has delivered the contact sheets, until, together you have chosen the best shots for your purpose, and he or she has delivered the final prints.

Mechanics for Submitting Photos

Always submit glossy, 8- by 10-inch (or larger) color or black-and-white photos, unless the newspaper you are shooting for has a different size preference. A 5- by 7-inch head-and-shoulders shot is appropriate to accompany the announcement of an individual's election or appointment to a new position. Some smaller papers use an electronic engraving process that calls for photos to be the same size as they will be when they appear in the paper. Find out in advance what size photographs your newspaper's editor prefers, and whether they even use black-and-white shots, and don't expect to get them back.

A word of caution in the event that a photographer is assigned from the newspaper. Do *not* request prints for your own use unless you know the newspaper has a policy that allows you to *purchase* them.

One of the great problems for editors receiving publicity prints is the quality of the prints. Newspapers that must reproduce photographs on porous newsprint demand top-quality, crisp, high-contrast prints to start with. If a subject's dark clothing blends into a dark background, the picture will look like a smudge when it is printed.

The Caption as the Photo's "Story"

Caption information is important and must be accurate and complete.

An otherwise usable picture often must be discarded because of inadequate or inaccurate information. Pictures are discarded if, for instance, they show seven heads but list only six names in the caption or, just as bad, six heads and seven names.

A typical caption very briefly tells what the picture is about. Here is an example:

> *ABC Inc. senior vice president Jeanne Jones and president Lawrence Smith, in front of the new sculpture at the entrance to corporate headquarters. The carving by well-known artist Henri Johanssen symbolizes the vigor and enthusiasm with which the company serves its customers.*

- Study captions in the publications to which you will send your releases, and use their individual form and style.
- Use a summary headline above the caption's text, centered rather than aligned flush left as in your news or feature releases.
- Identify the people as they appear in the photo from left to right. If the subjects can't be identified in a left-to-right direction, draw a diagram of the photograph and number the heads. Then list the names by number.
- Spell out the full names. Initials for first names are not acceptable.
- Always include the name of your organization in the caption, along with as many pertinent points from the accompanying news story as are compatible with caption space. This way, if the news release itself doesn't make it, the picture and caption can stand alone and still be effective as publicity. Remember, however, to keep captions brief.
- Do not double-plant within a newspaper. Don't send identical or similar photos to different people or to different sections at the same newspaper. If you send photos to two newspapers in the same area, be sure the photos are not identical.

Final Preparation of Photo and Caption

Neatness counts. A typed caption is essential. Follow these guidelines to prepare your photo and caption:

- Include all the proper identification of your organization: its address, your name (as contact), and your telephone number, all single-spaced. The caption itself must be double-spaced.
- Use letterhead if the identifying logo is small enough that it and the caption information require only about a half-sheet of paper. It is better to use plain white paper, but be sure that your organization's name, address, and phone and fax numbers, and your name (as contact) and phone number head up the typed information on each caption.
- Type the caption, double-spaced, on the lower *half* of a sheet of plain white paper, or leave enough space at the top of the paper to tape the caption, face up, to the bottom of the print. Do this so that picture and caption may be studied by the editor simultaneously. (Place the tape on the back of the print.)
- When the caption is ready to be mailed, fold it up over the photo to protect it and to fit into a mailing envelope. (This is why letterhead usually is not as useful as plain paper. Seldom is there room above a letterhead to provide space for taping the sheet to the photo.)

Photo Safeguards

Do *not* attach anything to the print with paper clips or staples, and do *not* type directly onto the back of a photo or write on it with pen or pencil. These practices damage the print for reproduction purposes. As insurance, you may wish to attach a pretyped, gummed label, with your name and phone number, just in case the caption becomes separated from the photo.

Most editors prefer to receive publicity photos by mail or carrier. Enclose them, along with your release or your fact sheet, in a large, strong envelope with sheets of cardboard protecting the front and back of the photos. On the envelope, in large letters, write plainly for the post office, "Photo. Do not bend."

Finally—and this is very important—avoid phoning a busy photo desk. It won't be noticed that you didn't phone, but it surely will be noted, negatively, if you do.

Photo Syndicates

There are outlets that can distribute your photos nationally for you, *if* the quality is outstanding and *if* the content has widespread appeal. (*Editor & Publisher International Year Book* lists photo syndicates.) These syndicates will make no compromise in quality of content, and they are probably the most demanding and exacting among any in the news business. Amateurism is not tolerated.

Suppose, however, your photo can meet the impeccable standards and a syndicate does distribute it. The gains will be greater than those achieved by any other means of distributing publicity material, because so many publications use syndicated photos.

Whereas newspapers don't appreciate receiving the identical photos that have been given to their competition, syndicates do not object. You can, therefore, supply identical photos to all syndicates on your customized media list.

Most photo syndicates have offices in major cities throughout the country. If you believe your publicity photos can qualify, contact the office nearest you and request information about the specific requirements of each. It will be worth the extra effort, and, because demand is so great for the syndicate's pictures, they are always receptive to any that can qualify.

Color It Read

"Black and white and read all over!" You may remember that saying about news-papers from when you were a kid. No more! Even "The Gray Lady"—*The New York Times*—and the *Wall Street Journal* at last have moved to color.

This is the final phase of a trend that began as far back as 1891 when *The Milwaukee Journal* used a color bar on its front page to commemorate the inauguration of a new governor.

It was as late as 1991 when a group of *The Philadelphia Inquirer's* readers were shown a prototype of an edition in color—and "were horrified." But *The Inquirer* went ahead with plans, built a $300 million printing plant to handle color, and began running full-color photos on the front page almost every day. Those horri-fied readers? "Virtually no comment" about the change, says Gene Foreman, deputy editor.

As for the *Wall Street Journal*, it began using color for the first time in Septem-ber of 1991, but *only* on the front and back pages of any fourth-section advertising supplements. Not for editorial content!

Today, according to *The New York Times*, more than 97 percent of North American newspapers now print some of their news pages in color, up from 12 percent in 1979. That means, of course, that the newspapers to which you send photos may no longer consider black-and-white photos. And don't take it for granted that only the biggest dailies are demanding color photos. "Across the country, smaller newspapers have routinely pressed their big-city competitors [to] be getting into color faster, taking advantage of technical and financial complexities that have slowed the process at major urban newspapers," says *The Times*.

When you run your periodic media list checks for up-to-date personnel names, request information about the use of black-and-white photos.

New Technology

High tech doesn't really explain it. What's already in use might be called "ballistic technology!"

The Associated Press now has what it calls PhotoStream, a high-speed digital photo service that carries in color many photos that go out only in black and white on an analog circuit. The additional service is made possible by the change to compressed-format transmissions on the satellite photo delivery service.

As for still frames from videotape, according to a report in *Editor & Publisher*, AP is making two improvements: "Permissions for use can be regulated better and faster and higher-quality pictures can be gained if images are taken direct from the original signal and cleaned up prior to transmission, eliminating frame-grab technology on the user's end."

A London newspaper group says it has moved beyond the use of Kodak's Photo CD for news photo production and is using another Kodak "interactive CD which can incorporate text, still and moving images, and voice."

After years of developing digital cameras, Eastman Kodak together with Associated Press, has produced a model strictly to meet the needs of news photographers, so that no longer must quality be sacrificed for speed. The new camera includes a microphone and voice recorder, which permit hands-free, on-the-scene captioning or note taking.

Printing has also moved into the new age. Color can be printed on a dedicated press that uses heatset inks and drying ovens to provide the polished "look of magazine color printing not ordinarily obtainable on absorbent, grayer newsprint," according to *E&P*.

There are some concerns about all this, though. Robert Schnitzlein, Reuters' Americas picture editor, is worried that technology may undermine the integrity of the genre, he says in *American Photo* magazine. "I hate to think that picture editors are thinking 'bits 'n' bytes' instead of pictures."

But, again on the plus side, Gamma-Liaison's executive vice president, Jennifer Coley, says, "Technology has completely changed the way we deal with deadlines. The quality of electronic photographs has improved to such an extent that recently I was unable to tell a computer reproduction transmitted to us digitally from an original chrome."

The word here is—it's all moving along so fast that not only must your photos be top quality, you must move them faster. The only way you can be sure your publicity photo releases meet up-to-the-minute standards is to keep informed.

11

Hard-Copy Press Kit Preparation

How to help reporters so they can help you

They're Baaack!

In fact, they never left. Until newspapers and other news media actually become fully electronic, the need for feet-on-the-ground hard-copy press kits will continue. In Chapter 16 you'll learn the how-tos for preparing so-called electronic press kits for television releases, whereby the information that otherwise would be sent in a press kit is put on videotape and built into a video news release (VNR).

So what exactly is a press kit?

The Press Kit Defined

What newspaper people and many publicists still call a press kit, some call a *media* kit, or a *media information* kit, in acknowledgment of electronic news media. Whatever you choose to call it, if you hold a press conference or any activity to which newspeople are invited, you should have such kits on hand to give them.

Press kits are special packages that include one or two news releases, photographs, fact sheets, backgrounders, quotes sheets, clip sheets, and other information related to an event or to the purpose of a press conference. Sometimes—when appropriate—they contain or accompany samples of a product or a device. The kits can include comprehensive information about your organization and its products or services. They can serve a more prolonged publicity purpose if they are constructed so that recipients find them valuable enough to keep on file as reference tools—think of them as on-demand references, like candy bar machines.

Simply stated, a press kit is merely a collection of materials that can help reporters do a better job reporting *your* story.

The Press Kit as a Publicity "Tool"

A press kit can be a powerful instrument in an organization's publicity "tool kit." One press kit, with an enclosed plastic trash bag and informative data, produced 19 column inches of publicity in one of the country's largest metropolitan daily newspapers for a local chapter of Keep America Beautiful Today.

Nineteen column inches! That's the amount of space that extends from top to bottom of a standard-size newspaper. And this particular paper divides each page into five columns instead of the usual six or seven, which increases the number of words in each column inch. That is a lot of publicity space, probably achieved only because a press kit that was enclosed with the press release gave additional information the reporter could use to lengthen the newspaper story. Few publicity releases without supporting material ever produce such a publicity windfall.

Purpose of a Press Kit

The primary purpose of a press kit is to help newspeople report your story more thoroughly and equitably. It can be an excellent means of saving a reporter's, and your, time at a press conference or event. Instead of giving a lengthy verbal presentation that requires extensive note taking by reporters, you can briefly summarize your project and then hand each reporter a kit. Tell them that you believe all the information required is inside. The savings in time will be appreciated by busy press people. The rest of the time can be spent in answering questions or serving coffee, tea, and soft drinks as a way of getting better acquainted with those attending. Or reporters with tight schedules can keep to their timetable and still get all the information they require to do a notable report.

Reporter Perspective. Not everything in a press kit will be used by the newspeople reporting your story, because reporters prefer to develop their own stories if they have the time. However, something in your kit may be the item or tidbit that allows them to add interesting information or to present slightly different perspectives or approaches than other newspapers' stories offer on the same topic.

Reporters are almost always pressed for time. They seldom have the luxury to research or explore additional sources of information that will flesh out a story to make it a more interesting, more comprehensive report. A press kit gives reporters the extra information they don't have time to dig for, and provides insight—from *your* point of view—that might not otherwise be available.

Presentation of Positives. A press kit gives reporters—or others who may receive the press kit—the *positives* you want to present to the public. Some call this slanting a viewpoint, but as the person responsible for your organization's image, you want the public to lean favorably in your direction.

Herb Baus, the late nationally known journalist, public relations practitioner, and author of several publicity and public relations books, said, "What people believe is to them the important thing, because it is to them the truth . . . [and] the job of public relations is to make people believe the truth."

When the end result—the printed article in the newspaper—provides not only immediate particulars of your announcement, but also substantial added information about your organization, that is indeed highly profitable publicity and excellent public relations.

Press Kit Format

A press kit can be an elaborate, custom-designed folder with your organization's name imprinted or embossed on the front cover. It can also be a very simple, inexpensive folder with pockets that is identified by typed stickers.

Any format is acceptable if it is capable of containing the contents you decide are essential. The most favored formats are folders with inside pockets (the most popular), loose-leaf notebooks (sometimes with divider tabs), spiral-bound booklets, and even large envelopes. Your publicity budget may dictate which format you will use.

If your firm or group has a special, distinctive logo, you may wish to include that on the exterior. It is not the cover that matters, though; it's the contents.

Cover

How often have you heard, You can't judge a book by its cover? But many people do, particularly when it comes to *press kit covers*.

If your press kit is issued by a business whose income is generated by its own initiative, such as through sales of products or services, then the cover and its contents—and just about anything else about it, for that matter—can be more elaborate than for an organization that is funded by public monies. Anticipate any criticism of your group's fiduciary judgment that might come as a result of too ostentatious an offering. If yours is a charitable organization funded by grants or donations, modesty may be your best approach so that no one questions how the monies you seek and receive are being used.

A press kit cover can often be used for several additional purposes merely by changing the contents according to the circumstances. You can use press kit covers at seminars or workshops for employees; send them to potential donors; give them in advance to visitors on a plant tour; mail them in a promotional campaign; and file them as material reference for speakers, sponsors, or another, later, press conference. Your executives and employees undoubtedly will think of many, many uses for such a cover. So consider the uses it may be put to before you make a final decision about yours. Design it accordingly. Also, if you anticipate other uses for the same cover, producing a larger number of them can substantially reduce per-unit printing costs.

Contents

Your press kit should contain as much information *as will be useful* to the recipient. Make sure that you don't forget to include information that will be crucial to the success of your package. The following list contains some examples:

- The most important pieces of information in a press kit are the name of your organization, its address and phone number, and your name (as contact) and phone number (if different from that of the organization). It is amazing how many press kits have been issued without this essential data. Someone just wasn't thinking! Some kits attach the contact's business card to the inside pocket, where it is easily seen and not easily misplaced. Others make the organization name, address, and phone number a permanent part of the cover information. The latter method requires that the contact's name be prominently displayed inside the kit so that recipients can easily locate it if there is a question of any kind.
- For a news conference, always include a "stand-alone" news release. A stand-alone release provides all the essential, principal facts or purpose of

the news conference and can stand alone to be used by recipient newspapers as presented. This news release should tell the complete story without causing the reader to want additional information, and it should be written in the inverted pyramid, five Ws news style.

- A publicity calendar of upcoming events can be a worthwhile enclosure, particularly for nonprofit organizations with a schedule of ongoing community events.

- A *fact sheet* may be included. A fact sheet can substitute for a news release and may be used by a writer who is unsure about how to write a release. However, the chances that a busy editor will assign a reporter to write your story from a fact sheet are considerably less than that the editor will pass a news release to the copy desk for editing or rewrite.

  A fact sheet lists the information you would include in a news release: the basic information about your company or nonprofit group; the event, announcement, or purpose for the release; and pertinent background information. (There are examples of fact sheets in Chapter 8, Figure 8.12, and in Figure 11.1 at the end of this chapter.)

  Be sure the heading on your fact sheet includes your organization's name, address, telephone number, and a contact's name.

  Use a bullet (•) to set each item of information apart and make reading and reference easy.

  Single-space the copy, but double-space between bulleted items.

  Classify each main point with an identification in boldface type to highlight the item of information.

  Try to include all information an editor or reporter requires to write the story, and try to answer all questions the editor or reporter would ask in preparing to write it.

- A *backgrounder* contains all the information the recipient could possibly want about your organization. Or it can provide additional information about the product, service, or event that is the subject of your principal release.

  For example, if you are announcing a new product or service, you might include a separate sheet that outlines the product's or service's development since inception, and the reasons for that development. The backgrounder can provide information about the field as a whole including when, where, and by whom it was introduced; what its impact has been over the years, and what its previous successes or failures have been. You might even include a backgrounder sheet outlining the research-and-development efforts that went into your product or service.

  As another example, a backgrounder for a nonprofit organization might very well summarize goals and objectives, list some significant accomplishments, describe when, how, and by whom it was founded, detail its area of influence within the community, and so on.

  A Los Angeles nonprofit orphanage headed its backgrounder, *The Who, the What, and the Why?* of its fund raising drive, and followed with subheads that asked and—more important—*answered* the following questions:

  —Who is asking for this money?

  —What sort of children do they care for?

—What does (the organization) do for these children?

—What do they need this money for now?

—Didn't I give to this last year?

—Am I allowed tax exemption on my gift?

—Why should I give?

Each answer was a powerful pitch on behalf of the group and its work.

- Include a *history* of the organization. Essentially, this also is a backgrounder. It provides additional information for reporters to draw on in describing the group responsible for the announcement. Keep it a concise compilation of key highlights about your organization that can help establish reputation and standing in the industry or community.

  If the announcement involves another entity, as in the case of an acquisition or a merger, the kit should also include a separate history of the other organization.

- A *quotes sheet* is an excellent means of providing interesting information that will expand a news story written by a reporter. Quotes dress up a news story; they can turn an otherwise dull recitation of information into an interesting, readable news piece. Also, names make news and sell extra newspapers, so be sure to attribute each quote to a company official or outside person and always identify the person by title and function. Attribution provides insurance as to the accuracy of the quotes used, rather than dependence upon the reporter's memory or scribbled notes.

  Here is where you can logically provide the information about the organization's past efforts to achieve the result that now is being announced or to give testimony for a product, for a service, or for your group.

- Include biographies (*bios*) of organization officials or leaders who are important to the announcement or the event. The bios should be brief and should give only pertinent information.

  If the announcement is about an event that includes a speaker or speakers, the kit should include a bio of each person and the text of each speech, if available in advance. You must make arrangements to acquire copies of speech texts in advance.

  A 5- by 7-inch head-and-shoulders photo can accompany each bio. Each photo should carry a caption to identify it in the event that the photo becomes separated from the bio.

- A *clipsheet* is not a "must" in a press kit, but it can produce excellent, sometimes unexpected, results. A clipsheet is a roundup of a variety of stories, illustrations, charts, and "filler" items that are arranged in column widths. (Fillers are described and explained in Chapter 7.) Smaller newspapers are particularly receptive to clipsheet material and keep them for use when a news hole must be filled.

  Some clipsheets include a choice of glossy photos or graphics, which are appreciated by newspapers that could or would not otherwise afford the reproduction costs.

- Previously printed news or feature stories about the organization can provide insight for reporters. Reproductions should *prominently display* the date the article appeared and the name of the publication in which it appeared.

- Brochures may be included if they contain data germane to the announcement. For instance, an annual report is often an excellent provider of information and data you wish the publication to use and, possibly, to keep on file for future reference. An operating manual for the product is another helpful piece of information for a reporter writing a story about a complex product.
- Photos of a product, with descriptive captions, are usually included. Photos of the exterior, or pertinent parts of the organization's interior space may also be included.

Other than mug shots, all photos distributed to print media should be 8 by 10 inches and have a glossy finish; they may be either black-and-white or color photos. (No glossy photos should be sent to television news departments, however.) Each should carry an attached caption. (Information about photos and captions is included in Chapter 10.)

Organization of the Press Kit

The most popular press kit is a folder with interior pockets. Information can be organized and divided between the pockets. For instance, the left pocket can contain background information such as history, bios, and so on; and the right pocket can hold current data about the event, product, or service being presented. Place the news release on top in the right pocket so that it is the first thing seen by the user, or attach it to the front of the cover with a paper clip.

If all the information is contained in a large envelope, you should probably cut down on the contents and use some method of coding, such as using various colors of pastel paper for different types of information. No dark or neon colors, please—not even for emphasis!

An index of contents is a possibility, but that calls for a three-ring binder with dividers so that the contents remain in the order in which they are listed in the index.

Another popular method of organization is to present various types of information on varying lengths of paper in a two-pocket folder. All papers are the standard $8^1/_2$ inches wide, but each set of information is a different length so that when the sets are placed in the folder, headlines on each can be seen and easily read. This type of kit is probably the most functional for reporters, but it is not readily adaptable to other uses, inasmuch as each section must be specially sized and printed.

Long-Term Use

Newspeople will often keep a well-constructed press kit on file. That's a plus you should aim for. If your kit is well organized and contains valuable information, there is greater likelihood that it will be kept by anyone receiving it. Make it a point to design your kit and its contents so that it will be a valuable addition, not only for filing in the publication's *morgue*, or library, but by any others who receive it.

One thing to keep in mind—as a six-month or annual personal assignment (mark your calendar!)—is a check of contents to be sure they are *current*. If there have been changes, if updated information is important to future stories, if there is any new information, send a *new* press kit. With it, attached to the front, include a note in large, boldface type, indicating that this is new material and should replace any previous information on file.

The Press Kit as a "Blueprint"

There are added uses for press kits, such as to provide other executives or committee members in your organization who are responsible for publicity, with the organization's official, authorized history, facts, and details (especially if yours is an organization with franchisees, branches, chapters, or affiliated memberships). It should also include canned copy for releases, but those who use such copy as how-to examples should be urged to convert them for local use by inserting local names and facts.

When the kit is used for other than press purposes, it should be expanded to include the following:

- A basic model news release about the organization.
- Copies of logos, stationery, or other organization identification graphics.
- Photos of and background information about other organization products, services, or functions, and copies of previously distributed releases about them.
- Photos of equipment, people using the equipment or performing tasks relevant to the organization's purpose, or appropriate interior and/or exterior shots of the organization's facility.
- A history of the organization, written so that each division or committee can extract and use the portion that pertains to it.
- Appropriate bios and mug shots.
- An instruction sheet with precise details and examples of the rules and mechanics of publicity.
- Fillers. (See Chapter 7 for more about fillers.)
- Suggestions for local participation in organization-wide events, anniversaries, contests, and so on.
- Reprints of previously published news or feature stories.
- The standard closing paragraph you wrote earlier, which succinctly states the purpose of your organization and gives pertinent information and data about it. Describe its uses and explain how it can be edited and tagged onto each future release.

Other Uses

Well-prepared press kits might also be used for business meetings, as a tool for salespeople, and for seminars or workshops.

It should be obvious that not everything listed must or should be included in each press kit. The nature of a kit's use dictates its contents. But if you have doubts about an item, it is probably better to err on the side of including it and risk its not being used, than to exclude it when staffers or reporters might use the information.

More About Fact Sheets

A fact sheet can substitute for a news release if you are reluctant to try your hand at writing a release. As mentioned previously, however, a fact sheet may be a poor substitute for a release.

A fact sheet can also provide additional information when you do not wish to send a press kit. Attach the fact sheet to the news release with a paper clip; do not use staples.

There are no hard-and-fast rules about a format for fact sheets. There are strict dictates, however, about including certain information, and about typing on only one side of a regular 8 1/2- by 11-inch sheet of paper. Every fact sheet must include the following:

- Your organization's name, full address, and telephone number. If you have a fax number, it too should be included for the convenience of those who wish to reach you by this means. As in your news releases, this information may be typed at the top of plain sheets of paper, or you can use regular or "instantly created" letterhead.
- Type the words Fact Sheet in a prominent position near the top of the page, so that this is not misconstrued as a release.
- Also in a prominent place near the top of the page and above the body of facts, type Contact:, then your name and your telephone number if it is an extension number or is different from the one listed for the organization. (As in your news releases, it is wise also to give the name of a knowledgeable alternate contact, along with his or her telephone number if it is different from the number listed for the organization.)
- Include the date on which the information is distributed—but not as a release date—so that the age of the information in this particular fact sheet can be easily recognized as outdated and discarded if you issue a new one at a later time. It is also helpful when you update and produce new fact sheets to see that the new fact sheets have a different appearance from those previously distributed. A change in paper color (always a subdued color) is one method of changing the appearance.

This is the information required on every fact sheet. The body of information can be presented in any way you consider to be easily read and understood.

The Facts. Just the Facts

If a fact sheet is to substitute for a news release, it should present the information you would set down in your preliminary outline for the news story. It should give answers to the five Ws: who, what, where, when, and why. If how—the H—is appropriate, also include that information. As a way of distinguishing the kinds of information, the Ws and H can be bulleted, typed in boldface, and used as lead-ins to the information that follows.

If the fact sheet is to accompany a news release rather than substitute for one, it should provide important information about your organization. Or it can give additional data about a new product, new service, or about the industry in which your organization operates.

A Fact Sheet by Any Other Name . . .

A professional public relations firm whose press releases are used as examples in Chapter 8, on copycatting, calls a fact sheet it produced for Visa Olympics of the Imagination, a "Media Alert."

Edelman Public Relations included the fact sheet in a two-pocket press kit folder. In addition to a three-page press release, the kit also contained a six-page backgrounder and a slide that presented the name of the local sponsor and the local person to contact, along with her telephone number, prominently displayed beneath the logo for Visa Olympics of the Imagination.

The facts were presented in a Who, What, When, Why, and How format. See Figure 11.1.

FIGURE 11.1　A Fact Sheet from Edelman Public Relations, Headlined, "Media Alert"

Contact:	Brad Hennig	Contact:	Ann Morley Wool
	VISA International		Susan Donnelly
	(415) 358-2435		Edelman Public Relations
			(212)704-8118/8166

MEDIA ALERT

VISA OLYMPICS OF THE IMAGINATION

WHO:　Ten children from the U.S. will win spots on an international team of student artists traveling to the Olympic Winter Games in Norway in February 1994.

Ten children from Norway and five from Canada will also be part of the 25-person team.

WHAT:　VISA and ten major U.S. newspapers are challenging youngsters, ages 11 to 13, to draw or paint a picture depicting their vision of what the Olympic Games will look like 100 years from now.

One winner will be awarded the grand prize by each of the following participating newspapers:

The Atlanta Journal-Constitution	Boston Herald
Chicago Tribune	The Denver Post
Fort Worth Star-Telegram	Houston Chronicle
Los Angeles Times	The New York Times
San Francisco Chronicle	The Seattle Times

NEWSPAPER
PARTNERS

The Atlanta Journal-Constitution

Boston Herald

Chicago Tribune

The Denver Post

Fort Worth Star-Telegram

Houston Chronicle

Los Angeles Times

The New York Times

San Francisco Chronicle

The Seattle Times

WHEN:　September 1, 1993 -- Nationwide contest kick-off
October 15, 1993 -- Contest entry deadline
December 7, 1993 -- Winners announced
February 11 - 16, 1994 -- Trip to Olympic Winter Games

WHY:　The contest marks the 100th anniversary of the founding of the Olympic movement.

HOW:　Entry forms, announcements and rules will appear regularly in each newspaper during the contest period, and contest kits will be distributed directly to schools in the readership area. Additionally, newspapers will select a local panel of judges to nominate the finalists and winners.

VISA INTERNATIONAL　Post Office Box 8999　San Francisco　California　94128

12

Press Conferences

*How to offer something in person that
you can't offer in a press release*

"Doonesbury" on Press Conferences

"Doonesbury" cartoonist, Garry Trudeau, in four comic strip panels picturing the White House (each with a few lines of dialog) presents his pithy view of press conferences and subtly gives us a rule about when *not* to call one:

> "I'm telling you, Dan, I've had it! If Ziegler doesn't give us a decent briefing today, then I'm quitting the White House press corps for good!"
> "Sshh . . . Keep it down! . . . Here he comes . . ."
> "Good afternoon, Gentlemen! Today the President had lunch at 12:30. Later, he made many important phone calls! Thank you."
> "THAT DOES IT!!"

"Doonesbury" doesn't need translation. The message is clear, and it is as true today as when the strip appeared in 1973 and Dan Rather was chief White House correspondent for CBS: Even the president's publicity representative shouldn't call in the media without good reason.

Advice on When to Call a Press Conference

Public relations specialist John T. Gillan tells us that the typical financial editor of a major newspaper gets an average of 20 invitations a week to attend press conferences. That's more than a thousand press conferences a year!

There is general agreement among editors that there are far too many press conferences called on subjects not worthy of a meeting. The editors say that a press conference just isn't necessary unless a product requires demonstration. "If a product can be adequately described in words, a news release can do the job—and the story will receive just as much consideration in this form as if presented at a full-blown dog and pony show," Gillan states.

Add to Gillan's wisdom a bit more advice: Hold press conferences only when the news is so notable and dramatic that in-person communication between the organization and the media is needed to convey the message.

For organizations—large and small—this means a new product or a new service, a cause, a technological breakthrough, a merger or acquisition, perhaps the appointment of new top-level management *if* meeting the new executive is interesting and stimulating for newspeople.

And, of course, a press conference may be warranted to handle bad news (handling "bad press" is examined in Chapter 5).

Still a further extension of Gillan's advice is that you will not make media friends if you call a press conference that reporters feel is a waste of their time, or if they find your conference *boring*. These feelings will extend to a reluctance to accept future invitations.

However, once you've presented a well-thought-out and meaningful press conference, the media will welcome the next one you call. Not only will they welcome it, they'll give it space . . . unless . . .

Unless there is a major news break, such as an earthquake, a tornado, or the assassination of a well-known local or national figure—the happening dreaded by every publicist. If such a spontaneous event does occur, there is nothing you can do except to set the news aside for the time being and decide later when and if another conference should be called.

Boring Is Bad

Boredom is an absolute guarantee that reporters will either not report your news or merely give it a minimum amount of space, and that your future conferences will be ignored. Celebrities can help to spice up a dull conference.

Of course, there must be a logical tie-in between the news story and the celebrity's presence at the news conference. The tie-in can be the celebrity's association with a cause, his or her scheduled appearance at an event related to the conference, enlistment of the person to launch a campaign or a drive, his or her acting as the advertising spokesperson for the company's product or service, or any number of other appropriate relationships.

Another way to prevent boredom among media is to make the conference a hands-on affair. Sometimes such events are called editor's—or media—workshops, rather than press conferences, and are designed to give those attending something to do instead of sitting and listening to a potentially dull presentation of facts and statistics. This type of conference works particularly well to demonstrate a new product. If use of the product is even the least bit complicated, or if the event is merely a tasting opportunity, you should have sufficient numbers of company personnel to assist the participants and make the experience an enjoyable one.

Is It a Press Conference or a News Conference?

Perhaps a few words of explanation are needed here about the seemingly random use throughout this book of the terms "press conference" and "news conference." Those who deal extensively with both print and electronic news media try to call such events "news conferences." Because this book is focused on the interests of small businesses and nonprofit organizations that rarely have news of sufficient magnitude to attract television representatives (most radio stations obtain their news reports from national services), the term "press conference" is used. It is preferred by newspaper people, but you should use the term with which you and your organization are most comfortable.

Reasons for Holding a Press Conference

Televised presidential press conferences have given most people a familiarity with the basic concept of a press conference, but they may have misled many too. Press conferences do not have to be of the size and splendor of those prime-time choreographed "specials." In the real world, the smallest organization can and should hold a press conference *if* a situation warrants it.

A press conference should be called for the following reasons:

- To provide personal presentations, explanations, descriptions, and opportunities for the media to direct their questions to responsible organization people and thereby benefit more than they would from a press release.
- To provide an opportunity to view and experience personally the way a product or service works to encourage media interest and, ultimately, public interest.

  In this situation, some pros rename the conference a "Media Workshop," because it puts a product into reporters' hands where they can see, feel, experience, and perhaps taste and smell it, instead of just sitting and listening to a description and watching a demonstration. The biggest plus, though, is that this type of conference becomes an activity—a hands-on activity—that substantially reduces boredom and can actually be fun for those involved.
- To introduce a newly appointed or elected executive whose association with the organization will have impact on the organization's direction, employees, members, consumers, customers, and/or constituents.
- To declare an extensive expansion program.
- To announce procurement of important new financing, such as new funding for a business, or a grant or a donation for a nonprofit organization, if the financier or grantor will be present and available for comments and questions.
- To announce, describe, and pictorialize acquisition of a property.
- To give a progress report that is better presented with visual aids and opportunities for specific questioning.
- To review a crucial situation such as a labor difficulty, an actual or rumored financial difficulty, an allegation of misconduct by organization persons, and so on.

Questions to Help You Decide

The most important questions you should answer before scheduling a press conference are as follows:

- Can your organization offer something in person that can't be offered in a release?
- Do you have a real news story?

- Will the empathy and understanding of newspeople in fact be heightened (by holding a press conference)?
- Will this opportunity for the press to personally meet and question your people establish a friendlier relationship and boost esteem and respect for your organization and its individuals?
- Is the news value sufficient to warrant the time required to attend by busy reporters?
- Are the skills of the presenters—as speakers and persuaders—and the advance planning adequate to keep those attending interested?
- Are the time and effort required to organize and conduct a worthwhile conference warranted?

Press Conference Preparation

Unless the reason for a press conference is a crisis of some kind that requires the conference to be called immediately, sufficient time, thought, and effort should go into its preparation so as to produce a productive, well-organized event. The following pages offer guidelines for generating a successful press conference.

Who to Invite

Your list of guests should be as carefully drawn up for each conference situation as your media lists are adapted to fit each news release. For instance, if the news is of interest only to business publications and business page editors, eliminate all others.

Invite all reporters who regularly cover your organization or the general industry in which your organization is included. This may mean financial editors or specialists in certain business or nonprofit categories. If yours is a specialty field or a business of special interest to specific groups, locate and include reporters from those special-interest publications.

If you don't know which individual person to invite from any specific news outlet, send the invitation to a newspaper's city editor or to the managing editor of a specific publication. This then puts the responsibility on these executives to assign whomever they consider best suited to cover the story. (See the information about broadcast media personnel in Chapter 16.)

Invitation

The format of an invitation can be any of several businesslike printed forms. A letter on your organization's letterhead, however, is the most common style of invitation, and it should describe the purpose of the conference. It should be signed by the person best known to those invited, preferably the owner, chief executive officer, president, or chairman of the board.

Never telephone an invitation.

Include the date, time, and place and the name and phone number of one or two individuals who can provide additional information about the purpose of the conference. If directions are required or would be helpful, include a simple map.

Some organizations put the invitation into press release form, but this can create a problem. There is a distinct possibility that recipients will not recognize it as an invitation, and it could be processed as a release or even mislaid or thrown away.

Time the arrival of the invitation so that it isn't received so far in advance of the conference date that it is misplaced or so close to the date as to prevent or make difficult the assignment of staff to attend.

Figure 12.1 is a press *release* that can also serve as a press conference *invitation*. A small, handwritten note to the individual editor or reporter can give it the personal touch of an invitation and identify it as other than just a news release.

Schedules and Media Convenience

This is a press conference, therefore it should be timed for the convenience of newspeople and for widest coverage, rather than for the convenience of your own people. If your locale has both morning and evening papers, to avoid showing preference you may wish to alternate times and hold a midmorning conference for the evening newspapers and a mid- or late-afternoon conference for the morning newspapers.

If you include television reporters, a morning conference is suitable, and a midafternoon conference will accommodate both dinnertime and late-evening newscasts.

Conference times for Sunday editions of daily newspapers and for weekly newspapers should be set according to a specific day, rather than hour. Scheduling the conference for a Monday will allow the greatest number of weekly newspapers to meet their deadlines and will also accommodate Sunday edition staffers who usually work on midweek deadlines.

You may wish to schedule a separate, special press conference for monthly publications such as trade magazines and business journals. They have far greater lead time requirements, often up to four months. Established, respected publications can be expected to honor your release dates.

Principal Representative

In almost every case, your organization's owner, chairman of the board, or CEO should be the principal representative of your organization at the conference. He or she should lay the groundwork and then turn the conference over to a specialist in engineering, research, or finance, or whoever is best suited to offer the particular information called for and to field questions on the subject.

For instance, if the news is about a new product, your principal representative should present introductory information, then turn the conference over to a vice president or engineer in charge of development of the product. When the subject deals with finances or economics, the chief financial officer (CFO) should be present and called upon.

When the conference has been called to introduce an organization's new president, executive director, CEO, CFO, or comparable high-ranking executive, be sure that there is sufficient interest—in the individual, in his or her responsi-

FIGURE 12.1   Press Release Announcing a Press Conference
By merely attaching a small, personal note, it becomes an invitation to the reporter or editor to whom it is addressed.

BLACK AMERICANS FOR LIFE

419 7th St. N.W. (Suite 500)
Washington, D.C. 20004-2293
(202) 626-8833

For immediate release: For more information:
Wednesday, February 23, 1994   Mignonne Anderson, (713) 667-3383

THREE PACs TO HOLD PRESS CONFERENCE
TO ENDORSE BEVERLEY CLARK

Black Americans for Life Political Action Committee (BALPAC) will hold a press conference on Thursday to announce their endorsement of Beverley Clark for Congress in the Democratic Primary for the 25th District, Houston.

The event will be held on:

Thursday, February 24, 1994 in the Hidalgo Room of the JW Marriott Hotel; 5150 Westhiemer; Houston, TX.

The Susan B. Anthony List, a pro-life women's political action committee, and National Youth PAC, a grassroots pro-life PAC operated by and for young voters, are scheduled to announce endorsements as well.

For more information on the press conference, or for interviews please call Mignonne Anderson at (713) 667-3383, or Michele Arocha at (202) 626-8810.

BAL is a pro-life organization dedicated to educational, legislative and political activity to stop abortion, euthanasia, and infanticide.

"Our Children Are Our Future"

bilities, or in the group he or she represents—to warrant calling a conference. Then pray that the individual's speaking and presentation abilities are top level.

The decision about who should be on hand for the meeting is contingent on the reason for the meeting, but only *one person* should be in charge.

Press Conference Coordinator

Chapter 13 emphasizes the necessity to have a coordinator for a staged event. A press conference, after all, is an event staged to create news, and here also a coordinator is essential. The choice of coordinator depends not only on who within the organization has the ability, but also on who can give the amount of time necessary to do the job.

Seating Arrangements

Here is a word about the physical arrangement of tables and chairs for the seating of press people. Under no circumstances should you place your people behind tables or separate them from the audience as though by an invisible partition. A good seating plan helps to build rapport between reporters and your people. The principal representative can be seated in front of a table or desk or leaning comfortably against it, and other executives can be seated casually among the press representatives. In this type of arrangement, there can be no perception of "us and them" thinking on your part.

The presence of a rostrum or podium also can communicate a subconscious feeling to those attending that you're there to "preach to the unwashed" or to give a lecture. The less formal your physical arrangement is, the more friendly it will appear.

You may wish to do a little advance research on the effects of your people's body language on those listening and questioning them. Actions do speak far louder than words, and they too can give subliminal impressions you do not intend. For example, those in the audience will intuitively recognize an insincere smile on a speaker's face. The top portion of the face gives it away, because when a smile is genuine the muscles around the eyes can't help but crinkle. And arms folded across a person's chest not only signifies the individual's discomfort, but the stance sends the same "invisible partition" message that tables and podiums do when they separate presenters from an audience.

Excellent information has been written on this subject, and a consciousness of how to use body language as a PR "tool" is well worth the time and effort to review it.

Prepared News Releases

In certain situations, you should prepare a news release and in other situations a fact sheet will be sufficient. In a few cases, however, you should definitely *not* prepare a news release.

When the reason for the press conference is to present, demonstrate, or describe a new product or service, a press release is mandatory. In those situations, the release should give basic details, and it should be accompanied by added explanatory material, such as an operation manual (to give details and data that some reporters may wish to add to their stories).

When company policy is part of the reason for the meeting, there should be no release or statement for handout or as part of the press kit.

Photos

By all means encourage the media to bring their own photographers.

If television people are included, you will expect them to have cameras with them, so provide for special seating arrangements. Set up the room to enable the reporters to sit close and the television cameras to shoot over their heads.

When a press conference includes television cameras, it will probably be necessary to seat all of your scheduled speakers at the front of the room. But, please, do not sit them behind a table barrier that, in effect, says, "We need protection from you reporters; you intimidate us."

It is expedient to have a still photographer on hand, not only to provide file photos for your own records, but to provide photos to accompany press kits for reporters who are unable to attend. The photographer can also be enlisted for shots for a reporter who does not have his or her own photographer present.

Press Kits, VNRs and RNRs

A press conference is one of the most widely existing reasons for constructing press kits—in hard copy as well as in videotape format. These special packages are designed to give reporters the added information that allows them to make their stories different from those of their competitors. A press kit includes a release, if one is called for, or a fact sheet related to the purpose of the conference. It also includes appropriate photos of individuals, products, physical structures, or other pertinent visual depictions; background and historial data; and whatever else is considered appropriate. (If you do not yet have press kits, the ground rules for designing them are covered in Chapter 11, for the hard-copy print version, and in Chapter 16 for the videotape broadcast version.)

Location

Choose a place that is comfortable for everyone, that can accommodate sound and lighting equipment (if electronic news media are included), and that is as convenient as possible to all invited media.

Room size is important. Pick a room to fit the numbers expected to attend, but remember it is better to choose a place that is a trifle too small. If your room is too big, it may create a false impression that your conference is not well attended. As you watch the next presidential press conference on television, notice that the room always appears to be filled to absolute capacity. This establishes a feeling of high importance for the conference.

If your organization has a conference room of adequate size, this probably is your best choice, because staff can be included or is readily available.

The location of your conference should be easily accessible to the press. If your building is located in a suburban or rural area not handy for your guests, transportation to and from the conference should be offered.

Nonprofit organizations often have the advantage of being able to borrow—at no cost—well-located, nicely appointed rooms from other organizations or from corporations. For-profit organizations seldom have this privilege and must rent outside accommodations if their own facilities are inadequate or not conveniently located.

Drinks and Food

The question of whether to serve food and drinks is a difficult one to answer. Keep in mind that a press conference is strictly a business affair. Press parties and receptions are sometimes inaccurately thought of as press conferences because they often include, in a more social setting, a special announcement, a product showing, or the introduction of a notable figure. Press breakfasts and luncheons also are often held to make special announcements, but they are more businesslike than receptions or press parties. Press conferences, however, are no-nonsense business affairs.

A rather general rule of thumb is this: For a straight press conference, it is usually not necessary to serve food or drinks; for press breakfasts, luncheons, or parties held to generate a somewhat social atmosphere and to create some business-social relationships, food is expected.

Coffee and tea always are appropriate, even for straight press conferences, unless the conference is called for an "emergency" and time does not permit arrangements to be made. If the weather is warm and cool drinks would be appreciated, soft drinks or juice can be added. A bar for liquor or wine is wholly dependent on the attitude of the press in your area and on your organization's position in this regard.

A Pro Gives Advice

Gabriella Klein of Communication Concepts Unlimited in Racine, Wisconsin, one of our Chapter 8 Copycat Primer pros, offers some advice. "We recommend offering a variety of beverages (including ice water!) so that participants have a broad selection. With busy schedules, we've found most writers/broadcasters appreciate the option to stay for refreshments, a light lunch, etc., but value the opportunity to bow out after the main portion of the event."

Decisions about serving food can be calculated on the basis of timing. A 4:00 P.M. meeting is probably too close to the dinner hour even for snacks, but at 9:00 A.M. breakfast rolls may be appreciated. The part of the country in which you are located, the local customs, and the size of your budget dictate these decisions.

If you opt to include food, a refreshment table with sandwiches or finger food may be sufficient. If the food is to be catered, in your own or in a borrowed or rented facility, check in advance that equipment such as a refrigerator and a microwave or stove are available and operating.

Dress Rehearsal

If this is a first-time experience for the principals involved in a press conference, a run-through may be an excellent idea. It also may be a good idea to prepare a written statement, for your organization's participants, on the essentials of the announcement to be made, especially if it is complicated. You can expect plenty of questions from the press, so, together with your own people, try to anticipate as many of these questions as possible and figure out the best answers. It's wise to be better prepared than the person who once said that she could always come up with the perfect answer—an hour too late.

When the subject matter is controversial, it helps those who will be on the "hot seat" to be alerted for what to expect. These people then can be more at ease with their questioners, and they can reply in an informal, convincing, assured manner, which will create a much more favorable impression.

The Day of the Conference

The following guidelines will help ensure that your conference runs smoothly:

- Prepare an agenda ahead of time, assigning each topic to a specific individual and setting time allotments in advance. This is a requirement for a smooth-running, professional meeting. Remember the time constrictions of newspeople, and keep the meeting moving right along.
- Have your people in place a few minutes before the announced starting time. Then open the conference *on time* out of respect for those who arrive on time and for their often close-cut schedules.
- Provide name identification badges (with titles listed) for all of your people in attendance, whether or not they are scheduled to be speakers. For those who are speakers, make sure the badges are large enough to be read by reporters who will be sitting some distance from the speakers. This courtesy will be appreciated.
- Open the conference with a statement about the purpose of the meeting and a brief summary of the agenda. Then introduce the principal participants, the persons who are most closely identified with the subject of the conference.
- If you have press kits, samples, or any handouts, pass them out *after* all preliminary statements have been made, but before you open the meeting for questions. This is important *if* you want those attending to listen to what you and your people have to say, instead of thumbing through and reading material you hand out. Making materials available before the Q & A session may eliminate many questions and thereby shorten the meeting, which is always appreciated by busy newspeople.
- Open the meeting for questions after all preliminary statements have been made and after you've circulated handouts.
- Do your best to arrange exclusive interviews if there are requests for them, but do this only *after* the conference, so that there is no hint of preferential treatment for any one reporter or medium. Give everyone the same opportunities.
- Announce the availability of a photographer for reporters' use—if you have one—during the opening statements. Introduce the photographer so that those who wish to use the service can locate him or her. You may want to give the photographer a preliminary assignment to make photos for your own records.
- Do not bar, under any circumstances, any credible media representative from attending your press conference because that person or the medium he or she represents has committed some real or supposed slight against your organization or one of its members.

Follow-Ups

During the conference listen for and make note of any questions that were not answered or that were inadequately answered, note the name of the reporter requesting the information, and get back to that reporter as quickly as possible with answers. You may want to assign this task in advance to someone who has fewer responsibilities than you.

It can be helpful to tape the entire session in order to recall the questions that weren't adequately answered. A playback during more relaxed hours following the conference may also help to improve on the way that kind of information is handled in future meetings.

If the press conference was called in response to a crisis, you may need to schedule follow-up meetings. If the crisis extends over days or over a longer time period, a responsible official who can speak with complete authority should be available to the media throughout the entire period. Let the media know who the person is and how to contact him or her.

"Private" Press Conferences—A General Electric Innovation

John Gillan, who was with General Electric's Chicago News Bureau, tells of an innovative way that GE handled the conflicts of time and pressure on editors in that highly competitive news area. GE held "private" press conferences in the offices of each editor without a single GE representative being present!

Gillan says that the reaction of the press was nothing short of fantastic. The challenge was to use only a limited budget to get maximum exposure in the trade press for a new miniature battery-powered DC motor. The key media were headquartered in 10 cities around the country and represented such diverse areas as product design, appliance manufacturing, electronics, hobbies, toys, and automotive engineering.

At a previously arranged time, a messenger arrived at each editor's office with three packages and a cover letter. The introductory letter welcomed the editor to his or her own private press conference and directed the editor to open, in order, three plainly wrapped packages, marked "A," "B," and "C."

Package A contained a new-product release, six product photos, a short "talk" by the marketing manager, a product bulletin, and a bulletin release on the motor. (Even though audio tapes are widely used for many purposes, a busy editor isn't likely to hunt down a tape player just to hear what a marketing manager has to say. So, if you copycat this type of press conference, put your exec's "talk" on paper for the convenience of recipients.)

Package B contained a GE electric toothbrush and a $^1/_{24}$-inch-scale slot car (each with the new miniature motor installed), plus a separate motor, all of which the editor could use for photographs, testing, or otherwise. A cover note explained the significance of the package.

Package C included a closing letter advising the editor that he or she could secure additional information by calling collect that afternoon to the product department in Morrison, Illinois, where personnel involved in the motor's development were standing by to accept calls. The conference closing included an American Express "Be My Guest" certificate for lunch, bearing the greeting "Have lunch without us."

Shortly after the private press conferences, a letter was sent to each participating editor, asking how he or she liked receiving news of important products in this manner. The response was exceptional. Letters were received from all 28 editors involved, and phone calls for specialized information numbered more than 20.

Thus, the four basic steps of any campaign—research, planning, communication, and evaluation—were honored and bore fruit in the private press conference, says Gillan.

A Final Personal Word

A nonprofit volunteer, whose name and whose organization's name are now forgotten, gave some excellent advice. "Be professional. Only you should know it is your first press conference. It's okay to panic as long as no one, particularly the press, knows it." Tuck it into your memory for future use.

13

Staged Events

*How to stage an event to create news
and build image*

They Used to Be Called Publicity Stunts

The term *publicity stunt* achieved its bad reputation from early Hollywood publicity events—wild exploits that were staged by motion picture studio "flaks" to get headlines. Today there's a much more dignified term—special event— and these events attain equally vast amounts of publicity by being arresting rather than outrageous. (The term *flak*—the unflattering name given press agents who devised those outlandish things for actors to do or to take part in to achieve great amounts of publicity—has also been lynched and left swinging in the wind.)

Never refer to your event as a publicity stunt, even if it basically qualifies as such. Today's media are truly gun-shy about both the word and the type of event that it represents. Professional publicity practioners now work hard to achieve and maintain credibility and respect and to live down that earlier reputation.

These days, special events are more professional and dignified (except in cases such as amassing show-biz publicity for Madonna- and Roseanne-type personalities), and they frequently support local community interests or charitable concerns. But whether a special event or a publicity stunt, it's still a staged event.

Differences Between Press Events and Staged Events

Someone once said that media are the tools by which an organization tells its story to the public. And the event you stage gives you access to these tools. There are, however, distinct differences between press events held strictly for media and the staged events that are described in this chapter.

Whereas press conferences (Chapter 12), press parties, and press receptions are usually held to display and demonstrate something that cannot be as graphically presented in a news release, they all are media events meant to create news, but each is held strictly for and attended only by *media*. The majority of *staged events*, however, and particularly those presented in this chapter, are for and include the public as well as media.

Early-Day Staged Events

The Romans regularly staged events—chariot races, public debates, and luncheons for lions, where the entrees for the lions were malefactors and offenders. The Romans are believed to be the first to introduce staged events; although newspapers, radio, and television did not exist at that time, there is little doubt that many of the events were staged to mold public opinion. These events did attract the public and provided entertainment. They may even have been financially successful for their promoters. Certainly they provided word-of-mouth publicity.

This book produces no earth-shattering news in recalling early-day history or in revealing that nonprofit organizations have turned for years to staged events to attract public interest, create publicity, and make money.

Giant corporations have also become known for "the big event." What may be news to some readers, however, is the degree to which *small businesses* have come to depend on staged events for very similar reasons to those of big business and nonprofit organizations: to create publicity, build name recognition, project a specific image, and attract attention that ultimately translates into profits and raises public support.

Created News and Controlled Publicity

As mentioned earlier, there are two kinds of news—spot news and created news. Spot news is spontaneous and beyond your control, and sometimes it contains information you'd rather leave unpublicized. Created news most often comes from a staged event that produces controlled publicity. Dick Hitt, when he was a reporter for *The Dallas Times-Herald*, called them "the patter of little feats!"

It's the little feats creating the news that keep the name of a small business or an all-volunteer organization before the public—through the media. However, leave the big "fetes" to the giant corporations!

To keep your organization's name before the public, you almost have to rely on staged events to create news. When do you ever have enough news to be able to announce—in publicity releases—a new product or service, the appointment or election of a new executive, a new project, an expansion or location move, an award, or recognition of or by affiliates? There's only so much ready-made straight news that can come out of an organization. (Feature news, however, is another, much more productive means of creating news that results in controlled publicity—there is an almost unlimited fund of feature news within every organization. Producing news features is covered in Chapter 7.)

When special events are used in innovative ways, they can achieve extraordinary results that are far more productive than advertising or other forms of direct marketing. Events, creatively used, capture the interest and attention of the media and produce exceptional amounts of media coverage.

"Acts of news engineering" is the definition given special events by the late Herb Baus. The single most important point to remember, however, is this: Although news may be created, even engineered, *it must be news.*

Types of Staged Events

Media event, public event, publicity stunt—a staged event can be any one of these:

- Press conferences and press parties are strictly *media events*.
- Banquets, luncheons, bike-a-thons, seminars and workshops, auctions, lectures, and performances are all happenings used by charitable groups, and sometimes by businesses, to increase awareness and/or to raise money. They are *public events* that can also be media events.
- Open houses, plant tours, and building dedications are also public events and media events.
- Macy's Thanksgiving Day Parade is a public event and a media event that brings millions of dollars to the City of New York at the same time as it creates megapublicity for the department store.
- A rock concert in which celebrity performers speak up—and act up—for a cause, can be a *publicity stunt* as well as a media event and a public event.
- A barrel ride over Niagara Falls is a *cliché-type publicity stunt*, but it also is a media event that creates media attention for both the individual and a commercial or nonprofit sponsor, if there is one.

All of these are staged events designed to increase income by attracting public recognition, and to grab and hold the attention of the media. This is because the media are the key to reaching greater numbers of people than any individual event, no matter how large, is capable of attracting on its own.

A Staged Event That Did Several Things

Back in 1989, an Arkansan named Jerry Jones arrived in Dallas, bought the Dallas Cowboys football team, fired its beloved coach Tom Landry, and proceeded to fill his own mouth with both his feet every time he opened it in front of the press.

In 1993 Jones created a major event out of getting Tom Landry into the team's "Ring of Honor." It was a staged event that included press parties, press conferences, and a publicity stunt that was given respectful attention by the media and not only garnered huge amounts of national and local publicity for the Cowboys, but went a long way toward tamping down Jones's genius for attracting negative press. For a short time the event gave Jerry Jones some excellent publicity and a much better personal image. It all came about by the very nature of the person it honored and the way in which it was handled.

Unfortunately, Jones, a fast study in most every other respect, still didn't seem to have learned the basics of *not* creating bad press, even though it appeared earlier that he had learned his lessons. After wooing the media with Landry's acceptance into the Cowboys' Ring of Honor, less than a year later Jones again stepped on everyone's toes except his own (which he apparently has tucked back in his mouth) by telling reporters at the NFL's 1994 annual spring meeting in Orlando, Florida, that he planned to fire Landry's replacement, Jimmie Johnson, and naming a replacement for Johnson. That extemporaneous announcement, supposedly made "off the record" to several reporters but within earshot of numbers of nonmedia people, made headlines in sports sections all across the country. Notice that even the best results from a staged special event that turns a sour image into a good one can be neutralized by the businessperson who doesn't remember—and practice— the basics of good media relations.

Choice of Event

Your choices of staged events are limited only by the confines of your imagination and your budget. The kind of event you choose should be conceived to fulfill four fundamental ends:

1. To tell a publicity story
2. To influence public opinion
3. To show a strong community tie-in and service
4. To carry out your long-range goals, objectives, and plans (as set forth in Chapter 3)

If your staged event is creatively designed and produced to fulfill these ends, it can not only give you excellent publicity, but can help to *enhance* or favorably *change* your group's image. Furthermore, a worthwhile event that is well thought of by the media and the public can win prestige, dignity, approval, and credibility for your organization. Credibility is the *key* ingredient in attracting support: financial support, media support, and, ultimately, public support through the media.

Outline and Checklist

One of the all-time great publicists, Herb Baus, wrote the *Public Relations Handbook*, now long out of print. In this book, he uses the bedrock foundation of straight-news reporting (the five Ws and the H) to set forth the basic elements of a staged event. These rules are just as applicable now as when Baus wrote them.

What?   Name of event, its scope, necessary buildup, budget, elements of program.

Why?   Purpose and objective.

When?   Full schedule of timing, with deadlines for each preliminary, all worked out as to dates and hours.

Where?   Geographic locale, facilities, including ample facilities for every detail necessary to complete functioning.

Who?   Who will engineer, star, be invited, attend, follow up?

How?   How will all these things be done? Advance planning for full coverage. Announcements by press, [television,] radio, magazines, direct mail, outdoor advertising, and other media. Stockpile of stories, pictures, features. Mechanical arrangements for coverage—pressroom, typewriters, [word processors, copier, fax machine,] telephones, accommodations for press, provisions for photographic and video coverage, wiring for radio [and television]. Information arrangements— advance copies of speeches and reports, programs, interviews, press conferences. Checking coverage—stenographer to check details, photographer to get pictures for distribution afterward to publications not taking own pictures. Follow up—thank-you notes, scrapbook, final report.

Advantages and Disadvantages of Staged Events and News Media Coverage

Although the focus of this book is publicity, you may be considering other kinds of promotion. You should be aware that a staged event, which gets you both publicity and promotion, is often far more cost-effective than, for example, buying airtime for commercials or broadcast production or mounting a direct-mail campaign. For a company with a product or service to promote, a staged event can initiate more media and public notice than other types of publicity, public relations, or advertising.

Never lose sight, however, of a basic fact: If you stage an event that is overtly commercial, the media will not attend, nor will they report it. If it is lackluster, commonplace, or poorly conceived and managed and they *do* report it, the coverage may not give the positive image you hope for. An event that is enthusiastically received can become a regular, perhaps annual, event that, over time, builds, strengthens, and continuously reinforces the public's—and the news media's—perception of your organization.

Consider some of the advantages and disadvantages of having the news media cover your staged event:

- As careful as you may be, a reporter may put his or her own interpretation or slant on your story—and that slant may not necessarily be to your liking.
- You cannot always count on the news media to go along with your "great idea." On the other hand, if the media are cool to your idea, that well may be an indication of the public's acceptance!
- To get the press to attend, you must set the time and place well in advance. Unfortunately, your carefully planned date may just happen to fall on a day when the biggest news of the year breaks—such as the day of O. J. Simpson's freeway run, or the day the ATF raided David Koresh's cult headquarters in Waco, Texas, and it burned to the ground along with all the people within, or the day Nancy Kerrigan was attacked in Detroit, Michigan. The bulletins may fill every inch of available news space and knock your story right out of the ballpark, particularly if the happening is of national interest but actually takes place in your hometown or state, where it claims even greater amounts of space than elsewhere and continues for days or even months.
- On the other hand, the date of your staged event could easily turn out to be one of the slowest news days of the year—a much more likely occurence—and your event might be given undreamed of space and treatment for the simple reason that newspapers have so much space to fill on that particular day.
- Created news can be customized to suit your need and your budget.

Purpose for an Event

Before you decide to stage an event, a full evaluation should be made of *why* your company or group will have the event. Image—building it, changing it, or softening it—can be all that is needed to justify the decision. A specially created event can be designed to foster and mold a favorable public image for an organization that has been thought of as remote and cold. Any organization *can* change its image. Perhaps this is the time to consider it, take action, and make the change.

Event Timing

Timing is an important element in planning an event. If you are considering an event that can be held only on a specific day or date, check local calendars to be sure yours will not run head-on into another well-established event scheduled for the same date. The chambers of commerce in most cities have community calendars that list events for a full year in advance.

Newspaper Listings and Community Calendars

Local newspapers usually include listings of events and activities, and some radio and television programs also have calendars of events. These informational calendars are not set far enough in advance to provide solid information about possible date conflicts, but they do provide something else—another publicity outlet for your upcoming event.

As another means of getting your message to the public, send the information about your event to each outlet that has a community calendar. It will pay to check each station and newspaper for its specific calendar requirements. Most outlets require the same information that you would normally include as the lead of your announcement release—in the form of the five Ws.

Begin sending your calendar notices about six weeks in advance, and continue to send them weekly until the time of the event.

Brainstorming an Event

Brainstorming can help you decide on the kind of event you want to stage. Consider the following points when you prepare for your brainstorming session:

- Know the event's purpose and objectives.
- Choose an event that is right for your organization and complies with your organization's goals and objectives.

When these points are indelibly etched into the concrete tablet on which you will set forth strategies, call in the best brains in your organization and hold a brainstorming session.

Because brainstorming is such a productive means of arriving at solutions to numerous kinds of problems, Appendix C is devoted to it. Refer to this section whenever you need to produce results. Brainstorming is a creative problem-solving technique, an excellent description of which is included in *The Path of Least Resistance* by Robert Fritz. Fritz describes brainstorming as a process "in which you attempt to blitzkrieg through your preconceived 'mind-set' by fanciful free association. The idea is to generate alternative solutions by overcoming your usual manner of thinking." Fritz recommends that while brainstorming, you "suspend your critical judgment so that you can be more inventive."

Imagination, creativeness, and inventiveness are the fundamentals for designing a successful event. If it's "old hat," or dull or overdone, no one—media or public—will want to attend.

The Enjoyment Factor

The enjoyment factor is an important one to consider in your brainstorming session. For an event to be successful, it must also be entertaining. Yet making enjoyment a major purpose may appear to give an almost unprofessional or unseemly luster to something as earnest as an effort to attract publicity that will build integrity, image, and recognition for an organization. Without a substantial enjoyment factor, however, neither the media nor the public will be pleased with any event. For truly serious events such as seminars or training sessions, enjoyment by participants can come from productive learning; an event needn't be thought of as "show time" in order to be enjoyable.

If your staged event is perceived by the media and the public as pleasurable, different, unique, and worthwhile, it will successfully fulfill all your requirements and could very well become a regular event that attracts a following for your organization. With such success will come the certainty that others will copy your brainchild. For you, that merely means it's back to the brainstorming sessions. You must continue to innovate and update to stay ahead of the pack.

Store Unused Brainstorms for Later Events

If your brainstorming sessions succeed in producing creative ideas, you may find that some are off-the-wall thoughts, but within even the most "creative" idea there's a germ of a usable event. And what may seem off-the-wall today may be the kind of high-interest event you might consider another time.

Every brainstorming session has a by-product that can pay off later: ideas that were generated but not pursued can be reconsidered, updated, and perhaps "piggybacked" onto the successful event to renew or revise or to create an entirely new event at a later time. Here is a suggestion: Tape and transcribe all brainstorming sessions and retain them in your files for future reference.

Something to consider when you are finally choosing your event is whether it is interesting enough and newsworthy enough to compete against all the syndicated material—features and such—available to all media without any expenditure of their time or effort.

An Event That Broke All Rules

Nothing could be more blatantly commercial than an event staged by the Miller Brewing Company—yet it attracted thousands of onlookers and was so interesting that media reported it almost as if it were the world soccer games. It's still being referred to by media, and bits are still shown occasionally on news programs.

The event? The *Weinerdog Winternationals*! This was a contest sponsored by Miller Lite beer in which dogs ran a 50-yard track, encouraged by their cheering owners and favorite toys. Some 2,000 entries were received from dachshund owners from Florida to Arizona. Thirty-four were chosen to compete.

Media were told that the idea for the race was, in part, a spinoff of the Miller

Lite campaign in which nontraditional events are combined, and that the commercial that combined a dog show and drag racing created the concept for the "Weinerdog Winternationals."

All through this book you've been told, *don't try to pass advertising off as publicity*. Here's proof that every rule can be broken. In this case, the event was interesting and about as much fun and memorable as anyone could imagine, which made it newsworthy.

Ideas to Get Your Brainstorm Session Moving

There are too many possibilities for feasible events to list them here. What follows are a few well-known kinds of happenings. Some may be a bit overdone, but they are worth consideration to get ideas rolling:

- All manner of shows, from product and business shows to home shows.
- Ethnic galas that celebrate with foods and cultural exhibits.
- Exhibits such as art, crafts, or manufacturing.
- Concerts for serious music lovers, teenagers, or families.
- Tie-ins with local events (a particularly effective type of event), such as special days, holidays, or weeks.
- Plant or company tours. Unless this is a rare occasion when the public and/or media are permitted to tour the facilities, and unless there is a truly interesting aspect to the tour such as an exciting new product being manufactured, or the manufacturing process itself is intriguing, or an orphanage is highly unique in the way it houses children, a plant or company tour can be deadly *dull*. Beware of just opening the doors and expecting all to rush in. If you do decide on such an event, be sure to have tour guides who are completely informed and enthusiastic about your product or service.

  A tour doesn't have to be just for media. Tours can be used to acquaint people whose support you want or need.

  Before deciding that a tour is the event you wish to use, you should be aware of some conditions required to make them successful: Stick to groups of no fewer than 20 and no more than 35. This keeps single tours manageable, the number of tours down, and the public exposure factor up.

  Each tour should have three parts: An advance briefing of what guests will see; the tour itself; and a debriefing to answer questions, to recap what was seen, and—to help them remember—to provide a souvenir or inexpensive booklet or brochure.

- A company open house. The general purpose of an open house is primarily to gain goodwill and educate the public. The exact purpose(s) should be put into writing so that everyone understands what the organization is trying to accomplish. The purpose should then be publicized.
- Unveiling or previewing an *important* new product, a product breakthrough or disclosure, or a landmark achievement.
- Workshops, which can serve your own needs as well as those of other small businesses or nonprofit groups. For example, specialists can be recruited

from PR, advertising, publicity, or whatever area of information participants require. Your organization will be given the credit through publicity,
and those who are recruited as instructors are likely to offer their services
for minimal or no charge, because the workshop puts them in touch with
those who may need and pay for their services at another time.
- Social events such as fashion shows, dances, coffees, or formal dinners.
- All manner of sports events.

Market Assessment

It seems only logical that you assess in advance the market you want to attract.
Sometimes, however, the desire for a certain kind of event by those developing the
plans conquer this common sense.

Some people are avid golfers, others live for tennis or biking, and there are
those who believe that anything of an artistic or crafts nature will provide enjoyment for everyone. Heed the old Indian admonition (in this slightly edited version) to "walk a mile in the moccasins of those you want to attend your event."
It is excellent advice. To ignore the desires and interests of those you want to
attract is to risk choosing an unappealing event that requires much work and expense
and offers few, if any, rewards.

The people you want to attract may have specific interests. To establish what
those special interests are, talk to potential patrons. There is no need for a full-
fledged survey or analysis, although either can be vastly productive. Merely talking
with people who make up your potential market can give you excellent insight
into their reactions—both positive and negative—and assure a more positive response to your event.

Benefit Events and Profits

There are some very good reasons for a commercial enterprise to back or support
an event to benefit a local charity. And obviously, it's highly beneficial for nonprofits
to be recipients of proceeds from commercially sponsored events—in terms of both
dollars and image. For businesses, such an event can result in substantial publicity
and even in financial assistance.

First, the fact that proceeds will go to an established, popular charitable cause
almost assures that publicity about and for the event will be used by the press.
However, Federal Communications Commission regulations prevent all mention
(in the form of public service announcements on television) of a commercial sponsor
of an event that benefits a nonprofit organization. There is a little more le-
niency in regulations for radio. (Additional information about PSAs is presented
in Chapter 18.)

Second, a tie-in with a nonprofit organization can possibly mean that space
in a centrally located, large corporation's building can be obtained free, or that
rental charges for a large facility may be reduced and subsequently deducted by the
grantor as a charitable contribution. It is worth exploring the possibility of additional "in-kind" contributions, which can cut costs considerably.

Third, a portion of the receipts from a ticket charge can be used to offset event
costs, with the rest going to the charity. For the sake of media and public approval,

make the percentage given to charity substantial enough that no criticism will reflect on your organization.

Considerations for Staged Events

Careful thought must be given to plans for staged events. The following paragraphs discuss some of the considerations you should be aware of.

Newsworthiness

When is an event news? Herb Baus spelled it out in *Tested Public Relations and Publicity Procedure*, a manual that he edited for The National Research Bureau, Inc.:

- When it is new
- When it is novel
- When it is related to famous persons
- When it is directly important to great numbers of people
- When it involves conflict
- When it involves mystery
- When it is considered confidential
- When it pertains to the future
- When it is funny
- When it is romantic or sexy

Cost Estimates

How much your staged event will cost may be the first question you must ask—and answer. After several successful events, you may be able to estimate costs based on previous experience. However, there is only one way to project a monetary figure for your first media event: Get valid estimates.

Figure the number of people who will attend, including the news media, the public, and your own people. The number is much easier to gauge if the event is invitational rather than a public-invited event. After you have listed every item that will be used, get solid per-person cost estimates for each item, and multiply these figures by the number who are expected to attend.

Your total cost estimate will provide you with enough information to decide whether the event is financially manageable.

Items to Budget For

There are several items to consider when you budget for a staged event.

- Location. Will the event be held at a "no-cost" organization location or in local rented space? You must consider not only the size of the space but also whether the location provides easy access for the media you plan to invite.
- Food and drinks. If the event is to be held on your organization's property, there undoubtedly will be catering costs. If it is held in a public facility, can the facility provide the food or must it be catered? Shop for caterers

and check restaurant prices if you do plan to serve food. If there is to be a bar, the costs of soft drinks and/or liquor or wine must be estimated. Compensation for service people is often a forgotten expense.

- Invitations. You must decide whether invitations are to be printed and whether they are to be simple or elaborate. Postage or the cost of more ostentatious hand-delivery must also be figured. (An example of an invitation to news media people is reproduced in Figure 13.1 at the end of this chapter.)

- Press kits. Every member of the news media who is invited should receive a press kit. Some people may request more than one, so plan to have plenty on hand. Television people will have a far greater appreciation—and be more likely to use the information—if press kits for them are on videotape. If you have not yet prepared a press kit for your event, check Chapter 11 to get an idea of what press-kit for the print media should contain. Check Chapter 16 on preparing what a press kit on videotape for television news people and what it should include. With this information, you can estimate the cost of producing the press kits you will need for the event.

Evaluation Questions

Before you make final decisions, there are some questions you should ask yourself and others concerned with producing a successful event. Insist on honest answers, even when the answers may not be what you and they hope to hear.

- Is this event appropriate for your community? Will the community like and respond to it?
- Will the news media respond positively to it?
- Will it produce the returns you have set as goals?
- What will your returns be?
- Do you have the resources and capabilities to carry out the event successfully? Do you have the budget, staff, enthusiasm, and organizational ability?
- Finally, and perhaps most important to achieve real success, are your own executives, line staff, and members enthusiastic about the event? Will they support it wholeheartedly?

Staff Members

A minister of a small church in Texas was attempting to enlist volunteers for a project that is a major fund-raiser for the congregation. It requires many people to organize it, staff it, and mop it up afterward. He used his pulpit as one means of making the appeal and included the following as part of his invocation:

This is the Tale of Four People named Everybody, Somebody, Anybody, and Nobody. There was an important job to be done and Everybody was asked to do it. Everybody was sure that Somebody would do it. Anybody could have done it, but Nobody did it.

Somebody got angry about that because it was Everybody's job. Everybody thought Anybody could do it but Nobody would do it.

It ended up that Everybody blamed Somebody when Nobody did what Everybody could have done. At least, now Everybody understands that Nobody cares.

And the moral to this Tale may very well be that, in this life, you can only depend on Nobody and Yourself.

The lesson from the "Tale of Four People" probably should be put into question form: Do you have an adequate number of people to organize and staff the event and to mop it up afterward? Or do you have only the infamous "Four People" to assist you?

Event Coordinator

If you are the head of an organization, you probably don't have time to arrange a successful staged event. You must find someone whose assignmment with regard to the event is very much the same as yours as entrepreneur: organizing, operating, and assuming the risk.

There's an excellent definition of a coordinator: someone who brings organized chaos out of regimented confusion. Actually, it is the coordinator's job to plan, organize, *and* coordinate the plans and the event staff. If the event is small enough, perhaps only one person is needed. If the event is complex or of any size greater than small, the coordinator will probably need assistants. A full-scale event requires an extraordinary amount of advance planning and preparation. The number of people needed is directly related to the complexity and size of the event. Don't underestimate the amount of work involved or the number of people required.

Press Contact

A person other than the coordinator should be designated to be in charge of the press at the event; the best person for the job is the person whose name is listed as a contact on press releases. If you are the head of your organization, you may and perhaps should be able to afford time for this special assignment, and that can be an excellent decision for two reasons:

- You know the answers to questions that reporters may ask.
- You can get to know the press, and they can get to know you.

Tips for Assisting News Media at Planned Events

None of the following tips is more than commonsense advice, but the list can be used as a reminder.

- When you schedule an event, make plans to invite the media.
- Send complimentary tickets in advance. Make arrangements for media people to be included as guests—individually seated with persons from your organization whom they know or would like to know.
- Assist members of the media in every way in covering the event, or assign a capable staff person to do so.
- Prepare a press release in advance if the occasion warrants.

- A day or so before the event, call the editor and ask if there are any special arrangements he or she or a reporter may require—a backstage pass, an interview with a speaker, or contact with specific individuals who will attend. Do your best to make arrangements for all that is requested.

Event Publicity

The information that follows is best directed to the event coordinator, whether that person is the executive in charge of the organization or a specially appointed person.

Inasmuch as the primary motivation and justification for holding this little bash is to attract media attention, it is time to zero in on how to assure worthwhile results. What do you do to get their attention?

There are three stages in an event's publicity plan:

1. Advance publicity
2. Day-of-the-event coverage
3. Follow-up coverage, roundup of results, and evaluations

Advance Publicity

Yes, it is publicity of the event itself that has been dominating your thinking up to this point. But why pass up the opportunity for additional coverage? Actually, you must have advance publicity to assure satisfactory attendance and success for your main event.

Advance publicity can come merely through sending out advance news releases. Or it can come through special advance events and their subsequent press coverage. These decisions depend on the size and kind of main event you are planning.

A number of events precede the Pasadena Rose Parade, which range in size from small luncheons to a preparade ball to the Rose Queen's coronation and her attendants' presentation. The smaller events begin months in advance, and each produces publicity for the main event. You undoubtedly are not thinking of an event of a comparable size, but the concept is the same for an event of any size.

A small event, such as a workshop or training seminar that brings in a well-known person to conduct it, may profitably be preceded by a publicity-producing advance event, such as a press luncheon or a coffee or cocktail party, to introduce the personality to the press.

(A word here about cocktail parties, or the use of alcohol at any event: Do a current, careful, thorough, advance check of both press and public reaction to offering liquor, wine, or beer at any event under your sponsorship. Both public and press reactions are becoming increasingly less tolerant in this regard.)

Advance events can be as simple or as elaborate as you wish. Some events don't call for any kind of advance happening, but every event calls for advance publicity.

Advance press releases should go out to attract an audience to the event. Details can be distributed over several releases to announce time, place, purpose, celebrity participation, and other relevant newsworthy details; or all the information can be included in one release.

Memos as Reminders

In addition to advance publicity releases, there is a certain amount of insurance in sending reminder memos to all local media on your media list. Give the time, place, purpose, speaker and celebrity names, event features, and provisions that will be made for reporters. Also state whether a photographer will be in attendance for the reporters' convenience, and give the names of the persons who will be there to assist them, along with telephone numbers at which these persons can be reached prior to the event. A reminder phone call a couple of days before the event can help too. If the reminder call is made by the person named to assist the editor or reporter at the event, it becomes a pre-event opportunity to get acquainted. It may also encourage the invited person to attend, based on the friendliness of the call.

Day-of-the-Event Coverage

An unknown author gave the following advice: "How many of you have been bitten by an elephant? By a lion or a tiger? By a dog or cat? By a mosquito? The moral here is, It's the little things that'll get you!"

In the same vein, some people cite Murphy's Law: Anything that can go wrong, will.

Now that you've been warned by such profound advice, be prepared for something to go wrong on the day of your event, no matter how fully you and your staff have planned for it. Whatever does go wrong probably will be a seemingly inconsequential "little thing" that was overlooked in your preparations.

With that negative thought behind you, look to your plans.

Press Badges.   Members of the press should always be supplied with tickets or passes to all event functions. If there is reason to differentiate media representatives from others at the event, you must provide them with specially printed press badges. If everyone will wear name cards, the differentiation can be shown by providing cards of a different color for the press, or by marking a regular card or badge with a color-coded stick-on star or dot.

A Room for the Press.   Events of less than two or three day's duration do not require elaborate setups, such as a press room with all the accoutrements that reporters need to report their stories (telephones, word processors and typewriters, a copier, a fax machine, perhaps a satellite feed, and informed and knowledgeable staffers on hand. Gabriella Klein says that now, with expanding technology, CCU, Inc. also offers on line modeming services).

It may be helpful, however, if the public attends and if there is a special speaker or celebrity whom reporters will want to interview, to provide a separate room for such interviews.

Press Kits.   Have plenty of hard-copy press kits on hand for both print and broadcast media. (Chapter 11 guides you in preparing them.) If there is high interest by television media in your event, you may also want to have videotapes available.

Hard-copy press kits are appropriate for television reporters who do not attend, along with videotapes.

Each hard-copy press kit should contain the following:

- News release giving the event's major points for reporters to flesh out and use, or to draw on for their own stories.
- Fact sheet for those reporters who wish to write their stories from scratch.
- Backgrounder about your organization (and of the sponsoring organization and the beneficiary, if the event is sponsored by a for-profit organization to benefit a nonprofit).
- Concise history of your organization (or include two: a history of the sponsoring organization and of the beneficiary group).
- Bios of celebrity speakers or special personalities, as well as organization executives in whom the media would be interested.
- Quotes sheet of quotable remarks by event participants.
- Operating manual, if the event's purpose is to introduce equipment or a product.
- Photos of the product or equipment and people using it, of the speakers or participating personalities, and any other appropriate subjects.
- Attractive, well-prepared brochure, such as an annual report, that gives additional background information (optional).

Support Staff.   Remember to provide adequate support staff for day-of-event coverage:

- Assign a sufficient number of *informed, knowledgeable* representatives from your group to meet, greet, and assist the press.
- Assign a sufficient number of "gofers" to run errands, so that you will not have to abandon your post and your responsibilities.
- Assign a special assistant to meet and greet the celebrity who will speak and to assist that person in any way that is requested.
- Plan ahead for traffic and crowd control (if the event is large). If police are required, check to be sure that they are on hand.

Follow-Up Coverage

When the event is over, you may be surprised if you think you are finished! No, there is more, and this part too must be coordinated.

Mop-up.   Your plans should include provisions for returning the facility to its original state, particularly if the place is on free loan or in a company location that will be used again shortly after the event.

Publicity.   A more important task than mop-up is that of follow-up to publicity. Use the following guidelines to ensure that your publicity efforts will be successful.

- Offer additional information or extra photos or videotapes to reporters. Send these items in plenty of time to make the reporters' deadlines.
- Immediately deliver or send a press release, a press kit, and a cover letter to each invited media representative who did not attend. Mention to each that he or she was missed.
- Write and distribute a "following-the-event" news release to those who attended and those who didn't. Include in it a roundup of information about the event and its success, the amount raised (if for charity), a few quotes from the speaker or notable persons present, a quotable remark or two of your own, and any other appropriate new news about the event.
- Send thank-you letters to all media representatives who attended.
- Send thank-you letters to all who assisted, including those who made contributions of space and those who contributed time.

Final Evaluation

Another essential follow-up assignment entails looking back on the event to assess it fully, before sharp recollections fade. Whether or not you believe you will repeat the event, it is important to make a comprehensive evaluation of it and to keep a complete file of that evaluation for future reference. *Keep everything!* Chances are good that you will have another event of some kind, and records from this one can provide valuable information for a future event, even if it is of a totally different type.

Follow-Up Meeting

Call a meeting of all who assisted in the event and, together with your assistants, assess the event's successful aspects and decide which of these can be repeated another time, in part or in whole. An appraisal should also be made of any weaknesses and of any areas in which improvements can or should be made in the future.

Make a rating of the quality of the program and of the speaker or celebrity. Request, from anyone and everyone who participated, individual, candid feelings and reactions about the event; be sure to include your own. Include feelings of disappointment, boredom, and other less-than-positive reactions, as well as feelings of satisfaction related to portions that were well done.

Return on Your Investment.   One of the most important after-the-event assessments is whether there is and will be a return on your investment. Not only were significant amounts of time used in planning and executing the event, substantial amounts of money undoubtedly were also spent. It's just good business practice to demand that these expenditures eventually provide a favorable result—in terms of goals reached or in predicted future business. Therefore, ask and answer questions such as the following:

- Is it likely that the additional press coverage and public notice will result in greater customer interest and thus a greater share of the market?
- Did this event result in direct orders? Or can we realistically expect an increase in future business as a result of these expenditures?

- What dollar return can and should we expect? How much? How quickly?
- Was there a boost in image, and was the impact on image substantial?
- Were we able to stay within our budget? If we exceeded the allotment, was it a small or a significant expenditure?
- Finally, was the outcome worth the time, effort, and money spent?

Tape the entire follow-up meeting, and transcribe it for easy reference.

Written Evaluation

When you have completed your follow-up meeting, get its results down in *writing*, so you will have records to refer to later. Do this while the project is still fresh in your mind and in the minds of your assistants.

Include the following in your written report:

- Evaluation of whether and how the project met your group's goals and objectives
- Evaluation of whether attendance—by the public and by news media—matched prior estimates
- Comments on how press coverage stacked up against expectations
- Narrative report of both media reaction and public reaction, gathered from everyone who had any contact with either group

Keep file copies of the following items:

- Media list(s) used
- Invitation list(s) with addresses and individual identifications or titles
- All releases—advance through follow-up—dated to show date of delivery
- Invitations, letters of invitation, and all correspondence related to the event
- Projected budget(s) and final costs, with comparisons
- Press clippings or a scrapbook of press clippings
- Set of photos or negatives or slides from which the photos were made
- Anything and everything that was used in planning or carrying out the event

Later, when memory has blurred, you or someone else with the responsibility of coordinator will have a full and valuable reference file. You can use the file and its supporting documentation to follow the same path to an identical event or to shift in another direction.

FIGURE 13.1   Example of an Invitation to a Media News Event

The Dallas Museum of Art

cordially invites you

to a news media preview of the new

MUSEUM OF THE AMERICAS

and the

NANCY AND JAKE L. HAMON BUILDING

Friday, September 24

Tour and remarks at 12:00 p.m.   Lunch served at 1:00 p.m.

R.S.V.P. (214) 922-1347

1717 North Harwood
Please enter at the Hamon Tower Entrance
facing Woodall Rodgers Freeway.
Enter underground parking from either
St. Paul or Harwood.

14

Wire Services and Syndicates

How they can help you reach readers and viewers you couldn't otherwise contact

Once upon a Time . . .

There was a time when news was transmitted by teletype. But that was once upon a time. Today, United Press International (UPI), through its Global News Network, delivers the news at a superfast 20,000 words a minute! And editors can view and analyze the news through UPI WorldView, a computer software program that lets them retrieve only the news they want—just by clicking a button. Today, in addition to the words, the news by UPI WorldView includes photographs, clip art, audio sound bites, and will quite soon include video. This was the first multimedia delivery system to bring the news directly to newsroom PCs, often within seconds of an announcement or event. UPI is the largest privately held global news agency.

The Associated Press (AP) hasn't been dozing either. According to CEO Louis Boccardi, AP has "up-speeded" its slowspeed news wire to 150 times its old rate of 66 words a minute. A calculator says that's 9,900 *words a minute!* The slowspeed service was for smaller daily newspapers and college papers, some of which will stay with the slower transmission because, they say, it gives them a choice of copy without overwhelming their small-staffed newsrooms.

AP went into the video news business in November 1994. The service, based in London, was created because of the need for an independent, comprehensive source of global video news, according to AP chairman Frank Daniels, Jr. A by-product will be still pictures taken from video.

Communication Links to the World

Aside from the local and area news that newspapers' own staffers are able to cover, wire services provide the bulk of the stories in daily newspapers across the country. And that includes straight news as well as newsfeatures. Therefore, if a news release has broad interest beyond that of the local media, wire services can be a boon to your publicity efforts.

AP and UPI are worldwide news and information services that operate 24 hours a day, 365 days a year, with staffers reporting from nearly every country on the globe.

These news and newsfeature services—and there are many more than UPI and AP—provide broader distribution than can be managed by mail servicing, and there are no mail distribution costs. There also are wire services that concentrate on business news, such as Dow Jones News Services and Bloomberg Business News. All welcome news from publicity people. They often pick up such news from newspapers and other media. Be forewarned, however, that the content and writing of a news release must be especially good to be accepted by a wire service.

Syndication

Trains and airplanes put the Pony Express out of business. Wire services did for newspapers what trains and planes did for mail service. Even with the arrival of satellite transmissions, wire services are still performing essential services. There are, however, significant improvements in the way these services are currently transmitted.

Wire services are in fact *syndicates*. There are straight news and feature news syndicates and picture syndicates; there also are specialty syndicates that distribute articles on travel, entertainment, human interest, business, personal finance, lifestyle, health, legal issues, and just about anything else that interests the reading public.

Not only do newspapers subscribe to wire services, magazines, radio, trade journals, college and business newspapers, but tabloids also subscribe.

Amazing Place

At small newspapers the process of receiving wire news may work much as it did when teletype was the means of transmission. The city editor, news editor, or wire editor (who is solely responsible for incoming wire material) evaluates the story, decides whether it should be used in that day's edition, and designates it for a particular page and position. The story is then sent to the copy desk, where it's edited, trimmed for size, and headlined.

At the majority of newspapers, however, transmission to and within the newspapers is through computers. John Davenport, whose title is Special Assistant to Management, describes how the process works at *The Dallas Morning News*.

No longer is there the clickity click and the clackity clack of hard copy coming in. Now we write and edit all of our stories on computer screens, and that is the same way we receive wire copy. Every terminal has access to the computers, and each news person has a set of commands that call up whichever wire is needed. In other words, if I want what's running on the state wire, I type in "DS fifty forty." The computer then accesses that wire right to my desk. I can do this from any desk that has a computer terminal.

In answer to the question, are there wire editors anymore? Basically the answer is yes, although that isn't a title at our newspaper. In effect there are individual wire editors: the assistant national editor scrolls the national wire, the assistant international editor scrolls the international wire, the features people scroll the features wires. Editors in various departments are responsible for the news on their wires, and each is virtually a wire editor. There is, however, one person who performs some of the functions of the old wire editor. Although she is primarily responsible for international news, and her title is assistant international editor, she is also responsible for seeing that all departments are made aware of news that is germane to their work. She is the gatekeeper, and if she sees something that is of interest to a specific department she alerts that person. Unlike the earlier wire editor, however, she doesn't print out hard copy and carry it to those she alerts, she flags them by computer. For them, it's like having incoming baskets on top of their desks.

Benefits of Wire Services

Without assistance from wire services it would be impossible for newspapers to provide the amounts of information that readers receive each day.

Staff Extension

For newspapers, wire services (that provide news) and syndicates (that provide other kinds of information) are projections of the newspapers' staffs. Not even the largest newspapers can have reporters and photographers everywhere in the world where news is breaking.

The size of a newspaper largely determines the methods it uses to cover news happening beyond the field that its newsroom reporters can physically reach. Large newspapers often have news staffs or bureaus in their state capital, in Washington, D.C., and, perhaps, even in other cities in their state and other states. Small newspapers usually rely on the wire services for news both from Washington, D.C., and from within their state. Newspapers of medium size, if unable to afford a full-time reporter in the state capital, will try to have one of their staff present for important events, such as legislative meetings. These papers rely on wire services for broader coverage, including news from the nation's capital.

Financial Advantages

Savings for Newspapers. At very small cost, each newspaper can print the writings, photos, and drawings of the most talented men and women of America, because the cost is spread across many subscribers.

In an article in *Saturday Review*, Boyd Lewis, former president of one of the largest basic newspaper feature services, described the advantages of syndication:

[Each subscriber newspaper] can present articles by the foremost authorities on medicine, psychology, child care, nutrition, cooking, and other specialties. It can expose the thinking of the finest thinkers in the land. It can use countless comic strips, panels, and colored pages. And it can get all of these for a tiny fraction of what the originators are paid.

Savings for all Media Forms and Corporate Clients. The savings that newspapers realize extend to magazines, radio, and television as well. What may not be known is that corporate clients, which customize their coverage requirements by choosing specified lists of topics, also receive the cost-effective subscription rates. And both small market media and corporate clients can receive this select news by fax.

Contributor Earnings

Syndicates work to the advantage of the contract contributors too. It has been estimated that Charles Schulz, who draws "Peanuts" for United Features Syndicate, grosses more than $20 million a year. It also is estimated that more than 250 million people around the world follow the daily doings and sayings of Snoopy and his pals.

Although you are, in a sense, a "contributor" when you submit your feature or news story to a wire service, you will not receive payment for it (any more than you would from the newspapers to which you send your releases). As a matter of convention, it is considered unethical to receive compensation from both the media and the organization you represent.

Style Differences

If you believe your news stories or photo releases merit wire service or syndicate distribution, it will be a wise move on your part to contact the nearest office for each service and to request information about how to conform to its standards and requirements. There *are* differences in preferences between wire services and newspapers, and even among wire services. For instance, one difference is that photo syndicates usually prefer negatives rather than prints. Some prefer chromes. They usually do not mind, however, if other photo syndicates receive identical pictures.

If you believe that your news story or feature has broader appeal and interest than a straight news release provides, and if national or worldwide publicity is a paramount objective, you will want to make personal contact with the nearest wire service office; these services frequently will work with you to develop a story you have in mind.

If a wire service has expressed potential interest in your news release, a copy should be sent to each service at the same time you distribute it to local news media.

Types of News Wire Services

The principal news wire services are UPI, AP, and Reuters Information Services (for worldwide news distribution). Along with independent news-gathering agencies, some cities have *city news services* that provide only local news, and there are several other categories of news services.

Business-News Services

Specialized business-news services such as Dow Jones News Services, Bloomberg Business News, Business Features Syndicate, Business Newsfeatures, and Business Wire handle news of interest to business publications and to the business pages of newspapers.

One business-news service focuses specifically on news for small-business owners and independent retailers, and others have broader business news interests integrated with other types of news and features.

Feature-News Services

Syndicated newspaper features cover many fields, from advice to the lovelorn, to cartoons and comic panels, to analysis of the weightiest issues of the day.

You probably recognize the names of the popular feature-news services that supply newspapers; you've doubtless seen their names as bylines or in credit lines on articles that have caught your eye. *Los Angeles Times Syndicate*, *King Features Syndicate, Inc.*, and *The New York Times Syndication Sales Corp.* are among the best known.

Information on Wire Services

If you decide to try for publicity through wire services, you probably can locate information about them in your library in the reference section. Look for the following resources:

- *Editor & Publisher International Yearbook* includes a section, "Syndicates & News Services."
- *Editor & Publisher Syndicate Directory* is an invaluable resource.
- *Writer's Market* not only lists names, addresses, phone numbers, and editor's names, it also describes the kinds of news and articles and the specialty interests of each service it lists.
- *Bacon's Publicity Checker/Newspapers* is another directory that gives wire services' names, addresses, and phone numbers, editors' or bureau chiefs' names, and, in some cases, the names of special-section editors.

Wirephotos Have Become High-Speed Technology

There are a number of wirephoto services—Associated Press, Reuters, and Agence France-Presse (AFP) are the largest—but none has more up-to-the minute technology than Associated Press.

In addition, AP has reach as a cooperative beyond other photo syndicates, through its access to the photos of its member newspapers as well as those of its own photographers and stringers (part-time photogs who usually cover a particular geographic area or subject).

Associated Press, Reuters, and AFP all offer digital photo delivery by satellite, but AP jumped ahead of the pack when it reduced image receiving time from 35 seconds to 8 seconds. The service also provides for a black printer, undercolor removal, and other enhancements.

A recent addition to AP's high-tech upgrades is a filmless, digital camera. It is compact, portable, and usable in varied and unpredictable conditions, but it also offers the economic advantages of digital photography: no film costs, no developing, and no chemical costs. It's called the AP News Camera 2000, developed by Kodak, with a Nikon mount.

Regardless of its quality, a photo is useless if it arrives late at its media destination. Portable scanner-transmitters with built-in photo-editing capabilities, still video transceivers, and digital cameras with modem links all are regulation equipment among photo syndicate photographers.

New Software Replaces Editors' Work

Because the electronic superhighway can now transport so much more news "baggage" than ever anticipated, it was inevitable that some kind of new conveyance had to be developed to meet new "highway" speed requirements—by performing the traditional editorial chores of finding, sorting, ranking, and culling information. Such a program has been developed at the University of Texas-Austin to do just that.

Training computers to analyze news content, judge the importance of each story, distinguish between business and sports stories, between banner-headline news from fillers, were the major challenges. Actually, UT-Austin journalism professor Wayne Danielson designed a program back in 1964 that ranked Associated Press stories, edited them to fit a specific news hole, and then printed them. This new software merely accelerates the speed of doing it all to match speeds of the other traffic on the highway.

Don't Give Up!

Achieving acceptance of your news and features isn't easy, and after several seemingly unsuccessful attempts you may feel as Reggie Jackson, one of baseball's great players, described it: "It's like trying to eat coffee with a fork." Don't give up, though. The results can provide your greatest publicity "coups."

15

Broadcast Publicity

Television and radio are different from
newspapers and why and how radio is
different from TV

So Little Time

Television news is inclined to concentrate on crises. In a cartoon strip by Tom Wilson, "Ziggy" tells it like it is. Sitting in front of his television set, Ziggy hears the lineup of the nightly news: "Welcome to the six o'clock news . . . I'll be reporting on the Middle East crisis . . . Barb will report on the budget crisis . . . and Bob Thurman and Skip Ramsey will be here later with the weather crisis and sports crisis!"

Television and radio news media have little time available for positive, image-building news. And they have even less time for business news unless it's about a giant corporation, a virtually incredible business happening, or exposure of misdeeds by a small business that the public should be warned about.

Beyond the time factor, television news is an intensely competitive business. The pressure for ratings has turned into the scream heard 'round the newsroom! Everyone in the country undoubtedly has heard the current cliché, "virtual reality." Well, let's coin a new phrase for TV news's highly competitive need to lure viewers by shocking them. Let's call it "invented reality." There are numbers of cases in which television news reporters and executives have been shown—after the fact—to have either rigged or distorted news, and even used rigged "teasers" to lure viewers to watch it. Such instances run the gamut from "dramatizing" a report that General Motors pickup trucks aren't safe in collisions because of improper placement of gas tanks, to staging a pit bull dogfight, apparently purely for shock value.

Print media aren't wholly blameless in regard to running misleading news, but they're not under the same intense competitive pressures. And newspapers are able to expand their news coverage to give good news space to businesses of all sizes merely by increasing the number of pages. Television and radio have only 60 minutes in an hour, so unless a station has an all-news format, it must stay within the confines of limited-time newscasts.

Now, however, there is cable television which, like radio, has a number of 24-

hour all news-stations that may welcome your news release *if* the news is of interest to their viewers or listeners, can be presented in a concise, crisp fashion, and has good *visual* elements.

The March of Times

News on television—both commercial and cable—is marching ahead, being put on television in some cases by *newspapers!*

The *Philadelphia Inquirer*, one of the country's leading newspapers, and the *Chicago Tribune*, a major metropolitan daily, have moved directly into the news-on-television business.

The *Inquirer* presents the "Inquirer News Hour," "tomorrow's newspaper tonight," which is called a nontraditional television newscast that goes far beyond a simple reading of articles that appear in the next day's newspaper, according to *Inquirer* executives. The program is broadcast at 10:00 P.M. seven nights a week.

One of the most extensive projects by a newspaper company so far is the two-year-old, 24-hour cable news channel owned by the Tribune Company. Its programming is produced by the *Chicago Tribune*.

Then there are national cable news channels: Headline News and Cable News Network (CNN), which debuted a decade and a half ago on June 1, 1980.

Do a little checking. You'll find that television and cable television news programs, along with all-news cable networks, are springing up like wildflowers. By the time you read this, there may be one or more cable news channels in your area.

Choice of Medium

Should you even include television in your publicity release schedule? And what about radio and cable news? Which would be more effective? Television reaches larger audiences than do cable, newspapers, or radio. Yet, radios are everywhere—in kitchens, bedrooms, and cars, and wherever kids are.

Television is not yet basic equipment in every car, but the amount of time most people spend watching television outside their cars is mind-boggling; 69 percent count on TV as their principal news source. That statistic is expected to take an enormous leap when cable levels out and finds the number of channels and the kinds of programming that meet the public's needs and desires.

Television and radio can do some things that print media cannot: They can put you right on the scene of a fire, at your favorite team's football game, or at the strafing of civilians by opposing factions in the Middle East.

On the other hand, the listener or viewer (at least a viewer with a regular set) cannot hear competing programs simultaneously, nor can he or she go back and review a program for better understanding or for study, unless it has been taped. And the viewer or listener can't clip an item and tuck it into wallet or tape it to the refrigerator door for reference, something that is often done with newspaper stories—and that gives extended publicity if the article is about your organization.

Among the three kinds of television—commercial, public, and cable—cable television pinpoints audience interest to the greatest degree: there are all sports, all music, all news (even all business news), and all weather channels. There's programming for Christians, for science fiction buffs, and for movie junkies. The term "narrowcasting" was born when cable television indicated its ability to target very narrowly defined, specific-interest groups. It's important that you do a consumer check, just as you would before placing advertising, to pinpoint precisely where your news should be circulated in order to reach the greatest numbers of your desired audience.

Although both types of television news require substantially the same production techniques, the kinds and amounts of news they look for may be very different. A station that presents its news within a half-hour or a one-hour format is able to use far fewer stories than one with a 24-hour-a-day pattern. And a cable channel that enlists viewers from, say, only the medical field may be able to use only *limited amounts* of news, but it probably is always hungry for the kinds of news that pertain to their special viewers. If well constructed, your news releases to such a medical channel will probably be used consistently if, for instance, there is solid information for and about pharmacists, doctors, nurses, and health care providers; about pharmaceutical products, medicines, or their preparation and uses; new treatments and breakthroughs, and other such topics.

Different Formats for Distributing Broadcast News

There are two forms in which news releases can be circulated to television and radio stations: (1) VNRs and RNRs, and (2) long-standing hard-copy press releases. Video News Releases and Radio News Releases require considerably more expertise and a greater knowledge of news gathering for use on television and radio, and they are substantially more expensive to produce. VNRs, RNRs, and so-called electronic press kits are the subjects of Chapter 16.

This chapter is devoted strictly to producing traditional news releases, constructed to fit the unique requirements of broadcast news departments.

News Versus Advertising

Like newspapers, most radio and television stations accept both news and advertising. Some cable stations, like public television, accept no advertising. Advertising time on commercial television, radio, and those cable stations that accept advertising *can* be purchased, just as paid advertising can be placed alongside news in newspapers.

Aside from elements of shock value called for by some news operations, a number of the same basic requirements apply as to the acceptability and value of straight and feature news in both print media and broadcast media. The principal differences are that television/cable news must be visual, and it is abbreviated because of time restrictions. In pointing up the degree to which TV news is abbreviated, no less a news figure than Walter Cronkite has repeatedly called TV news a "headline service." Print news has space to give details.

There's another difference, according to Charlie Gibson, former newsman and now co-host of "Good Morning America" on ABC TV. He says, "Newspaper reporters always ask who, what, where, when, and why. TV journalists ask, 'How does it feel?' " Television appreciates and looks for the human-interest angle.

Broadcast-News Operations

The methods of operation for television, cable, and radio news are considerably different from those of print media, and many operational methods among television, cable, and radio are different from each other. Some elements, however, are the same or similar for all three.

Formula for Electronic News

Your news items should follow the requirements for every good print news story: Give briefly and concisely the who, what, when, where, and why of your news. Leading off with "how it feels," as suggested by Charlie Gibson, could be the element that attracts editors' attention and gets the story on the air.

Unlike print news, however, electronic news allows no time to follow up those 5 Ws with fleshed-out details. Every word counts because there is such a premium on time, so every word that does not contribute to better understanding of the message must be eliminated.

Broadcast Editors' Titles and Functions

Broadcasting's counterpart to the newspaper's city editor is the assignment editor, who dispatches crews and field reporters.

The news director is the highest authority in the newsroom. Generally speaking, news directors are considered management and only in smaller markets do they roll up their sleeves and produce, anchor, act as assignment editors and/or do the editing. The line producer is the person who puts the newscast together.

If you think of the news director as the captain, the executive producer is basically his first officer. There's an executive producer for each of the day's newscasts—for the morning, the five o'clock, the six o'clock, and the ten or eleven o'clock shows.

In TV news you can count on chaos. If for instance there's a change in your news, it's important that you cover all your bases when you let the news department know about it. It's essential that you alert *everybody* who has any involvement in your news story. It's not unusual for a news director or executive producer to be given information that never gets relayed to the reporter working on the story.

If you're soliciting news, the person most interested in using your news via your VNR is the reporter who specializes in your turf. The second most likely person to be interested is a feature reporter who is always looking for any kind of story.

Otherwise, general assignment reporters are excellent contacts because they usually have a voracious appetite for stories. The percentage of general assignment reporters increases as markets get smaller, because in smaller markets there's little budget for specialty reporters.

As is true in any news operation—print or electronic—these are busy people. Before trying to sell the merit of your organization's news, listen to the station to find out its system. Make your call well away from the station's deadline (or deadlines, since some stations are on constant news cycles).

Suitable News

What are you going to give to the radio, cable, or television news department? Your story must be something that's happening soon, that deals with an interesting issue, has a strong visual ingredient, and, if possible, also has a strong human-interest ingredient.

Examples of suitable news might be your organization's march for abused children, a company-sponsored debate between teenagers and senior citizens or kids and parents, or your organization's unique method used to overcome a problem faced by many businesses. Don't bother sending the announcement of someone's appointment as CEO or CFO, or of yesterday's board meeting—unless you can provide something visually interesting, such as an on-camera interview, or something of real news value that came out of that meeting. And, if it did, yesterday's news should have been reported by you *yesterday!*

Differences Between Radio and Television News

Radio News

Changes in radio, to a great degree, have set the agenda for what's happening in television. Radio is a $9 billion industry with more than 10,000 stations, most of which are niche focused. From the standpoint of having your publicity message heard, keep in mind that 97 percent of Americans listen to radio every week. And it's a very personal medium, where you can listen in your shower, in the car, on a jog.

Radio news operations in many ways are unlike those of television. But the less understood differences are those among radio stations' news operations; they vary considerably. Some stations have all-news operations with large staffs; others may be strictly "rip-and-read" operations, with disc jockeys or station announcers who read wire service bulletins at specific times.

Like newspapers, radio stations get the bulk of their material from news services. All-news radio stations hire reporters and have fully staffed newsrooms to cover local and area news, whereas almost all rip-and-read systems rely only on wire feeds.

In many cases, instead of wire service news on paper, the news coming to radio stations is prerecorded by a news company that sells its services to the station, where it is played rather than read. There is so much variety among radio stations in the sources from which they receive their news that their methods must be checked to ensure greater acceptance of your publicity releases.

Most news received from wire services by broadcast stations has been especially written in a conversational style "for the ear"; it is then transmitted over a circuit different from that provided to print media.

An audiotape to accompany and augment your hard-copy news release, that consists of a short, interesting interview or two with persons pertinent to the news subject contained in the release, or comments by celebrities or local people, can often mean the difference between your news being carried or being relegated to a wastebasket.

You must know whether you should supply copy—with or without audiotapes—

directly to the station or to the services that furnish the station's news. A telephone call to the station should give you that information.

Television News

Television news is the glamorous branch of the news business. Dan Rather, Connie Chung, Peter Jennings, and Tom Brokaw are no less celebrities than the biggest motion picture and rock stars. And who doesn't know who Walter Cronkite is, even after all his years away from the news-anchor desk? Even news anchors in relatively small markets are considered stars and are invited to host various business functions, lend their names to sports tournaments, or head charity drives. You can expect that cable also will "grow" its list of news celebrities.

For some people, television news is the main source of information. Television can do something that newspapers cannot: show action. Always remember that television news editors think in terms of *visual* impact; therefore stories are selected for that reason.

Television News Time

Anytime you visit a television news room you will probably get a foot-high stack of news releases handed to you with a comment such as, "Don't these PR people know this is *television?*" There's probably nothing that disgusts a TV newsperson more than when he or she receives news releases presented in the manner in which possibly 90 to 95 percent arrive. Because this situation is so prevalent, you can really get your organization, yourself, and the news you submit noticed, remembered—and used—if you closely follow the "rules of the game."

This chapter addresses these objectives.

Advice from a TV Newsman

Maury Green was for many years a newsman for a CBS-owned television station in Los Angeles. Green offered advice about placement of news with television news departments in his book *Television News—Anatomy and Process.* His counsel is directed to professional public relations representatives, but it holds up well for anyone representing a commercial enterprise.

> In general, PR [representatives] do not "score" as well with television as with newspapers, for two reasons: (1) because of its time limitations television cannot cover as many stories as the newspaper, and many PR releases are therefore rejected as too trivial or too limited in interest, and (2) many PR releases are so promotional in nature that to incorporate them into a news show would constitute a "plug" [free advertising] for the PR client.

However, Green also concedes that public relations representatives "of business firms, governmental offices and agencies, political parties and candidates, foundations, civic and community organizations, and numerous other groups provide a large amount of news which appears on television in one form or another."

In other words, if the news is big, involves big names and big issues, and has broad interest value, television news departments are interested in your release. There is little time or place, though, for the average small organization's news dispatch unless its content would have major impact on *local* people or issues or will deeply touch the emotions of viewers.

Television Stations and Free Tapes

Maury Green stresses that achieving television publicity is difficult. There is, however, a means that may be productive: free videotapes. (A free videotape is far less expensive in terms of time and production costs than a VNR.)

Can you supply 30 seconds up to three minutes on tape of a noteworthy portion of a happening and perhaps a taped interview with someone pertinent to or a part of the news or happening? From your hard-copy press release, along with your videotape, the station's news department can put together a story complete with visuals, rather than merely a "talking head" recitation of some information by the news anchor or a reporter.

If a television news department uses video that accompanies your news release, it undoubtedly will pass it off as its own. Therefore, *it must be broadcast-quality video.* Most video is shot on BetaCam, which is the stuff you play movies on at home. It may look a lot like VHS, but it is not the same.

Before you attempt to shoot video to accompany a news release, read Chapter 16 on producing VNRs. The information will help you shoot a professional-looking tape and greatly improve the likelihood that it will be used.

If television news has a high priority in your publicity plan, and after reading about VNRs (Chapter 16) you decide you cannot go the VNR route, be aware that supplying a free videotape—called a handout—can provide excellent publicity returns, particularly from cable channels and smaller, independent television stations.

These stations are especially interested in such visuals because they provide on-screen action to go along with the story that the stations have neither staff nor funds to cover. If you do supply tape, be sure it is something that is visually animated, and in a horizontal format.

(Just as in still photos, take care to have life and action in your tape or slide; someone making an announcement with a lineup of standing executives or with the chairman passing a gavel will never qualify.)

Copy Rules for Both Television and Radio

The following rules are exclusive to radio and television copy.

Conversational Tone

If you are the writer of your radio or telvision copy, remember that you are not writing it to be read in a book, a magazine, or a newspaper. You are writing words to be spoken by an announcer and to be listened to by individuals.

Use everyday, conversational language, for both radio and television. Maury Green advises that the language must be casually conversational, even to the point of sounding "slangy." "It is spoken language, not literary language," he says, so write the way you speak.

Most commercial television news departments prefer to rewrite your news release into this conversational style. But if you're sending releases to cable channels, you undoubtedly will receive a better response if you do the writing for them. Therefore, your task is to put everyday spoken words down on paper so that the announcer will sound as though he or she is talking, not reading. Use the vocabulary and expressions of ordinary speech, not of written language. There's a big difference. For example:

- If you normally use the contraction *don't* when you speak, use it when you write.
- Use the contraction *let's* instead of the words *let us*.

Pronunciation Clarification

Newscasters should never have to worry about how to pronounce names. The correct pronunciation should be given right in the news copy.

If your organization's name, a person's name, or any word within the copy has an unusual pronunciation, spell it out, as in the following examples:

The Yo toon HAY man (Jotunheimen) Center that is on An goo LEEM (Angouleme) Street

If your organization is best known by its acronym, spoken as a word, write the acronym in capital letters. If the letters are spoken separately, type them separated by hyphens (e.g., U-S-A, G-E, or P-A-S-I). Hyphens (or dashes) are used to instantly alert the newsperson that it is not a word, but an abbreviation in which each letter is to be spoken individually.

News Ethics and Home Video Cameras

Some of the most dramatic moments on television these days are coming from amateurs with camcorders, or home video cameras. These amateur shooters are, on occasion, producing spectacular footage, such as parts of the 1994 O. J. Simpson freeway "chase," the California earthquakes, and the torrentials rains that caused homes to slide onto Pacific Coast Highway. This brings into question new ethics for news reporting and broadcasting.

It is believed by some observers that television's acceptance of such footage—and now invitations to amateurs to become extensions of news staffs—is also inviting opportunities for manipulation, distortion, camera trickery, and lies.

Fakery has already reared its ugly head. NBC and ABC believed they were showing audiences the first footage of Russia's nuclear disaster at Chernobyl. It turned out to be misrepresented amateur footage of a fire in an Italian cement plant. The networks were deceived, and their viewers were tricked. Matt York, editor and publisher of *Videomaker*, a magazine for home camera enthusiasts, expressed his concern. "The line between amateurs and professionals is becoming blurred, and soon it may be erased." Everett Dennis, executive director of the

Gannett Center for Media Studies at Columbia University, said he believed that when a news organization turns over its responsibility to another party—particularly to untrained newspersons—it is forfeiting its professional control to ensure objectivity in the ensuing report.

Newspapers do not permit self-serving representatives to cover events. Yet more and more television news services are accepting footage without asking who made it or what point of view is being championed. Activists representing narrow, specific viewpoints, even religious congregations, have geared up to present biased news footage showing only one point of view.

There is little question in many observers' minds that publicity and public relations professionals are already using this means for promoting their clients. The blurring of advertising messages as news undoubtedly will not be allowed because of the infringement upon revenues. But this obscuring of impartiality in news reporting can mean viewers will lose what has been the first tenet of journalism—unbiased, objective reports.

This development bears continuous watching. It has opened new avenues through which organization publicity now travels. But the public's desire for reliable news reports may force reconsideration of what will be accepted from amateurs.

16

What You Should Know About Video and Radio News Releases

How to prepare and distribute VNRs and RNRs—the electronic-age way to get broadcast publicity

It's Not Buck Rogers

It's not Buck Rogers—Buck never dreamed this far into the future. They could be Buck's great grandchildren, though!

Actually, VNRs and RNRs aren't all that new. Barry Kaufman, an Emmy Award-winning television reporter, says the NBC technicians' strike in 1987 was the turning point in *acceptance* of VNRs by broadcast media. Before the strike and the subsequent urgent need for air-quality video, VNRs were viewed as thinly veiled attempts at free product advertising. Larry Pintak, a former CBS correspondent who now makes VNRs at Pintak Communications International, is quoted in *TV Guide* about the reason for the escalation: "The news industry has been so gutted over the last few years that they don't have a choice [but to use VNRs]."

Professional publicists have begun to also recognize the power of RNRs as a highly productive substitute for traditional hard-copy radio press releases. RNRs provide interview sound bites in place of printed quotes, they greatly increase chances of a release being used, and they are used in much the same manner as VNRs. In addition to using them in newscasts, however, radio stations often use portions of audio release material in public service announcements and as lead-ins to talk shows.

Publicists in the entertainment business and in a few areas of the country sometimes speak of electronic press kits—but they're usually referring to VNRs. Some of the information normally included in a press kit, such as interviews, quotes sheets, and product photos are often included in VNRs or as part of RNRs. But broadcast time is so limited there's seldom need to provide great amounts of the extra information routinely contained in press kits.

Simultaneously with the cutback in TV personnel and dollars, more and more news shows are being added. Why? Because they are usually less expensive—and more profitable—than entertainment shows.

The bottom line is that fewer and fewer people must produce the same amount of, or even more, news "minutes."

This voracious appetite for video news also continues to grow because of the surge of cable and its news operations, ranging from CNN and CNBC to regional cable news networks such as the Orange County Cable Network in Los Angeles and News 12 Long Island in New York. Even the Entertainment Channel and MTV offer daily newscasts. Add to these a large number of television news syndications, ranging from "Beyond 2000" on the Discovery Channel to "Hard Copy." All are striving to fill added airtime created by the cable and independent television station boom.

Further need is shown by the fact that VNRs are now aired regularly on private, corporate, and industry networks, including IBM, DEC, and the Automotive Satellite Television Network.

Fast Forward to the Present

Medialink and Dow Jones & Co., Inc. have joined to feed corporate-sponsored videos into desktop computers connected to the Dow Jones Investor Network (DJIN). The "Desktop Business Broadcast" allows companies to transmit video about their operations directly onto the network. (Dow Jones publishes *The Wall Street Journal* and *Barron's*; Medialink distributes live and taped publicity videos.)

DJIN is a video broadcast news service for professional investors from Dow Jones MultiMedia Division. Video programs are delivered via satellite directly to PCs. DJIN is a subscription-based service with license fees that start at $750 a month.

The degree to which need for VNRs shows up is in the numbers of *new* places where they can be used. Hardly a week goes by without announcement of a new network. For example, the Interactive Distance Training Network (IDTN) offers a satellite technology that allows a corporation to train its people simultaneously, regardless of whether they're in a dozen different locations across the country.

Chrysler Corporation, through Westcott Communications, allows dealers to receive training, instruction, and current news and information on the Automotive Satellite Television Network. (Westcott creates and produces training and educational information programming, which it broadcasts through private satellite television networks.)

A survey by Medialink puts VNR newsroom usage at 100 percent. Not that 100 percent of all VNRs are used, but 100 percent of all stations, at one time or another, use VNRs.

This increased hunger for broadcast news in a video format means that even smaller businesses can expect a high percentage of acceptance and use of their publicity—*if* the material submitted is of professional quality.

A Professional to Guide You

Forget what you may have heard from E. F. Hutton! When VNR-1's Jack Trammell speaks, publicity pros listen.

Jack Trammell, who for years was a television news reporter and producer for an NBC affiliate and is now VNR-1's executive producer, is here to help you understand what VNRs are, what their content must be, how they are produced, the best ways to distribute them, and where to check on how, when, and where they are used.

A substantial portion of the information provided in this chapter comes from Trammell and VNR-1, a Dallas-based company with offices and production facilities in Los Angeles, New York, Chicago, Washington, D.C., Tampa, and London.

Understanding Is the Key

A double-truck ad for *Fortune* magazine asks, "Can you manage technology if you don't understand it?" A Hertz commercial provides the answer: "Well, not exactly!"

Understanding VNRs is essential if you think there's a possibility you may use them. But it's sort of like art—you can completely understand and appreciate it, but you can't produce a suitable piece of art because you don't have the talent, training, and technical knowledge.

As you continue through this chapter you'll learn whether or not you have the "three Ts"—talent, training, and technicality—or whether you should have the work done by professionals. Even if you contract for the work, it is essential that you *understand* the workings so you can recognize what should be done and when it has been done effectively. With understanding, you'll also be able to decide whether you can or should *afford* VNRs to achieve your company's or nonprofit's goals.

Jack Trammell says the biggest mistake most people make, even those who acknowledge they shouldn't attempt the do-it-yourself process, is that they hire people who also don't know what they're doing. This is an important forewarning. Don't confuse commercial production houses and industrial production houses with video news producers. As their name implies, commercial production houses are best at producing commercials. VNRs produced by them tend to look like commercials—which amounts to applying a red flag on the tape cassette you distribute, arousing resentments among newspeople who insist that news and advertising must remain independent of each other. Industrial production houses rarely, if ever, have trained newspeople or people who know how to produce news for television, so quality tends to be inadequate.

Update Your Thinking

When Henry Ford first began selling cars, he was asked, "What's it like trying to sell cars?" He said the problem is, it's like trying *not* to sell a horse. Ford explained, "Because people still think horses, the first thing you have to tell them is to forget about horses, we're talking about cars."

Trammell uses the story to explain that when he talks about VNRs to prospective clients, he has to tell them, "Forget about television being newspapers with pictures." Television news stories require a specific kind of attention—attention to individual style, approach, and substance.

So, Explain It, Please

It sounds simple when Jack Trammell explains it. "A VNR is any self-generated news on video tape, whether it's sent by satellite or distributed by mail, courier or overnight delivery."

But when you get into the details, it's not quite so simple. A VNR includes a "package" and/or "B-roll." It's not just the "package"—a complete, 1-minute, 20-second air-ready news report—that so many people think of as a video news release. (Later in this chapter you'll see an example of a purely fictious VNR with its "package" script.)

A VNR can be all or some of the following:

- An editor's note at the beginning, which explains—on-screen in a written format—the news story that follows.
- A tracked package—a news story that can run anywhere from 1 minute to 2^1/$_2$ minutes, but is ideally about 1 minute, 20 seconds long—with a reporter's voice-over telling the story.

  This segment also includes what TV newspeople call a "suggested anchor lead-in" that submits written copy on-screen that a station's news anchor could give to introduce the video with audio.

  And it often ends with an on-screen written suggested anchor tag, such as, "If you wish more information, call . . . "
- A "natural sound" package with the same video as used in the tracked package, but with only the natural sounds—no reporter's voice-over, just the background sounds of, say, factory equipment working or children playing. Voice audio is maintained in the interview portion of the untracked package, but the rest—with only background sounds—is designed so that a station can substitute its own reporters' voices reading the copy or giving the stations' comments. This gives each station's story the look of a purely *local* story reported by a station's own reporter, and is why you should *never* have the person appear on camera who voices the story.
- Then you have B-roll. "B-roll?" That expression is a film term left over from the late 1950s when film (instead of videotape) was used on television and a newscast had station access often to only two film playback machines. One was called "A" and the other was tabbed "B." The "A" machine seemed always to play the interview with the fire chief, and the film projector called "B" played footage of the fire. As the years passed and the use of film was eliminated, the B-*roll* remained as an accepted newsroom term meaning footage—not interviews—just footage of the fire or whatever.

  B-roll footage may show shots of a new product coming off the assembly line. And it may have some "archival shots" that show the business in its early days.

  Sometimes graphics are also included; for example, animation of a new kind of drug, showing how it affects the brain, or graphics such as a map of the United States showing where an infestation of fire ants is most intensive.

  And why do television newspeople like B-roll videos so much?

Marketing News says that "with B-roll, producers aren't locked into any-thing and can use the [videotape] however they please."

- Additional interviews follow the B-roll footage—most often those not included in the tracked package—with company executives and with product or service "users," or with anyone affected by or pertinent to the news being announced.

    Be sure to properly identify on the slate the names and titles of each person interviewed. (A "slate" is on-screen information. The editor's note at the very beginning of a VNR is really just a series of slates. For example, if there is an interview with John Doe, the president of the Acme Com-pany, sometimes the station's reporter or anchor must ask a question so that what Mr. Doe says makes sense. He may have said, "Well, we make a lot of things here . . . "

    So the question written out on-screen tells the reporter or anchor to ask, "What do you make here?" Then the answer makes sense.

- Contact data is always given at the very end of the VNR. This is the information that tells the newsroom whom to contact—with the name and phone and fax numbers of the PR contact person—if more informa-tion about the story is desired.

Five Requirements for a VNR

Before you ever consider preparing a VNR for a specific news release, ask yourself the following five questions:

1. Is it topical—of interest to a large number of viewers?
2. Is it timely?
3. Is it local?
4. Does it have a human element?
5. Is it visually interesting/animated?

The first four elements apply to all news media—without them you don't have a news item—although topicality has a much higher rating for television than for print media. The fifth is basic to television—without it you don't have a prayer that the release will ever appear.

Trammell puts that last requirement into perspective with the following ex-ample.

Let's say you're going to open a small manufacturing plant in Dayton, Ohio, to be a "sister" to your operation in Brooklyn, New York. And it's going to employ 50 people to make electronic parts. Now, what does the average publicity plan consist of? Inviting television to come out to shoot two fat, bald men dig a pail of dirt with a gold shovel, or stand behind a podium and talk. If television reporters and cameras show up at all, it's because they think the employment issue is impor-tant, and therefore they stretch their coverage to shoot maybe five seconds if they shoot at all. Dirt diggings, balloon launches, and marathons are poor, trite, burned out concepts, says Trammell.

What company representatives should do is to bring videotapes of what the plant in Brooklyn looks like and of its manufacturing operations. If nothing else, they should bring architectural renderings, even blueprints, of the new plant-to-be.

For even better coverage, let's say the Dayton operation has already hired a handful of people, who are in the process of setting up the new company. In that case, the company can and should arrange interviews with the new hires at their homes. Now the station has a local story. And think of the impact when, for instance, one of those interviewed—a mechanical engineer—has been unemployed for two years and now he has a job. The result is akin to an unsolicited testimonial on behalf of the company: "It's great to be working again, and I can only thank the XYZ company for hiring me. This is a wonderful thing that's happened in our town, and I can't wait to get back to work and . . . "

The station's reaction? Wow! This is human drama, it's employment, economy, money, dirt flying, building new technology. It's all there. But instead, what do they get? Two guys standing behind a podium or shoveling dirt. Later a company exec asks the station, "How come our event didn't get coverage?" The station isn't likely to give the real reason—because the real reason is that the company's actions look stupid, trite, flat, and worn out.

One Time Dirt Digging Worked

Sometimes a little ingenuity—and a lot of work—can turn the most ordinary, trite, burned-out concept into a preopening publicity windfall. It happened when Sydne Purvis, the professional public relations manager for Fiesta Texas, San Antonio, decided to "create a dirt round-up."

Instead of a dirt-shoveling ground breaking, Purvis had officials and entertainers go to the county seat of each of the state's 254 counties. In each county, according to *Amusement Business* magazine, they put on a media event that included scooping up a shovelful of dirt. That dirt became a part of the landscape at Fiesta Texas.

"The success was overwhelming," Purvis says. "The media [were] informed personally by phone and we provided a great, different type of photo opportunity"—a great, different spin on one of the oldest, most hackneyed photo ops in publicity history.

More Trammell Tips

Trammell adds another bit of important information regarding the use of a podium—or anything that separates speakers from their audience. He calls it "speaker armor," and says it's just an attempt to keep those wearing it from taking hits from their audience, and that newspeople recognize it for what it is and are annoyed by the negative "body language."

There are other things to be aware of—and *eliminate*—if you are expecting or wanting TV news coverage:

- Do not set up a group of people in front of a big, wide window—the light will blind the cameras and block out the people or show them as silhouettes.
- Do not put a glossy logo, that reflects bars of light from flashes or camera lighting, behind the people being interviewed.

- Be sure microphones are of professional quality, and that they are plugged into top-quality speakers.
- Don't wonder why your event isn't covered if you hold it 30 miles from where the action is and at a time when a station's staff have no chance of attending and getting back in time to use the material. Check out convenience factors in terms of the people you want to attend.

There's More to It Than Just Planning and Shooting

There are several components in the development of a VNR from concept to "playout." Basically, these are as follows:

- Planning, which includes preparing an outline, writing a preliminary script, and writing the final script.
- Production, which is shooting and assembly.
- Notification, which may be done by phone, wire, or fax.
- "Marketing" (for want of a better name), which requires phone calls to pitch the story to specific stations in specific markets.
- Distribution, which may be by ground delivery or by satellite. If distribution is by satellite—the most common practice for dissemination in large geographic areas—personal telephone calls are made immediately before launching to alert stations that "here it comes."
- Monitoring and verification, which most recently is done by special companies set up to "read" hidden coded symbols on VNRs to verify exactly where the tape played, how much of it played, the number of seconds that were used, plus the station's call letters and affiliation, as well as demographic and map analysis of each VNR airing.

Your Mission

As your organization's publicity representative, your mission is to get the *attention of newsrooms by convincing news management that your story affects people*—their viewers—on a local basis for local stations and on a national basis for the networks.

What to Give Television News Departments

When you plan a VNR, accept the fact that the story—as you prepare it—may not be used. The trick is to be sure your VNR includes something a station can readily, and rapidly, adapt for its own local area. It must be something that has a story that is timely, and has a sense of topicality that under normal circumstances the station's personnel wouldn't have time to create.

In other words, be aware that they may not have time to use your entire VNR, or they may not wish to use it as you've prepared it. But their abbreviation and adaptation of your taped video and/or sound with their own on-camera shots or announcer's voice is far better than having the tape end up in the news director's "round file." Whatever is used will still be publicity for your organization. So, give the news editors maximum flexibility by giving them a selection of shots in the footage and material they can modify with maximum ease, such as interviews, graphics and charts, animation, or whatever you send.

Interview Tips

Try always to include interviews in a VNR. Interviews are people, and people are human interest. But when you shoot an interview, shoot cutaways so that stations have room to maneuver. And try to give them a selection so they have different types of people and different kinds of action to choose from.

There are business geniuses who are uncomfortable or may even become tongue-tied when being interviewed live for television or radio. The solution here is to *pretape* the interview. This strategy allows you to put the individual with people he or she is comfortable with, and you then can even ask truly *tough* questions. The person can respond without feeling severe pressure, or, if the remarks do not come off sounding as desired, the interview can be redone.

News Is a Story

A video news release is basically a story. News on television is telling—and show-ing—stories.

Television newspeople will tell you that there is an immense difference be-tween press releases for television and for newspapers. They'll also tell you that news is not a list of facts, it's not a speech, and it's not a sermon. But what is news today has changed from what it was in past years.

Trammell explains that a TV story about a city council meeting 10 years ago would have shown the announcement that it had approved plans for a parking lot downtown. Then there would have been the "obligatory shouting back and forth between a citizen and a city councilman," plus a politically correct statement about how the parking lot will benefit low-income minorities, ending with the reporter standing on the city hall steps saying, "This is Action News . . . "

All that has changed at more progressive news departments. Now, Trammell points out, a wide-angle view shows a little house on one section of the proposed parking lot. When the reporter knocks on the door, a little old lady answers, who's lived there all of her life, who lost her husband two years ago from cancer, and is now being kicked out by a ruthless, evil city that doesn't care or even know that she's there. Now the story is edited to start with the reporter telling listeners that "72-year-old Ethel Winters, who's lived here all her life, will soon be on the street." That makes the announcement a story—a human story!

A secret: start your video with a real person and end it with a real person. Sometimes the pattern is bad news-good news, and sometimes it's good news-bad news. In either case, there's a human beginning and end to the story. Television newspeople call this "bookending." This technique is considered by many profes-sionals to be the best way, but networks seldom use it, only local stations do. There's a reason—there is much higher interest among local viewers when a local person appears in a news clip than for other viewers across the country.

Whatever your news, be sure you recognize the *story* in it.

A television news editor tells an unlikely tale about sending a photographer out to shoot a circus. The reporter came back early. When asked why, he said, "I didn't shoot a single frame the entire time I was there." "Why?" "Well, because the circus burned down right in front of my eyes." It's not likely that you'll have that kind of trouble recognizing your organization's news, but think visually and think "people" the entire time you're planning or preparing it for broadcast.

The "Ultimate" VNR

According to Trammell, the ultimate VNR is a news story that reflects positively on the client as it appears seamlessly in a newscast. It is such a smooth part of the newscast that viewers cannot distinguish between the VNR and the news that came directly from the station's newsroom. "That's the ultimate video news release," he says. "The ultimate!"

If We Build It, Will You Come?

There's one more process that can be done before expending so much time, effort, and money to assemble a VNR. Advance research consists of calling a television station and explaining the story you plan to put together, and asking, "Would you be interested?"

Trammell says that it's difficult to gauge in advance what TV newspeople will want, but it's fairly safe to expect they will be interested in anything that deals with health, money, or what "in the old days" was called Tips, Tots, Pets, or Vets (or sex, children, animals, or flags).

Advance phone calls can provide a small amount of assurance that your ultimate effort won't be in vain, particularly if you are dealing with local or regional television stations.

Recycling Ad Footage

If you have plans for television advertising, you may also want to do what some of the big boys sometimes do—reuse footage from a TV commercial in a VNR.

Pepsi took shots from a commercial featuring basketball pro Shaquille O'Neal for a VNR that had more than 150 airplays in newscasts at 95 stations, according to data from MediaLink. The VNRs offered behind-the-scenes footage of the making of the Pepsi commercial.

McDonald's turned its TV commercials with basketball stars Michael Jordan and Larry Bird into a VNR package that aired on 73 news shows.

Note that in each case, newsworthy people were the subject of the VNRs. If your television commercials don't include such newsmakers, come up with something else that is newsworthy. Perhaps you can use something interesting or humorous that happened during the shoot, or something that provides worthwhile guidelines for other businesses. That can only be done if you plan for it *before*, or at least recognize its potential *during*, the shooting of the commercial.

Patrick Pharris, partner at Perri Pharis Productions, in an article in *O'Dwyer's PR Services Report*, explains: "After incurring the expenses of advertising production and placement, advertisers are beginning to seek alternative ways to more fully capitalize on these costly investments."

VNR Production Staff, Crew, and Credentials

Preparation of VNRs requires a knowledge of news and its production—specifically, knowledge of how broadcast news is produced and of the people who produce it. The following is a list of these TV newspeople.

- **VNR Newswriter.** Newswriters write the actual story in coordination with the organization and the VNR's producer. Most VNRs are rewritten after shooting is completed in order to accommodate location changes and to "write around" selected sections of completed interviews. It is important that the writer is a trained *news writer*. Freelancers are available for hire.

Trammell cautions that television news styles differ. For daytime newscasts the news is written as if it were for radio because people, particularly in the morning, are listening, not watching. The style for the 6:00 P.M. and 11:00 P.M. news recognizes that people are sitting in their recliners, *watching and listening*.

- **VNR Producer.** A producer is in charge of all aspects of production, ranging from directing interviews to overseeing the video crew. The producer answers to the organization for which he or she is constructing the VNR, and all crew members answer to the producer. The producer is your contact about any phase of production.

- **VNR Photographer and Crew.** Video photographers (don't call them cameramen!—cameramen operate studio cameras) are the eyes and soul of the VNR. Close rapport between the producer and photographer can turn an ordinary report into an exciting, human story. Photographers occasionally have assistants (more common where unions operate) who handle audio and tapes as well as help in carrying and setting up gear.

- **VNR Makeup.** A makeup person is optional but is occasionally provided in consideration of the comfort of a nervous spokesperson who indicates his or her anxiety about "looking bad" on television.

- **VNR Actors.** This is a no-no. Actors work well in commercial spots, but "real people" are an integral part of news stories. Besides, newspeople can spot an actor immediately and just as quickly will tab the release a concocted story not fit for airtime.

- **VNR Editor.** This is the person who puts it all together, who assembles the interviews, audio, key information, and pictures into a single, cohesive, and logical VNR. VNR editing does not permit such techniques as dissolves and "peels," often seen in commercials but which instantly alert television newspeople that this is a commercially produced product. An editor's job is to be sure the VNR gets its message across clearly.

VNR Production Equipment

VNR production gear varies widely, but should include the basics of a lightly armed news unit. It is the producer's responsibility to make sure that the photographer has the equipment needed for the project. This equipment includes:

- **Camera.** Up-to-date news crews shoot with BetaCam or BetaCam SP. BetaCam cameras are preferred because they are always dependable. There are some other formats that are now being used in small markets, but their quality is questionable and their use is impractical for mass distribution. A quality tripod is a must.

An adequate supply of BetaCam recording tapes must be available. (These BetaCam tapes can cost a total of $20 to $30 each later when you have them duped one-on-one for distribution to as many as 20 or 30 stations. If you plan on distributing to more than that number of stations, you should consider satelliting as a less expensive, less troublesome way of distributing the VNR. If your VNR is satellited, the receiving station records it on its own videotape. There is more about satellite transmission later in this chapter.)

- **Audio.** Most news photographers supply one hand-held microphone, a pair of lavaliere microphones (to clip to a lapel or dress collar), a boom microphone (for long-range sound shooting), and often a wireless microphone (for interviewing highly mobile subjects).
- **Lighting.** News crews generally carry a standard lighting kit containing three or four 1,000-watt stand-up lamps, plus "barndoors" and diffusion materials to help highlight dark areas or to softly light the hard creases in the forehead of your spokesperson.

What to Bring to the Shoot

From experience (and perhaps with a little tongue-in-cheek humor), Jack Trammell suggests that you as the company's rep come to a location—or field—shoot with the following equipment: legal pads, extra pens, tennis shoes, plenty of aspirin, stopwatch, portable telephone, and, most important, a microcassette recorder to co-record interviews for references back at the office.

A Suggested Efficient Shooting Outline

VNR-1 gives its clients the following information. The same information can serve your purposes.

- Consolidate as many interviews and location shoots at the same place on the same day as possible. Interviews look best when shot outside of an office setting. Most video crews operate on straight 8- to 10-hour days. Overtime for such crews is generally less expensive than hiring crews for a second day.
- From time to time, VNR-1 employs an interview technique known as the "CNN style" of remote interviewing. The subject moves to an office location with a speakerphone. Looking off-camera at a seated assistant, the subject answers the questions heard over the speakerphone as if the person doing the questioning is present. The only crew on-site is the photographer and the assistant. This is the least expensive remote interview method.
- Flight arrangements are far less expensive for interview subjects than for video crews. We recommend that whenever possible interview subjects be transported to the shooting site.

    Many organizations plan video shooting sequences in conjunction with preplanned conventions or conferences so that costs can be shared with other activities. Satellite media tours, however, can be conducted out of many cities in the United States, precluding the need for any travel at all.
- Because of video crew time and availability considerations, locations in major cities are more efficient than those in rural areas.

Television News Management

Who are the people you must convince? Jack Trammell explains the hierarchy in a TV newsroom and then tells us that "these are the people who eat unqualified, inexperienced publicity reps for lunch and pick their teeth with their bones in the evening."

Here's the lineup in most television news operations:

- **News Director.** Virtually every television station with a news operation has a news director (ND). The responsibilities of the ND become more and more rooted in day-to-day news operations, ranging from the largest to the smallest markets. In the smallest markets, he or she often is also the assignment editor, and even the anchor. In most midsize and large markets, the news director is not the person to be contacted by a publicity representative.
- **Executive Producer.** This is the person at most stations of any size who determines the day to day course of news coverage. It's the EP's job to determine whether more features or more hard news is needed and which stories should or should not be covered.
- An executive producer is an excellent contact, *but* usually difficult to reach by phone. Send a notice about your event by mail.
- **Line Producer.** This person is an excellent contact, because he or she is specifically responsible for one or more newscasts, depending on the size of the market. It is the job of the LP to make his or her newscast the most visual, timely, topical, and exciting possible.
- **Field Reporters.** The *best contacts* are field reporters, particularly if they specialize in the field that your news relates to—such as business, environment, or health. The number of **specialty reporters** at a station drops in direct proportion to the size of the market.

  The majority of reporters are **general assignment** reporters, and they are often hungrily looking for stories.
- **Assignment Editor.** This person is a cross between a field sergeant and an air traffic controller. Assignment editors (AEs) work terrible hours, are usually exhausted, and are the least-thanked group in the news department. They often respond by answering phones gruffly and otherwise making any publicity representative feel that the call is an imposition.

"My suggestion," advises Trammell, "to any public relations person trying to get through to a newsroom with a story idea is to locate the appropriate reporter first. If this fails, talk to the executive producer or the assignment editor. Don't bother the news director except in small markets."

Some Advice

Trammell gives some valuable advice that serves as a warning when contacting television newspeople: "Do not send letters addressed to unnamed assignment editors or reporters or 'To Whom It May Concern.' Bother to find out their names, then address the envelope *by hand* if there's time. Personalize all faxes, otherwise, faxed news releases are treated as junk mail in television news departments. Federal Express will no more get someone's attention in a newsroom than if you call on the phone and tell them you are calling long distance."

When to Call

It's a good idea, Trammell says, to call the newsroom only after their morning story meeting (usually between 9:00 and 9:30), and prior to 11:30 A.M.

There are two other call-time windows—in the afternoon from 1:00 to 2:00 (afternoon story meetings usually run from 2:00 to 2:30), and then from 2:30 to 4:00 P.M. (prior to the evening newscast crunches). If you're calling from another time zone, translate the times above to the recipient's time zone.

Step-by-Step Advance Notifications

"I recommend calling the reporter several days before the event and following up with a fax and a letter," says Trammell.

A copy of the letter should also go to the assignment editor with a note saying it is also being sent to a specific reporter.

Next step: Call the day before the event to ensure that the reporter has everything he or she needs to report the story.

Then call the assignment desk on the morning of the event. Contact the executive producer as well if he or she will take the call.

The trick in getting cooperation from the executive producer, an assignment editor, or a reporter is gentle persuasion and an ability to detect instantly any exhaustion, frustration, or anger in his or her voice. "It's very easy," warns Trammell, "to go too far in trying to encourage interest in your project." Always ask first, "Are you under a deadline?" This shows a respect for the person's time. If it is deadline time, tell the person that you will call later when things calm down a little—*then get off the phone quickly!*

Now, with Tongue Firmly in Cheek, Let's Script a VNR!

Just in case you're a little curious about what a standard package VNR script looks like, Jack Trammell put one together as an example.

It will take you but a moment to recognize that this script is pure fiction. However, it's written in broadcast style and shows how a for-profit company can cooperate in a joint publicity effort with a nonprofit that has a cause directly related to that particular company's product.

Trammell emphasizes that everyone reading this script should remember that there are about 10 right ways to write a good script and about 100 ways to write a bad one. Then he tells us that this example is what VNR-1 considers a standard package format (although it runs a little long in order to incorporate all the standard elements):

- It utilizes "bookending" of a human being involved in the story;
- It adds reinforcing interviews with a "third-party neutral authority";
- And, of course, it includes an interview with the for-profit client.

This sample is minus the "Editor's Notes" that usually precede a package, explaining the nature of the story in an abbreviated press release format.

A Snapshot of a VNR:

1. *Announcement:* "The following video news release is distributed by . . . (etc.)."
2. *Editor's Notes:* "National Hiccup Association Announces Cure" at a news conference.
3. *Suggested Anchor Lead-in:* "Good news for hiccup sufferers . . . "
4. *Tracked package:* "That is a sound Jeri Brown has . . . "
5. *Anchor Tag:* "If you would like more . . . "

The feed is then followed by B-roll and additional interviews and other information, not indicated in this script. (In scripts, "keys" are the words you see brought up on screen to identify people and places.)

`Zestland/Nat'l Hiccup Association Script`

SUGGESTED ANCHOR LEAD-IN

> "Good news for hiccup sufferers today. A treatment that can slow down Hiccupitis. There are some fourteen million Americans who are forced to live with this illness every day. Reporter Jack Trammell says it's a misunderstood health problem that has destroyed lives, but a new drug recently approved by the FDA is already making a difference."

(VTR PACKAGE FULL)

(Shot of Brown in laboratory setting, wearing smock and hiccuping)
(Natural sound open, closeup of Jeri Brown)

> "Hiccup"

(Trammell)

> "That's a sound 34-year-old Jeri Brown had heard all too often . . . eight years to be exact. Jeri suffered from Hiccupitis, an acute and sometimes deadly form of the common hiccups."

(Brown on camera)
(Key: Jeri Brown
      Hiccup Sufferer)

> "It started years ago as a kid when I drank a cola too fast. It never stopped."

(Interview with Darcy Jones, Spokesperson for the National Hiccup Association)
(Key: Darcy Jones
      National
      Hiccup Association)

- more -

Zestland/Nat'l Hiccup Assn. script - page 2

"Hiccups is a serious and debilitating illness that shatters people's lives. It affects young and old, black and white—and contrary to popular opinion, can be extremely difficult to overcome. The National Hiccup Association estimates that one out of every five Americans has had recurrent hiccup attacks, or RHA's, at one time in their lives. And for the first time, we have taken a major step forward in the war against hiccups."

(Brown in laboratory setting, wearing smock and hiccuping)
(Trammell)
(Key: National Hiccup
      Research Center
      Bethesda, Maryland)

"This was two months ago, at the National Hiccup Research Center, Jeri was averaging one hiccup every 10 seconds."

(Brown in labortory setting, taking medication)

"But a new medication called ZESTLAN has changed everything."

(Interview with Dr. William Blake, spokesperson for Acme Laboratories)
(key: Dr. William Blake
      Researcher
      Acme Laboratories)

"We discovered that hiccups is caused by a bacteria that is found in the skin around the "belly-button" area of the body. Zestlan suppresses that bacteria and relaxes the spontaneous abdominal reflexes that cause a person to hiccup uncontrollably."

(Microscopic footage of the bacteria)
(Trammell)
(Key: Courtesy Acme Laboratories)

"The bacteria are most commonly found lying close to the muscle tissue in the stomach. When they generate too much oxygen . . . you hiccup."

(Brown at home playing with her little girl in backyard)

"To Jeri Brown, what really counts is that she can now lead a normal life."

(Interview with Jeri Brown)

"I can breathe again. I can have fun with my children . . . and most important, I have my self-esteem back . . . see . . . no hiccups!"

- more -

```
(Brown at home playing with
her little girl in the backyard)
(Trammell)
```

> "Although there is still no cure for
> hiccups . . . doctors believe this new
> medication is a major step forward. I'm
> Jack Trammell reporting."

```
(end package)
```

```
SUGGESTED ANCHOR TAG:
(over graphic with 800 number)
```

> "If you would like more information
> regarding hiccups, you can call the
> National Hiccup Association at 1-800-
> HICCUPS."

Monitoring

In the early days of video news releases, there was little if any means of checking on whether a VNR was used. There were just a handful of services that employed people to watch TV.

Now there is computer technology that does the watching 24 hours every day and is 100 percent accurate. As Jack Trammell points out, people used to do the monitoring but people go for snacks or their brains may tune out, and they definitely cannot calculate precisely the number of seconds a specific video plays. Computers don't snack, they don't fall asleep, and they *can* calculate exact measurements and register specific play times.

It's all done with what is called electronic encoding, a sort of electronic blip placed on the videotape that stays there through replaying, dubbing, reediting, or any other change. You might call it a barcode placed on the VNR tape, much like those on food items at the grocery store. In the case of electronic encoding, the "barcode" is invisible on TV screens, but it triggers computers that monitor each television station.

When a station pulls down a tape, the barcode is there; even if the tape is edited, dubbed, or rebroadcast, the barcode is still there. Computers can catch anything that is given more than six seconds of play.

Computers are able to report time, date, place, audience, and just about whatever other information you wish. For example, the report might say that your tape aired on KABC-Los Angeles, an ABC affiliate, at 6:08 on the evening of September 28, and played to 243,000 viewers. Furthermore, such a report by Neilsen or MediaLink can also give you a demographic breakout of the age, gender, and ethnicity of the audience that watched the tape.

Nielsen currently monitors every television station in the top 200 U.S. markets, with a system they call Sigma.

Burrelle's, a national news summary service, records and logs news programming on 448 television stations in the top 174 markets, including ABC, CBS, NBC, and FOX affiliates, as well as major cable networks.

Radio/TV Reports, a national news summary service, provides data base search capabilities for TV news programming in 10 markets, including 7 in the top 10 markets.

Video Monitoring Services (VMS), a national television taping service, provides information about your project's usage on TV news programming in 31 markets.

There's also a new, competing system called Vericheck, which works a little differently. It pulsates the visual on the screen. You can't see it with the human eye, but computers can detect whether a video is being pulsed. Vericheck operates only in the top 75 markets in the United States.

The amount of publicity being distributed has grown to such a point that even large, multioffice companies like MediaLink do nothing but service that particular industry's distribution, notification, marketing, and monitoring.

Some professional companies, such as VNR-1, use more than one system to maximize tracking.

(Just so there's no confusion: Companies such as VNR-1 convert publicity messages into acceptable/usable news releases for television and radio, and companies such as MediaLink are the delivery and monitoring mechanisms.)

Newspeople Express Outrage—But They Use "Recycled" VNRs

In late 1990, *Marketing News* said "Every once in a while there's a story expressing outrage about newspeople using footage that viewers think was produced by a news station when actually it was sponsored by a corporation. But it's no different from a printed press release. They have the option of accepting or rejecting, editing or changing it."

The news story goes on to say that overall, VNRs get a good reaction from stations, but videos do get flak when they're too long, too commercial, or too light. The recommendation: "Try to keep it to one visual and one verbal mention of the [company]" in the approximately 1-minute, 30-second time allotment.

Another strategy is to establish a problem and present the company's product or service as a solution. "That way," says *Marketing News*, "the product comes in naturally."

Look, Ma! No Paper!

As computer programs advance to include video, there will be no hard-copy paper press releases. It will be possible to store VNRs on computer, so that in the future it will be very easy to reissue a press release, or alter it, or update it, by accessing the old video—the data that are stored in the computer—rearranging it on the computer screen, and then transmitting it.

At this time, technology doesn't permit good reception—computer to computer—of motion videos. Broadcast video operates at 30 frames per second, which allows it to look exactly like live action. The highest-grade computer system presently available to the public operates at 20 frames per second. So, what you see when you look at video on the computer monitor from a CD drive is a sort of shaky, staggered action, something like a Max Headroom effect.

But a VNR does not necessarily mean motion video. It can be simply photographs, which doesn't require anything more than a standard CD drive. A computer VNR like that will probably be cheaper than the regulation hard-copy press release/press kit package.

After several VNRs have been put together, everything that's needed for an "average" electronic press release is stored in the computer, including a picture of the CEO, a picture of the new plant, plus some extra interviews. "An individual can put it all together and transmit it to everyone simultaneously," says Trammell. "No mailing, no labels, no stamps, no anything. And the only paper used will be attached to the copy for the boss upstairs, saying, 'By the way, I sent this out over the financial on-line computer service.' "

Actually, this system already exists for investors through DJIN—the Dow Jones Investors Network, which began operation in mid-1994.

What Makes DJIN Different

The DJIN is a private broadcast entity that pinpoints investors. For instance, if the Acme company wants to send a press release about its third-quarter results—which are less than wonderful because Acme just built a new plant—Acme has the option to send its news directly to the media or to completely bypass them.

If the Acme story appears on local television, the report probably would say, "Acme company took a financial hit in the third quarter . . . now more news after this commercial break." Undoubtedly there would be no explanation about the costs of building the new factory and of its effect on quarterly returns.

Regular media can be bypassed, however, and through a twice-a-day news segment called "Desk Top Business Broadcast," traders can be alerted that an announcement will be made at, say, five o'clock today. In essence, "Desk Top Business Broadcast" takes video news releases and adapts them into what you might call investor video releases.

Another Technology Has Arrived

We interrupt this newscast to bring you information that may be valuable.

There is new technology you might call "computer public relations." Its initial use is by stockbrokers and companies that are in the financial market, but it will be rapidly extended to focus on other aspects of business.

This example may explain: Previously, if your company showed a record third-quarter profit, you might distribute a little one-page paper release, which might be used in the business section of the local newspaper. With this new technology, your company has the opportunity to send a computerized press release over an on-line financial computer system. The benefit is that not only would it contain the printed data that say how financially profitable the company is—all the regular news release information—but it could also include a digitized interview with the CEO, who might say something about how proud the company is and how it plans to continue to move forward, and so forth.

Here is another example: You're planning to build a new plant, and you want to get the word out to a core audience in the financial world. The new service extends the information contained in that one-page paper release to include aerial shots of the new location, or action shots of new equipment that will be installed, or whatever is available to extend publicity and promotion for your company.

VNRs Can Be Cost-Effective

According to *Marketing News*, the cost of producing a VNR can run anywhere from $15,000 to $80,000. (Jack Trammell says the average cost is $18,000 to $20,000. Of that, $12,000 to $14,000 is for production, and $4,000 to $6,000 is for distribution. Strictly local distribution of a VNR can run as little as $500.)

Amusement Business magazine reports how one public relations manager turned a most difficult assignment into a winner. Ann Parker knew that getting publicity for a new roller coaster at Beach Boardwalk in Santa Cruz (California) was going to be tough. She says she was looking at the fact that the coaster wasn't going to be the fastest, the tallest, or the steepest coaster in the world, or even in the area, so someone had to come up with a different angle.

The hook? Pretty simple, really. It was that with the addition of Beach Boardwalk's coaster, the states of California and Ohio would now be tied at 22 coasters each in the race for being the state with the most coasters.

Then Parker created a video news release that showed the staff riding the coaster and giving testimonials on camera. She helped edit the piece, and, counting production, distribution, satellite time, and tracking to see who used the piece, she says it cost less than $15,000.

"Our coverage was [worth] tenfold what we spent on it," she said. "CNN and 'Entertainment Tonight' both picked it up, along with scores of other stations."

Parker also told the magazine that there is a company that, for $350, will take your idea and pitch it to stations and outlets across the country to see which would be interested in picking it up. She also advises that video news releases are particularly valuable when you have a message that positions your event so it attracts national or regional interest.

VNRs Can Be Great for PR

Public relations is pretty much the same as it's been for years. There are more messengers now but the message is the same. Getting there is another matter entirely. One of today's vehicles is called Video Public Relations (VPR), and VNRs now are the foundation of VPR.

Many companies use VNRs for crisis communications. Exxon used them during the Valdez disaster. At that time, Exxon had a public relations fiasco on its hands. All the nightly news programs seemed to be showing were dead ducks and sea animals on their backs gasping for breath—directly tied to the name "Exxon."

To overcome, or at least to mitigate, the PR damage, Exxon issued daily VNRs that showed Exxon people working intensely to clean the beaches—doing all the right things—and explaining the special technologies they were using. In addition, they showed interviews with environmentalists who gave credible testimony on Exxon's behalf.

Exxon also provided interviews with its own executives. This circumvented the possibility that those executives would be cornered and questioned in a way they would have difficulty handling. Moreover, it offered control in case an executive said "damn" or something he'd like to retract. When that happened, they merely reshot the video. The VNR method, in effect, told the media, "Look, here's an interview with our CEO—you can take it or leave it."

Video PR Can Be Great Marketing Too

Jack Trammell tells of the way a supermarket used VPR to introduce itself to a local community.

About a week before the store opened, homeowners in the area received VHS cassettes in the mail. (The same kind of cassettes you rent from movies-for-rent stores.) Each had a card explaining what the video was about and telling recipients there was a coupon on the tape—but it didn't say what the coupon was for.

Each tape was a tour of the store, with an attractive woman as a guide, telling how the store made its fresh bread, that its seafood was absolutely fresh, that the store is open 24 hours, and so forth. At the very end there was a video coupon worth five pounds of shrimp, redeemable at the meat department—which, of course, was at the very back of the store.

The supermarket had only a few cassettes made, and they sent them by standard—low cost—mail. In order to claim the gift, recipients had to return the tape, which means the supermarket undoubtedly was able to remail the tapes to others in the neighborhood, which kept costs at a rock bottom level.

Radio News Releases

RNRs are a lot less expensive than VNRs—they cost about a third to a fourth of what it costs to produce a video news release. And they are preferred when you wish to zero in on narrowly defined audiences. Radio, much like speciality magazines, targets specific groups of people, whereas television—except for certain cable channels—reaches a mass audience.

Big considerations on the plus side are that radio is fast, it's spontaneous, and it's instant. VNRs for television require a day or more to produce, but in an emergency an RNR can be produced in a matter of hours.

Three Distribution Methods

There are three ways to distribute RNRs—by tape, by telephone, or by satellite.

When you use the telephone method, the person being interviewed sits in a professional radio studio with high quality phone lines. (The quality of the phone service, which is of prime importance, is not regularly available outside broadcast stations.) The radio stations on the media list are contacted and "booked" in advance. This process that literally turns phone calls into interviews is called a radio media tour.

There also are radio satellite tours. Stations that want to participate are queried and booked in advance, but instead of giving the tape feed by telephone they turn their satellite dishes to a certain satellite insert coordinate and the stations come on line just as they do for a television media tour.

Generally, radio media tours go faster, because radio is a much simpler medium and it's much easier to connect a phone call than a satellite. For organizations wishing to connect only with local and regional media, the business or nonprofit offers connections by phone. Only one station at a time is connected, but the difference is that, unlike an ordinary phone call whereby the company is merely calling Station A, it's not calling on an open line. Satelliting, however, unlike telephone tours, is broadband casting. A satellite isn't like a laser or a phone line— it literally "broad" casts, covering the area like a rain shower.

Seldom do small or even mid-sized businesses have reason to distribute news nationally or internationally, which is when "satellite tours" are generally used. But with new technology seeming to make almost anything possible, it may pay for you to understand both satellites and satellite media tours, and perhaps initiate such a tour for your oganization. Here are the definitions given by Webster's *New World Dictionary of Media and Communications*, by Richard Weiner:

> *satellite*   a relay station for audio and video transmission, orbiting in space or terrestrial. A *satellite station* is a radio or TV station used as a relay, broadcasting on the same or a different wavelength as the orginating station. Almost all communications satellites . . . hover in the same place in the sky, 22,300 miles above the earth, in *stationary orbit.*

> *satellite media tour*   several interviews, generally on TV but sometimes in other media, during a specific period, such as one hour, in which a celebrity or spokesperson in one location is interviewed via satellite by journalists elsewhere; also called *satellite tour* or *satellite press tour.*

The only difference between a radio media tour and a television media tour is that on a media tour for television you also send pictures. For radio you just send sound. Most radio tours, however, are done by phone.

Tapes are used when distribution is purely *local.* It's cheaper to handle *regional* or *national* distribution by satellite or by telephone. When the audience is strictly local, or the content may be used over an extended period, distribution by tape is the most cost efficient means.

Moreover, if your spokesperson—the president or the CFO—is uncomfortable being interviewed live, a prerecorded tape is by far the best choice.

The same is true if one of the people you want to include in your media tour is in another city. In this case, there's no choice—the RNR must be on tape.

Interviews are the mainstay of RNRs because—as with VNRs— injecting the human element is basic. But interviews are *not* the only thing that makes a radio news release, as so many people who aren't fully knowledgeable about radio are inclined to think. Radio people want *sounds.* Be sure your tape includes sounds beyond that of a person talking—background sounds, natural sounds, manufacturing sounds, whatever is appropriate.

A Recommended Way to Handle Distributing an RNR

Radio newsrooms have far fewer people than television newsrooms. Years ago, in the late 1970s, the FCC cut back its regulations, which allowed radio news to cut back on staff. Aside from a few stations, all in major markets, there are a minimum number of newspeople in each newsroom. Most stations have either a single newsperson or no one at all (they conduct what's called "rip-and-read" operations).

Even no-staff news operations want sounds with their stories so they don't give the impression they're just ripping pages from a wire service and reading them. A large number of stations have satellite capabilities, but even those that don't, do have the ability to record from a telephone feed.

Make a call to the news director or the producer at the radio station of your choice. Have your tape machine with the taped message ready to play. Then tell him or her, "I have a story that's just happened," describe what you have in mind, and ask, "Would you be interested?"

The answer probably will be, "Yeah, I think so."

You then tell the person, "Okay, go ahead and roll your tape. We'll feed you some remarks from the president of Acme Company, and after that there are sound effects of the funny-sounding noise of the Acme Widgit being manufactured."

The station runs its tape, you run yours, and it's taped right over the phone lines.

Of course, a tape can be mailed if time permits.

17

Do-It-Yourself Advertising in Print Media

It gives you a "buy-line" when your message doesn't qualify for news space

How's Your Ept?

How's your ad savvy? Feeling a little inept? Fair warning! The technological revolution has hit advertising as solidly as *anything* traveling the "infobahn." And yet another alert! Print advertising is far easier and less expensive to produce than video commercials. But with cable television busting its buttons and offering an almost pinpoint means of reaching specific niche groups, electronic advertising now may not only be within your financial margins, but may be a productive way to go. Like niche magazines and radio stations, today's niche cable stations zero in on the special interests of specific groups, some of which may be exactly the groups you want to target.

Newspaper advertising, however, is still the medium of choice by small businesses—and by manufacturers and vendors who offer co-op arrangements. Newspapers reach a mass market much like commercial television, they are affordable, they reach a defined geographical area, and they offer hard copy for readers to cut out and keep for reference and for advertisers to reproduce and circulate as direct mail at minimum costs.

Only print advertising is discussed in this chapter; broadcast advertising is presented in Chapter 18.

What Is Advertising?

Whoever said it gave one of the best—and shortest—descriptions of advertising: "Advertising is the mouthpiece of business." Even the smallest business needs a big mouthpiece so that in good times people don't forget it, and in less-than-good times people will buy—buy its product or their service, or accept the image the organization wants them to perceive.

Advertising's sole purpose is to sell a product, a service, or an image. Selling is the name of the game. Country singer Ricky Skaggs says, "America is the land of milk and honey that's been turned into the land of mink and money"—doubtless accomplished through effective advertising!

"Advertising is what you do when you can't go see somebody," was Fairfax Cone's explanation. Cone was a partner in Foote, Cone and Belding, one of the country's largest advertising agencies. Aldous Huxley said it is "an organized effort to extend and intensify craving."

But, according to one of the foremost newsmen of the century, Adolph S. Ochs, the late publisher of *The New York Times*, "Advertising in the final analysis should be news. If it is not news it is worthless."

So often, even professionals who should know better, call publicity "free advertising." Perhaps a good explanation for advertising, then, is it's "paid publicity." A quarter-page ad for Infiniti carries a two-line headline that, in its way, says the same thing:

You can't buy this kind of press. But you can
certainly buy the car they're talking about.

It's true. Advertising *should* be news. It also should and can be excellent publicity to promote a product, a service, an image. All of these observations tell you that the publicity-news skills you've learned and are polishing can be put to good use on behalf of your advertising program.

Copycatting Works for Advertising Too

One of the *most effective* uses of copycatting is in do-it-yourself advertising. Collect, collect, collect. Save, save, save. Keep a copycat file of ads that impress you, arouse interest, inspire a desire to buy. Also collect those that you reject for any reason. As you gather them, make notes about why each ad caught your interest, impressed you, created a desire to buy, or produced a negative reaction. Make the notes right then, because reactions fade as time goes by. This file can be your source for ideas that will work with your target audience. For more about copycatting, see Chapter 8.

Worth Its Wait

High tech has elbowed its way into the advertising departments of newspapers. Electronic Data Interchange, Heliogrammes, the ability to accept ads on disk and on line, and electronic shopping information and transaction services are only a few of the many changes that have come out of the techno-age.

Electronic Data Interchange? A complex, confusing term for something that the director of advanced computer science for the Newspaper Association of America says "is not rocket science!" John Iobst says it's merely an electronic way of managing information. Iobst explains its increasing use in the advertising departments of newspapers: "Most advertisers that I've talked to are interested in doing electronic remittance with newspapers . . . because they are moving to as paperless an operation as they can. There are three things they [advertisers] ask for: electronic purchase orders, electronic copy, and an electronic invoice."

Some Denver advertisers no longer must rely on the *Rocky Mountain News* for ad makeup services. And they no longer supply the Colorado daily with camera-ready art. According to *Editor & Publisher*, "Electronic files of display ads created on advertisers' computers can be delivered to the *News* on floppy disks and removable hard drives or directly over phone lines, via modem at up to 14,400 bps." Ads supplied in digital form range from black and white one-quarter page to four-color spreads across two tabloid pages.

Then there's the introduction in this country of the "Heliogramme," from England. Here, we spell it "heliogram," and recognize that it's a message sent by heliograph.

Heliograph? Well, explaining it is pretty complex, but it's a signalling device, orginally used to photograph the sun, that now uses sunlight and mirrors to flash coded messages. According to the companies that market the service, a heliogram provides enormously better quality than a halftone photo and is cheaper than paying for an illustration. The first claim is a distinct plus for illustrations that must be reproduced on coarse gray newsprint. These companies also maintain that the process provides greater realism, better definition and depth, and that it's "ideal for automobiles, electronics, food, packaged goods. Anything."

Topping off all this is a brand-new service offered by the *Los Angeles Times* and a new subsidiary of the San Francisco-based Pacific Telesis regional Bell. The joint venture is meant to combine business listings, classified and display ads, and editorial material. It will give users access to in-depth information ranging from home upkeep and real estate to auto, travel, and entertainment services.

Far less high-tech, but equally or perhaps more important to business advertisers, are newspapers' recent abilities to target specific subscribers, located through data base searches, and to deliver a specific message or product to these subscribers.

Precisely selected subscribers of one newspaper, for example, received a full-size grocery bag, which gave customers a discount of 25 percent on all the groceries they could get in the bag.

The Four Basics of Advertising

As the architect of your organization's advertising, you must play the game like a soccer player—you've got to use your head. And it's best to play by the rules. Once you've learned the rules of advertising—at least what works *best*—then it's okay to break them.

This chapter takes you through only the basics in producing effective advertising. But, as advertising copywriter Scott Nosenko says, "Advertising isn't brain surgery or a mental mind game. Its sole purpose is to sell a product or a service [or an image] by speaking to the market. Period."

The fundamental guidelines explained here include (1) knowing whom to advertise to, (2) knowing your own product or service and that of the competition, (3) locating media to reach a defined public, and (4) designing messages that sell—your product, service, or image.

1. Know Your Customers.   It's not exactly smart business to peddle shampoo to bald-headed men! But you could peddle sunscreen or hats, if you know how and where to find a pod of bald-headed buyers. It doesn't require an advanced university degree to realize that if you want your advertising to work, you must know *who* your potential buyers are and *where* to find them.

You must decide on the population to whom you want to direct your message. Do you need to reach men, women, young people, mature people, retired people with time on their hands, parents with children—bald-headed men? They all *buy*. But, specifically, who are the people who can use and benefit from *your* product or service? Or who are the people you want to influence in regard to your organization? (There are sources for locating just such narrowly defined clusters of potential buyers.)

You must identify your desired audience as precisely as possible. You can't just say "the working Mom" anymore. You need to know her age, whether she is the sole support of the family. What does she do? What does she buy? How does she consume media? When you are able to direct your message to a clearly defined group—say, people with cars that are five years old or older—you will catch their interest far more readily. A rifle is better than a shotgun when you are out for big game.

There are a number of ways to discover who is your target audience:

- Through questionnaires, circulated in-store or by mail
- Through in-person questioning
- With telephone surveys
- Through focus group sessions

Questionnaires.   Designing a questionnaire requires some thought and consideration. The contents, to one degree or another, will be used in all of your preliminary research. Call a meeting of your staff and set down the details required to produce an accurate profile of your consumer.

When you have a concise, efficient questionnaire, you can use any means you prefer to acquire the answers, but one of the easiest is merely to talk to the people who already are your customers. You can find out *why* they buy and *how* their purchases fulfill their needs, wants, or desires.

Perhaps you also need to know *where* people live or work. If, for instance, you're an auto repair shop you want to know zip codes of the people who live within three, or five, or ten miles of your shop. The post office can help you with this information.

2. Know Your Product or Service—And the Competition's.   As important as knowing your customers is knowing exactly what you are offering them. Not only must you know the benefits of your own product or service so you can tell the buyer, you must also know how the competition's product or service stacks up against yours. With information about competitors you can establish your place on the success ladder. Moreover, in your advertising messages you can tell prospects about the benefits and advantages they receive from your product or service over those of the competition, or about the benefits and advantages your product/service offers that the competition doesn't have.

3. Locate Media That Reach Your Customers.   Choose the right medium for your message, and you will be able to knock on the doors of only potential buyers. Pick the wrong medium, and regardless of how great your ad is, it will fall on deaf ears and be a complete waste of money.

There are perils in locating and purchasing media: the possibility of falling prey to overenthusiastic, sometimes unscrupulous media salespeople; and the difficulty in properly assessing and comparing audience-reach statistics and costs. Set your advertising budget *now* before you ever see a sales rep and become a victim of impulse buying. Make yourself a promise now that you will stay within the designated amount. Be certain to ask probing questions of the reps that give you information on which to base comparisons.

One thing to keep constantly in mind when talking to media reps is that each will present his or her information so that it appears that this medium (this newspaper, this radio station, these outdoor boards) is best in its field and best for your purposes. Demand validation of claims. And never forget that any claim—for example, that this rep's station reaches more people than any other medium—must be followed by the answer to your question as to whether all those people it reaches are *your* true prospects.

4. Design Productive Advertising Messages—"Advertising 101."   Now that you know exactly who you are directing your message to; what you have to offer them in terms of benefits and comparisons with other similar products or services; and where these potential buyers can be reached, let's get about the job of preparing the message you want to deliver.

Hard Sell Versus Soft Sell

Before you can frame your message, you must decide how you should tell it. Is a hard-sell approach the best way to reach your selected audience? Or do you prefer to appeal to the emotions of the reader to solicit aid or approval? Do you plan to soft-sell the message strictly as an image builder?

Hard sell is most often used when there is a high degree of competition, as for sales of used cars. Soft sell is used when a business wants to build and maintain an image of dignity, honor, character, and integrity.

Outline

Most ads are conceived in isolation on a doodle pad, so start roughly designing the space you have to work with and the illustration, headline, and copy elements to go in it.

Be prepared to write leaner and cleaner than perhaps you thought possible. Every word counts in advertising, no matter whether message length is measured in inches or seconds.

As you did with your first news release, make an outline of what the ad will contain. To begin, don't write any copy other than doodle notes until you know what you are writing about and what you want the ad to achieve. Then write your first draft. Don't be concerned with word perfection yet. Just get the idea down in rough-draft form.

Headline for a Print Ad

It's true! The headline for a print ad is vital.

The headline must grab the attention of readers and bounce them into the copy and make them want to read on. If writing this critical lead-in to your ad intimidates you, write the body copy first. Your headline will come more easily when you've trimmed and tailored the text into its final form.

If you do have trouble writing headlines, take a moment for a smile, courtesy of Johnny Hart's "B.C." cartoon. Know however, that it has absolutely no instructional value here except to illustrate attention-grabbing value.

> In the first panel, the copywriter says, "I need a headline for this [ad], and he's asked, "What's it about?"
>
> In the second panel he explains, "Naked people qualifying to run in the marathon."
>
> Third panel: "How 'bout "All the nudes that's fit to sprint?'"

Indeed, that's a head that might catch more than a few eyes! And it definitely could cause a lot of readers to dive headfirst into the body copy.

As you write the first draft and each revision, strive for conciseness and vividness. Avoid useless words. Advertising space is expensive and, equally important, readers won't bother reading wordy copy.

Text

Your first paragraph should be short, and it should tie in with the head. (You may want to hold off on writing both the headline and the first paragraph until after you've written the rest of the copy.)

Start with the strongest possible appeal—the point that will be of greatest interest to the reader. You and your organization may have a stronger interest, but readers don't care about that. They respond only to appeals that relate to their own interests and concerns.

Include other appeals in diminishing importance, but don't use so many that you will water down the reader's interest. Use no glittering generalities. Be specific. As you write your copy, it is helpful to visualize one person and write as you would talk to him or her. Try to answer that person's arguments, questions, and needs.

Use action verbs and few adjectives. Be persuasive.

The "Do Something" Appeal

The last paragraph of your body copy should be a "do something" appeal. Unless the purpose of the ad is merely to build an image or to boost recognition of the organization's name, its chief objective is to stimulate action of some kind. You may want the reader to write or call for a brochure, place an order by phone, send in a coupon, volunteer time or expertise, or make a contribution of some sort. Whatever it is you want the reader to do, come right out and ask him or her to do it in the last paragraph, then spell out exactly how to do it.

An Ad That Missed Its Target

A survey by Starch INRA Hooper, regarding a double-truck ad for Hyundai, showed that not many readers stopped to read it. The report, in *Advertising Age*, said the reason was that the flow of the ad was wrong. "The stunning photograph was on the right-hand page, and the headline and copy on the left didn't give the reader enough reason to 'swim back upstream' to the left-hand page," was the assessment made by Philip Sawyer, editor of Starch's *Tested Copy*. His conclusion was that a lot of advertising "would be more effective if it stuck to basic principles."

The report was about automobile advertising in magazines, but the commentary applies to print advertising for just about any product or service.

Sawyer developed a list of seven principles of effective auto ads based on his analysis of Starch surveys conducted over each of the preceding three years. Merely substitute *your* product wherever Sawyer uses the word automobile, car, or vehicle, and the principles can become your ad copy "rules."

- **Go with the flow.** The layout creates a flow of action that directs a reader's eye to a particular spot. The best-read ads flow to the copy.
- **Use powerful illustrations.** It sounds obvious, but a surprising number of print ads show a car in static position or against a backdrop that tends to camouflage the vehicle.
- **Emphasize the headline.** A provocative headline gives the reader an excuse to get into the copy.
- **Create visually inviting copy.** Few will read copy if it's small and crowded into a corner.
- **Avoid internal competition.** Copy will lose out if it's competing for attention with an illustration.
- **Heighten the contrast between automobile and background.** Outstanding print ads make the vehicle stand out. At least make sure the car and background aren't shades of the same color.
- **Add some drama.** Drama elicits emotion, getting a reader personally involved in the ad.

Nine Ad-Writing Points

It's how the blank white space or the airtime you've purchased is used that spells the difference between being successful and being ignored. Some of the following nine points repeat, in effect, Philip Sawyer's principles, but rephrased restatements tend to build better understanding. The following list applies primarily to print advertising and is adapted from a booklet produced by the Bureau of Advertising of the Newspaper Association of America. It's called *How to check your ads for more sell*, and is used with permission.

1. **Be sure your ad has a theme.** State the sales message with a simple declarative sentence.
2. **Make your ads easily recognizable.** Studies show that ads that are distinctive in their use of art, layout techniques, and typefaces usually enjoy a higher readership than run-of-the-mill advertising. Try to make your ads distinctively different in appearance from those of your competitors, then keep your ads' appearance consistent. This way readers will recognize your ads even before they read them. If you've built a good image, the recognition will create a feeling of wanting to hear from a friend.
3. **Use a simple layout.** Ads should not be crossword puzzles. The ad layout

is nothing more than the arrangement of (*a*) headline; (*b*) illustration; (*c*) body copy; and (*d*) signature.

The layout should carry the reader's eye through the message easily and in proper sequence, from headline to illustration (or vice versa), to explanatory copy, to price (if applicable), to your organization's name with address, phone and possibly your 800 and fax numbers.

Avoid the use of too many different typefaces, overly decorative borders, reverse plates (white on black), or copy overprinting a photo or graphic. All of these devices are distracting and will reduce the number of readers who receive your entire message.

4. **Use a dominant element.** Use a large picture or headline to ensure quick visibility. Photographs and realistic drawings have about equal attention-getting value, but photographs of real people win more readership. So do action pictures. Photos of *local* people or places also have high attention value. Use good artwork; it will pay off in extra readership.

5. **Use a prominent benefit headline.** The first thing a reader wants to know about your ad is: What's in it for me? [known in the advertising business as the WIIFM (pronounced "whiffem") strategy]. A good headline states a reader benefit and should try to include the advertiser's name. It also should be selective—addressed to a specific audience—so the reader knows immediately whether or not the ad is directed to him or her. Otherwise, readers may jump to the conclusion the message is not for them.

    Select the main benefit that your service or product offers and feature it in a compelling headline. Amplify the message in subheads. Remember that label headlines do little selling (whether of a product, a service, or an image).

    Always try to appeal to one or more of the basic desires of your readers: safety, beauty, fun, thrift, leisure, popularity, and health.

    "How-to" headlines encourage full copy readership, as do headlines that include specific information or helpful suggestions.

    Avoid generalized quality claims.

    Your headline will be easier to read if it is black-on-white and is not superimposed or overprinted on part of the illustration. And, of course, the headline should be simple enough to be clearly understood.

6. **Let your white space work for you.** Don't overcrowd your ad. White space is an important layout element in newspaper advertising because the average news page is so heavy with small type or cluttered with ads. White space focuses the reader's attention not only on your ad, but it will make your headline and illustration stand out.

7. **Make your copy complete.** Know all there is to know about the product, service, or image you sell, and select the benefit(s) most appealing to the audience you wish to reach.

    Your copy should be enthusiastic and sincere. A block of copy written in complete sentences is easier to read than one composed of phrases and random words.

    In designing the layout of a copy block, use a boldface lead-in.

    Small pictures in sequence will often help readership.

8. **Urge your readers to act now**. The closing text should urge the reader to act *now*. Chances are, if the reader sets the paper or the ad aside, he or she will forget it regardless of the degree of initial enthusiasm felt about responding.

   If a mail-in coupon is included in your ad, provide spaces large enough for customers to fill them in easily. As part of each coupon, include the name and address to which it is to be mailed. And place the coupon alongside the edge of the ad, and request that the ad be placed as close to the edge of a page as possible—for readers' convenience in cutting it out.

   If a check is to be enclosed, tell the reader to whom the check should be written and the address where it should be sent. In other words, don't make your reader search throughout the ad for information. Make it easy for him or her to act now, while enthusiasm is high and before he or she forgets.

9. **End with the signature**. Readers expect to find the signature at the bottom of an ad because that is where most advertisers have placed it for years. You can also try to work it into the headline, and wherever else it is appropriate, but when you sign off the ad, be sure the name stands out loud and clear, complete with address (and ZIP code), phone number, and business hours.

Points to Improve Readability

The following points cover design mechanics for producing your ad:

- The typeface (font) should be simple and unencumbered, but not stylized or drastically different from most of the copy in the newspaper. Sans-serif faces tend to be easier to read. (The advertising representative from the newspaper will have a typeface book from which you may pick a type style and the sizes you prefer. He or she also should know which ones are preferable.)
- Headlines in all-capital letters are harder to read than those with an initial capital letter followed by lower-case letters.
- Flush-*left* type (*justified*, or aligned, against the left margin) is easiest to read. There is little difference in readability between blocks of copy that have both margins justified and copy that has a *ragged right* margin. In most cases, fully justified copy uses more space than ragged right copy.
- Related illustrations help pull the reader's attention to the copy or fix the text content in the reader's mind more clearly.
- The length of the lines of type should be between $1^1/_2$ to 2 "alphabets" long, or between 39 and 52 characters long, for ease in reading. If you've chosen a large ad space, break your copy into blocks that are no wider than 2 "alphabets" (52 characters).
- A moderate amount of space between lines of body copy may make it easier for the reader's eye to keep its place as it skips across the page.
- Put lots of white space around your copy. Here's why:

Copy is much harder to read
whenwordsarealljammed together. It is also hard to read
big blocks of type that are jammed together, with the
lines of type on one side
set flush right
instead of flush
left.

Five "Don'ts"

As you write your advertising copy, remember the following tips:

1. Don't forget basic information. Check every ad you produce to be certain you have included your organization's name, address, telephone number, and business hours. If you want readers to respond by fax or by an 800 number, be sure to include your fax or 800 number. And if you want them to visit your place of business, include a location identification such as "at the corner of Seventh and College Streets."

   Even if yours is a long-established name, make it easy for readers to find you or to call you. According to U.S. government statistics, one or more of every ten families in your town moves each year, so you can count on a large number of readers who do not know where you are located. One-tenth or *more* is a large chunk out of any number.

2. Don't be too clever. Many people distrust cleverness in advertising, just as they distrust salespersons who are too glib. Headlines and copy generally are far more effective when they are straightforward than when they are tricky or smart-alecky. Clever or tricky headlines and copy are often misunderstood.

   Softened humor, however, can be a plus. Bo Pilgrim, who glorifies his Pilgrim's Pride Chicken with numerous benefits, ends one commercial with a rib-tickler that doesn't cause distrust: "I march to a different drumstick."

3. Don't use unusual or difficult words. Many of your potential customers may not understand words that are familiar to you. Trade and technical terms, big words, or jargon may be confusing and easily misunderstood. Everybody understands simple language and nobody resents it. Use it.

4. Don't generalize. Be specific at all times. Facts convince.

5. Don't make excessive claims. The surest way to lose customers (or supporters, if your ad is for a nonprofit organization) is to make claims that you can't back up. Go easy with superlatives and unbelievable values. Remember, if you claim that your prices or achievements (or anything, for that matter) are unbelievable, your readers are likely to agree.

Spot-Check Questions

With the foregoing input, plus help from the newspaper's advertising representative and its creative staff, your ad should be highly effective. After you have written, rewritten, edited, and reedited your copy, try testing it on an imaginary reader. If you were the reader you had in mind as you wrote the copy, how would you respond to the following questions?

- Would you clip the ad?
- Would you get up, go to the telephone, and call?
- Does the copy hold your interest all the way?
- Is the ad clear and understandable?
- Is the purpose direct?
- Are the statements honest?
- Are there words that could use a little strengthening, a little more action and impact?
- Is the message interesting and enthusiastic?
- Does it answer the WIIFM question—what's in it for me?

Was each answer a positive? If not, work on that element until your ad can successfully pass the spot check.

Eye-Catching Ads

Just to be sure that your horse is before your cart and that you have a good handle on what makes for the highest readership of your ad, here is additional information that should be helpful. These data were developed over more than 25 years of newspaper-readership research—by the Bureau of Advertising, the Advertising Research Foundation, Daniel Starch and Staff, and many other organizations—through ongoing programs that conduct and analyze research projects.

Eye-camera research shows that not only do people note more ads that reflect their interests, they even see more of such ads. As the eye scans the page, it is unconsciously drawn from the edges of vision to those items that are relevant to the reader. The eye avoids the irrelevant. Together, the eye and the brain are engaged in a constant and rapid filtering process.

Key Elements to Advertising Success

A report published by Standard Rate & Data Service, Inc. (SRDS) confirms that the qualities that most strongly influence advertising readership are the layout, the ad's ability to key into the reader's interests, and the freshness of the message. The report states that the key elements "should be considered as carefully as placement. Even the best placement or 'media buy' cannot guarantee an ad will be read."

The study that produced the results quoted by SRDS was conducted by Starch Inra Hooper and addressed such issues as why two ads placed in the same publication produce different results.

"It's no secret that basic human needs and interests are the prime movers in human behavior," says the SRDS report. "They are also, of course, the basic motivations behind what people read."

One finding showed that ads with a dominant single picture and caption (as compared with those that had several line drawings and multiple sections of copy, none of which dominated), scored approximately one and a half times higher.

"A dominant focal center, however, does not necessarily assure a high noting score," states the SRDS report. As many as 4 out of 10 advertisements with dominant focal centers did not secure high noting scores, which "points to the presence of a second important factor in determining the size of the observer audience. It is the operation of a quick perceptual-meaning interaction." The SRDS report explains that a "perceptual-meaning interaction" is an ad's ability to provide a momentary challenge to the curiosity or self-interest of the reader.

In summarizing the requirements for achieving high success, the SRDS report states, "The physical impact of a dominant focal center is highly important in attracting a reading audience. [However,] the psychological impact of a challenge to curiosity, self-interest or cue to a meaningful explanation is equally important. To create an ad with a dominant focal center, but without a perceptual cue to curiosity, self-interest or unexpected explanations can cut down the reader audience considerably."

"Co-Op" Can Be a Magic Word

Enlisting co-op advertising can mean you double the amount of advertising you place and, in some cases, it can mean you don't have to design and write the ads. Not incidentally, newspaper advertising is the medium of first choice for by far the great majority of co-op "underwriters."

Cooperative advertising, according to the *Dictionary of Advertising and Direct Mail Terms*, is an "arrangement between a manufacturer [or a vendor] whereby the manufacturer [or vendor] will reimburse the retailer in part or full for advertising expenditures."

What more could you ask? You'll be reimbursed—partially or fully—for the ads you run!

Don't worry about the manufacturer or the vendor. They definitely get their money's worth because co-op advertising allows them to take advantage of your ability to buy space or time at a much lower local rate than they must pay as national advertisers, and they get exposure in what for them can be the friendly, favorable surroundings of a community medium, linked with a respected community business. Of course, they refund only for advertising that promotes and sells their products or services.

The most common cost sharing is on a fifty-fifty basis. For every dollar you spend, there is another dollar to expand your advertising program. Cost sharing can range from 25 percent to 100 percent of your advertising space or time costs. And the extra ad dollars you spend may qualify your program for media volume discounts, thereby stretching your ad dollars even further.

As described in *The Advertising Kit: A Complete Guide for Small Businesses*, "Specially prepared advertising material, logos, graphics, and precise wording sometimes are required. But when such conditions are called for, the manufacturer or vendor usually provides the professional layouts, scripts, or recordings." That can add up to sizeable savings in production costs.

For more information contact either of the following:

Co-op News
45 South Park Street
P.O. Box 633
Hanover, NY 03755-0633
603/643-2667

Newspaper Advertising Co-op Network
1180 Avenue of the Americas
New York, NY 10036
212/704-4566

You should know that every year there are billions of co-op advertising dollars that go unused. Check it out. It's well worth your time and effort, and it may be a gold mine that funds an impressive advertising program for your business.

18

Do-It-Yourself Broadcast Advertising

How to prepare affordable television and cable advertising

The Eyes Have It!

Motivational speaker Joe Griffith tells this story:

> A restaurant customer summoned his waiter and said, "Look at this small piece of meat. Last evening, I was served with a portion more than twice the size of this."
> "Where did you sit?" asked the waiter.
> "I sat by the window," replied the customer.
> "The explanation is simple," the waiter explained. "We always serve larger portions to customers who sit by the window."

The story not only says that there are a number of ways to advertise (including "word-of-eye" as well as word-of-mouth!) but also that visual impact is priceless. If the advertisement includes movement and color, the impact is even stronger.

Those are reasons that television has become a preferred advertising medium among megasize corporations. But for years it has been beyond the budgets of small businesses.

Enter Cable

Fineman Associates built a news release based on the problem of most small businesses in being able to afford television advertising. Following are excerpts from the news release distributed by the San Francisco public relations firm.

> *Contrary to conventional wisdom, small retail businesses can afford broadcast advertising. But they have to be cagey about why, where, when and, perhaps most importantly, how often.*
> *Carriere Clothing, a Southern California-based upscale men's clothing chain which operates a store in Westlake, provides a textbook case in point.*
> *As a smaller advertiser, Carriere found Westlake, with its affluent professional*

*population, a retail advertiser's dream—but one that was a nightmare to cost-effec-
tively reach over the airwaves because of its isolated location in the Southern California Conejo Valley.*

Enter cable.

*Westlake may not have its own TV station, but it does have a cable TV com-
pany that airs locally targeted ads along with national and regional spots on its
channels. And these ads reach almost everyone in Westlake—because of the city's
geographic barriers, most households subscribe to cable service to obtain better reception for local and network TV as well as cable programming.*

*"For the smaller advertiser—and not just the ones trying to reach isolated ar-
eas—cable often is a better buy than general market broadcast because you can run
commercials more frequently on more channels—and really reach the channel changer
who often zaps the advertiser," says Inter/Media [cable network] Executive Vice
President and COO Robert Yallen.*

*Bob Carriere, president of Carriere Clothing, says he's convinced of the effec-
tiveness of cable advertising for the smaller retailer, citing a 35 percent increase in
business since his ad campaign started.*

*However, Carriere adds a caveat for other advertisers: "The greatest creative
in the world won't do a thing for your business unless you can afford to get your
message out to the right people over and over again."*

For this book's readers, the Fineman Associates release gives more information
than merely about the affordability and value of cable for small businesses. As a
seeker of publicity for your own business, it is an example of a type of news release
that editors love, a type that you may wish to emulate: one that contains educational information of vital interest to their small business readers.

The Future Is Here

Let's take a look at where cable is now. Many networks produced by the cable
explosion are still blustering and stretching. But the nation's largest cable TV
company jumped headfirst into the digital revolution in April of 1994. According
to a report in *The Dallas Morning News*, Tele-Communications Inc. "took its first
crucial step toward the much ballyhooed '500 channel' future, when cable systems
will be able to substantially increase capacity"—and revenues. The action allows
TCI to increase the number of available channels *tenfold* by converting from analog
to a compacted digital format.

TCI is calling its approach "single-subject cable" and plans a heavy emphasis
on advertiser-sponsored shows and high-quality infomercials. TCI expects to introduce channels that will cover men's interests, women's interests, sports, business, and entertainment.

The future for cable has arrived!

Much, however, including advertising rates, hasn't been resolved yet. But rates
should not be used to compare regular commercial television with cable, or to
make decisions about whether cable is affordable *and effective* for your operation.
The depth of programming the channel offers that directly targets your potential
customers should be the determinant.

Perhaps the best buying method at this time is Time Warner's ultra-

*un*sophisticated buying technique. Time Warner now buys advertising based on which station makes the phone ring!

Because there are so many channels and so many more to come, all competing for viewers, cable has gone the way of magazines and radio—it has zeroed in on viewers' special interests. Viewers can choose channels that offer all movies, all news, all comedy, or all education. And within education there are tightly targeted channels, for instance, those strictly centering on the interests of doctors, nurses, and caregivers. (If you sell pharmaceuticals, how better to get your sales message to the people who recommend and prescribe them?) A channel called NET (National Empowerment Television) is a round-the-clock procession of political and public affairs programs. And there's the Golf Channel, the Cooking Channel, the Military Channel and the Truckers' Channel.

"Bizarro's" creator, Dan Piraro, couldn't resist taking a swipe at just how far cable has gone in fragmenting the interests of specific groups of viewers. His cartoon shows a television set beneath which is written, "The Shoplifting Channel," and the woman on the screen is pulling something hidden from her sleeve. "When I first saw this lovely pearl necklace in Macy's I *knew* I just *had* to have it! So I waited until the salesperson was busy with someone else. . . ."

A shoplifting channel? No way! But Dan Piraro is right—you *can* find just about *anything*, and the so-called 500 channels aren't even all in place yet. The reason the advent of the channel explosion has slowed a bit is the persistence of regulatory uncertainty, concerns about the high costs involved, and various technical issues.

There is a network that offers foreign-language programming from around the world, including news and entertainment from China, Japan, Korea, the Middle East, and Europe. If you have a concentrated ethnic group, speaking to its members in their own language is a powerful way to catch their attention.

There is another fledgling cable system from Hughes Communications called DirecTv, which offers every home in the country up to 150 crystal-clear channels of entertainment, news, and sports. *Advertising Age* says this new medium "holds tremendous potential for advertisers, who will be able to digitally pinpoint exactly which DirecTv subscribers they want to reach."

There's also a sci-fi cable network that broadcasts only science fiction, science fact, and fantasy 24 hours a day. The network is avidly looking for advertising and maintains that it targets "difficult-to-reach, highly sought-after core audiences . . . audiences [that] are not just viewers, they're avid fans, so your message will be delivered in an environment where viewer involvement has no equal."

What this degree of narrowcasting means to you is that if you take time now to draw from your earlier research and evaluations about precisely who your audience is, there undoubtedly is a cable channel in your area that will virtually let you right into the viewers' homes to sit down with them, and deliver an advertising message that says what's in it for them, as no doorbell-ringing salesperson ever could.

The doctors' education channel may claim only 5,000 viewers in an ADI (area of dominant influence) where the mass audience television station claims 250,000 viewers. But you can count on paying considerably less for time on the highly vertical-interest cable channel than for the same amount of commercial time on the mass appeal commercial television station. The enormous plus for you—and your budget—is that you've tapped into a concentration of people it might take weeks and months to reach among the quarter-million viewers on the mass-audience station. With "menu" cable there's no scattergun shooting. It's almost like going big game hunting inside the fences at the zoo—and the cost of your hunting license is comparable to buying peanuts.

What's Ahead for Cable?

As the cable industry grows, there will be no "channel surfing," as it's called, because viewers can pull up the Prevue Channel, already in close to 50 million cable TV homes. It uses a split-screen technology, whereby you can watch a continuing scroll of program listings while the other half of the screen shows previews or commercials.

This 24-hour-service channel charges $500 for a 30-second national spot. The split-screen technique allows local tags to run on national spots. Prevue expects to have an interactive version in place quickly, allowing viewers to use a remote control to scan through the menu and take specific ad messages and coupons directly from the channel.

Television or Radio—Or Both?

The time is here when small businesses can and possibly should afford cable television advertising. Immediately the question arises: Should I use both cable and radio?

Television does what no other communication medium can: It adds visual motion and thereby is more effective than radio or print in some instances. It is, however, more costly and difficult to produce. Television production can be a budget buster.

If you use only radio, then you are employing only the spoken word, and your production task is simplified significantly. Radio also has the advantages of short lead times and limited production costs. A radio commercial can be written, given to a station announcer in script format, and prerecorded or read live on the air—all within a matter of hours.

Radio, like cable, gives you the flexibility to target specific groups: teens, home workers, retirees, business people, ethnic groups, and so on. Each radio station may attract a completely different audience, and each audience may be a highly vertical group. There are rock stations, classical music stations, news stations, "talk" stations, religious stations, foreign-language stations, and many others. Each aims its programming to specific listeners.

To answer your question about which to choose—radio or cable: When visual impact is essential, by all means choose cable television. However, "Advertisers should think of radio as a *visual* medium," advises veteran advertising agency executive George Arnold. "Radio is a kind of little theater of the mind for that 30 or 60 seconds . . . and a much more imaginative medium than television. A good radio message," he says, "will completely absorb and involve a listener. The best radio spots are the ones where you can see what's going on in your mind's eye." So make your decision based on two things: the need or desire to save expensive television production costs and your ability to "write pictures."

A Way to Trim "Budget-Busting" TV Production Costs

Public service announcements are used by nonprofit organizations as an inexpensive means to produce what might be called their advertising messages. Small businesses will do well to pay attention to—and perhaps copycat—these techniques. Public service time is a valuable option for nonprofits, and information about PSAs is included here for use by *both* nonprofits and businesses.

Writing Television Commercials

Whether we're talking about spots for cable or for purely commercial television, both cost more to produce and are more difficult to construct than ads for other media forms. Knowledge and experience are required, but if yours is a nonprofit group, you undoubtedly will have the station's cooperation and assistance. If you represent a commercial enterprise, however, you are urged to locate either an agency or a trained professional to produce your commercial, or at least to counsel and assist you if you choose the do-it-yourself method.

Adapting the PSA technique permits small businesses to produce lower-cost, acceptable commercial messages, particularly in light of a current trend whereby commercials are developed to give the impression of being PSAs for use on cable and smaller local stations.

Public Service Announcements (PSAs)

"Commercial" PSAs

First, before there's any misunderstanding—there is no such thing as a commercial PSA. The FCC doesn't allow it, because *PSAs are the strict domain of nonprofit groups.* (A list of station requirements and policies pertaining *strictly to nonprofits* appears later in this chapter.)

Commercials now mimic public service announcements. Aetna Life & Casualty is the trendsetter in this category, with a campaign, according to *The New York Times*, "that delivers what most insurance advertising tried to avoid—straight talk about some of the thornier problems facing the public and insurance companies, issues like AIDS, drunken driving, and long-term care for the elderly."

"We want to be seen as a leader on the important issues of today," said Christine Farley, assistant vice president of advertising at Aetna, as quoted in *The Times* article. The commercials are meant to look and sound like public service spots.

The drastic stylistic departure from other commercials has another advantage: it is likely to catch viewers' attention.

The main point in including information here about how to contruct a PSA is that it's the least expensive production method, and it can be followed by both nonprofit and for-profit organizations.

PSA Defined

It helps to understand exactly what a PSA is and specifically whom it benefits. There are major—and obvious—differences between print and broadcast. One of the critical differences lies with FCC-dictated free airtime, which is called public service time. PSAs fall within the constraints of government-dictated public service time. Print media are not required by government to provide free space to nonprofit groups.

The definition of a PSA, according to the Federal Communications Commission (FCC), is as follows:

> [A PSA is] *an announcement for which no charge is made and which promotes programs, activities, or services of Federal, State or Local Governments [e.g., sales of bonds, recruiting, etc.] or the programs, activities or services of non-profit organizations [e.g., Red Cross] and other announcements regarded as serving community interests.*

If a newspaper grants free advertising space to a nonprofit group, a business working with, sponsoring, or otherwise allied with that group in supporting its charitable efforts finds no limits and no penalties for receiving full company name credit. But there is absolutely no commercial name credit permitted in like situations for PSAs on television. Radio appears to have some leeway in this regard. For television, the restriction extends even to mentions of places at which an event is held, such as hotel names, restaurant names, and such.

Free Airtime Versus Purchased Airtime

Broadcasting, like print media, is under no obligation to grant free airtime to any *specific* nonprofit organization. Unlike print media, however, broadcast stations are required by FCC regulations to make a certain amount of free airtime available for public or community service.

Generally speaking, stations give about one-fourth of their commercial time to public service. The station chooses the form its public service will take and decides who will receive the free airtime.

Format.   The format for public service airtime may be through hosted, regularly scheduled programs with segments devoted to projects by nonprofit organizations. Or television stations and radio stations may opt for PSAs. The format of a PSA is similar to that of a broadcast commercial.

Control.   While receiving free airtime has a definite monetary advantage, purchasing airtime also has its benefits. Purchasing airtime gives you control over the exact time period in which your message will be seen and/or heard, so that you can reach certain types of listeners or viewers. You can vary the number of purchased spots for different degrees of intensity and impact.

On the other hand, PSAs are scheduled at the radio and television stations' discretion—to play at *their* chosen time, which may be 2:00 A.M. And the message you had hoped would be aired many times may receive only a couple of exposures before it is shelved.

If a station gives your nonprofit group free PSA airtime for your message, don't cancel out the possibility of future PSAs by buying newspaper space or airtime elsewhere. Broadcast people not only read newspapers, but check out other stations (a practice called monitoring). They will find out about your purchases elsewhere and close their medium to you for anything other than the purchase of commercial time.

Preparing PSAs and Commercials the PSA Way

If your public service appeal is to be effective, you should have the answers to certain key questions even before you contact your local station. The same questions apply in preparation of advertising for a for-profit organization.

For A Better PSA—or Commercial, answer these questions:

- What is your message? Are you sure of the basic idea you want to get across?
- Who should receive your message? Is it of general interest to a large segment of the listening and/or viewing audience? Can it be tailored to those you want most to reach?
- How can you best put your message across? If yours is a nonprofit group, does it have enough general interest for a special program? Would a brief announcement serve just as well?

Your answers to these questions, particularly to the *what* of your message, will largely determine your success in getting free public service airtime.

Points for an Effective PSA

Writing for broadcast, whether using purchased time or public service time, takes salesmanship, and you can't sell something unless you are completely informed about your commodity, whether it is a commercial product or service, an event, or a plea for volunteers. Your job is to overcome the listener's or viewer's apathy, to create interest in your story, to motivate the listener to do something.

- Determine the objective of the total campaign—the specific goal for the radio and television announcements or spots.
- List all the pertinent facts to be included in the order of their importance.
- Decide on the single most important thing you want to say.
- Think about how you would say it if you were talking face-to-face to one person. Then write it that way, *in a conversational manner.*

Television PSAs and PSA-like Commercials

When you watch television, the PSAs look easy and sound easy, but they are not. Perhaps you have in mind just running down to the nearest television station so it can videotape you while you read or recite your message. Forget it! You will be courting disaster, unless you are a professional television actor or announcer. Holding the attention of viewers is most difficult and becoming increasingly so, as new technologies are used by national advertisers with jillions of dollars to spend making commercials that will be in direct competition with your PSA-type spot.

Try to remember the last political campaign period on television. Remind yourself of how many times you switched away from an announcer merely reciting copy—and those people are highly paid professionals. If they have difficulty competing for viewers' attention, think how difficult it is for nonprofessionals.

When Mary Alan Bonnick was Community Affairs Director at a CBS affiliate station, KDFW-TV, she prepared a brochure that was circulated to local organizations that were granted PSA time. The information also applies to buyers of commercial time. The following excerpts are adapted in order to present information that is more or less universal. And if you're considering only cable television, the standards may not be as stringent. To be safe, check to verify that the following guidelines and instructions meet your station's requirements.

Artistic, Creative, and Technical Standards

PSAs must be of acceptable artistic, creative, and technical quality as perceived by station management (generally the public service director, in the case of PSAs for nonprofits).

In its brochure about PSAs, KDFW-TV issues a warning in this regard: "If you produce a PSA at a cable television facility, do not automatically expect it to be aired on commercial stations. Most cable equipment is not [regular television] broadcast quality because it does not have to be. The technical quality does not [always] meet FCC standards when using cable equipment."

Video and Audio Format Requirements

Video and audio formats may be completely different from one station to another, depending on each station's equipment. Be sure to check your local station's requirements. One network affiliate accepts the following:

Video
>   2-inch videotape
>
>   1-inch videotape
>
>   3/4-inch videocassette (not 1/2-inch, as used in home recorders)
>
>   35-mm color slides
>
>   Super card or artwork [to be superimposed on the screen to replace a verbal reading].
>
>   8-by-10 [*horizontal*] prints (color or black and white).

Audio
>   1/4-inch audiotape (reel to reel)
>
>   Sound on tape (2-inch, 1-inch, 3/4-inch)
>
>   Record album (no cassettes or eight-tracks)

PSA Script Guidelines—Applicable to Commercial Spots

Mary Bonnick gave definite and specific instructions for writing PSA copy that, to a great degree, is applicable to small businesses.

Scripts
>   1. What do you want to promote?
>   A. A generic PSA for the organization [or a commercial to promote the name of the business]

   B.   A specific event benefiting the organization [or for a business, the company's product or service]

   C.   A program offered by the organization

   D.   A campaign [in the case of a business, perhaps to build image, integrity, or name recognition]

2. The copy must fit the video. Think visually as the script is written.

3. Keep it simple. Stay away from difficult medical terms or tongue twisters.

4. The name of the organization [or business] should be mentioned at least twice in the copy. However, if some information has to be edited for time, the name, address, and phone number of the organization can be superimposed on the screen during the last five seconds of the PSA [or commercial].

5. Don't omit essential information. Check the copy to be sure it tells who, what, where, when, and why.

6. Don't get carried away by trivialities, superlatives, and overenthusiasm. Omit adjectives and avoid nicknames. Think economy; your PSA [or commercial] time is a valuable commodity. Use it wisely.

7. Do not write scripts up to the 10-second, 20-second, 30-second, and 60-second limit. Leave 2 or 3 seconds to spare.

Visuals

1. Studio Camera

   A.   The studio is confining, so keep it simple.

   B.   Normally, no more than two cameras can be used.

   C.   Often live talent is used: talking, singing, acting, or simple dancing.

   D.   There are several factors to consider when choosing talent:

   (1) In how many other PSAs [or commercials] is the talent already appearing?

   (2) Is the person at ease on camera?

   (3) Will the talent be a good spokesperson for the organization?

   (4) Will the message be convincing to the public not only by the talent's image, but by how well the lines are delivered?

   E.   Props are provided by the organization (plants, director's chair, etc.).

   F.   A background can be created by using creative lighting(black limbo, blue or green, star filter) or a process called chromakeying, where a picture is inserted behind the talent. A blue or green backdrop is replaced with a video source (camera, tape, film, slide).

   G.   Costumes can be worn. If chromakeying, no blue or green can be worn. (Chromakeying is an electronic process used in television for matting one picture into another.) If talent is Black, bright white and black should not be worn. Actually, bright white should not be worn by anyone. Avoid plaids and checks.

   H.   A teleprompter is used for the talent so they can look directly into the camera lens and say their lines.

   I.   Other video can be shot in the studio to be used as cutaways from the studio talent. These visuals match the script and keep the talent from a straight "talking head" look. Existing video or slides can also be used for cutaways.

2. Slides
   A. 35 mm
   B. Color
   C. Horizontal format (action from side to side rather than top to bottom).
   D. TV system will crop edges on all four sides so titles and action must be within the center, ³/₄ inch high and 1 inch wide.
   E. Only top-quality slides will be used (e.g., in focus, good color contrast because light color will wash out on television, correct exposure, tells a story).
   F. One slide with 10 seconds of copy is not acceptable.
      Minimum number of slides:
      Per 10 seconds—2
      Per 20 seconds—4
      Per 30 seconds—6
      Per 60 seconds—12
      (A word of caution here about slides. They should never be sent to television newsrooms for *publicity* purposes. They are obsolete for that use, just as are print news releases and hard copy photographs.)

3. Prints
   A. *Minimum* size 8-by-10.
   B. If the subject calls for it, black and white photographs can be used.
   C. Use same quality standards and numbers as for slides.

4. Taping on Location
   A. The studio is confining, so in certain instances location shooting is preferred.
   B. Pick a location keeping these factors in mind:
      (1) Find a visually pleasing background.
      (2) Secure permission from the appropriate person(s).
      (3) If taping inside, check the lighting and electrical outlets of the locations.
      (4) If taping outside, check the lighting as well as the noise level of the location.
   C. Location shooting often involves talent. Use the same guidelines for choosing talent for location tapings as for studio tapings.
   D. Cue cards are often used on location. The cards are clumsy, because the talent does not look directly into the camera and often the talent has a problem reading the cards. If possible, request the talent to memorize the script. Also, visuals of the talent in action or in special surroundings can be shot with no natural sound. A voice-over is used in place of talent talking on camera.
   E. Visuals of the surroundings or the talent can also be shot to be used as visual cutaways to avoid the talent talking on camera for the entire PSA.

5. Existing Footage
   Footage that has been shot previously can be used to create an entire PSA [or commercial] or to create visual cutaways to add to a PSA [or commercial].

6. Artwork
   A. Artwork (color or black and white) is usually provided by the organization.
   B. White lettering on black camera card is used to superimpose information on the screen.
7. Tagging
   A. It is an FCC regulation that the name of the nonprofit sponsor be mentioned in the script or superimposed on the screen. Normally, the name and phone number of the sponsoring organization is supered [superimposed] the last five seconds of the PSA.
   B. Tools used for tagging
      (1) Camera card (white lettering on black) used for supering or full screen
      (2) Electronic Character Generator at the station (super of full screen)
      (3) Slide (white lettering on black background slide or color slide for supering or full screen)
   C. It is an FCC regulation that if a nonprofit organization buys commercial time, "Paid for by. . . ." has to be superimposed somewhere during the commercial. This is to distinguish between commercials and PSAs.

Audio
1. Talent talking on camera.
2. Voice-over using a celebrity (Be careful choosing talent. Does the person have a pleasing professional voice?) or the professional voice who records for the station.
3. Natural sounds from footage shot on location.
4. Sound effects (usually taken from record albums).
5. Music
   A. Music enhances a PSA.
   B. Copyright laws are not strictly enforced with PSAs. The stations pay BMI and ASCAP a large sum of money for use of the music. Most classics are public domain, and there is also library music which is not copyrighted. [Copyright laws are enforced for profit-making businesses.]
6. Combination of any of these.

Post-Production Hints
1. Copies of the PSA, for other stations, are made at no charge to the organization. Extra copies are made for the organization to distribute as it chooses. However, after seven copies, the organization will be charged a fee to be determined by the station. The station producing the PSA usually keeps the master tape. [For-profit businesses should arrange for "dupes" to be made elsewhere than at the station where airtime has been purchased.]
2. When picking up PSAs from the producing station, be sure to also pick up any slides, artwork, props, or music used in producing the PSA.
3. Personal delivery of the PSA to Public Service Directors is highly recommended.
4. There is no guarantee for public service time. Do not beg, plead, threaten, or demand public service time. Be brief, courteous, and friendly.
5. If the PSA is to be returned to the organization after airing, tell the Public

Service Director. (Generic PSAs are usually aired for six to nine months.)

6. Most Public Service Directors can give the number of times the PSA was aired in a week or a month, but not the times of day it was aired.

Airtime Scheduling

1. PSAs are scheduled [at most stations] by the Public Service Director about a day in advance, except for weekend PSAs, which usually are scheduled on Thursday and Friday.

2. There is no guaranteed Public Service time. Public Service availabilities change daily depending upon the amount of commercial sales and station promotional announcements. After commercials and promos are scheduled, the remaining time is filled with public service.

3. Public Service availabilities are seasonal—not so for purchased time. For businesses, the following information tells you when your commercial will be up against the strongest competition from other businesses.
   A. Heavy commercial sales mean less Public Service time.
      (1) September starts the new TV season.
      (2) October, November, through December 21 are ratings months and Christmas sales are heavy.
      (3) November, February, and May are national and local rating sweeps months (blockbuster programming and specials).
   B. Lighter commercial sales mean more Public Service time.
      (1) December 22 through January 1 is heavy Public Service [time] because advertisers traditionally do not buy as much time between the two holidays.
      (2) January—advertising slacks off slightly after Christmas.
      (3) June, July, August sales slack off because there are not as many viewers. Repeat programming, vacations, and good weather keep the viewer level down during the summer.

The "Smash" List

Alva Goodall, Public Service Director for another network-affiliated station, offers the following memory jogger for writers of PSAs. It is used with permission.

- **S**tudy each station. Watch how they handle PSAs and public affairs programming.
- **M**eet personally with the Public Service Director. Introduce yourself and acquaint him or her with your organization.
- **A**sk questions. Don't be shy. The PSA Director is there to help you. Find out the requirements for submission of material.
- **S**ubmit your material as required by the station. Be on time for deadlines; make appointments.
- **H**elp the Public Service Director help you. Mark your material clearly, including any start and end dates that are necessary.

If you are professional, prepared, patient, and polite, you will be a *SMASH!*

Tips for More "Insurance"

The following sections add a few tips to those shared by Mary Bonnick and Alva Goodall, to provide greater assurance that your PSA—or PSA-like commercial—will be effective.

Slides: Use slides that are visually stimulating, that show your organization—nonprofit or for-profit—at work, or that picture a problem with its possible solution relating directly to your spoken message.

If you are doing your own photo work, get in tight with what television people call a CU (closeup), or ECU (extreme closeup). Avoid medium or long shots. Showing action makes your slides more compelling.

For a 30-second PSA or a paid commercial, use from 5 to 15 slides. Using several slides puts a feeling of action and movement into the spot. Nothing is more deadly to watch than less than a minimum number of slides. Research shows that the viewer's eye will wander after seven seconds, no matter how compelling the audio portion of the message.

Calling for *cuts* from slide to slide produces an animated, lively feeling. Using *dissolves* (the overlapping fade-out of one slide and fade-in of another) produces a slower visual change and a more relaxed effect.

Professional Announcers.   A voice-over narration can be done by someone in your organization who is capable of reading copy in a professional manner. But it is far better to have it done by a real professional. Sometimes the station will assign one of its announcers to read the copy without charge to you if yours is a nonprofit group, but if there is a talent fee and it is within your budget, you are better off using this service.

Minority Representation.   FCC regulations require broadcast stations to provide a certain amount of minority programming. So, if it is a PSA, include pictures of minorities in your slides if possible. The same works well when appropriate for commercials. However, don't force it, and don't use exploitation. If such inclusion is appropriate in a PSA, stress this in your message. It may help your PSA to get better play, because it can help the station when relicensing applications come due.

Station Requirements and Policies Strictly for Nonprofit PSAs

Find out individual station requirements and policies, and keep an updated list. The specifications definitely may be different in other geographical areas, or markets, as broadcast people say.

These are the usual station requirements and policies for nonprofit PSAs:

- The sponsoring organization must be tax exempt and able to prove it.
- No shared commercial message (visual, aural, or both) may be included in a [PSA] for television, and any hint of commercialism such as "charges to cover expenses" of a product or service being offered is strictly unacceptable.

- Names of commercial ventures such as sponsors of events cannot be mentioned even if all proceeds benefit a nonprofit organization.
- Names of hotels, ticket agencies, and individual stores cannot be mentioned as that constitutes commercialism. However, names of shopping malls can be used.
- No event will be publicized that is not open to the public or that does not have broad-based audience appeal.
- PSAs will not be aired using personalities or members of the broadcast media of another station or personalities from another network.
- PSAs will not be aired for membership drives for clubs, civic or social. [Nor will it air messages] for colleges/universities promoting registration days and holidays; [nor] for political organizations or special interest groups; [nor] for individual churches.

Make the Spot Entertaining

There are two requisites in advertising that have almost become mandates:

- Tell a story.
- Bring a smile.

Motrin IB tells a story to make its point and does it in an entertaining, convincing way in a 30-second spot. No recitation of facts, figures, or benefits. You watch it happen.

> A boy wearing a pitcher's glove asks, "Any kids around, Aunt Jane?"
> An announcer—voice over—explains that Jane Stewart suffers from arthritis and that she takes the pain-relief medicine.
> Then there is Aunt Jane, wearing her catcher's mitt, saying, "Okay, kid, let's see what you've got."

Soft-sided humor is valuable as an attention-getter and important in building remembrance.

But There's A Wrong Way!

We're well aware of junk mail, so it probably is not surprising that there are junk radio and TV spots too.

Actually, they're not really junk spots. That's just what TV and radio people call them. They bring a very negative reaction. It's something to think about.

Larry Powell, a columnist for *The Dallas Morning News*, says there are some spots that have left bad tastes in his mouth, one of which is for AT&T's 800 number service. It's a radio commercial with twangy music and a real folksy voice—to be run in the Dallas market.

"I can almost see a roomful of ad wizards nodding and agreeing, 'This will play to those hayseeds in Dallas,'" Powell says. The copy, as he tells it, is as follows:

> *THIS HERE OFFER! Why, shut my mouf, if ah didn't hop in the flatbed and run over to the filling station where I borried two-bits from a pump jockey and gave a holler to the opratur for uh 800 nummer for muh new bidness, "Dialogue R Us."*

What Powell's comments say is that advertising of this kind isn't cute, isn't entertaining, but is, in effect, insulting to Texans. Keep his comments and example in mind when you devise commercials for anyone, and particularly for an ethnic group.

Powell points out another advertising blunder that shows up in a Cadillac spot. "The company wants to sell the most finely engineered, most dependable automobile on the road today and mentions that it comes with free towing service. Well, what on earth for?" he asks.

That last would seem to be a breach of common sense. As we mentioned in another chapter, it's only common sense *not* to mount an advertising campaign to sell shampoo to bald-headed men. The same kind of common sense tells you not to open a drive-through bank or cleaning establishment *on the second floor of a building.*

No matter how smitten you are with the words you've written, *listen* to them while wearing your intended consumers' shoes.

Formulas for Timing Your PSA or Commercial Spot Copy

Because copy for both radio and television is written to be heard (whereas print copy is written to be read), the timing formula is the same for all broadcast copy. And while newspapers deal in column inches as their form of measurement, radio and television deal in seconds and minutes.

It is important for you to time your copy for broadcast spots precisely, whether they are purchased commercials or free public service announcements. The following table will help you estimate the length of your copy by number of words per second.

Seconds	Number of Words
10	20
20	50
30	75
60	150

Most people use a stopwatch to time spots. But because some people read faster than others, KNBC-TV in Los Angeles devised a more accurate method for timing spots: five syllables equal one second.

Time is so controlled by today's state-of-the-art electronics that a poorly timed spot that runs even one second too long will be automatically cut off the air at the point it overruns its allotted time slot. Be as precise as possible.

(If you're wondering whether you should time *news releases*, the answer is no. A news release will be rewritten at the station to fit time consignments, so that timing is not your responsibility.)

Preparation of Copy for Radio PSAs

The following are guidelines and instructions that apply to radio public service announcements.

Radio PSA Guidelines.   Just as for print media, your typewriter, word processor, or computer printer must be in first-class shape and your typing must be neat and accurate.

- Use one announcement per page.
- Type on only one side of the paper.
- Double- or triple-space announcement copy on 8¹/₂- by 11-inch white paper.
- Use a clean typewriter or a new printer ribbon.
- Use upper- and lower-case letters for regular copy and upper-case letters for emphasis. For instance, use upper-case letters to emphasize your organization's name.

Radio PSA Instructions.   For greater understanding of the following instructions, refer to the example in Figure 18.1.

1. If you are not using letterhead or "instantly created letterhead," type and center (at the top of the page) the following information about your organization:
   Name
   Address
   Telephone and fax numbers
2. Space down two to four lines and type the contact information at the left margin. As in a press release, try to provide two contact names.
   - Type the word "Contact": then your name, then space down one line.
   - Type your telephone number if it is different from the one listed in the letterhead. (In the example in Figure 18.1, the first person listed can be reached at the organization's telephone number, so no telephone number is listed.) Space down one line.
   - Type the words "Alternate Contact:" then the name of a knowledgeable staff member or volunteer, then space down one line and type his or her telephone number if different from the number given for the organization.
3. Alongside the right-hand margin and opposite the contact information:
   - Type the words "Start Date:" and space down one line.
   - Type the date on which the PSA is scheduled to start playing, and space down a line.
   - Type the words "End Date:" and space down another line.
   - Type the date on which the PSA is scheduled to stop running.
4. Space down two lines and, aligned with the left-hand margin, type the word "Time:" followed by the number of seconds the PSA is set to run.
5. Space down two more lines and type "Words:" followed by the number of words in the PSA announcement.
6. Space down four lines or so and type the announcement copy, double or triple spaced.

Videotaped Productions

No one disputes that moving pictures move viewers. They are the preference of most large advertisers, because they are the most effective visual method of

FIGURE 18.1   Format Example of Radio PSA Copy
(When no letterhead is available, use plain white business-size paper.)

THE RESOURCE ASSISTANCE CENTER
1234 South Sixteenth Street
Dumont, Kansas 85123
Phone: 111/456-7890 Fax: 111/456-0987

Contact: Mark Whitmore   Start Date: February 2

Alternate Contact: Deb Wilson   End Date: February 8

          111/222-3333

Time: 20 seconds

Words: 47

This is HELP A SENIOR CITIZEN WEEK. This week join THE RESOURCE

ASSISTANCE CENTER to help Dumont area seniors prepare their tax

returns. Over the years, TRAC has helped people of all ages.

Now TRAC needs your help. Call today . . . TRAC's number is in

your phone book.

                # # #

---

presenting a sales message. But video production, of even a very short commercial, is expensive.

There is a way you may be able to have your commercial spot videotaped affordably. If there is a motion picture, advertising, or broadcasting department at a university or college in your area, sometimes a student will work free or for a small fee to acquire the experience he or she needs and to provide a sample for a portfolio. Be sure to check out the student's ability and have a firm advance agreement for tapes, camera rentals, and other costs; ownership; delivery dates; and contingency plans for unacceptable results. Also be sure that the correct videotape, as dictated by the station's requirements, is used.

If you are able to arrange for a handsome, well-produced video PSA, you undoubtedly are assuring that the spot will receive an exceptional amount of airtime. This does not apply to the number of uses for a commercial—the numbers of times it will be used is a part of the advertising contract.

19

Anatomy of a Newspaper

How the newspaper business works

Extra! Extra! Now It's the E-Paper!

"What is black and white and technicolor and digital and read all over?" asks William Glaberson in *Editor & Publisher*.

"It's one of the most sophisticated electronic newspapers yet—the *Atlanta Journal and Constitution's* 'Access Atlanta,'" he says. The "E-paper" is available over Prodigy Services' computer service for $6.95 a month, with additional charges for services such as electronic mail.

True, it's high tech gone ballistic as compared with the news-on-paper we've known and read in this country since John Campbell first published *The Boston News-Letter* back in 1704. The *Atlanta Journal's* E-paper gives readers easy access to illustrations as well as text and a chance, at the touch of a button, to have their computer screens "painted" with color graphics and photographs that accompany news articles.

"Local"—It's as Big as High Tech

More important in terms of survival for newspapers is a concept that you should keep in mind regarding your publicity efforts. "Local, local, local," is how David Scott, publisher of electronic information services at Atlanta's *Journal and Constitution*, describes it. That means the service will concentrate on detailed neighborhood information that is not now found in most other large metropolitan newspapers.

So now we learn that even E-papers must have a heart that's truly *local* in nature. But you already know that—you know that the news with the highest interest level for readers of any newspaper is local news. And the best newspaper publicity releases accentuate local aspects because newspapers, unlike most other media, are, first, local publications.

Apparently not all newspaper publishers have been getting this "local" message as well as they should—or they haven't recognized the dangers of ignoring it. At a recent conference on the future of print journalism, newspaper editors and publishers were drubbed for "throwing out the baby with the bath water," by scrimping on local news as a means of reducing costs.

"In the future, it won't be good enough for local papers to offer a smattering of local news and fill the bulk of the paper with wire service copy," warned Steven Ross, a former magazine and newsletter editor, author of several books, and now a professor at the Columbia University Graduate School of Journalism. "The public will figure out . . . they can get AP on Compuserve," he said. The story was reported in *Editor & Publisher* magazine.

E-Papers Will Be Everywhere

As you read in Chapter 1, large newspaper companies, such as Knight-Ridder and its subsidiary the *San Jose Mercury News*, have been furiously reinventing themselves. They, along with the Times-Mirror and Media General companies will offer their services through Prodigy, while the Gannett and Tribune chains will present their E-papers through America Online and Compuserve. An ad for the *San Jose Mercury News* explains how it all works:

> *Using a personal computer and modem, readers can browse the full text of the Mercury News, search back issues of 15 newspapers, plus read thousands of articles and features not found in the Mercury News. Mercury Center is also interactive—with electronic mail, conferencing and bulletin boards. Plus, many of our editors and reporters are online to answer questions and discuss issues.*

Newspapers—Long Before High Tech—Were Highly Unique

Newspapers have always been unique. People who have read them all their lives feel they understand them and are comfortable with them. Actually, newspapers always have been—and will continue to be—complex and complicated free-enterprise operations that, in many ways, are totally unlike other businesses.

For one thing, newspapers are strictly profit-making operations, yet they disregard some basic business canons, such as in selling their product for less than their manufacturing costs and in giving free delivery for less than the cash-and-carry price.

Understanding how newspapers operate is interesting, but more significant, that understanding can help you learn and practice better publicity skills. And regardless of the degree of reinvention and technological changes, their missions, purposes, and aims remain constant.

The Many Purposes of Newspapers

Of all media available, only the newspaper serves people of so many different education levels, ages, personalities, interests, and concerns.

Even after it has informed, educated, enlightened, entertained, amused, instructed, enriched, enlivened, stimulated, convinced, activated, involved, saddened, gladdened, and perhaps angered, the newspaper still makes the reader think.

Anna Quindlen, a reporter for *The New York Times*, describes newspapers' functions this way: A newspaper is "portable and reusable. If you don't get the gist the first time, you can reread. If you don't care about one gist, you can turn to another.

"And when you're through with gist," she says, "you can pack up old dishes and line bird cages." She neglected to mention that newspapers have for years been useful for swatting flies, covering schoolbooks, wiping paintbrushes, training puppies, and, of course, wrapping fish. What other medium offers such a spread of services?

Newspapers Serve Many Needs

Almost everyone reads a newspaper, even in these days of time dominance by television and radio. Newspapers are the key to jobs, housing, movies, television shows, bargains, sports events, and such close-to-home questions as why the fire sirens sounded during the night.

Jeff Greenfield, Universal Press Syndicate columnist, describes it in his own way. "An old adage about news consumers goes like this: When someone wakes up in the morning, the first questions she asks are, 'Am I OK? Is my family OK? Is my neighborhood OK?' Then she will permit herself to think about bigger things."

People count on radio to find out about immediate things, such as whether to take an umbrella or whether the interstate is backed up for miles. And even though people may witness events firsthand or see them on television, the first thing they do the next morning is reach for the newspaper. Why? Because the newspaper fills in the gaps. It explains, reports, narrates, and reviews. In short, it interprets the scene by answering people's questions about the event. Newspapers try to tell the reader the *why* of what has happened, since he or she has already learned the *what* from the television screen.

Newspapers as Information Factories

Today's newspaper is the biggest information factory in the world! And it offers many kinds of information—from front-page news that presents current history and becomes tomorrow's past, to biographical data supplied in obituaries and feature stories.

People turn to newspapers to be able to make valid judgments after being given both sides of an issue and to analyze for themselves what has been read so they can draw their own conclusions.

But you can ask any group of people—including newspaper people—the question, What is a newspaper? Then look up the word in a dictionary and in an encyclopedia. Chances are there won't be one answer exactly like another. This is because a daily newspaper is so many things, and it is different things to different people. It is uniquely different from other news media (magazines, television, radio). It also is different from other businesses.

Fulfillment of Individual Needs

The *Centre Daily Times* in State College, Pennsylvania, told its readers how it believes a newspaper serves different purposes for different readers.

- To opinion searchers, it stimulates thought.
- To the voter, it is guidance; to a politician, friend or foe.
- To the seller, it means a quick response; to buyers, many selections.

- To some, it brings good news; to others, sad tidings.
- To front porch sitters, it describes life beyond the horizon.
- To the immigrant, it is a schoolbook that helps him [or her] learn English; to hunters of truth, it translates the customs from which the immigrant fled.
- To the living, it is a source of freedom and hope; for the dead, a tribute to their virtues.
- To the homemaker, it is ideas for new menus and new clothes and sensible buying.
- To the mother, it is suggestions for raising the youngsters.
- To the lonely diner, it is a companion; around the family dinner table, a topic of conversation.
- To sports and theater lovers, it's who and what is playing, when and where.
- To athletes and actors, it's scrapbook material.
- To an unknown, it brings fame; to a well-known, it furthers his [or her] name.
- To the publicity seeker, it is a haven; to the publicity shy, a source of annoyance.
- To friends and neighbors, it tells about promotions, school achievements and who got married, who was born, who died.
- To all who read the newspaper it means uncensored news; in some countries it means censored propaganda.

As Howard Kurtz, press critic for *The Washington Post*, says, "Newspapers help us make sense of the blur of televised images racing by. [Newspapers] provide the context, the explanations, the fine print. When it comes to finding out things that government and business leaders don't want us to know, newspapers remain the last bastion of what used to be called muckraking."

The Newspaper Paradox

A newspaper is a private business enterprise that makes a product and sells it for a profit. But the kinds of material it sells—information and news—make it a quasi-public utility. Actually, a newspaper could be described as a private business that performs as a public institution.

A newspaper has five basic responsibilities. The first is selfish; the remaining four are social:

- To preserve itself
- To provide information
- To offer guidance and advice
- To entertain
- To serve and represent the public

The People's First Right

Uniquely, a newspaper carries the distinctive honor of being one of the four major freedoms guaranteed by the Constitution of the United States—the only private business mentioned in the Constitution. It is the people's first right in the Bill of Rights.

However, the First Amendment to the Constitution does not protect only the "responsible" press. Recognizing this, many years ago, the American Society of Newspaper Editors (ASNE) set down what it believed were the obligations of a responsible press in its "Canons of Journalism: A Code of Ethics."

To be truthful, accurate, and thorough.

To be fair, decent, and impartial.

To defend the public's right to know without invading individual privacy under a guise of public curiosity.

The role of the press is to report events and what they mean; to provide leadership with responsibility and integrity.

Free Press Issues in the 1990s

An update by ASNE in November 1992 interprets free press policy this way:

The framers of the Constitution believed a free press is essential to a democratic government, and they expressly enjoined Congress to "make no law . . . abridging the freedom of speech, or of the press."

The role of the press is not always understood or appreciated by government officials, members of the bar and bench, the military or the public at large.

The press thinks of itself as a watchdog, and the role is well taken. In the United States, it is the people who possess absolute sovereignty, not the government. People, and the press on their behalf, thus enjoy the right to freely examine what their government is doing, in all its manifestations.

. . . A free press may sometimes be an annoyance, but a tamed press hurts democracy.

Service to All

Each newspaper has what seems an insurmountable task—to furnish its services for all of the people, no matter how varied their ages, personalities, interests, and concerns.

A book is written in a single style and is often read by many people for the same kinds of reasons; in addition, those people usually have similar interests and levels of education. This is not true of a newspaper.

A newspaper is written for a wide variety of audiences and in a variety of writing styles. It is written for people who like sports, people who read only the comics, people who want to know who is divorcing whom, people who follow the stock market, and people who want to know details, beyond the headline service television is able to give, of the really important things that have happened in the last 24 hours. To make it even more difficult, newspaper readers may have reading and education levels that range from minimal to scholarly.

A newspaper is also written for people who want to be informed, but who don't have much reading time, for people who have plenty of time and demand everything in depth, for people who cannot comfortably begin their day until they know what the stars say, and for people who must feed and outfit a family for school on a limited budget and need to know where food and clothes cost least. It must satisfy people who want pro and con opinions, people who want details about products, people who want to be entertained, people who want to know what's playing at the movies and what each movie is about, and people who want to find new jobs, buy second-hand cars, or give away puppies.

Almost unbelievably, each edition of an average daily newspaper contains as many words (not including advertising) as a full-sized novel or a couple of paperbacks. And it all comes together and is in the hands of its readers within a matter of hours. It seems like an impossible job, but it is done day in and day out, usually every day of the year.

Information for Pennies a Day

The free press issue—not as we know it—comes up in Johnny Hart's "B.C." comic strip. The editor of *The Daily Mud* is asked, "Do you believe in a free press?" The editor replies, "Darn right I do." Then the editor is asked, "Then what are you doing charging six bits for a newspaper?"

Let's ask another question: where today can you get the world on a platter for even less than the cost of *The Daily Mud?* The following are the single-copy sales prices charged by newspapers across the nation:

New York Daily News	40 cents
Newsday	50 cents
The New York Times	50 cents
New York Daily News	40 cents
Staten Island (New York) Advance	35 cents
The Dallas Morning News	25 cents
San Francisco Examiner & Chronicle	35 cents
The Des Moines (Iowa) Register	35 cents

Factor in the reality that readers are used to paying cheap prices for mounds of information in their newspapers because advertising subsidizes most of the costs. Now, subtract advertising as it exists, and E-papers and prices to subscribers will skyrocket.

There's not much available these days for only 35 cents. Even Snoopy's brother Spike acknowledges this. In a "Peanuts" strip, Spike is flanked by paintings and a sign that says, "Western Paintings for Sale," and he remarks, "Did I tell you I got a grant from the National Endowment for the Arts?" Then he adds, "You can't do much, though, with thirty-five cents."

Try giving yourself—or your six-year-old, for that matter—an allowance of 35 cents a day, and see what you get. You can't buy a Coke from a Coke machine for 35 cents. And where in the metropolitan area are there bus rides under 50 cents one way? (This doesn't even consider the return trip!)

The astonishing thing is that those 25, 35, or 50 pennies don't begin to cover the cost of producing a newspaper, let alone give the owners some margin of profit. The paper and ink alone that go into a daily newspaper cost more than the price of the newspaper. Actually, the sale of the product is only about one-third of a newspaper's revenue.

Business and Competition

A newspaper is the only product that is sold to the consumer for less than the cost of manufacturing it. Top that with a newspaper's practice of delivering its product daily with no charge for the delivery, and often for *less* than when sold on a cash-and-carry basis at a newsstand.

Be it a weekly or a daily serving a small community, a major megalopolis, or even the entire country, as in the case of such newspapers as *The Wall Street Journal*, *The Christian Science Monitor*, and *USA Today*, every newspaper operates under the checks and balances inherent in a competitive economy. If, for long, a newspaper irritates its clientele, it writes its own obituary. If it offends morals or mores, it loses favor. If it caters to special interests, it risks loss of confidence, respect, and integrity. If it grows meek and fails to champion what benefits the people it serves—in the community, the state, or the nation—it may be replaced by a more courageous competitor.

So, how does a *business* not subsidized by government or any funding agency continue to operate under a process that is completely contrary to the market formula for business success (that retail sales prices must include all costs of manufacture and distribution and still allow for profit)?

Advertising as Financial Mainstay

Advertising provides the largest chunk of a newspaper's revenue—about two-thirds for most newspapers. Advertising revenue is imperative so that newspapers can retain their freedom from government control of news content. Without it, newspapers would fail or be forced to accept government funding, which would remove their private-interest status and make them merely voices for government.

Yet why are advertisers willing to carry this lopsided cost burden? In reality, it's not so one-sided. Newspapers and advertisers are dependent on each other.

- Newspapers provide an editorial setting for advertising to enable it to do its best job.
- Advertising provides product and service news and the other information readers want that is so necessary to the success of a newspaper. The importance of advertising to readers has been tested and proven over and over whenever there have been newspaper shutdowns or strikes.

The Forecast Isn't All That Cloudy

Howard Kurtz gives perspective to what made newspapers all over the country sit up and take notice of what was happening to their revenue, their readers, and their advertisers—and to begin their dance of the dinosaurs.

> *The industry's bottom line never looked better than in the Roaring '80s. [Then] the bottom fell out in 1990, with newspaper earnings plunging by 30, 40, or even 60 percent.*
>
> *Classified advertising stalled with the collapse of the real estate and employment markets. . . . Less advertising invariably means less news. . . . [and ultimately] circulation took a nosedive.*

"Just when it began to look as if telecommunications developments would overshadow and inundate newspapers, a rejuvenated newspaper business is gearing up for future expansion with fire in its eyes," *E&P* reported in the summer of 1994. "Rebounding advertising and profits for newspapers are breaking up a logjam of pent-up demand that has accumulated since the worst newspaper recession in decades forced many papers to cut their staffs and to shelve much capital spending."

NAA's annual survey showed newspapers planned to spend nearly $1.1 billion in 1994, 13.3 percent more than they spent in 1993. And the president of the International Newspaper Marketing Association says newspapers' use and approval of new technologies and new techniques together with their new attitudes make the forecast for the next five years "about the most positive in newspaper history."

The results of a recent market study indicates that newspapers have 10 to 15 years of "breathing space" in which to position themselves before significant competition emerges in interactive video systems.

But the study by consulting firm Clark, Martire & Bartolomeo Inc. of Englewood Cliffs, New Jersey, also states that while publishers "may have begun to 'talk the talk' they are not yet prepared to 'walk the walk.' "

That statement is disputed by the Newspaper Association of America. VP and COO Len Forman says, "We are getting our act together, and that's pretty impressive when you consider how diverse the industry is."

Forman also disagreed with a prediction that total circulation would drop by the turn of the century. Most papers are gaining circulation, a fact masked by the decline in aggregate numbers stemming from papers closing.

Newspapers Then and Now

In 1690, Ben Harris probably could have collected most of the news he needed for the first newspaper published in the colonies, *Publick Occurrences, Both Foreign and Domestick*, from a centrally situated bench on Boston Common. In fact, Harris gathered the news for his paper from Bostonians who met in his coffeehouse to read the London papers and "to converse and argue as well as sip."

Later, in 1704, when John Campbell published the first regular weekly newspaper, *The Boston News-Letter*, he could have gathered the information without ever leaving his post as postmaster. Either man alone could have converted the news into the publications they published.

Today's newspaper staffs may roam cities, counties, countries, and continents to find and report daily news. In addition, newspapers have access to wire services and syndicate agencies for features and news analysis. And all newspapers receive additional important information from publicity releases distributed to them from organizations and publicity agencies.

Newspaper Operations

Newspaper practices and mechanics vary greatly, according to the size of the city, the newspaper's circulation, its frequency of publication, and its access to new-age technologies. *The New York Times*, The *Los Angeles Times*, and The *San Jose Mercury News*, for example, are as dissimilar as the Army, the Navy, and the Marine Corps. Because of this, any generalized picture of newspaper operations is subject to some distortion by omission. A broad picture can be drawn, however.

Today newspaper chains—which in the sixties claimed less than half of all daily newspaper circulation—now in the nineties account for more than three-quarters of the 1,580 newspapers in the country, which means differences in fiscal and financial accountabilities.

Even a small newspaper requires a relatively large capital outlay; some of the largest are multimillion-dollar corporations. All must be well organized if they are to be financially successful, and although they generally do not have a rigid method of organization, all usually consist of five departments:

1. Editorial
2. Advertising
3. Circulation
4. Business
5. Production

Chain of Command

Generally, a flow chart for a newspaper would be as follows:

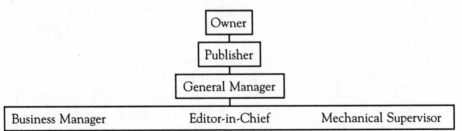

Publisher

For 80 percent of daily newspapers, the owner is a newspaper group such as Knight-Ridder, Capital Cities/ABC, Inc., or The Ogden Newspapers, and the corporation hires publishers for each of its newspapers.

For an individual newspaper that is not part of a group, the owner is almost always the *publisher*. (Although most daily newspapers are incorporated and may have a president and chairman of the board of directors, the publisher often functions somewhat as chairman, president, chief executive officer, and chief operating officer.)

For larger papers and those that are members of a group, a publisher is hired to supervise the many details of publishing. He or she is responsible for operating the newspaper so as to make a profit, for seeing that it is accepted by the readers, and for ensuring that employees are satisfied with their working conditions. The publisher is the authority with regard to decisions concerning the advertising, circulation, business, and production departments.

The publisher is the person who formulates broad policy for most newspapers. Generally, however, he or she has no part in day-to-day editorial matters. (It should be noted that in many groups each newspaper is a separate corporation, with little or no central direction of editorial policy.)

The *general manager* is the publisher's assistant. Often he or she is the chief financial officer. A general manager must have widespread knowledge of all departments within the newspaper.

Editor

How does an editor handle the constant tightrope walk? (Bet you didn't know that Ann Franklin was the first female editor of an American newspaper, the *Mercury*, published in Newport, Rhode Island, in 1762!)

The *editor-in-chief* is in charge of the editorial departments. (Note: The designation "editorial department" does not cover merely the editorial and opinion page(s) section, where editorials, opinion columns, letters to the editor, and so on, appear. "Editorial department" denotes all news departments and all printed content that is *not* advertising.)

Rarely is the editor-in-chief's entire title used; the simple title *editor* most often denotes the highest news official in charge of all editorial departments.

The Wall Street Journal, in its "Pepper . . . and Salt" feature, calls an editor "a line tamer," but in reality, he or she is much more. As a matter of fact, the editor has copy editors who do the line taming. The editor is responsible for everything that appears in the paper except advertising. He or she works closely with the business manager and the production manager, determines the amount of space to be allotted to local, state, and national news, and decides on the features, columns, and cartoons that are to run in the newspaper.

There is probably no other single person in town who knows more about what makes your community tick—past, present, and future—than the editor of your local newspaper. In many towns, nearly every significant piece of data about every citizen, from birth notice to obituary, passes across the editor's desk.

Newspaper editors often walk a tight line in deciding what to put in the paper and what to leave out. They know, for instance, that reporting certain disturbances may lead to more violence by leaders who like to see the disruption they cause. But when this is weighed against the right of the people to know what is going on, the latter usually wins out. Newspapers are often accused of printing such information for its sensation value. There may be merit to the allegation with reference to scandal tabloids and those offbeat publications that practice check-book journalism. But conventional, traditional, respected newspapers don't have to print sensational news in order to sell papers, because home-delivered papers are paid for in advance and home deliveries make up about 75 to 85 percent of the sales of the majority of newspapers.

Reporters

News reporters are news gatherers, not ventriloquists. Anna Quindlen, in *The New York Times*, said that a newspaper is given its voice by the people who write and edit it, and then added, "Ventriloquists won't cut it."

Reporters are the heart of the news-gathering operation. Most editors, editorial writers, and columnists were once reporters.

A want ad that appeared in a publication of the American Newspaper Publishers Association (now NAA) spelled out a reporter's qualifications:

> WANTED: *Individual with innate curiosity, intelligence, college education (not merely degree), writing ability, typing proficiency. Must have capacity to dig for news and to write it accurately, fully and intelligibly even under deadline pressure. Must possess interest, versatility and skill to reduce complex issues to lucid, simple English for demanding readers seeking not merely facts but comprehension in era of unparalleled complexity, perplexity, ferment, change.*

A reporter's reward and gratifications—or the opposite—are built into the job. He or she is on the "inside" of news and in the confidence of newsmakers. The reporter must demonstrate initiative, independence, and judgment. The unexpected is to be expected. The relentless pressure of a deadline rides like a monkey on the reporter's back, and, at times, personal plans give way to emergency job demands. His or her priceless prose may be slashed to accommodate space. Being accurate, factual, honest, and objective about a story and refusing to take no for an answer sometimes create enemies.

David Casstevens, when he was a reporter for *The Dallas Morning News*, added some thoughts of his own about his job as a reporter: "There are times I feel jealous of athletes. . . . A football player scores a touchdown, and the feedback, the roar of the crowd, is instantaneous and exhilarating. Writing is solitary work. If words born from one's keyboard touch a reader in a positive way, the response, whether it be an agreeing nod or a touch of a smile, goes unseen by the one who produced it."

However, for most, the greatest reward is seeing the results of the day's work in print almost immediately, often even with a byline.

Revenue Producers

The advertising and circulation managers may report to the business manager or directly to the general manager or publisher. They are the revenue producers for the company.

The *advertising manager* is responsible for selling advertising space in the newspaper and for supervising all advertising copy. He or she may have assistance: a classified advertising manager and national and retail advertising managers. The advertising department, which produces about two-thirds of the company's revenue, has salespeople who have regular customers on whom they call to sell advertising.

The *circulation manager* is in charge of distribution of the newspapers by a number of methods. He or she is responsible for promoting sales campaigns and for overseeing the carrier salespeople and the newspaper-delivery functions. The circulation department produces about one-third of the revenue.

The circulation manager performs somewhat like the general of a small but highly efficient army of specialists. Under his or her command are drivers, carriers, district field managers, a skilled clerical force, solicitors, troubleshooters, and supervisors.

Distributing the newspaper is a daily triumph in logistics and over obstacles of geography, traffic, weather, and train, bus, air, and post office schedules.

There is something of an irony here, though. No other business in the world functions at jet-age speed right up to the shipping dock and then turns over its product to be delivered by a boy or girl on a bicycle (or, at best, to someone in a car tossing it out the window onto your lawn). (It wasn't until 1972—210 years after Ann Franklin broke the gender barrier in the newsroom—that federal and state laws permitted girls in the 10-to-16 age group to be newspaper deliverers.)

The number of boy and girl carriers is dropping dramatically, however, in a large part because of fears of crime on the streets. The International Circulation Management Association reported that the number of young carriers in the United States had dropped from 823,746 to 362,470 in the ten years from 1980 to 1990, while the number of adult carriers rose from 88,788 to 188,886.

Future Delivery—On Paper?

Jerome Rubin, a pioneer in on-line research services, believes that "in the future, we may be able to use flexible on-line computer displays that approach paper—*or may even be some form of paper.*"

Rubin says that advances in delivery technologies indicate that the familiar look and feel of a newspaper may be preserved, even as the abilities to present information is increased dramatically.

Rubin is chairman of the News in the Future Consortium at the Massachusetts Institute of Technology Media Laboratory. The consortium envisions news delivery on large, even wall-sized, screens, receiving the information from satellites, fiber optics, or even the common twisted-pair copper wire of phone lines.

Does it sound as though the Consortium is a dream team plotting a "Terminator" movie? Hardly. It may be one of the most serious such groups anywhere, with 20 sponsors, including the largest newspaper chains in the business: Chronicle Publishing Co., Gannett Co. Inc., Globe Newspaper Co., Hearst Corporation, Knight-Ridder Inc., Pulitzer Publisher Co., Times Mirror Co., and the Tribune Company.

Editorial Content

A newspaper has two basic parts—editorial content and advertising. Editorial content is anything that is not advertising. The editorial department includes not only the editorial pages on which the policy of the paper is set forth, but every other kind of editorial matter.

Editorial space is never for sale; advertising space is always for sale. If an ad looks like a news or feature story, it is carefully labeled as advertising so there is no mistake in interpretation.

There are, however, what news and advertising people call "advertorials." The word comes from a combination of the words *advertisement* and *editorial*, and these pieces are usually contained in special sections meant to instruct or entertain readers. These are used more and more frequently as a special kind of advertising to generate additional revenues.

Separation of Fact and Opinion

Within the normal editorial content of a newspaper there are two main categories—fact and opinion. There is no place for opinion, unless it is labeled as such, in the news columns of a newspaper. Opinions of the newspaper, of its opinion writers, and of its readers go on the editorial and op-ed pages.

Interpretive reporting is also appearing more often these days in newspapers, necessitated by the fact that radio and television get the big news first but provide merely a headline service in reporting it. However, *interpretation* is not a synonym for *opinion*. An opinion is a judgment; an interpretation is an explanation. This is a major reason that even the most loyal broadcast-media fans turn to newspapers. The reporter who has covered one particular *beat* (news area) for any length of time knows more about it than his or her readers or even his or her editors. A reporter's interpretation of events in the light of his or her beat-knowledge and experience is invaluable to the reader entering the situation for the first time.

The difference between interpretive reporting and editorializing was brought into focus by Allen H. Neuharth while he was president of the Gannett Company, the largest newspaper chain in the world: "Interpretive reporting, if done well, explores all angles related to any part of a story, and then puts them in perspective as the story develops, without expressing the views of the writer. An editorial, however, must be opinionated; it must say whether something is good or bad . . . there is no 'on the other hand.' "

Individual Newspaper "Personality"

One of the editor's important jobs is to give the newspaper its "personality"—and every paper has its own. You understand what this means when you visit other cities and read their hometown newspapers. They just aren't like the "old friends" you read at home. The arrangement of stories in the columns is distinctively different, and the typographical appearance also may be totally different. The format may be six columns to a page, or even five or eight columns. The paper's size may be unique. For instance, the *Rocky Mountain News* in Denver, Colorado, the *Chicago Sun-Times*, and *Newsday* in New York—all major metropolitan dailies—are tabloid size, while *The New York Times*, the *Los Angeles Times*, and the *Chicago Tribune* are standard size.

News Placement

A newspaper is arranged to enable a reader to digest its contents within a reasonable time. *Placement* of news is the primary method used. News of universal interest goes on the front page. News of lesser importance or of more specific interest goes on inside pages. Commentary, analysis, and pros and cons of issues are gathered on the editorial and op-ed pages.

Sports news, women's and family news, business and financial news, comics, fashion, and food and cooking information can usually be found in their same places in a newspaper each day or on special days of the week. Familiarity with a newspaper cuts reading time because you know where to find the information of special interest to you.

In making up the newspaper's pages, the editor for a specific page or section works from the top of the page down. The last column to the right on page one is considered the position of greatest importance, since the reader scans the *banner* head (the headline across several columns or often run across the entire page) from left to right. Then the reader's eye naturally drops into the last column. The most important story of the day goes there.

Headlines tell you what each story is about. The lead—or first paragraphs— of a news story contains the most important details. Each succeeding paragraph contains elaboration or addition of details to the information in the lead.

The editor of page one (like every other page or section editor) wants an orderly variety of stories and pictures on each page, not a jumble, so he or she usually follows a tested formula. The editor alternates the size and type styles of headlines and uses stories of varying lengths. Subheads and short paragraphs are used to break up the gray look of solid columns of regular-size type. Pictures and drawings provide greater contrast and interest.

Makeup on inside pages is more complicated because of ads. Page by page, news and advertising space is worked out according to *dummy* sheets (miniature page layouts), which indicate the placement of each ad and the amount of space on each page to be filled by stories and pictures. The production department works from dummy instructions as to where to place ads and arrange heads, pictures, and columns of type.

Readability Aids

Readability aids for readers may be either subtle or obvious. One readability aid is the placement of news by category (business, sports, family, and so forth).

Other readers' aids are of a more obvious nature:

- *Cross references.* "Reefers," as they are called by newspaper people, appear across a column of type, or possibly across several columns, and are set apart from body copy by lines. The following is an example of a reefer that directs a reader to page 33 in section A for a photo that relates to the news story in which the reefer appears.

{ } Related photo 33A

- *Explanatory notes.* These notes are called precedes, tags, or inserts. One type of precede might be an editor's note that explains the contents of the information that follows. It is enclosed in parentheses, is usually set in a different type style, such as italics, and may be indented. An example might be an editor's precede above a column in the business section:

(Editor's Note: This is the eighth in a series of 16 articles excerpted from The NEW Publicity Kit: A Complete Guide for Entrepreneurs, Small Businesses, and Nonprofit Organizations.)

- *Jumplines.* These include the line that uses a key word from the headline to direct the reader to where the story is continued. Jumplines may be worded differently, according to individual newspapers' styles. One newspaper may set its jumplines in italics; another may use boldface type, with the key referral words in capitals. Whatever the style it is used consistently throughout the newspaper. The following examples show different wordings and type styles:

  Please see 2 GROUPS on Page 16
  Continued on Page 8, Column 1

A line at the top of the continued story, in the same style as the jumpline, tells the reader he or she has located the continuation. Following are examples of continued lines:

  Continued from Page 1A
  Continued from Page 1

Newspapers often help to make a story clearer by having pictures, charts, maps, and diagrams accompany the story. A more complete understanding of a story is possible for a reader who takes the time to read the chart, study the map, or scan the picture.

You will find many more readers' aids when you look for them.

Types of Writing

If a newspaper is to be read, it must please an enormous range of people with a vast assortment of interests. It must be read in order to remain in business. But a newspaper is a public trust as well as a commercial enterprise. In other words, a newspaper must provide information that people want to know as well as information that people need to know.

Because audiences vary so much, a newspaper's writing must also vary. What appeals to some people will not be read by others. Sportswriting is completely different from the writing on the business and financial pages. It also is different from much of the straight-news writing that appears on the front page.

The Editorial Department

All reading material except advertising is assembled in the editorial department. Medium- and large-size newspapers generally have five divisions within the editorial department:

1. Newsroom
2. Copy and rewrite desks
3. Editorial pages
4. Photo department and lab
5. Library, or morgue

News Flow

The typical flow of news follows this order:

Managing Editor.   The managing editor is the editor's chief-of-staff and may even serve in both capacities, as editor and managing editor. He or she hires and fires and makes innumerable production decisions throughout the working day. The managing editor's job might be described as the task of seeing that every day, when readers receive their newspapers, the package is complete.

City Desk.   (Local and state news.) City editors assign reporters and photographers to cover news events.

Wire Desk.   (World news.) Each editor (national, international, sports, family, business, and so forth) receives news and photos from wire services and syndicates and decides what to use and what not to use.

Copy and Rewrite Desk.   Copy editors read copy for accuracy and sense, and they write headlines. Rewrite people have the responsibility for taking phone calls from reporters and writing their stories to meet deadlines, and for rewriting press releases.

Editorial, or Opinion, Pages.   The editorial page is the place where the newspaper's opinions appear, along with "editorialized" cartoons expressing the cartoonists' opinions. Editorials present issues of interest to readers, take stands, make judgments, and present attitudes that would not be found in news stories. Op-ed pages contain the personal viewpoints of readers—through letters to the editor and local and syndicated opinion columns.

Photo Department and Lab.   Photographers are assigned by the city editor or by a special photo editor, and they often accompany reporters on assignments. An on-premise photo lab permits rapid development of film and printing of photos for reproduction in the paper. (New technology is replacing this method. See Chapter 10 for details.)

Library, or Morgue.   The "final resting place" for news stories and photos that run in the newspaper is the *morgue*. It's the librarian's responsibility to clip and file the news stories so that reporters may easily have access to background information when writing about the same person or subject at later times. At most mid-size and large newspapers such information is filed and located by means of computers.

Special Departments.   Other editors head special news departments: fashion, food, business, family, and entertainment. The sports editor has a separate department with reporters working for him or her and is usually responsible for covering all sports events on the local, state, and national scene. Much national sports coverage, however, is available through wire services. The sports editor and other special-department editors may report to the managing editor or directly to the editor.

Columnists.   Newspapers also employ columnists, chosen for a particular style of writing to round out the content of the paper. These columnists are free to choose their own material, but they are responsible to the managing editor or editor.

Editorial Decisions

Newspapers' decisions about particular editorial positions vary from paper to paper. At some newspapers, the editor *is* management. He or she may be the owner or co-owner, or, often, in the case of small papers, he or she serves as both editor and publisher. In these situations, the editor represents the thinking of the paper and is able to speak for it. Large newspapers usually have editorial boards that meet each day as a committee and arrive at judgments in a formal manner.

"An editor, who must or should take vigorous editorial positions on the great issues of the day, is not to be loved," said John S. Knight, when he was editorial chairman of Knight-Ridder Newspapers, Inc. "If he seeks affection and popularity, he should be in public relations. Newspapers must base their conclusions upon the facts at hand. The unvarnished truth is frequently unpleasant reading since it so often differs from the reader's preconceived notions of what the truth should be."

Another publisher expressed it this way: "Newspapers that don't express strong editorial opinions that can cause some readers' emotions to explode like throwing fat into a fire, are like a dish of boiled oatmeal."

E. B. White, coauthor with William Strunk, Jr., of *The Elements of Style*, said it in a simpler manner: "There are three things no one can do to the satisfaction of anyone else: Make love, poke the fire, and run a newspaper."

Yet, as still another editor asks, "Did you ever think about the fact that a newspaper is the only business that is expected to jeopardize its income from advertisers, and even its very existence, by taking strong stands on highly volatile public issues?"

Newspaper Duties

A newspaper should be expected to do the following things:

- Supply accurate, objective information about national, international, state, county, and local issues and events.
- Provide factual information, as well as news commentary to help its readers evaluate the news.
- Include material to interest a wide variety of readers with an enormous assortment of interests and concerns.
- Take an active part in supporting worthwhile community projects by printing news stories and perhaps editorials about needed improvements or projects.
- Be attractive and easy to read; make a sincere effort to eliminate errors and misspelled words.
- Guard the freedom of the press: withholding news from the public makes for an ignorant public; sensationalizing the news makes for a cynical public.

Newspaper Rights

A newspaper should not be expected to do the following:

- Support a private interest that is contrary to the general welfare.
- Suppress news that one person or a particular group does not wish to see in print. (A person may support freedom of the press only until he or she becomes personally involved in a news story and feels that his or her privacy has been invaded.)
- Search out and publish details of prominent persons' private lives that do not directly concern or affect the public.
- Operate at a loss.

Some Famous Names in Journalism

Many people whose accomplishments made them legends served periods of their lives as newspaper publishers or reporters.

- Charles Dickens was a reporter for the London *Chronicle*.
- Rudyard Kipling was seventeen years old when he launched his literary career as a reporter for a paper in India. According to the late newspaper columnist Walter Winchell, Kipling carried on in Sahara temperatures and covered everything from murder trials to sporting events. He had a remarkable memory and never bothered making notes while covering a story. Winchell wrote that Kipling said, "If a thing didn't stay in my memory, I believed it was hardly worth writing about."
- Carl Sandburg, Ben Hecht, and Vincent Sheean were reporters on the *Chicago Daily News*.
- Gail Borden, a newspaper publisher who invented canned milk, was the man whose headline in the *Telegraph & Texas Register* immortalized the cry, "Remember the Alamo."
- Charles H. Dana started as a $10-a-week reporter on Horace Greeley's *Tribune*.
- Don Knox, a graduate of the University of Kansas and a reporter for The *Dallas Morning News*, knows more than a little about Kansas's most influential journalist, William Allen White. "His writing somehow managed to leap off the pages of *The Emporia* (Kansas) *Gazette*." White knew the journalist's credo, Keep It Simple, Stupid, according to Knox, who says that White chiseled his commentaries to a manageable size if only to ensure their wide distribution over wires of the Associated Press.
- Winston Churchill was a war correspondent when he was 21, and Britain's highest paid newsman of that period.
- Authors Ernest Hemingway, Kenneth Roberts, and John P. Marquand once were news reporters.
- Few people are aware that novelist Irving Wallace learned his writing skills as a reporter and editor for the *Wisconsin News & Southport Bugle*.
- Even some of the infamous were once reporters. Syndicated columnist L. M. Boyd wrote that it wasn't until after the famous Bat Masterson left the western frontier to return to New York City that he bought a gun in a

pawn shop there, filed 22 notches in the handle, then manufactured his own legend while a reporter for the *New York Telegraph*.

OTHER FAMOUS JOURNALISTS

Robert Benchley	Horace Greeley	Edgar Allan Poe
Heywood Broun	Bret Harte	Joseph Pulitzer
William Cullen	William R. Hearst	Ernie Pyle
Bryant	O. Henry (W. Sydney	Will Rogers
Art Buchwald	Porter)	Damon Runyon
Al Capp	Thomas Jefferson	Jonathan Swift
Marquise Childs	Sinclair Lewis	Dorothy Thompson
Frank Irvin Cobb	Jack London	James Thurber
Norman Cousins	Don Marquis	Mark Twain
Theodore Dreiser	Christopher Morley	E. B. White
F. Scott Fitzgerald	Thomas Paine	Walt Whitman
Benjamin Franklin	Dorothy Parker	

YESTERDAY'S NEWSPAPER CARRIERS
WHO BECAME HISTORY'S LEADERS

Entertainment

Art Linkletter
Danny Thomas
John Wayne
George Goebel
Dick Van Dyke
Joe E. Brown
Richard Boone
Frank Sinatra
Glenn Ford
Jack Webb
Emmett Kelley
Bing Crosby
Ernie Ford
Arthur Godfrey
Bob Hope
Fred MacMurray
Lauritz Melchoir
Red Skelton
Ed Sullivan

Business Leaders

Walt Disney
Benjamin F. Fairless
Crawford H. Greenewalt
Eric A. Johnson
W. Alton Jones
Garvice D. Kincaid
Mervin LeRoy
Elmer L. Lindseth
George Eastman
David Sarnoff

Sports

Joe DiMaggio
Jack Dempsey
Rafer Johnson
Ben Hogan
Sam Snead
Ken Venturi
Gil Dodds
Yogi Berra
Stan Musial
Mickey Mantle
Rogers Hornsby
Knute Rockne
Willie Mays
Jackie Robinson
"Duke" Snider
Red Grange
Mick McCormick

Statesmen

Lyndon B. Johnson
Harry Truman
Dwight D. Eisenhower
Herbert Hoover
Glenn H. Anderson
Harold S. Stassen
Ralph J. Bunche
Anthony J. Celebreeze
Tom C. Clark
Jack G. Diefenbacker
William O. Douglas
Lester B. Pearson
Abraham A. Ribicoff

Religious Leaders

Rabbi Edgar J. Magnin
Francis Cardinal Spellman
Dr. Norman Vincent Peale

Military

Walter Cunningham
John W. Glenn
John W. Young
Michael Collins
Gus Grissom
Alan Shephard, Jr.
Scott Carpenter
Gen. James Doolittle
Gen. Omar Bradley
Gen. Nathan Twining
Rear Adm. Jack P. Monroe
Capt. Eddie Rickenbacker

Law Enforcement

J. Edgar Hoover
William H. Parker

Education

Glenn T. Seaborg
Roy E. Simpson
Robert Gordon Sproul

Literary

Carl Sandburg

Appendix A

Photo-Release Form and Photo Guidelines

Photo-Release Form

I, _____, being of
                              (photo subject's name)

legal age, hereby consent and authorize _____
                                              (name of your organization)

_____, its successors, legal

representative and assigns, to use and reproduce my name and photograph(s) (or

photographs of) _____, taken by _____
                    (name of minor and relationship)   (photographer)

on _____, and circulate the same for any and all purposes,
          (date)

including public information of every description. Receipt of full consideration of

_____ is hereby acknowledged and no further claim of
whatsoever nature will be made by me. No representations have been made by me.

\
_____   _____
(signature)   (address)

\
_____   _____
(signature)   (address)

Guidelines for Color or B&W Still Photos

Following is a memo sent to agency staff members by an international advertising and public relations firm.

If you are going on a photo shoot or have any production activities that can be used for publicity purposes on behalf of the client or this agency, please bear in mind that the following points should be addressed:

- If the shot includes participants who are not agency staff or the agency's hired people, *get a signed release* from each "outsider."
- When the photo is taken, be sure that the people look presentable for a publicity release—particularly the agency's own representatives. (No cut-off tee shirts, untied shoes, or shorts, no matter how hot the temperature or how difficult the shoot.)
- Poses, too, should be of a "professional" quality;
  People doing something representative of the client's purpose for the shoot. (Please remember that the intent of the release is to publicize [agency's name]'s advertising professionalism—and to give the client added publicity exposure). No all-in-a-line-face-the camera-and-grin shots, *please*. Have people *doing something*. No more that three—at the very most four—people in a photo.
- The format of most publications calls for vertical shots whenever possible. A horizontal shot most often must be cropped, which frequently cuts a person on the end or kills the shot entirely.
- If possible, take both black and white shots as well as color slides. Any standard b&w film is fine; but try to use a 100 or 200 ASA/ISO color slide film-not one of the new high-speed slide films.
- There is no need for the photographer to supply prints of the b&w shots; a contact sheet will be sufficient. But be sure to include the photographer's name and phone number, so that we may order the print(s) we require.
- All shots for publicity purposes should be made by a professional photographer, if possible. Otherwise, be sure that all publicity stills are made with a 35mm SLR [Single Lens Reflex] camera [not a point-and-shoot viewfinder camera]; with camera mounted on a tripod to achieve tack-sharp images that are acceptable for either newspaper or magazine reproduction.

(These guidelines are effective this date, and until further notice.)

Appendix B

How to Write Effective Publicity Goals and Objectives

Well-Defined Goals and Objectives

As the Cheshire Cat told Alice, "If you don't know where you are going, then any path will take you there."

Lack of well-defined goals create the kinds of problems in attaining success that you encounter with a map on which the names of the roads cannot be easily read. Or, as Ashleigh Brilliant unequivocally states in a "Pot-Shots" cartoon, "The greatest obstacle to achieving my goals is that I don't know what my goals are."

Every organization and every division or committee of that organization needs goals and objectives. Other terms, such as *targets*, *statement of purposes*, *strategies* and *tactics* (lumped under the current buzzwords *strategic planning*), may be used interchangeably by some. But everyone understands the old standby term: goals and objectives.

"Values determine needs;" says William F. Christopher in his book, *The Achieving Enterprise*. "needs determine goals; needs and goals together determine the function and the future of our business enterprises." This assertion is equally applicable to nonprofit enterprises.

You can achieve substantial, recognizable results if you know where you're going. Your publicity efforts will be much more effective if you set well-defined goals for what you wish to realize and specific objectives for how to get there.

Broad Participation

Who should establish your major goals with their objectives?

Some organizations adhere to the belief that goals and objectives should be handed down from on high, formulated by the board of directors or the company" czar." Even if you *are* the board of directors, you will achieve far greater success in accomplishing your goals and objectives if *everyone concerned* actively participates in planning and defining them. This includes the board, management, line staff, and volunteers.

An added bonus to broad participation is the insurance that everyone involved with the creation and execution of goals and objectives fully understands them and thereby trusts and is loyal to them.

The Necessity for Goals and Objectives

If you are wondering why you should bother with goals and objectives, the answer is this: Well-circulated and well-understood goals and objectives accomplish highly desirable results. No organization can operate efficiently, productively, and profitably without them. Nor will the results of your publicity be efficient, productive, and profitable without solid goals and objectives.

This is what well-defined goals and objectives can do for your publicity efforts:

- Cut down or eliminate much of the time and effort wasted on unproductive tasks.
- Set courses of action and stimulate performance.
- Guide efforts.
- Eliminate other goals or objectives that do not work to further the major purpose of your organization.

Definitions and Differences

The following sections clarify and explain the distinct differences between goals and their objectives and describe how to formulate them.

Goals

Goals are long-range plans. They are determined by *needs*. It is important that you set well-expressed publicity goals for a proposed plan—explicit specifications of the *results* that you are looking for.

Goals are the ends toward which efforts are directed. Though they may change as time requires, they are a necessary first step in the planning cycle.

Each goal should supplement other goals, and, at the very least, no cross-purposes should exist. More specifically, goals for your publicity program should be set to supplement the organization's goals as well as any other existing publicity goals. There must be no conflict between your publicity plans and overall organization plans.

Goals are general statements of end results.

Objectives

On the other hand, good objectives contain explicit, specified results. Goals can be lofty and visionary (but not unrealistic). Objectives, however, must be practical, specific, and attainable, but set to require some stretching and extending.

Side-by-Side Definitions and Differences

In order to make it easier to recognize the distinct differences between goals and objectives, they are defined here side by side. It's academic, my dear Watson—at least the definitions sound so.

A goal is a statement of broad direction or interest which is general and timeless and is not concerned with a particular achievement within a specified period
(Caution: It must be attainable.)

An objective is a devised plan for action that can be verified within a given time and under specific conditions that, if attained, advances the system toward a corresponding goal.

(Caution: It must be measurable.)

Examples of Goals

Any one of the following are considered goals. Not one could be considered an objective.

- To devise and conduct a publicity campaign to achieve greater public recognition.
- To conduct a fund-raising program to finance organizational expansion.
- To increase the number of volunteers and the greater use of their donated time and participation in a nonprofit organization's activities and programs.
- To create public awareness of a for-profit organization's new service or product.

They are goals, not objectives, because none state precisely *what* is to be accomplished; *who* is to accomplish it; *when* it will be accomplished; or *how* it will be done.

Components of Objectives

A well-written objective should include the following components, in whatever order you prefer:

- *Who.* Specific statement as to the *individuals* who will perform the objective.
- *What.* Specific *accomplishment* when the objective has been achieved.
- *When.* Specific *point in time* when the objective is to be achieved.
- *How Well:* Specific *criteria of success* to be obtained.

Measurable Words.   Inexperienced writers of objectives often ensnare themselves in a common pitfall: They fail to state their objectives in measurable terms. They use words such as To *know*, To *understand*, To *appreciate*, To *enjoy*, and To *believe*.

How do you measure understanding, appreciation, or belief? Usually you can't, and when you can it is with great effort and difficulty! On the other hand, objectives are easier to measure when you use the following words in your statements:

To construct	To eliminate
To identify	To differentiate
To maintain	To solve
To increase	To compare

To decrease	To list
To reduce	To recognize
To improve	To lessen (the problem)
To develop	To better (a condition)

Five Objective Measurements.   Objectives formulated with words from the above list can be measured, and they will state the following:

- what will happen,
- to whom,
- to change them how much,
- by what time, and
- how we will know.

Sample Publicity Goal and Its Objectives

Goal: To devise and conduct a publicity campaign to achieve greater public awareness of and recognition for (your organization).
Objectives:
1. By (date), I (the publicity staffer or committee chairperson) will have gathered all data and pertinent information for a media fact sheet, including names, addresses, and phone numbers for the organization's headquarters, board of directors, and staff; brief descriptions of accomplishments and achievements of the organization to date; long-range goals; founders and founding date; a brief statement of philosophy of the group's purposes; and all other pertinent and important information about the organization.
2. By (date) I/staffer/chairperson will have defined, listed, and personally contacted all news media personnel who are important to furtherance of creating greater public awareness for the organization, and will have distributed to each the media fact sheet for his or her files, along with a letter introducing him- or herself and suggesting a future meeting to discuss publicity plans for the organization.

A goal as broad as the example shown above would require many more objectives to adequately create the plans for achieving it. But because goals and objectives must be customized to the individual organization, examples are difficult to offer.
Remember though, emphasis in objectives is always on *accomplishment.*

The SMAC and SMART Formulas

Here are some last suggestions. The following two memory crutches will help you write your objectives and test whether they will perform as they are meant.
First, SMAC 'em! SMAC stands for the following:

S Specific	A Attainable
M Measurable	C Compatible

Second, out-SMART 'em! SMART stands for the following:

S Specific   R Reasonable

M Measurable   T Time (frame)

A Achievable

Your objectives will fly, and they will return success to you, if you follow the SMAC and SMART formulas.

Appendix C

The Basics of Brainstorming

Some people might tell you not to call it *brainstorming*. Their argument is that the word is out of date. Today it's called problem solving or crisis management. But the technique of brainstorming isn't used exclusively on solving problems and overcoming crises. It is also a splendid, positive means of generating *ideas* that has been around for a very long time, and it holds great promise for being used productively for years and years to come.

The word *brainstorming* describes this technique best, but if it must be renamed, how about calling it creative thinking? Probably the greatest fear among businesspeople is that they will run out of the food that feeds their abilites—ideas! Your cupboard never will be bare if you brainstorm.

Brainstorming is a technique with which an issue, literally any issue, can be vigorously assailed—"stormed," if you will—by a volume of ideas.

The Mechanics of Brainstorming

1. Form your group. Involve as many individuals (up to 12) as can creatively contribute. You can even brainstorm by yourself, but the group process is far more productive as a rule.

2. Be the discussion chairperson, or facilitator, or appoint one. The chairperson's principal responsibilities are to see that the "rules" are followed and to get the process started. A good method for getting the flow of ideas started is to ask some questions. "What-if" and "how" questions are good ones with which to stimulate this creative-thinking process. Here is a word of caution: The *first* rule that must be followed is that anything goes. So if your strengths are inclined more toward logical, judicious thinking that, more or less, automatically suggests objections and says that something can't logically be done (as opposed to more creative, "far out" thinking), then make someone else the facilitator. This person should be able to ensure wideness of suggestions and be capable of blocking negative, inhibiting reactions. Robert P. Levoy, in *The Toastmaster*, explained the necessity when he quoted a plaque in the boardroom of one of America's largest corporations: Nothing will ever be accomplished if every possible objection must first be overcome.

3. Appoint someone to record ideas. This should be someone who is not part of the "think tank," but whose sole responsibility is to record *every* idea, even duplicates, and who does the job without editing of any kind.

4. Set time boundaries. This is important because there inevitably will be lulls in the session. When this happens, it is natural to assume that ideas have run out and to call an end to the meeting. However, a period of silence most often is followed by an explosion of ideas. The chairperson should be prepared, if the group becomes fidgety during these quiet times, to offer an idea to trigger further thinking.

Four Rules

1. Encourage freewheeling expression, The wilder the idea, the better. You can edit ideas later. Let free thinking flow, even if the ideas sound dumb, silly, crazy, or useless and even if the person submitting the idea is second only to Miss Piggy among deep thinkers. The "worst" or the wildest idea may be the very trigger on which someone else piggybacks to toss in one that works.

2. Do not criticize anyone's ideas. No adverse judgments are permitted. Anything goes.

3. Quantity—not quality—is desired. The more ideas you generate, the better are your odds for finding good, workable, profitable ideas.

4. Combine ideas for strength. Urge everyone not only to piggyback on others' ideas but to combine ideas to produce still other ideas.

Postsession Practices

After you have completed your brainstorming session, it is time for logical, rational, and sensible minds to take over.

Previously banned judgments now must be made about whether an idea is practical, which ones may have been tried before, what is too expensive, what is against policy, and so on. Common sense, experience, and sound judgment must take over. Stable, sensible evaluation of the ideas is as *important* as generating those ideas.

A Big Company Makes Brainstorming Pay Off Big

The Adolphe Coors Co. in Colorado has a special employee group called the Right Brainstorm (which takes its name from the theory that the right side of the brain is the creative side). This group has been saving the company large sums since 1980.

Members of the pioneer group acknowledged that they initially viewed the idea "as so much lunch meat" and signed up merely to ensure their next raise. "We knew our supervisor was real enthusiastic about this thing, so we just did it to get in good with him," said one Right Brain member.

Within the first two years, they produced ideas that saved thousands of dollars. One idea put into practice cost only $56 but resulted in annual savings to Coors of $38,000. Also within that two year period, they handed the company a "3-to-

1 payout"—their suggestions saved three times more than they cost. Another idea was projected to cost $2,400, including the brainstorming meeting time, with a savings to the company of $17,000. In actuality, the savings mounted to $29,000. That idea was followed by one that cost $27,000 but produced a savings payout of $146,000.

The group claims that productivity, rather than financial gain, is their real goal. The financial aspect is "nice," said one group member, "but we're not out to prove that we can save so much money. Our goal is working together as a team to produce the highest quality ideas we can."

Right Brainstorm's "Code of Conduct"

The following 14 rules for conducting brainstorming sessions, as set by Right Brainstorm, can help you set forth your "Code of Conduct" for your group's sessions.

1. Encourage the ideas of others.
2. Make positive constructive comments.
3. Encourage the participation of all members.
4. Solicit input from others in the department.
5. Ensure that credit is given to those to whom it is due.
6. Maintain a friendly and enthusiastic atmosphere.
7. Attend all scheduled meetings.
8. Rotate tasks on a voluntary basis.
9. Mail the minutes of the meeting within a reasonable time.
10. Assist other group members as necessary.
11. Follow the rules of brainstorming.
12. Follow "Robert's Rules of Order."
13. Maintain equality among all members of the group.
14. Accept the decision of the majority.

So, if developing exciting, productive, new ideas makes you feel a little like you're sticking your finger in a pail of water and pulling it out to see what kind of a hole it leaves, you may want to try organizing a brainstorming group.

There is no attempt here to pass off Adolphe Coors Co. as a small-business enterprise or as a nonprofit organization. But if brainstorming works so handsomely for such a large corporation, think how much easier it can be applied by smaller organizations.

Brainstorming can also help you develop ideas for the staged events described in Chapter 13. Using it for such an event can also provide the practice and conditioning you will need to apply this technique throughout your operation.

A book first published in 1958, and revised and updated in 1988, can provide valuable information about brainstorming: Brainstorming: *The Dynamic New Way to Create Successful Ideas*, by Charles H. Clark.

Appendix D

Directories and Other Information

Directories

EDITOR & PUBLISHER INTERNATIONAL YEAR BOOK
Editor & Publisher Company, Inc.
11 W. 19th St.
New York, NY 10011-4234   212/675-4380

This directory in both print and CD-Rom formats gives the most complete and reliable information about newspapers that is available. It is the encyclopedia of the newspaper industry and is presented in an easy-to-use format with section tabs. It lists daily and Sunday newspapers (in the United States and Canada), and weekly newspapers; foreign daily newspapers, special-service newspapers; news services; industry, foreign-language, college, and Black newspapers (in the United States); news, picture, and press services; feature and news syndicates, clipping bureaus; and more.

For daily newspapers, the entries include publisher's name, address, and phone, as well as the names of executives and departmental editors (business, financial, book, food, etc.).

Also presented are circulation and advertising data and production information, including the format of the newspaper and the equipment used.

Editor & Publisher magazine issues a special edition each year in July, which is devoted to syndicates. It is a directory of newspaper columnists and can be purchased for under $10 or is part of any annual subscription to the magazine.

BACON'S PUBLICITY CHECKER
Bacon's Information, Inc.
332 S. Michigan Ave.
Chicago, IL 60604   800/621-0561 or 312/922-2400

Bacon's Publicity Checker is a comprehensive two-volume coil-bound guide to magazines and newspapers in the United States and Canada. It is published annually.

Volume 1—Magazines, lists more than 7,000 magazines and newspapers, organized into 195 market classifications and subgroups, from advertising though woodworking.

Volume 2—Newspapers, lists all daily, weekly, and semiweekly newspapers in the United States and all daily newspapers in Canada. Daily newspaper listings include the names of editors, managing editors, and city editors, and some departmental editors.

Radio/TV Directory is a separate listing of more than 9,000 radio and 1,300 television stations. It is organized geographically and includes station call letters, phone numbers, formats, programming, target audiences, network affiliations, and more.

STANDARD RATE AND DATA SERVICE (SRDS)
Standard Rate & Data Service, Inc.
3004 Glenview Rd.
Wilmette, IL 60091   312/256-6067

SRDS publications are most useful when frequent rate and circulation updates are required. The Business Publications directory provides good information about business, professional, and trade magazines. Other than rates and circulation data, SRDS Newspapers directory provides little information about news operations. SRDS Newspaper Rates and Data is published monthly, and, as for all SRDS publications, it primarily provides advertising and market data.

SRDS Business Publication Rates and Data also is published monthly, in two parts. Part 1 includes an index to business publications, while Part 2 includes an index to international publications and to direct-response advertising media.

SRDS Spot Television Rates and Data, published monthly, lists television stations in the United States, Guam, and the Virgin Islands.

DIRECTORIES IN PRINT
Gale Research, Inc., Dept. 77748
835 Penobscot Bldg.
Detroit, MI 48226-4094   800/877-GALE or 313/961-2242

This is an annotated guide to approximately 10,000 business and industrial directories, professional and scientific rosters, directory databases, and other lists and guides of all kinds that are published in the United States or that are national or regional in scope or interest.

ULRICH'S INTERNATIONAL PERIODICALS DIRECTORY
Order Dept., Box 1001
Summit, NJ 07902-1001   800/521-8110

Listed is information on magazines, especially foreign publications, including publishers' and editors' names and data on circulation and frequency of publication.

GALE DIRECTORY OF PUBLICATIONS & BROADCAST MEDIA
Gale Research Inc., Dept. 77748
835 Penobscot Bldg.
Detroit, MI 48226-4094   800/877-GALE or 313/961-2242

O'DWYER'S DIRECTORY OF PUBLIC RELATIONS FIRMS
J.R. O'Dwyer Company
271 Madison Ave.
New York, NY 10016   212/679-2471

Basic data on more than 1,400 individual firms and more than a thousand individual public relations counselors are provided to give quick access to experts in public relations, public affairs, investor relations, employee communications, corporate advertising, all forms of product publicity, issues analysis and management, forecasting, lobbying, proxy solicitation, TV speech training, and international PR.

Stylebooks

THE UNITED PRESS INTERNATIONAL STYLEBOOK
NTC Business Books
4255 West Touhy Avenue
Lincolnwood, IL 60646-1975   800/323-4900 or 708/679-5500

The UPI Stylebook is a standard reference for the communications field that is used by UPI editors and writers, newspaper reporters and editors, and PR personnel. It includes information about writing style, courtesy titles, usage, spelling, punctuation, nuclear terminology, and capitalization.

THE ASSOCIATED PRESS STYLEBOOK AND LIBEL MANUAL
Dell Publishing
666 Fifth Avenue
New York, NY 10103   800/255-4133 or 212/765-6500

The *AP Stylebook and Libel Manual* is more than the traditional stylebook. It aids in spelling place names and brand names, identifying the correct form for government agencies, military titles, ship names, and corporation names. It also verifies correct punctuation, capitalization, and abbreviations. In addition, it provides a libel section for people writing for newspapers, newsletters, or anything that goes to the public in print.

THE ELEMENTS OF STYLE
by William Strunk, Jr., and E.B. White
The Macmillan Company
866 Third Avenue
New York, NY 10022   212/702-2000

This tiny book is a result of the principal author's "attempt to cut the vast tangle of English rhetoric down to size and write its rules and principles on the head of a pin," says E.B. White, coauthor. The book is perhaps used by more writers than any other of its kind.

U.S. NEWS & WORLD REPORT STYLEBOOK FOR WRITERS AND EDITORS
by Robert Gover
U.S. News & World Report
2400 N St., NW
Washington, DC 20037   202/955-2000

This stylebook by *U.S. News & World Report* news desk deputy chief Robert Gover is listed for those who wish to extend their publicity programs to news magazines. This stylebook is unique inasmuch as most magazines do not publish this information. The information is applicable to other magazines of the same genre.

Clipping Bureaus

Listed below are clipping bureaus that read and clip nationally. The following paragraph provides you with a means of preserving those clippings, so they won't yellow or become brittle, thereby permitting you to reproduce them into promotional and advertising material or for any other purposes. The method was developed by Richard Smith, when he was an assistant professor at the University of Washington.

Rx FOR PRESERVING NEWSPAPERS: Dissolve a milk-of-magnesia tablet or one tablespoon of milk-of-magnesia emulsion in a quart of club soda, recap tightly, and let stand in the refrigerator overnight. Pour into a pan large enough to accommodate the flattened newspaper. Soak newspaper for one to two hours; remove and pat dry. The solution cannot be reused. Estimated life: 200 years. Chemically, the magnesium oxide combines with the carbon dioxide in the soda to form magnesium carbonate, which neutralizes acids in the paper that cause deterioration.

Editor & Publisher Yearbook lists 3 news-clipping services. Some are primarily regional; others are national and international. The best known are as follows:

BACON'S CLIPPING BUREAU
332 S. Michigan Ave.
Chicago, IL 60604   800/621-0561 or 312/922-2400

LUCE PRESS CLIPPINGS, INC.
420 Lexington Ave., Suite 203
New York, NY 10170   212/889-6711

Note: Luce offers an additional service called "Impact," a monthly reporting system that tracks publicity efforts and results.

Nonprofit Information

SOCIAL SERVICE ORGANIZATIONS & AGENCIES DIRECTORY
Gale Research Co.
835 Penobscot Bldg.
Detroit, MI 48226-4094   800/897-GALE or 313/961-2242

This publication lists approximately 6,500 national and regional social service organizations. Entries include publications which they publish. *Note:* THE DI-RECTORY OF DIRECTORIES, published by Gale Research Co., lists other social services directories.

"How-to" Booklet for Radio and Television

"IF YOU WANT AIR TIME . . ."
NAB Services
1771 N St., NW
Washington, D.C. 20036   202/429-5300

The National Association of Broadcasters publishes a how-to booklet that is designed to help community leaders, civic groups, organizations, and individuals to use radio and television to get their message to the public. It contains specific advice, check-lists, rules, "do's" and "don'ts," and examples on writing creative public service announcements (PSAs), producing news releases, appearing on-air, and more.

Glossary

ad   short for "advertising

ADI   area of dominant influence: an area in which a TV station has a commandingly large share of the viewing audience. This phrase, like "designated marketing area," was coined by a market research firm.

advertising   messages printed in newspaper space paid for by the advertiser.

advertorials   a relatively new, controversial type of advertising intended to instruct or entertain readers and produce additional revenue for the publication. They consist of promotional and editorial material, jointly produced for the advertiser, and usually are contained in a separate section of the publication.

anchor   a person who anchors a television news broadcast, narrates news, and introduces reports presented by reporters.

assignment   a single or continuing story a reporter covers for his or her newspaper.

assignment editor   the person at a television or radio station who is responsible for dispatching camera crews and reporters to cover news events.

Associated Press (AP)   a cooperative news-gathering agency, encompassing more than 4,500 newspapers, TV, and radio stations worldwide.

audience   the number of people reading, watching, or listening to a particular medium.

audiotext   voice information services, such as those used by new high-tech "talking newspapers."

backgrounder   a story or news release that summarizes the history or background of a current matter in the news; also, a meeting with the press in which a source gives information not for direct or immediate attribution.

banner   a large headline that runs across the entire width or most of the newspaper page, used more frequently across the front pages of "street editions." They are large and bold, and written to attract the eye and interest of the street buyer who may be offered several choices in racks standing side by side.

beat   the report's regular assignment, such as the police or courthouse "beat."

bleed   an advertisement in which all or part of the graphic material runs to the edges of the page. There usually is a premium charged for a bleed advertisement.

blind lead   a short, punchy introduction to a news story that is "a way of showing readers the forest before plunging into the trees" (Jack Hart). A blind lead holds back on the 5 Ws to present concisely the central theme of the story.

body, body copy   all of an article that follows lead paragraphs.

body type   type used in the story, not in the headline.

boldface   applied to type, meaning heavy or dark type.

bookending   a television news term indicating that the news story begins and ends with a person, so that there is a human beginning and ending to the story.

box   a story with a border around it, or a rectangular space marked off in a story.

break   a period when a broadcast is interrupted, such as when a commercial plays on the air—a commercial break.

breaking news   news that is developing at the moment.

B-roll   a term left over from the 1950s when film (instead of videotape) was used by television stations that had only two film playback machines. One was "A," the other was "B." The B-roll played footage of the news event. Today it means footage of the event—not of interviews.

byline   the name of the writer printed at the head of a story.

b&w   black and white; usually refers to photos supplied to newspapers or to film for television.

call letters   a broadcast station's name. Usually four letters starting with W east of the Mississippi and starting with K west of the Mississippi.

camera cue light   a red light on the front of a TV camera indicating it is the one in use.

caps   abbreviation for capital letters.

caption   descriptive matter accompanying an illustration; sometimes referred to as a *cut line*; also sometimes used to signify a headline used over a picture or group of pictures.

center spread   two facing center pages, on one continuous page in a newspaper.

chromakey   an electronic process used for matting one picture into another. For example, a background scene affecting the foreground action. The work is sometimes hyphenated: chroma-key.

city desk   the desk where the editor (often flanked by other editors and assistants) process local news.

city news service   a syndicated news service that distributes only city or local news.

circulation   the total number of copies of the newspaper distributed to subscribers and news vendors in a single day.

classified advertising   advertising space usually purchased in small amounts by the public. The ads are "classified" into various categories such as jobs, autos, apartments for rent, etc. Also, sometimes referred to as the "want ads."

clipsheet   a collection of news stories, illustations, charts, and filler items arranged in newspaper columns, that can be reproduced and used in newspapers.

co-op advertising   an arrangement with a manufacturer or vendor whereby the advertiser is reimbursed in part or in full for costs of advertising that promotes or sells the manufacturer's or vendor's product, service, or image.

column   the arrangement of horizontal lines of type in a news story; also, an article appearing regularly written by a particular writer or "columnist."

compose   an old term meaning to set type.

commercial   a broadcast term that, when used technically, means an advertising message broadcast during a program that advertiser sponsors. Most of what people call commercials, are, in a broadcast parlance, advertising spots.

composing room   where copy, headlines, advertising, and illustrations are set and assembled in preparation for printing.

contact proof print   a positive photographic trial print, to be "read" by an editor and marked to indicate content and size of the final print for in-paper use.

controlled circulation   for business papers this is now usually called *qualified circulation*. It is nonpaid. For suburban newspapers it means delivery of nonpaid copies to everyone in a specific area, regardless of whether they are subscribers or not.

copy   any written material to be published or reproduced; a single newspaper.

copycat   one who imitates or simulates. In this case, a method of using published news stories or previously produced advertising as an "idea factories" for constructing similar publicity releases, advertising layouts, and advertising messages.

copy editor   assistant to city or national editor, edits reporter's copy and writes headlines.

copy desk   horseshoe-shaped desk at which copy editors sit.

copyright   legal protection to an author from unauthorized use of his or her work.

cover   to go and seek information for a story. "He covered the fire."

coverage   in print media, the number of copies (assumed to be greater than the "circulation") physically received by people in the mail, from carriers, at newsstands, and as pass-alongs. In broadcast, it's an engineering measurement of how far and where a station's signal can be received. Coverage describes only potential. It doesn't tell you how many people actually look into that publication or tune in to that station. There is mass coverage (for example, a TV network program with wide appeal) or *specific* coverage. Specific coverage may be directed geographically (state, region, locality, etc.) or toward selected groups of people assumed to have the same interests (teenagers, sports fans, and so forth).

created news   controlled news that comes from a created event or happening such as appointments or elections of individuals, meetings, performances, new product or new service announcements, new programs, and so on.

crop (photo)   trimming the edges of a photo to fit space.

CU   broadcast term: closeup of individual's face only, or of a small item with a signature card and price card.

cue   a sound or action noting the start or conclusion of a show. The signal to someone to say or do something.

cue card   a television term meaning a card placed out of camera range for someone to read from.

cume   a television term meaning as frequency increases, new people who have not seen or heard an advertisement are exposed to it. Reach, thus, increases. Cume is short for dumulative audience.

cut   to shorten newspaper copy, more often referred to as *trim*; also, another word for *illustration*, derived from the days when all newspaper illustrations were woodcuts.

cut   broadcast term used for an instant camera change, from one camera to another.

cutaway   a television method to abbreviate too-lengthy news clips. For example: a shot of the fire chief endlessly rambling on about how and why the fire ladder caught on fire. An editor is able to find two clips that, together, have the fire chief saying, "I don't know what happened." But the break produces what is called a "jump cut," whereby the first cut shows the fire chief on screen right with his helmet on, then suddenly — midsentence—he's shown on screen left with his helmet off. If shown without any other visual it can become distracting and disorienting to a viewer, so a cutaway is used to cover the transition. A cutaway is a visual bridge most often used to cover an edit within an interview.

cutline   written text accompanying an illustration or "cut," more often called *caption*.

cybernetics   the global web of computer networks; the mathematical analysis of the flow of information on electronic systems.

cyberspace   a web of public and private computer networks.

data base   a collection of information—data—about a specific subject or a group, such as demographic or psychographic data about a group of potential consumers.

dateline   precedes the first sentence of the lead, telling the reader the location and often the date of the story.

demographics   statistics about people: their occupations, incomes, educational levels, and the like to help you identify your prospects among the total population. If you know the kind of people you want as customers, demographic information can help you better target your advertising by helping you select the media that best reaches them. Demographic editions of publications are aimed at specific groups of people based on one or more of the above criteria.

desk   desk at which journalists edit local sports, national, fashion news, etc.

deskman   copy editor.

display advertising   large, frequently illustrated advertisements usually purchased by retail stores, manufacturers, and service companies; as distinguished from classified advertising.

dissolve   a slow take out of one camera as the other camera is brought in. It is possible to use a fast dissolve or slow dissolve, and they can be slowed or speeded up for effect. With a slow dissolve, for example, you can actually see a wrapper coming off a loaf of bread.

dolly   to move the camera in on the subject or away from the subject. However, to go from a long shot to a CU, it is advisable to change cameras.

double planting   to give the same photo or news release to more than one person at the same newspaper.

double truck   two full facing pages or a center spread.

drive time   the early morning and late afternoon/early evening hours when radio has its largest audiences and highest rates.

dummy   a diagram or layout of the newspaper page that shows the placement of headlines, stories, pictures, and advertisements.

ears   space at the top of the front page on each side of the paper's name; usually boxed in with weather news, index to pages, or an announcement of special features.

ECU   a television term meaning extreme closeup. Indicates filling the screen with an item and is used primarily on small objects (watches, rings, small cans of food). As an example, it can be used on tires for a good look at the tread design. It also can be used for a face-only shot of a person.

edition   one day's run of the newspaper; "today's edition"; some newspapers print several editions per day, each containing news of a different locale, such as"city edition," "northeast edition"; large circulation papers break up long press runs with several numbered editions updating the news of preceding editions; the most recent news is contained in the "final edition."

editor   the person responsible for deciding what news goes in the paper and where it will appear; one who reviews, corrects, and, if necessary, rewrites the stories submitted by reporters.

editorial   an expression of opinion by the newspaper's editors, usually reflecting the opinion of the publisher or owner of the newspaper; also the department of the newspaper where news is gathered, written, edited, and readied for publication.

editorial cartoon   cartoon art that expresses opinions on the news.

electronic encoding   similar to an electronic blip, placed on a video (news release) tape that remains on the tape through replaying, dubbing, reediting, or any other change; a kind of invisible barcode to trigger computers that monitor TV stations.

E-mail   short for electronic mail; the exchange of messages on a computer network. E-mail systems use "electronic mailboxes" to direct messages to specified receivers.

ENG   electronic news gathering. Television coverage of news using minicams at remote locations.

face   the part of the type that comes in contact with the paper; also the style or family of the type, such as boldface or italic, Caslon, or Bodoni.

fact sheet   a set of data or information about a specific event or happening that contains all of the information from which a news story can be written. It replaces or amplifies a news release.

fade   one camera is faded out before the other is faded in. There is a fleeting moment of black on screen.

feature   a story that deals with something other than late-breaking news.

filler   a very short, interesting, and perhaps humorous news item that an editor can use to fill space below or between longer articles.

five W's   who, what, when, where, why, (some people add "H" for how); the major questions answered in the "lead" of a well-written news story.

flag   the name of the newspaper appearing on page one.

flak   a disparaging out-of-date name given to publicists who create publicity by means of staged stunts.

flush left/right   copy that is "justified" on either the left, right, or both edges so that the copy is aligned evenly. Traditionally, newspaper columns are aligned flush left and right (justified) except at the beginning of a paragraph where the first word is indented.

First Amendment   the first article of the Bill of Rights, granting freedom of religion, speech, press, assembly, and petition.

focus group session   a group interview of 6 to 12 specially selected people, conducted by an interviewer to elicit information about their perceptions, needs, or reactions to a specific product, service or organization.

follow-up   a story that adds more information to a story already printed.

font   a complete alphabet of type in one size and style.

fourth estate   an eighteenth-century phrase describing the press. During a speech in Parliament, British statesman Edmund Burke pointed to the reporters' gallery saying, "There are three estates in Parliament, but yonder sits a fourth estate, more important than all of them." He was referring to the three classes of people recognized under British law: the clergy, the nobles, and the commons. Thus, newspapers became the Fourth Estate.

freedom of the press   the freedom granted in Article 1 of the Bill of Rights, "Congress shall make no law respecting an establishment of religion or prohibiting the free exercise thereof; abridging the freedom of speech, or of the press. . . ."

fringe time   the periods immediately before and after TV "prime time": generally, 4:30 P.M. to 7:30 P.M. and after 11:00 P.M.

general assignment   a reporter who covers a variety of stories rather than a single "beat."

geographics   the segmenting of a group according to geographic location(s)—such as urban, suburban, rural, climate—rather than by socioeconomic demographics.

glossy, glossy print   a smooth, shiny-surfaced photograph required to produce a sharp, clear reproduction on newsprint.

graf   newsroom jargon meaning paragraph.

handout   a press release; a prepared statement for the press. Also a free film clip or videotape of a news event, supplied to a television station.

hard copy   copy that is in touchable form as opposed to verbal copy, copy on a computer screen before it is printed, or on a VNR or RNR.

head   news room jargon, short for headline.

headline   display type placed over a story summarizing the story for the reader.

home editions   newspapers that go to subscribers do not have to vie for the buyer's interests, so small headlines can be used, often with separate headlines topping each front page story. The banner-type headline usually is omitted, although the lead story may carry a three- or four-column head if the story is important.

human interest   elements in a story that appeal to readers' emotions, that have to do with events in human life.

index   table of contents of each newspaper, usually found on page one.

infobahn   a metaphor coined to use in place of the cliché "information superhighway."

information superhighway   two-way fiber-optic communication systems such as Internet, Prodigy, America Online, and other computer-linked systems; includes the breakdown of voice, data, and video into indistinguishable bits that can be transmitted simultaneously.

interactive media   interactive TV is most widely known, as a service whereby consumers can play games, shop, bank, or vote. Other forms include some newspapers, cable, computers, fax on demand, cellular telephones, CD Rom, and audiotex.

issue   all copies of a newspaper produced in a day.

inverted pyramid   a method of writing news stories in which the parts of the story are placed in descending order of importance.

jargon   the special vocabulary of a particular business; the language of that business.

jump   to continue a story from one page to another (usually from page one to inside).

jumpline   the line that tells readers the page where a story is continued.

jumphead   the headline used on a story continued from another page, which repeats key words from the original story.

justification   type set to fill the entire line so that margins are flush left and flush right— as different from "ragged right" margins.

keys   in television vernacular, the on-screen words that identify people and/or places.

kill   to discard all or parts of a story before it is printed.

l.c.   lower-case letters as opposed to capital letters.

lead   the first paragraph or two of a story, which usually contain(s) the "5W" information (pronounced "leed").

letter to the editor   a letter in a newspaper in which a reader expresses his or her views, frequently printed on the editorial page or the page opposite the editorial page.

libel   a false communication that injures the reputation of an individual.

library   file of stories, biographies, pictures, etc., available for reference at any time; the place where these materials are kept. Also called the *morgue*.

line   a line of type; uniform method of measuring the depth of an advertisement; newspapers sell advertising by either a line or column inch; there usually are 8 lines to the column inch; advertising people refer to the total amount of advertising sold in a given period as "lineage."

logo   short for "logotype"; a design bearing the trademark or name of a company or business, or of a newspaper feature.

long shot, cover shot, full shot   television terms: can be used interchangeably; takes in the complete set or a full shot of the announcer.

makeup   the arrangement of stories, headlines, pictures, and advertising on a page.

managing editor   the editor at most papers who directs the daily gathering, writing, and editing of news, and of the placement of news in the paper; working for him or her are the city editor, the national editor, etc.

masthead   the formal statement of a paper's name, officers, point of publication, and other information, usually found on the editorial page.

media   plural of *medium*, a term used to depict the combination of a variety of communications including newspapers, television, radio, magazines, direct mail, etc.

media event   an event designed to create news that attracts media news coverage.

media kit   also known as media information kit; see press kit.

media list   a list of newspaper, radio, and television people to whom news releases and other information is sent for the purposes of acquiring publicity or good will.

menu publishing   a slang expression denoting magazines and other publications whose content keeps strictly to a specific topic or special interest, such as rap music information for rappers, information of interest to computer users, or investing material for investors.

MCU or MS   (medium closeup or medium shot) television terms: usually used interchangeably. It can be a bust shot of the announcer. Or it is used for larger items, such as a dryer where the top is shown, but not a closeup of the controls.

minimax principle   minimizing the negative while maximizing the positive.

mobile unit   television broadcast equipment used outside the studio.

monitoring   a television term used to indicate checks of competitors' programming, commercials, and transmission quality.

morphology   usually spoken of as "morphing"; a high-tech method sometimes used in TV commercials by which something happens that may actually be impossible, such as when a car climbs a wall, crosses the ceiling, and descends on the opposite wall, or a screen drops behind a car and it drives off into the scene on the screen.

mug   a photograph of a person's face.

multimedia   a term used in marketing to denote the use of different media: newspapers, magazines, billboards, radio, television; or the combined used of diverse elements such as slides, computer drawings, videotape, and audiotape.

morgue   an old term for the newspaper's library where files of clippings, photos, microfilm of past issues, reference books, and other material are contained.

narrowcasting   television programming that targets a very narrowly defined specific-interest group of viewers.

national editor   "wire" editor, in charge of selecting and editing the news of the nation outside the newspaper's circulation area.

network   a link-up of many stations by cable or microwave for simultaneous broadcast from a single originating point. The stations may be owned by or affiliated with the network.

news director/news editor   dispatches broadcast crews and field reporters; puts a newscast together.

newsfeature   a news story that doesn't follow the structure of straight news reports, is timely but doesn't have the immediacy of straight news; it emphasizes human interest or is entertaining or informative.

news hole   the space in a newspaper allocated to news rather than to advertising.

newspeg   the main element of a news story; the "peg" upon which the story is hung.

newsprint   a grade of paper made of wood pulp, used primarily for printing news-paper, delivered in rolls weighing up to a ton.

news release   see press release.

news services   news-gathering agencies such as AP and UPI that gather and distribute news to subscribing newspapers.

niche publishing   directly targets a specific, individual audience, often very narrow in terms of its interest(s), such as a magazine for single mothers with small children, for recreation vehicle users, or for retirees who desire to continue working or volunteering.

obituary (obit)   a biographical account of a person's life published at the time of his or her death.

off the record   information given by a source that is not for publication.

on location   broadcast programming produced outside of a studio.

on the air   the time a programming is being broadcast or recorded. Signified by signs in the studio and outside the studio doors.

op-ed page   means "opposite the editorial page"; some newspapers use this page to print reader opinions, articles by columnists, and other nonnews features.

page one   the first page of a newspaper; also, "important" as in "page-one news."

pan   from the word panorama, meaning to move sideways from one item to another in the same shot. It means merely turning the camera, not necessarily to move the wheels.

pasteup   prepared advertising copy and art for reproduction. All elements are in the proper position. Also called me*chanical* or *camera-ready art*.

peel   a rarely used television term that calls for it to appear that the image on the screen is peeled back—as one would peel a sheet of paper from a sticky-note pad—to reveal another scene directly beneath the first image.

penetration   another term for "reach," it means the extent to which a publication or broadcast station has gotten audience attention in a given area (market). If a publication or station gets half a potential audience, it is said to have a penetration of 50 percent.

photo release   signed permission from an individual giving permission to use his or her name and photo likeness for the purposes stated in the release.

pica   unit of linear measurement of 12 points, equal to $1/6$ inch.

pica pole   a ruler that measures in picas.

plant/double plant   a term used to mean that a story has been placed—planted—with a particular news outlet. Double planting is taboo practice, meaning to place the same news release with two editors or two sections within the same publication.

PNs, Personal Newspapers   electronic newspapers such as those being developed by Knight-Ridder newspapers.

point   designating the size of type, one point representing about $1/72$ of an inch.

position   the location of an ad on a page.

precede   a reader's aid, an explanatory note, that precedes and explains, such as an "editor's note."

press association   an organization that collects news from around the world and relays it to subscribers. Best known are the Associated Press, United Press International.

press conference   special meeting called to give information to the press.

press junket   an especially arranged trip for press/media only- a strictly media event.

press kit   a special package of information related to an event or for the purpose of a press conference: a collection of selected materials to help reporters write a more complete news story.

press release a specially prepared statement for the press (see handout).

prime time when television has its largest audiences and highest advertising rates. In the Eastern, Mountain, and Pacific time zones it is from 7:30 P.M. to 11:00 P.M. In the Central zone it is from 6:30 P.M. to 10:00 P.M.

professional paper a classification of business papers edited for people who buy very little themselves, but whose recommendations influence the expenditure of large sums of money. Architects are an example.

proof an impression of a printed page or story; a printer "pulls a proof" so the "proofreader" can check for errors before the final version is printed.

proofreader one who reads proof and marks errors.

psychographics a segmentation process used in marketing research to denote life styles, buying habits, and personality types of potential consumers. It can include needs, motives, perceptions, attitudes, culture, and social class.

publicity newsworthy information distributed to media to gain public notice or support.

publicity stunt an unusual, preposterous, often inane event staged solely to attract public and media attention.

public relations activities and attitudes of an organization intended to create and maintain worthwhile relations with the public.

public service announcement see PSA

public service time free airtime that broadcast stations must allot according to FCC definitions; includes public service announcements and special programming in the interests of the community.

publisher the chief executive and often the owner of a newspaper or other publishing enterprise.

put to bed printer's term for the final steps taken before the presses start to run.

PSA a broadcast term standing for public service announcement; an announcement for which no charge is made and which promotes programs, activities, or services of nonprofit organizations and other announcements regarded as serving community interests.

quotes sheet a page or more of fully attributed quotes by organization officials or outside persons qualified to speak about the subject or purpose of a press conference or a news release; usually part of a press kit.

radio media tour a prescheduled phone interview between an individual and a radio station, using special high-quality phone lines.

ragged right type set in a newspaper column that is not "flush right."

reefer a cross reference, referring a reader to an item or photo.

release to specify the publication of a story on or after a specific date.

Reuters the first news-gathering service, founded in Great Britain in 1849.

review an account of an artistic event such as a concert or play that offers critical evaluation, the opinion of the writer.

rewrite man a newsperson whose job is to write a news account from information supplied by reporters at or near the scene of the story.

ROP run-of-paper news and advertising appears in any position convenient to the make up of the paper.

satellite media tour a means of bringing together people in different locations, using broadband casting—literally "broad" casting that covers an entire area—whereby both voice and pictures are transmitted by satellite.

scrawl a line of type running across the bottom of a television screen as opposed to a scroll, which runs vertically down the screen.

scroll   information that runs vertically on a television screen; different from a scrawl, which runs horizontally across the bottom of the screen.

set   type is set when it is arranged into words and lines.

shopper   what shopping guides are called. Consisting almost entirely of advertisements, they have nonpaid "controlled circulation" and are distributed in specific geographic areas to give complete coverage. Most are weeklies.

sidebar   a secondary story presenting sidelights on a major news story.

(a television) slate   on-screen information to "cue" reporters or news anchors about what questions or remarks to make prior to running a prerecorded video.

source   supplier of information, such as a person, book, survey, etc.

spin doctor   a trained expert who puts a desired "spin" on a situation that is or could be seen in a different light; a public relations expert who specializes in crisis communications.

spot news   news obtained first-hand; fresh news.

stand-alone news release   a news release that provides all the essential principal facts or purposes (as for a news conference) and can stand alone to be used by recipients as presented.

still video   a new technology for newspapers that produces newspaper photos from a camera that records up to 50 images on a computer disk; requires no developing before the image can be seen on a video screen.

street editions   often have "ears"—small boxes on one or both sides of the "flag," nameplate—to give further information that is meant to attract the single-copy buyer. Only the top half of page one is visible in a street rack. The editor uses this portion to catch the interest of street buyers.

stringer   a part-time writer usually covering a particular area or subject, often paid according to the amount of his or her copy printed by the newspaper.

stunt   see publicity stunt.

style, stylebook, style manual, style sheet   the rules and rulebook governing writing, spelling, etc., which most newspapers provide their writers and editors.

subhead   a one- or two-line head used to divide sections of a story.

super   a television term often used to mean superimposing information such as an organization's name, telephone number, address, or other essential information on a slide, film, or video clip.

syndicate   a company that sells news, features, comics, drawings, or photos to newspapers, magazines, radio, trade journals, business newspapers, all for a fraction of the amount paid to the contributor; syndicated features material such as comics, advice columns, etc., supplied nationally to newspapers by news syndicates.

tabloid   a newspaper format that is a little larger than half the standard size, usually with five columns per page.

target audience   a specific group to which marketing messages are aimed; a group previously defined by its geographic, demographic, or psychographic nature.

tear sheet   a sheet torn from a publication to prove insertion of an advertisement.

teaser   an announcement placed prominently in the newspaper, often on page one, which tells of an interesting story elsewhere in the paper.

telecommunication   an electronically transmitted message via television, cable, radio, or telegraphy.

Telephoto   the United Press International service that transmits pictures to subscribing newspapers.

tip   an item of information that might lead to a news story.

tracked package   a videotaped news story, 1 minute to 2$\frac{1}{2}$ minutes long, with a reporter's voice-over telling the story. In comparison, an untracked package is a "natural sound" package that uses the same video but with only the natural sounds—no reporter's voice-over—of perhaps factory equipment working or children playing.

trade publication   a publication edited specifically to reach members of a specific occupational group. Such newspapers (or magazines) contain articles and advertisements directed to the group's interests.

truck   means almost the same as dolly, except the camera is moved, as around a car or along a large set.

type   the physical letters used by the printer to produce readable material.

typo   short for "typographical error"; a mistake made during the production rather than the writing of a story.

u.c.   upper case, another term for capital letters.

United Press International (UPI)   one of several worldwide news services.

untracked package   see tracked package.

videotex   a means of transmitting computer-stored information by an electronic communications system, or by telephone or cable, to a specially adapted television set or computer terminal.

visuals   any and all visual elements in a television program.

video news release; VNRs   any self-generated news on videotape, whether sent by satellite or distributed by mail, courier, or overnight delivery.

VNR package   a complete, 1-minute, 20-second air-ready news release. Also known merely as a VNR.

VPR   video public relations.

want ads   classified advertisements.

widow   a single word or a partial line at the end of a paragraph that appears alone at the top of a column of type.

wire editor   edits news supplied by the news agencies or "wire services."

Wirephoto   The Associated Press service that transmits pictures to subscribing newspapers.

zone edition   an edition of a city newspaper for a specific geographic area, which may be within the city or a group of suburban communities. A zone edition is for both news and advertising . It may consist of localized pages, a separate section, or a tabloid insert. It may be published every day or only on certain days, but almost always on Sunday. Big City newspapers often use zone editions to meet competition from suburban newspapers both for readers and advertisers.

"30" or ###   signifies end of copy.

Many of the definitions in this glossary are reproduced with permission from a booklet printed by American Newspaper Publishers Association Foundation. Additions have been made.

Index

If you're going to walk the walk, why not talk the talk. It helps to know what media people mean when they use the jargon of their trade. For example, most professionals use acronyms rather than the spelled-out meanings of those initials, so references in this index are listed under acronyms.